BUYING
RESPECTABILITY

Philanthropic and Nonprofit Studies

Dwight F. Burlingame and David C. Hammack, editors

BUYING RESPECTABILITY

PHILANTHROPY AND
URBAN SOCIETY IN
TRANSNATIONAL PERSPECTIVE,
1840s TO 1930s

THOMAS ADAM

INDIANA UNIVERSITY PRESS
Bloomington and Indianapolis

This book is a publication of

Indiana University Press
601 North Morton Street
Bloomington, IN 47404-3797 USA

http://iupress.indiana.edu

Telephone orders   800-842-6796
Fax orders   812-855-7931
Orders by e-mail   iuporder@indiana.edu

The paper used in this publication meets the minimum requirements of
American National Standard for Information Sciences—Permanence of
Paper for Printed Library Materials, ANSI Z39.48-1984.

Manufactured in the United States of America

Library of Congress Cataloging-in-Publication Data

Adam, Thomas, date
  Buying respectability : philanthropy and urban society in transnational
perspective, 1840s to 1930s / Thomas Adam.
    p. cm. — (Philanthropic and nonprofit studies)
  Includes bibliographical references and index.
  ISBN 978-0-253-35274-3 (cloth : alk. paper) 1. Philanthropists—History—
19th century. 2. Philanthropists—History—20th century. 3. Charities—
History—19th century. 4. Charities—History—20th century. 5. Public
institutions—History—19th century. 6. Public institutions—History—20th
century. 7. Social status—History—19th century. 8. Social status—History—
20th century. I. Title.
  HV25.A33 2009
  361.7'409034—dc22
                                                        2008032107

1 2 3 4 5   14 13 12 11 10 09

For Wentworth Walker

Contents

Acknowledgments   ix

Introduction   3

PART ONE

CHAPTER ONE

Cultural Excursions: Museums, Art Galleries,
and Libraries in a Transatlantic World   13

CHAPTER TWO

Heavy Luggage: The Intercultural Transfer
of Models for Social Housing Enterprises   39

PART TWO

CHAPTER THREE

How to Become a Gentleman: Philanthropy and Social Climbing   89

CHAPTER FOUR

Bountiful Ladies: Philanthropy and Women's Place in Society   126

CHAPTER FIVE

Giving for Good: Philanthropy and Religion   153

Conclusion   181

Notes   183

Index   229

Acknowledgments

This book is the result of ten years of research and writing in various places of the transatlantic world. Following the traces of intercultural transfer in the nineteenth century, the inquiry into the exchange processes between various cities within the transatlantic world brought me from Germany to Canada and finally to the United States. It all began with my curiosity for philanthropy in nineteenth-century Leipzig and the realization that Leipzig was part of a much larger transatlantic discourse on philanthropy. I am deeply indebted to Hannes Siegrist for his insight, suggestions, and encouragement to deepen my work by incorporating newer research on philanthropy with the older German research on the leisure class (Bürgertum). Margaret Menninger too deserves my gratitude for sharing not only ideas but also her comprehensive knowledge about cultural patronage in Leipzig. The idea to see cultural and social philanthropy through the same lens derived from our continued discussions about Leipzig's philanthropic establishment. Tobias Brinkmann, Martin Daunton, Robert Fairbanks, David Hammack, Bernard Harris, Andrew Lees, Alf Lüdtke, and Kathleen McCarthy have read various segments of this book at various stages of its completion and provided important critique. In many cases, these readers have raised questions that inspired me to pursue new directions and to expand my manuscript into directions not envisioned before. Gabriele Lingelbach, further, encouraged me to apply the theory of intercultural transfer to the transatlantic exchange of philanthropic concepts and practices. In addition, our continuous discussions helped me to broaden my understanding of the phenomenon of intercultural transfer. Kerstin Wolff and Ortrud Wörner-Heil pointed me in the direction of women's involvement in philanthropy, and they are responsible for generating a deeper interest that resulted in more intensive research in this area. Johannes Frackowiak was extremely helpful in locating sources about Therese Rossbach. The archivists at the State Archive of Saxony in Leipzig and the State Archive of Lower Saxony in Bückeburg saw to it that I received copies of the relevant materials about Rossbach. Rüdiger Zimmermann from the Library of the Friedrich Ebert Foundation arranged for me to receive copies of rare publications that were nowhere else to be found. Without this logistical help and support, I would never have finished this book. With the support of the German Historical Institute in Washington, D.C., and in collaboration with Eckhardt Fuchs and Simone Lässig, I was able to co-organize two international conferences on the topic of philanthropy in 2001 and 2006. These and other conferences on both sides of the Atlantic allowed me to present my findings to an academic public.

From the very beginning of this project, the support of the Alexander von Humboldt Foundation was essential for this project, and a large part of this success I attribute to the efforts of James Retallack for having invited me in 1999 to the University of Toronto and for having supported my application for a Feodor Lynen Fellowship. His unwavering support not only allowed me to carry out this research project but also paved the way for my professional future in North America. The Feodor Lynen Fellowship and the financial support from the University of Toronto, which included the George C. Metcalf Postdoctoral Research Grant 2000/2001 from Victoria College, allowed me to undertake the necessary travel in order to pursue my research interests. I want to thank here Rod Carruthers for having introduced me to the Arts & Letter Club of Toronto and more specifically to Wentworth Walker, who was indispensable for this project for not only having provided many documents from his family archive but also for having arranged meetings with the descendants of those Toronto philanthropists who were so central to my work. His phone calls opened doors of private homes and social clubs to which I would otherwise not have had access, and it is for this reason that I have dedicated this book to him.

The study and research of transatlantic history involves a great deal of travel on both sides of the Atlantic in the hunt for archival sources, published and unpublished materials. The generous support of the Fritz Thyssen Foundation enabled me to visit various archives and libraries in Berlin, Hamburg, Leipzig, and Dillingen in the summer of 2003. Since my return from research abroad, I have had to rely more and more on the Interlibrary Loan services at my university and the willingness of archivists and librarians at various institutions, and the National German Library in Berlin in particular, to send copies of materials I needed for my research. The librarians at the Interlibrary Loan services at the University of Toronto and the University of Texas at Arlington often worked miracles when it came to locating and receiving the one copy of a book that was available in that distant library. Last but not least, I would like to thank Beth Wright, the Dean of the College of Liberal Arts at the University of Texas at Arlington, for providing the necessary funding for the inclusion of images in this book.

BUYING
RESPECTABILITY

PART ONE

Introduction

This book introduces the concept of intercultural transfer to the study of transnational and modern transatlantic history.[1] The subject of this book is not American, British, Canadian, or German history per se but the entangled and interconnected histories of urban communities in these four countries. The aim of this book lies, therefore, not in the reconceptualization and normalization of one particular national history but in writing a "history in between and beyond" the national histories of Germany, Great Britain, Canada, and the United States and thus to present an alternative to writing history in the age of the nation-state. Focusing on a phenomenon such as philanthropy across several countries uncovers lost connections and contexts and allows for an investigation of intercultural transfers across the British Channel and across the Atlantic with their social and cultural repercussions for urban societies in the transatlantic world before World War I.

The cultural and social infrastructure of nineteenth-century cities within the transatlantic community did not emerge in isolation but was a result of intensive contacts and transfers across geographic, linguistic, and later "imagined" national borders. London's social housing companies inspired similar enterprises in continental European and North American cities. Museum associations and libraries in German cities impressed American visitors so much that they returned home with a passion to create similar institutions in their hometowns. These institutions in turn became the subject of observation by German travelers, who at the end of the nineteenth century searched for inspiration for urban and social reform in American cities.

The Concept of Intercultural Transfer

The approach of intercultural transfer, developed in the 1980s by Michel Espagne and Michael Werner for the investigation of cross-cultural contacts between Germany and France, provides a new theoretical framework for the investigation of transatlantic exchanges and cultural borrowing.[2] Intercultural transfer refers to the movement of material objects, people, and ideas between two separate and clearly defined cultures and societies.[3] According to Kirsten Belgum, the concept of intercultural transfer presumes "three things: (1) that something is being transferred, (2) that there is a point of departure for that transfer, and

(3) that there is a point of arrival."[4] For Bernd Kortländer, intercultural transfer happens as a three-step process of selection, transport, and integration.[5]

Intercultural transfer always occurs below and beyond the level of the nation-state and connects regions and places in distant areas. This concept assumes an openness of societies that allows for outside contacts and the import/export of ideas. In the process of intercultural transfer, societies acquire ideas that undergo modification and in the end contribute to the diversification of the societies involved. Espagne and Werner reminded historians that intercultural transfer always includes the adaptation and assimilation of foreign ideas, which in the process of transfer are integrated into the receiving society and thereby contribute to the stabilization of regional and local identities.[6]

In contrast to traditional ways of writing history, transfer history does not serve to legitimize national cultures or groups. History written along the lines of intercultural transfer undermines national stories of exceptionalism and uniqueness. The goal of transfer history, for Espagne, is to uncover the interconnectedness of various cultures and societies. To be clear, transfer history is concerned with the excavation of foreign influences and the appropriation of such influences within a given culture but not with the study of political or diplomatic contacts between different nations.[7]

Although the study of intercultural transfer breaks with old notions of the dominance and distinctiveness of nation-states, it still assumes the existence of distinct and different communities, between which the transfer occurs.[8] That might be problematic, since communities in the making, which have been the arrival and departure points of intercultural transfers, have never been as stable as the proponents of transfer history and comparative history have suggested. Furthermore, the occurrence of intercultural transfer reflects cultures, which are not static but in a constant flux of change, making it challenging to identify homegrown concepts and outside influences. Since intercultural transfer often works both ways, and thus changes the structure and character of the arrival and departure points, the distinctiveness of both societies is called into question. Ideas traveling between two societies and their successful integration in the receiving society should alert us to the fact that both cultures possess a degree of openness and compatibility that might outweigh their perceived distinct character. In other words, if nineteenth-century German cities provided concepts for the organization of American metropolises, does the successful integration of such concepts tell us something about the compatibility of urban society on both sides of the Atlantic? Or would it be better to speak of one culture that spanned the Atlantic and included middle- and upper-class urban societies on both sides?

When Felix Warburg, a wealthy Hamburg banker, went in 1895 to New York City, where he was to join his future wife, it took him twelve days to cross the Atlantic. And although Warburg was new to New York City, this American metropolis did not feel alien to him. As Sven Beckert pointed out, the elites of New York and Hamburg shared common values: they read similar books, followed similar social conventions, expressed similar ideas about social organization and responsibility, and enjoyed a similar urban culture including museums and operas. Although thousands of miles away from Hamburg, Warburg felt right at home.[9]

Agents of Intercultural Transfer

Transfer history depends on individual agency. Thus this concept offers a unique opportunity to combine an investigation of social structures with the study of individual agency. Agents of intercultural transfer were not ambassadors or political functionaries of nation-states but acted on their own and often in concert with larger local social and cultural organizations. They did not, however, belong to transnational religious, political, or cultural organizations. As private nineteenth-century citizens, they were concerned with the improvement of their hometown. To become an agent of intercultural transfer was not a choice or a profession, but it could become a well-respected career. It happened by chance and was always related to travel and social privilege. It was the wealthy citizen traveling for education and enjoyment who encountered models for the creation of an urban infrastructure. Travel was essential but did not always result in transfer and in learning about the different ways of creating an urban infrastructure. Agents of intercultural transfer were very selective in their observations of other cultures. Their "selective eyes"[10] were predetermined by their social and cultural experience and by the contacts they were able to employ for observation and study.

However, it seems to be questionable that travel did not have any impact on the agents of intercultural transfer themselves. It is certainly true that they perceived Europe according to expectations and stereotypes formed long before their arrival. These psychological structures, in turn, influenced how they perceived the world they encountered. In his journal, for instance, George Ticknor insisted on calling the Royal Saxon Library simply a public library[11] and he praised it for its unrestricted access to the public without ever investigating who exactly entered that library. When he returned to Boston from his second trip to Germany in 1835–36, he wanted to re-create what he thought he had seen and experienced in Dresden. And while his perception of Dresden's society was certainly predetermined by social and cultural stereotypes, it was not American stereotypes that influenced his perception of Germany but the stereotypes of Dresden's nobility and royal court.[12]

Nineteenth-century intercultural transfer differed fundamentally from earlier colonial encounters (e.g., missionaries) in that the agents of intercultural transfer in most cases belonged to the receiving culture. Although agents of intercultural transfer may have been filled with a missionary zeal too, they were certainly not missionaries in the traditional meaning of the term. They did not represent a superior culture and were not guided by the negation of the receiving society. And although they admired the giving society, which they perceived as superior to their own, they were still concerned with the transformation of the object of transfer to make it fit into the receiving culture. Intercultural transfer always depended on perceived or real differences between two cultures. Feelings of inferiority and superiority played an important role as motivating factors for intercultural transfer. For wealthy New Yorkers, it was exactly the feeling of cultural inferiority to such poor and politically backward places as Spain and Saxony which, nevertheless, possessed museums that every American traveler wanted to visit before he left the European continent that spurred the founding of the Metropolitan Museum

of Art in New York.[13] Without a feeling of inferiority and without a clear acknowledgment of the superiority of the other culture, intercultural transfer would not
have occurred.

In the process of transfer, agents of transfer became the authors of the object
of transfer, since they selected certain concepts and further transformed them to
make them compatible with the receiving culture. This was necessary because
agents of intercultural transfer returned with their object of transfer to the society
they had left and were confronted with a virtually unchanged society and the challenge of integrating an alien object into this culture in order to transform society according to their visions. Thus agents of intercultural transfer engaged in the
observation, the transfer, and the replication of a model they created in the process
of transfer.[14] According to William Stowe, this role allowed "nonproductive" members of society "to justify their privilege" and to "minimize their guilt feelings"
toward a society that had made the neo-Puritan work ethic the norm. They could
take up positions of teachers and experts and "act out their desires for authority
and importance."[15]

Knowledge about concepts and the direct experience during travel, however,
were never sufficient preconditions for a successful transfer. Sometimes it took
decades before certain models were replicated in the receiving culture. In the case
of Ticknor's free lending library, it took thirty-two years to create the Boston Public Library.[16] The desire for the establishment of such institutions by the receiving
society is as important as the availability of models that could be implemented and
the necessary funding. Although the desire for a public library was prevalent, and
although Ticknor lobbied friends and city government for some time to create a free
lending library, it took the pledge of Joshua Bates to finally realize Ticknor's dream.

It would be wrong to assume that intercultural transfers occurred only in one
direction. After Ticknor had established the Boston Public Library and George
Fisk Comfort had created the Metropolitan Museum of Art, these institutions
became the object of observation by Canadian (Sir Edmund Walker) and German
(Constantin Nörrenberg and Adolf Bernhard Meyer) travelers who advocated the
transfer of these perceived models (in the case of Nörrenberg free lending libraries and in the case of Meyer the museum association) to their hometowns. It was
not unusual that one particular model traveled several times across the Atlantic
and across continents. It should be clear that transformations and modifications
sometimes changed these models to a degree that they were barely recognizable by
members of the giving society as having originated from within their own culture.
The circle of intercultural transfer was thus complete. The replica had become the
model that was replicated in the country of origin and sold as something amaz-
ingly new and alien.

Philanthropy and Leisure Class

The challenge for any comparative study is to find a level of comparison that allows
the scholar to discuss similarities, differences, and (in the case of transfer studies)
influences between two or more distinct cultures and societies. The decision for
a particular level of comparison is determined not only by comparable historical

phenomena but also by the current state of historical scholarship. As historians in the United States, Germany, Great Britain, and Canada have begun to study the history of philanthropy for their particular national culture, they have developed very different concepts, theories, and explanations for philanthropic traditions and actions. American and British historians have come to see philanthropy as a general social phenomenon that transcended class boundaries.[17] German historians, in contrast, have conceptualized philanthropy in the context of research on class society and focused on philanthropy as a constitutive element of elite culture.[18] Although one can certainly disagree with either of these two interpretations, for the purpose of a comparative study scholars have to rely on previous research and interpretations. Since there is an extensive body of research on elite philanthropy in Germany, Canada, Great Britain, and the United States, it seemed to be logical for this comparison to focus on philanthropy of the affluent leisure class. This is not to say that philanthropy was limited to this social formation.

A further decision was necessary with regard to the terminology. Those scholars who investigate philanthropy of the wealthy in various national historiographical cultures have developed their own concepts of social stratification. German historians speak of the Bürgertum, which is more than just an economic formation, since it includes economic elites (Wirtschaftsbürgertum) as well as educated elites (Bildungsbürgertum).[19] Further, German historians have come to believe that this formation has developed a specific value system that provides the glue to hold its two factions together. Philanthropy is one element in this value system. In contrast, most American historians shy away from clear concepts of social stratification of American society.[20] Elites, middle class, and upper middle class are just a few of the many ways American historians identify the wealthy. Since it will be argued in this book that motives for engagement in philanthropy were similar in the communities under investigation, it seemed problematic to use different terms for socially privileged groups in European and North American contexts. Such differences in terminology imply differences in analysis that are not there. For this reason, Thorstein Veblen's underused concept of the "leisure class" has been adopted for this comparative study.

In his observation of late-nineteenth-century American society, Veblen acknowledged the importance of ostentatious consumption of the elites for their self-assertion and claim to social leadership.[21] In contrast to Karl Marx's reasoning about the emergence of social classes, Veblen came to acknowledge that it was the sphere of consumption and not production that provided the basis for the formation of distinct social classes. The consumption of goods became, in Veblen's thinking, a display of wealth, and the failure to consume an acknowledgment of inferiority. Since Veblen traced the emergence of the leisure class through all of history from tribal to modern society, he concluded that with the growing accumulation of wealth, different factions with an elaborated system of ranks and grades within the leisure class emerged. "This differentiation is furthered by the inheritance of wealth and the consequent inheritance of gentility. With the inheritance of gentility goes the inheritance of obligatory leisure." In this context, Veblen pointed to an interesting aspect, since "gentility of a sufficient potency to entail a life of leisure may be inherited without the complement of wealth required to maintain a dignified leisure."[22] Leisure and good reputation are the two cornerstones for identifying the leisure class in any given society. "The basis on which good repute in any highly organised industrial community ultimately rests is pecuniary strength; and the means of showing pecuniary strength, and so of gaining or retaining a good name, are leisure and a conspicuous consumption of goods."[23] Conspicuous consumption and leisure are both a "waste of time and goods." But it also demonstrates the possession of wealth to the public.

Although some scholars might object to classifying philanthropy as part of conspicuous consumption and therefore as a waste of time and goods, it is the basis for legitimate and necessary support for charitable and cultural projects. There is no doubt that many philanthropists acted out of religious feelings and humanistic motives. However, elite philanthropy was always a public and much publicized event. The wealthy and rich gave not only out of feelings of responsibility but also out of a desire to be recognized by their peers. Elite philanthropy shares many elements with Veblen's concept of conspicuous consumption. Both were a display of accumulated wealth, both were a public performance, and both helped in defining the class structure of nineteenth-century society. Within the context of nineteenth-century urban culture and the struggle between old and new elites for dominance over urban society, philanthropy played a significant role in asserting positions of cultural and social power. With an eye on the position of women in early American society, Kathleen McCarthy has pointed to the role of philanthropy "in enabling even politically disadvantaged groups to shape American society." She asserts, "Participation in voluntary associations ultimately gave women a voice in local, state, and national legislative debates, as well as the distribution of charitable resources. Women—especially (but not exclusively) middle- and upperclass white women—used the parallel power structures that they created through their charities to influence legislation."[24]

While McCarthy focuses on the empowering function of philanthropy for women, one might consider her argument in a larger context. Women were not the only disenfranchised or disadvantaged group in the nineteenth century. Jews shared the experience of discrimination and of engaging in philanthropy to attain recognition and integration.[25] And if philanthropy worked for disadvantaged groups, it must also have provided power to those majority groups which dominated philanthropic practice.

The involvement in the creation of major public institutions in nineteenth-century cities offered philanthropists an opportunity to define the public sphere according to their desires and value systems. In museums, philanthropists decided about the objects on display by donating entire collections and imposing restrictions on their presentation. In libraries, they tried to shape public taste with their decisions about the books to be purchased. And in the case of social housing enterprises, they set standards for the architectural design and thus attempted to define the modern family. Even if the success of these imposed norms is questionable, philanthropic institutions provided their founders with a cultural power structure that runs parallel to the political power structure. They may have overlapped for a significant period of time, since old elites dominated both city government and the boards of various philanthropic institutions. However, as in the case of women, a significant group of citizens, although excluded from participation in political life, could still influence the shaping of their city through charitable work. Such actions could be seen as a first step toward inclusion of women in political life. But, as Kathleen McCarthy reminds us, most women involved in elite philanthropy were no suffragettes.[26] Therefore, one might be tempted to reconsider philanthropy as a countermodel to emancipation.

It would be wrong to consider philanthropy with its ability to function as a social mechanism for exclusion and inclusion only as part of a progressive movement. Since philanthropy offered to its proponents a cultural countergovernment, it could, as in the case of Boston's Brahmins, also serve as a retreat for social elites who lost direct control over political life. Losing city hall to the Irish was tolerable to the Brahmin caste because they considered their hold over the many philanthropic institutions they had created and dominated for so long as a counterweight to political power. In both scenarios, philanthropy emerged as a parallel world in which social relations were negotiated and in which members of an elite attempted to exercise power through cultural and charitable institutions.

STRUCTURE OF THE BOOK

The first part of this book traces the intercultural transfer of museums, libraries, and social housing enterprises between English, German, American, and Canadian societies from the 1840s to the 1910s. The second part compares the emergence of philanthropic cultures in Leipzig, Boston, New York, and Toronto. Using extensive socioeconomic data, it analyzes the conflicts between groups and factions of the leisure class for dominance in philanthropy and thus society.

The first chapter introduces the reader to the intercultural transfers that occurred in the cultural realm. Tracing American museum associations back to their German roots, it will be shown how European concepts of supporting cultural institutions influenced the emergence of an American and later Canadian cultural cityscape. New York's museums, which were deeply influenced by German and English concepts of museum organization, occupied a central position in the intercultural transfer and mediation of such models. After the Metropolitan Museum of Art had successfully introduced the concept of a museum association, it became a model for subsequent creations in other American and Canadian cities. Agents of intercultural transfer, who had traveled to Germany and collected information about the functioning of museums, were essential for this transfer. The same holds true for the transfer of the free lending library from Dresden to Boston, which was the outcome of George Ticknor's experience during his travels in Germany and his extensive lobbying for such a library after his return. This chapter also turns the reader's attention to the reimport of these concepts from the United States to Germany at the end of the nineteenth century. By that time, Germans came to the United States in search of ideas for reorganizing their own cultural and social life. They found the free lending library and the museum association to be enticing models for a modern city. Little did they know about the German roots of both concepts. And little thought was given to the origins of these ideas, which were sold as American in nature back home.

While these transfers in the cultural sphere follow a pattern of mutual exchange in which ideas travel back and forth between Europe and North America, the second chapter about housing reform sees North America only at the receiving end. This chapter examines the extensive transnational network of social housing reform that spanned Europe and the Atlantic. With London and its pioneering role in social housing reform as a focal point, this chapter follows the travels of German and American housing reformers from the 1840s onwards. It tells the story of various individuals who came to London in search of solutions for the overcrowding of apartment buildings and the emergence of slums. Three waves of observers can be distinguished:

1. From 1840 to 1860, German agents of intercultural transfer arrived in London to study its nascent social housing enterprises. Upon their return to Berlin and Frankfurt, they engaged in the creation of similar institutions in their hometowns. From here these ideas spread to all corners of Germany. Grand Duchess Alice of Hesse-Darmstadt found herself in the unique position of being a translator for Octavia Hill's ideas and thus helping in the proliferation of social housing reform in Germany.

2. From the early 1870s, American social reformers joined their German colleagues in traveling to London to study its social housing enterprises. They then produced texts about their experiences in London and founded social housing enterprises inspired by the London examples.

3. The third wave of intercultural transfer occurred between 1880 and 1910 when German housing reformers traveled again to London for inspiration and when American observers cast a wider net and studied social housing enterprises in various cities of continental Europe. Around this time, Canadian housing reformers also grew concerned about the housing conditions in Montreal and Toronto. However, in contrast to the United States, it was English social reformers who influenced the Canadian discourse on housing reform.

Based on this extensive transnational network of social reformers and the complex processes of intercultural transfer within the transatlantic world, local urban cultures of philanthropy emerged which relied on each other for innovation and proliferation. The three chapters in the second part of this book investigate the contested philanthropic cultures in Leipzig, Boston, New York, and Toronto. Based on the evaluation of extensive biographical data for those individuals who founded and supported major public institutions in these four cities, it will be shown that philanthropy played a part in the struggle between new and old elites for power and domination over urban communities. Depending on the strength of the new elites and the resistance of the old elites, two basic patterns emerged: divided philanthropic culture (New York and Leipzig) and unified philanthropic culture (Boston and Toronto).

A divided philanthropic culture emerged from the presence of at least two competing factions of the leisure class which aspired to domination of urban society. In the case of New York, old and new elites were equally strong, and the old elites furiously resisted integration of members of the new elites into their ranks. Both groups embarked on creating their own philanthropic infrastructure, which reflected the divisions within the leisure class.

A unified philanthropic culture emerged from two starting points: the absence or weakness of a new elite that could challenge the old elites (Boston), and the successful integration of selected newly rich individuals to prevent the emergence of a coherent new elite (Toronto). In the case of Boston, the new elites were no match for the old elites' power and, furthermore, did not challenge the old elites' grip on their philanthropic institutions. In the case of Toronto, old and new elites were equally weak and simply could not afford to establish competing philanthropic networks. With the help of Sir Edmund Walker, selected financially powerful members of the new elites were integrated into the old elites, further weakening the new elites and preventing a standoff between factions of the leisure class.

The lines of conflict run not only along the lines of various elite groups, old and new money, but also along gender and religious lines. Throughout the nineteenth century, women played an increasing role in the founding, financing, and running of philanthropic institutions. For Kathleen McCarthy and Richard Stites,[27] this philanthropic engagement seemed to provide women who were excluded from political life with an opportunity to shape urban communities according to their dreams and desires. The same was true for Jews who, largely excluded from political and social life, saw in engagement in nonsectarian philanthropy a way to gain recognition from their Christian peers and to be accepted into the leading circles of society. Philanthropy offered both disadvantaged groups a way out of social isolation and discrimination.

By studying philanthropy in these contexts, this book will expand our understanding and concept of philanthropy. While the book focuses on a rather limited section of philanthropy—the actions of the wealthy—it casts philanthropy in a new light. Philanthropy is conceived as a social tool for the integration and exclusion of various social groups (defined by gender, religion, economic power, and heritage) and contributes to the formation of hierarchies in modern societies. Thus philanthropy reflects the need of economic elites for social distinction and status even in egalitarian societies such as the United States. While not every member of the leisure class contributed to philanthropic projects, philanthropy became a key element of elite identity.

CHAPTER ONE

Cultural Excursions: Museums, Art Galleries, and Libraries in a Transatlantic World

S ince the German social welfare state entered a period of crisis and reconstruction, both Conservatives and Social Democrats have encouraged the revitalization of private funding for public cultural institutions such as art galleries and museums. The reconstruction of the Frauenkirche is the most visible sign of this new political climate. Destroyed in World War II, the ruins of the church in downtown Dresden were left untouched because the East German government declared this pile of rubble a powerful monument to the horrors of war. After German unification in 1990, the newly elected government of the state of Saxony under its conservative premier, Kurt Biedenkopf, decided to resurrect the Frauenkirche in an attempt to revive a regional identity and create a civil society in which the citizens and the state share responsibility for cultural icons. A private foundation was created to secure two-thirds of the construction costs from private sponsors. Between 1993 and 2005, roughly 600,000 individuals contributed 100 million Euros to this project.[1]

Inspiration for the current privatization of cultural sponsorship is drawn from a perceived American model. Since the early 1990s, German politicians, intellectuals, and social scientists have looked admiringly to the United States and its privately funded museums, universities, and libraries.[2] However, as in all cases of intercultural transfer, the perception of a foreign model is highly selective and, as Gabriele Lingelbach has argued, guided by the interests of those who advocate changes. References to a "prestigious" foreign model often serve just as an instrument for achieving reforms and are not always connected to any actual transfer of ideas.[3] This is not to suggest that such an intercultural transfer is highly unlikely, as Lingelbach seems to imply. The cultures and societies of Central and Western Europe and North America were connected by large-scale migration and cultural exchange and borrowing. As Daniel T. Rodgers notes, none of the cultures within the transatlantic world developed in isolation.[4] Migration and travel were the engines of intercultural exchange, transfer, implementation, and assimilation of cultural institutions. The experience of traveling in Europe influenced well-off Americans, as Neil Harris has suggested:

Many Americans learned abroad to look at their own country for the first time, and many were unhappy with what they saw. Out of their sense of native deficiencies grew a new respect for European institutions and commitments to the artistic enterprise in America. Americans once had idealized individualism and pluralism, attempting in their polity to control the effects rather than the causes of faction; they now sought new means of engineering consent and molding the opinions, as well as the actions, of their fellow citizens.[5]

The enjoyment of museums, art galleries, and libraries in Europe as well as the many letters and reports about these institutions sparked interest in establishing a similar cultural life in American cities.[6] It will be suggested that the creation of museums, art galleries, and libraries in North America was influenced by the observation of similar European institutions by wealthy American and Canadian travelers who became agents of intercultural transfer. These travelers returned with ideas regarding how to organize a museum, how to arrange an exhibition, how to house an exhibition, and how to finance and support a museum and its construction. The founders of the Metropolitan Museum of Art in New York City were inspired by the Dresden and Leipzig art galleries. Toronto's museum makers sent emissaries to New York and Leipzig to explore the organization, architecture, and financing schemes of museums. Boston's Public Library would never have been founded if George Ticknor (1791–1871) had not been so impressed by Dresden's Royal Saxon Library. Major cultural landmarks in this country owe their existence to wealthy Americans who studied cultural institutions in Europe and founded museums, art galleries, and libraries employing European strategies, exhibition techniques, and financing schemes. However, intercultural transfer is never a one-way street; instead, it involves multiple transfers (both failed and successful) in multiple directions. At the end of the nineteenth century, German social reformers visiting the United States were impressed by the democratic character of museums and libraries. Often unaware of the German roots of these institutions, they returned home arguing that German cities needed to adopt these "American models."[7]

While we have some information on the application of American ideas in Germany, such as the free public library, the inspiration of German and British concepts for the creation of cultural institutions in North America has nearly remained terra incognita. One notable exception is Kathleen D. McCarthy's reference to the inspiration that Julius Rosenwald and John G. Shedd received from German museums for the founding of the Chicago Museum of Science and Industry. Rosenwald and Shedd had "commissioned studies of similar European ventures before publicly pledging their gifts, augmenting the investigators' findings with personal observations of their own." Munich's Deutsches Museum became the blueprint for the Chicago museum.[8] Even though Rodgers reminded historians of the interconnected character of European and American history, the investigation of intercultural transfers across the Atlantic has not attracted larger attention among German and American historians of the nineteenth century. Using the example of the Metropolitan Museum of Art in New York, the Boston Public Library, and the Toronto Art Gallery, the following pages will shed light on how major American and Canadian cultural institutions were created under the influence of their European predecessors. It will be argued that German museums, founded and funded by art associations (Kunstvereine), provided the organizational blueprint for the Metropolitan Museum of Art, which in return became a model for subsequent museum projects in other American and Canadian cities. Ironically, the very same North American cultural institutions served, in some cases, as models for the (re)organization of museums and libraries in Germany around 1900 and again in the 1990s.

"Yet beyond the Sea . . .": George Fiske Comfort and the Founding of the Metropolitan Museum of Art

For several decades, wealthy New Yorkers and Bostonians traveled to Germany to enjoy the rich social and cultural life in Berlin, Leipzig, and Dresden. The art galleries, libraries, universities, and concert halls of Dresden and Leipzig attracted large numbers of Americans who found there what they lacked back home. William Cullen Bryant (1794–1878) and George Ticknor spent much time in Dresden's art gallery, the Grünes Gewölbe, and the Royal Saxon Library. Back home, both advocated the establishment of similar institutions in New York and Boston.[9] The Metropolitan Museum of Art and the Boston Public Library were the results of their advocacy. After decades of having to cross the Atlantic in order to enjoy a rich cultural life, New York's leisure class became impatient with the quality of urban life in the New World. At the end of the 1860s, members of the elitist Union League Club took a lead in the creation of the Metropolitan Museum of Art.

The Union League Club was one of the most exclusive social clubs of New York. Founded in 1863, this club represented New York's exclusive society. Like the Union Club and the Knickerbocker Club, the Union League Club was modeled on London's social clubs. It differed from the Union Club and the Knickerbocker Club only in its political character. According to the standard account of the Union League Club's history, "The only requisite for membership" was an "unblemished reputation, [. . .] an uncompromising and unconditional loyalty to the nation, and a complete subordination thereto of all other political ideas." The members of the Union League Club came foremost from the old Dutch and English families, who had arrived on the shores of the New World during the seventeenth and eighteenth centuries. Many of its members were "men with colonial names" who belonged to New York's leading circles and had made their money in real estate and banking.[10] To ensure the social exclusivity of this political and social club, membership requirements limited access. Candidates for admission had to "be proposed by one member, seconded by another, and bulletined, before reference to the committee whose business it [was] to investigate as to qualifications or eligibility. At every monthly meeting of the club, it [was] the duty of this body to report upon the names of candidates submitted to its consideration, after which the members vote[d] by ballot upon names thus recommended."[11]

The admission fee was set at $100, the yearly dues at $60. Clearly, the members of the Union League Club belonged to New York's wealthiest and most exclusive circles. The European Grand Tour for cultural education was a shared experience among its members. William Cullen Bryant, one of the founders of the Union League Club, made several visits to the Old World and inspired other members to follow his example by traveling to Europe or sending their children. Washington Irving and James Fenimore Cooper, who gave us detailed accounts about their European experiences, shed some light on the custom of American travels in Germany.[12]

In 1835 and 1836, Americans like George Ticknor stayed for several months in German cities, and thanks to a favorable exchange rate they enjoyed a lifestyle they would never have been able to sustain back home. For wealthy Americans, this transatlantic Grand Tour "was a way of affirming the respectability of one's race, class, or gender."[13] Thus wealthy New Yorkers spent much time in Europe enjoying museums, art galleries, and libraries. From May through November 1845, Bryant visited the European continent. After arriving in Liverpool, he visited Cologne, Düsseldorf, Nuremberg, Berlin, Dresden, and Leipzig in August and September.[14] Bryant was especially impressed by the art museums found in the small Kingdom of Saxony. After John Jay suggested the establishment of a Metropolitan Art Museum in New York in his speech to Americans in Paris celebrating the ninetieth anniversary of American independence in 1866,[15] Bryant became involved in the attempts made by the Union League Club to popularize such an enterprise among his peers. He accepted George P. Putnam's invitation to preside over a meeting on November 23, 1869, in the Theatre of the Union League Club to which all individuals interested in establishing such an art museum were invited.[16] Some three hundred members of the Union League Club, the National Academy of Design, the New-York Historical Society, the Century, the Manhattan, and other social clubs attended this meeting. In his introductory speech, Bryant reminded his fellow citizens that in terms of cultural life and atmosphere New York could not compete with even the tiniest European city or kingdom:

> Yet beyond the sea there is the little kingdom of Saxony, which, with an area less than that of Massachusetts, and a population but little larger, possesses a Museum of the Fine Arts marvelously rich, which no man who visits the continent of Europe is willing to own that he has not seen. There is Spain, a third-rate power of Europe and poor besides, with a museum of Fine Arts at her capital, the opulence and extent of which absolutely bewilder the visitor. I will not speak of France or of England, conquering nations, which have gathered their treasures of art in part from regions overrun by their armies; nor yet of Italy, the fortunate inheritor of so many glorious productions of her own artists. But there are Holland and Belgium, kingdoms almost too small to be heeded by the greater powers of Europe in the consultations which decide the destinies of nations, and these little kingdoms have their public collections of art, the resort of admiring visitors from all parts of the civilized world.[17]

Bryant's emotional speech was followed by an enthusiastic but informed talk about art museums and the organizing principles of art collections by George Fiske Comfort (1833–1910), an 1857 graduate of Wesleyan College who had spent nearly five years (1860–1865) in Europe.[18] He traveled extensively from Trieste to Turkey, Greece, Italy, Spain, Austria, France, Belgium, Holland, Germany, and Great Britain. Not much is known about this travel or about how much time he spent in each country and which universities and museums he visited. However, we know from his letters and notes that he spent years in Germany. In a letter to Reverend John Makan (Allegheny College) in 1866, Comfort stated that he had spent "nearly five years in traveling through most of the classic lands of ancient and medieval art, studying the monuments and museums, and devoting nearly half of my time to formal study in the German universities."[19]

In his speech, Comfort pointed to the museums in Kensington and Berlin as possible blueprints for the Metropolitan Museum of New York City:

> The Kensington Museum has been organized within twenty years, and it contains a large number of casts of works of sculpture and architecture and many works of art that are owned by wealthy people in England, left there as loans for the inspection of the public without cost. They may be reclaimed by them or their heirs, but probably the larger portion will be given or bequeathed to the museum. This museum also contains a large collection of works, illustrating the application of the arts to industry. And there are schools connected with the museum—it is an institution of science as well.[20]

As this passage shows, Comfort favored the connection between the display of artistic work and artistic education. More important, he was very concerned with the property rights of the artistic works. And although the South Kensington Museum provided some inspiration for the founding of the Metropolitan Museum,[21] Comfort's eyes were fixed on the museums in Berlin and other German cities. He continued his speech with high praise for the museums of Berlin as the largest and most impressive cultural institutions of his day:

> The foundation of the old museum building was laid in the year 1828; and the building was finished some four years after. The foundation of the new museum building was laid in the year 1852, and was finished two or three years after. This building contains to day the largest collection of casts of works of Sculpture of any museum in the world. There is no place where a person can study to more advantage the progress of Sculpture, from its first appearance in Egypt down to its appearance in Greece and through the middle ages, and through the modern times, than he can in Berlin, and by all means of this valuable collection of casts. The casts that are in that museum, if I am rightly informed, cost about 300,000 thalers, which is equivalent to about 300,000 dollars in our present paper money.[22]

Comfort learned to appreciate both museums during his extensive study in that city between 1863 and 1865, "where he pursued his studies in the University, the Academy of Fine Arts and the Royal Library. He was received in social circles of leading artists, critics, connoisseurs, and the professors of art and archeology of that great literary capital of the world, as Cornelius Keinlbach, Lepsius, Waagen, Gerhart, Piper, Von Ranke, and others."[23] In the aforementioned letter to Makan, Comfort pointed out that he had "paid much attention to the organization of academies of art and museums of art."[24] While he studied in Berlin, Comfort visited art museums in Nuremberg, Munich, Leipzig, Dresden, Posen, and Bremen in order to collect information about the organization of art institutions in these cities and the objects shown.[25]

Traveling to these cities, Comfort encountered a rich, cultural urban life that included art museums, private exhibitions, and art associations. As Manuel Frey pointed out, by 1850 nearly every German city had its own art association.[26] Wealthy citizens founded these associations to organize exhibitions, support artists, and create art museums independent of royal/ducal control. Within the context of nineteenth-century German society, art associations represented the drive for bourgeois emancipation from a feudal monopoly over art. By establishing their own art scene, burghers claimed a leading position within urban society, and by financing artistic endeavors, they proved their economic power and their desire to produce a new culture. Such art associations represented a collective approach to philanthropy, since they could easily bring together several hundred members. The Leipzig Kunstverein, for example, received support from 980 members in 1837.[27]

Throughout the nineteenth century, art museums founded by royal/ducal authorities and by bourgeois art associations became the focal point of cultural life in German cities. According to Walter Grasskamp, art museums were founded in two waves. During the first half of the nineteenth century, dukes and kings financed royal art museums and collections. The Old and the New Museum in Berlin, the Art Gallery in Dresden, and the Art Hall in Karlsruhe are prime examples of this period. In the second half of the nineteenth century, Leipzig, Bremen, and Hamburg, which were not court cities and subsequently not dominated by the nobility, received art museums founded and financed by self-confident and economically and politically powerful burghers.[28] With the exception of the Städelsche Art Institute in Frankfurt am Main, founded in 1816 by Johann Friedrich Städel,[29] all other art museums resulted from the activities of local art associations. The first such museum was built in Bremen between 1845 and 1849.[30] Generally, these museums were financed by wealthy citizens.[31] Since American scholars who studied the emergence of art museums looked only to those museums created by royal/ducal rulers and ignored the new type of art museums that entered the cultural scene in the second half of the nineteenth century, nineteenth-century Germany came to be seen as a state in which art patronage remained a feudal privilege.[32] That also explains the absence of any inquiries into the intercultural transfer of museum concepts between Germany and the United States.

Influenced by what he experienced in Germany, Comfort

> expressed himself as "overwhelmingly impressed by the vast gulf, wider and deeper than the Atlantic Ocean, that separated the institutions and conditions of education and culture in continental Europe from those in America," speaking especially of that time, the early sixties. And he felt impelled to dedicate his life, as far as his circumstances should permit, to awakening a more active interest in higher culture, especially in esthetic and artistic lines, in his native country, particularly by establishing institutions, as schools and museums, for promoting and diffusing artistic education and culture in the people at large.[33]

His handwritten "Address before the Syracuse Chamber of Commerce Regarding a Museum of Fine Arts" (1897) not only provides some details about what Comfort encountered in Germany but also gives a plan for the establishment of a fine arts museum. In this speech, Comfort emphasized the importance of museums for attracting visitors from other countries. He noted that most American travelers after having arrived in Hamburg or Bremen immediately left for Dresden or Munich. Dresden attracted a large number of "cultured men" and travelers because of its famous art galleries. Large colonies of wealthy, transient residents from Russia, Great Britain, and the United States sprang up in the capital of Saxony. Comfort reminded his audience that "the possession of Raphael's Sistine Madonna alone, perhaps the most pleasing and popular picture in the world, gives luster to the fame of the city of Dresden, and adds to the material wealth of the city."[34]

Although Comfort was very impressed by the exceptional collection of the Dresden art gallery, he recognized that it would not inspire similar institutions in the United States, since a nobility was absent and the wealthy men of his days were little inclined to dedicate enormous amounts of money toward an art gallery. When Comfort suggested the creation of a museum of fine arts in Syracuse in the 1890s, he considered four ways. First, the museum could be established by one wealthy bene-factor who would provide the necessary finances for the building and the exhibi-tion. This proposal reflected the general organization of museums in German court cities, where the museum was supported by the local ruler, and in cities such as Frankfurt am Main, where extremely wealthy burghers provided sufficient financial and material wealth to fund an art museum on their own (e.g., Städelsches Art Insti-tute). Second, the city of Syracuse could establish such an institution as a munici-pal agency financed with tax money. Comfort's suggestion that a city government should assume financial responsibility for cultural institutions was somewhat ahead of his time, even for Germany. "A third method," according to Comfort, "would be the united voluntary contribution of persons who desire and enjoy the benefits of such a museum, as a kind of a club or a membership corporation, the collections being opened to the public." This proposal reflects the organizational blueprint of such cultural institutions as the Leipzig Art Museum, where several hundred citi-zens collectively financed the building and the art collection. The financiers decided about the museum's hours, entry fees, and accessibility to the lower classes. A fourth possibility, according to Comfort, was the "Metropolitan Museum Plan." Comfort considered this the best solution because it was based on the concept of private-communal cooperation. The Metropolitan Museum of Art in New York received financial support from both the municipal and state governments as well as from philanthropists who donated financial or material goods to this institution. Further-more, the museum was open to the public, and entrance was free of charge.[35]

While this sketch was written long after the Metropolitan Museum of Art in New York City was established, it shows that Comfort championed the system of collective philanthropy. In a letter to George P. Putnam, chairman of the organiz-ing committee of the Metropolitan Museum, Comfort suggested several German museums (Gotha, Berlin, Nuremberg) as possible models, but he mentioned the Leipzig museum of art before all others.[36] He probably visited the Leipzig museum during his stay in Germany. It was opened to the public in December 1858—two years before Comfort arrived in Europe—and displayed the paintings, casts, and statues purchased by the Leipzig art association. The museum building had been financed by Heinrich Adolf Schletter, a wealthy silk merchant. The art associa-tion funded purchases of art objects or donated paintings and drawings directly to the museum. The membership was divided into two groups: the shareholders (Aktionäre) who paid three taler a year and the subscribers (Abonnenten) who paid one taler and eight groschen a year.[37]

Comfort recommended forming a membership organization, the American version of the German art association, to collect sufficient financial and material

FIGURE 1.1. Leipzig Art Museum. Photograph by Hermann Walter, ca. 1890.
Courtesy of the Stadtgeschichtliches Museum Leipzig.

support from wealthy citizens. At the initial meeting in November 1869, a provisional committee of fifty prominent New York citizens was formed. Among its members were William H. Aspinwell, William T. Blodgett, George Fiske Comfort, Frederick Law Olmsted, and Rutherfurd Stuyvesant.[38] Within this committee a subcommittee of thirteen men under Putnam's leadership was appointed to prepare a constitution. In May 1870, this association was incorporated and its constitution was published.

The structure of this new association adopted some features from the German art associations and some features from the social clubs of New York City. Similar to the Union Club and the Union League Club, membership in the Metropolitan Art Museum Association was initially limited to 250. Those who aspired to become members had to be nominated by the trustees. Only if two-thirds of the members approved the nomination did the aspirant become a member.[39] This procedure was evidently copied from the Union Club and the Union League Club to ensure that only New York's well-established families would gain access. However, the new art association was even more exclusive. While membership in both clubs was limited in numbers and restricted to Knickerbocker families, it was sufficient that a new member was proposed by one existing member and seconded by another member. Neither of the two clubs required two-thirds of its members to approve. The nomination and election procedure would ensure the exclusion of newer families from this exclusive art association.[40]

The founding of the New York art association, which was in fact an association not of artists but of philanthropists who pledged to support the arts, was remi-

FIGURE 1.2. Leipzig Art Museum. Photograph by Hermann Walter, ca. 1895. Courtesy of the Stadtgeschichtliches Museum Leipzig.

niscent of Leipzig's art association, which differed from other art associations in the social/occupational profile of its membership. While the Dresden art association had a large number of artists among its members, the Leipzig art association was nearly exclusively an organization of wealthy citizens who were interested in the promotion and funding of art. Less than 7 percent of the members of Leipzig's art association had been artists. With 5 percent, New York's art association had an even lower share.[41] In Leipzig and in New York, the primary goal was to establish an art museum and to create a membership organization that would provide the financial basis for running it. Similar to Leipzig, the organizational committee in New York decided to establish more than one membership class. However, while the Leipzig organizers thought that two classes were sufficient, New York's organizers insisted on three. For a contribution of $1,000, one could become a patron of the museum, for $500 one became a fellow in perpetuity, and for $200 one was entitled to be a fellow for life.[42]

While German art museums and their art associations provided the inspiration for the organizational structure of the Metropolitan Museum of Art, the South Kensington Museum provided concepts about what to collect and how to arrange the collections.[43] This becomes evident in the decision to include "applied art" to the collections of the museum. A pamphlet about the future plans for the Metropolitan Museum published in March 1871 announced: "Officers of the Museum desire[d] especially to begin at an early day the formation of a collection of industrial art, of objects of utility to which decorative art has been applied, ornamental metalwork, carving in wood, ivory, and stone, painted glass, glass

FIGURE 1.3. The Old Museum in Berlin, ca. 1910. Courtesy of Landesarchiv
Berlin, Fotosammlung.

vessels, pottery, enamel, and all other materials."[44] While the creation of such
collections in German-speaking states was just under way and resulted in the
creation of separate applied arts collections and museums, as for instance the
Deutsches Museum in Nuremberg, which was founded with the idea of illustrat-
ing "the application of art to industry in Germany as well as other branches of
German history," the founders of the Metropolitan Museum attempted in a catch-
all approach to combine the art museum (collection of paintings and busts) with
the museum of applied arts (collection of industrial produced objects).[45]

Comfort's chief concerns were teaching, collaboration with artistic education, and integration of the museum into higher education. The Berlin museum,
which was built in close proximity to the Academy of Fine Arts, impressed
Comfort deeply. He had very fond memories of his education at the University of Berlin, where he could easily "go after the lecture and see the works of
which the lecturer has spoken" in the museum, which was built just around
the corner. Recalling his experience, Comfort told the individuals interested
in founding the Metropolitan Museum of Art in his speech for the first meeting in November 1869: "The Museum of Berlin is used as an appendage to the
University and the professors of the University of Ancient and Modern Art take
their classes from the University building to the Museum building, and there
standing before the work of art can show its good points and the position that
it occupies in the History of Art." Following the Berlin model of connecting
museum and university, Comfort suggested locating the Metropolitan Museum
of Art "in close proximity to a great university." Furthermore, he thought that it
would be desirable to provide the museum with "a few rooms in which lectures
could be given from time to time for the general public." Sharing the belief

that education of the masses would ultimately lead to the betterment of society, Comfort argued that such "an institution . . . would also indirectly stimulate and foster an increased interest on the part of our people in favor of a good municipal government."[46]

TAKING THE BEST OF TWO WORLDS: THE FOUNDING OF THE TORONTO ART GALLERY

The organizational structure of the Metropolitan Museum of Art became a model for many museums founded in the United States and Canada. During the following decades, wealthy citizens from Philadelphia, Boston, and Toronto traveled to New York and visited the Metropolitan Museum of Art. Among them was a young Canadian banker, Byron Edmund Walker (1848–1924), who had been sent to New York by the Canadian Bank of Commerce. After he had left school early, Walker entered the banking business. He joined the Canadian Bank of Commerce in 1868 and was first made chief accountant in Toronto before he was sent to New York as junior agent "with responsibilities which fall to the lot of few young gentlemen of twenty-five." Walker reached New York in the midst of a deep financial crisis. According to a biographical sketch by C. W. Colby, "The failure of Jay Cooke, with all that it involved, created pressing problems for the Junior Agent who had in charge all of the bank's New York loans of gold against currency. To maintain the proper margins and to recover gold that had been lent to firms which suddenly became bankrupt called for incessant vigilance and prompt action. To gain experience of a first-class panic at first hand was an invaluable experience for a young banker."[47]

However, Walker, who was very conscious of his lack of formal education, dedicated his free time to the study of geology and to "a systematic study of pictures and the art of painting."[48] Walker and his wife, Mary Alexander, joined a Browning society in Yonkers and enjoyed the cultural life of New York City. They attended concerts and plays and spent much time in the newly created Metropolitan Museum.[49] First housed in the Dodworth Building at 681 Fifth Avenue, the museum had just moved to the Douglas Mansion at 128 West Fourteenth Street.[50] Here Walker and his wife spent much time studying the paintings and observing the organizational basis for the museum.

During the 1870s, the museum underwent several important changes. First, after the state and city decided to finance the construction of the new museum building for the Metropolitan Museum of Art (and the American Museum of Natural History) in 1871, the city government further "agreed in 1873 to appropriate $30,000 a year for the Metropolitan and the American museums—$15,000 to each—to help pay their rent and other pressing expenses." This marks a sea change for state-public relations in America. For the first time, a city government considered it a duty to support a private but public cultural institution continuously by means of annual subsidies. As Calvin Tomkins points out, this "was an entirely new idea in municipal government, and it became the pattern followed by most of the major art museums in America (although not in Boston, where the Museum of Fine Arts neither solicited nor received any public funds at all)." Second, a fourth category of members was added to the three-tier system of membership. Starting with 1874, the Metropolitan Museum Art Association formed "a new class of membership, annual members, who by the payment of $10 each year should be entitled to a ticket admitting two persons whenever the Museum was open and invitations to all receptions given by the Officers of the Museum." Within a short time, more than six hundred annual members were added.[51]

Walker enjoyed the collections of the Metropolitan Museum as they were displayed in the Douglas Mansion during his first stay in New York between 1873 and 1875 and in the new Metropolitan Museum in Central Park during his second stay in New York between 1881 and 1886.[52] As Katherine A. Lochnan points out, "Walker developed tastes in art which were consistent with the educated anglo-saxon taste of the day. He was drawn to the 'Primitives' of the Northern and Italian Renaissance, in particular to Van Dyck, Van der Weyden, Cimabue, Ghirlandaio, Lippi, and Giotto. He was also interested in the 17th-century Dutch school and its 'modern' exponents, the Barbizon and the Hague Schools."[53]

Walker carefully observed how the Metropolitan Museum was founded and funded by New York's leisure class in collaboration with municipal and state government. The concepts of an art association with a multitiered membership system and of municipal and state support for museums are a theme that can be found in Toronto after 1900, when Walker and other wealthy citizens established the Art Gallery of Ontario and the Royal Ontario Museum.

In 1900, Walker, who was then general manager of the Canadian Bank of Commerce, agreed to chair a committee with the purpose of establishing a Toronto art museum. In contrast to New York and to Leipzig, the artists, not the philanthropists, were the instigators. Already in 1872, Toronto artists had formed the Ontario Society of Artists (OSA) with the goal of establishing an art museum and a school. It was George A. Reid, the president of the OSA, who persuaded Walker to take a leading role in the creation of an art museum. This was an excellent choice for two reasons: First, Walker had carefully observed the organizational structure of the Metropolitan Museum of Art and longed for the establishment of a similar institution in Toronto. Second, as Fergus Cronin argues, Walker had a "yearning for academic experience and for recognition as a man of culture."[54]

Walker was not alone in providing the necessary know-how. James Mavor, professor of political economy at the University of Toronto, used his business travels to collect information on art galleries in Germany.[55] When he went to Europe to examine the possibilities of European immigration to Canada and the effects of the German and Austrian workmen's insurance systems in 1899, he studied art collections and galleries in Dresden, Leipzig, Munich, Nuremberg, Prague, and Stockholm. Mavor ordered photos made of these galleries and their pictures, and he collected catalogs. A small red notebook from his voyage confirms his deep interest in all organizational aspects of these institutions. Like many American "tourists" before him, Mavor was captivated by the exceptionally rich collections of the Dresden art museums—the Green Vault, the Albertinum, and the Palace of the Grosse Garden. He made detailed notes not only about entrance fees but also about accessibility to the public.[56]

Influenced by the Metropolitan Museum Art Association, the membership of the Toronto Art Museum Association was divided into four classes—founders, benefactors, life members, and annual members. One could become a founder by

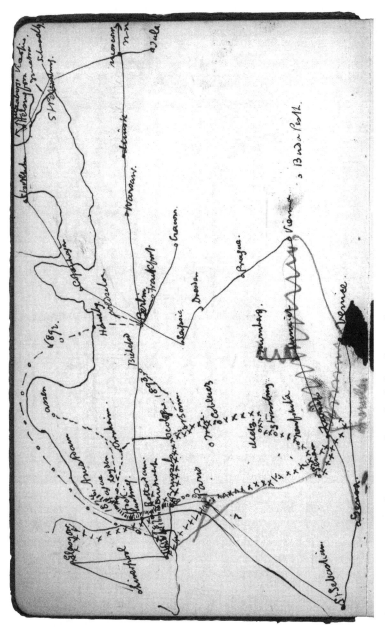

FIGURE 1.4. First page of James Mavor's notebook about his travels in Europe in 1899. Courtesy of the Thomas Fisher Rare Book Library, University of Toronto.

donating CAD$5,000. The founders "shall have their names inscribed on the walls of the Art Gallery and printed in every Annual Report." For $500, benefactors saw their names printed in every annual report. "The payment of $100 shall constitute Life Membership. . . . The payment of $10 a year by a layman, and $5 a year by any member of a recognized Art Body, or by anyone who has satisfied the Council that he is an Art Student, constitutes Annual Membership."[57] The inscription of the names of the founders on the walls of the museum as well as the listing of all supporters in the annual reports are traditions that go back to the Metropolitan Museum of Art. Since 1876, all annual reports of the Metropolitan Museum have listed all patrons, fellows in perpetuity, and fellows for life, but not the hundreds of annual members. The names of the patrons were inscribed on the walls of the new building in Central Park after it was opened in March 1880.[58] In both the Metropolitan Museum of Art and the Art Gallery of Ontario, the names of the patrons/founders can still be found engraved in stonewalls of the entrance areas visible to the visitor.

The most significant difference between the Leipzig and New York art associations and the Toronto art association is the role that artists played in the founding and support of the art gallery in Toronto. Between 1900 and 1925, the membership rolls of the Toronto art association included 35 founders, 87 benefactors, 254 life members, and 557 annual members. Among the latter were 130 artists. The Toronto art association had twice as many artists among its members as the New York or Leipzig art associations: nearly 14 percent of the members of Toronto's art association were artists.[59]

The main challenge facing the founders of Toronto's art gallery was acquiring a building. Walker and Mavor chose the path taken by German philanthropists— provision of the museum building by a wealthy citizen. Both were often invited to dinners at the Grange, a beautiful red brick house built in the early 1820s and owned by the wife of Goldwin Smith. During one of these dinners, Harriet Elizabeth Smith mentioned her thoughts about bequeathing their home for some public purpose. With the death of Goldwin Smith in June 1910, the art association finally received a building and a park, which in an agreement with the city council became a public park. Furthermore, inspired by financial support given by the City of New York to the Metropolitan and American Museum, Walker and Mavor were able to push the city government to subsidize the new Toronto Art Gallery. The city agreed to contribute $5,000 annually to the maintenance of the gallery under the condition that one day each week admission would be free of charge.[60] A similar provision had been arranged by the New York City Council. Already in 1873, the trustees of the Metropolitan Museum Art Association declared Monday the day when no admission fee was requested.[61] In the end, the founders of the Toronto Art Gallery received many ideas concerning the organizational structure of the new museum from the New York Metropolitan Museum and thus from the Leipzig Art Museum.

THE PROFESSIONALIZATION OF CULTURAL BORROWING

In the case of the Metropolitan Museum of Art and the Toronto Art Gallery, philanthropists obtained information about museums in other cities by traveling and spending time in these cities and their museums. They filled their diaries and letters with essential information about these cultural institutions so that these diaries were often written in a very dry and factual style. In many cases, these diaries are indistinguishable from official reports. After the turn of the nineteenth century, the acquisition of knowledge about how to construct, maintain, and finance museum buildings followed a more scientific approach. No longer did the philanthropists play the main role in collecting information; this task was undertaken by museum directors and academics. These professionals visited selected museums and investigated their architecture, collection principles, and financing schemes. After their return, they delivered a written report to the board of trustees. The prime example of this new approach is the survey of American museums by Adolf Bernhard Meyer (1840–1911), the director of the Royal Zoological, Anthropological, and Ethnographical Museum in Dresden.

Meyer was sent by the authorities of the Royal Collections of Art and Science in 1899 "to visit the museums and kindred institutions of the United States so far as they relate to museum affairs, and to pay special attention to the preservation of the collections from fire." Because of the large number of American museums and the limited time available, Meyer decided to visit only the eastern part of the country (New York, Albany, Buffalo, Chicago, Washington, Philadelphia, Boston, and Cambridge). His observations were published after his return to Germany under the title *Über Museen des Ostens der Vereinigten Staaten von Nord-Amerika* (*About the museums of the Eastern United States*) in 1900/1901. This volume includes information on architecture and building costs, the size and character of the collections, the financing schemes for the purchase of art objects and for the maintenance of the museums, opening times, entrance fees, and concepts of educational schemes targeted at the general population. For Meyer, American museums represented strong competition to European museums. He warned: "We Europeans must, each in his place, exert all our strength to avoid being outstripped."[62]

The educational work organized and carried out by American museums impressed Meyer the most. He admired the concepts regarding the integration of children into museum education—a tradition absolutely alien to Germany. Meyer reported that in "the large museums, a section may generally be found specially adapted to the comprehension of children." Furthermore, direct "efforts are made to induce pupils of both sexes to visit the museums by offering prizes for essays adapted to the different classes."[63]

Public lectures to popularize certain aspects of science were an integral part of the educational work provided by American museums, such as the American Museum of Natural History in New York. Summarizing his experience, Meyer emphasized that

> Americans assign a leading part in the activity of their museums to the exhibition collections, which they arrange for wide circles of the educated, half educated, and uneducated classes. At the same time, they foster the interests even of little children and try to stimulate the older ones by offering prizes; they make the museums contribute directly to the cause of education by series of lectures, by popular publications, and by lending collections; and they keep the doors of their museums open to everybody from morning till evening.[64]

The opening times were of particular concern to Meyer. While the Metropolitan Museum of Art was opened at "7, 8, 9, or 10 in the morning till 6," the Green Vault in Dresden, for instance, was open only between 9 and 2.[65] Furthermore, while American museums attempted to invite as many visitors as possible and to make the collections accessible to the average person, German museums tended to treat visitors as intruders and refused to help them understand the cultural and artistic objects displayed. In short, German museums were meant to educate the intellectual visitor while American museums were meant to entertain both educated and uneducated citizens. Obviously, Meyer was very much in favor of the attempts to work with children in museums, but he was also skeptical about whether "all this could be adapted to German conditions."[66]

This report, written in German and intended to provide a material basis for the reorganization of museums, influenced the practical work in museums in Germany less than it did in North America. Four years after the report was published in Germany, the Smithsonian Institution included in its 1903 annual report a translation of Meyer's account on American museums together with an account about European museums, which Meyer had published in 1902.[67] These two texts thus provided the North American reader with a survey of American, British, French, and Belgian museums. This publication inspired Walker to urge the provincial government of Ontario and the board of governors of the University of Toronto to establish a museum that would give a home to the already existing archaeological, geological, mineralogical, paleontological, and zoological collections. Following the example of the Metropolitan Museum of Art and the American Museum of Natural History, Walker was able to persuade the provincial government and the university to finance the construction of a museum building while most of the collections were purchased by wealthy Torontonians. In the case of the art gallery Walker had to rely on his own observation and knowledge of the Metropolitan Museum of Art, but in the case of the Royal Ontario Museum he could rely on a survey of American museums produced by Henry Montgomery.[68]

Montgomery, an outstanding geologist, received his early education at Upper Canada College in Toronto. After studying geology, mineralogy, and biology at University College and the University of Toronto, he held professorships at the University of North Dakota and the University of Utah at Salt Lake City. In 1894, he returned to Toronto to become head of the Department of Geology and Biology at Trinity University. With the federation of Trinity and Toronto universities in 1903, Montgomery became the curator of the new museum of the university.[69] It was Walker who urged Montgomery to visit a number of American museums in March 1906 to collect information about how to organize such a museum. Montgomery visited the Smithsonian Institution and its National Museum of Natural History in Washington, the American Museum of Natural History and the Metropolitan Museum of Art in New York City, Yale University in New Haven, the Art Museum and the Natural Science Museum in Springfield, Massachusetts, and the Harvard University Museum in Cambridge. His final report contains information about the organization, financing, and architecture of these museums.[70]

Montgomery referred in his report to the one provided by Meyer and published by the Smithsonian Institution, and he used this report in his recommendations to the founders of the Royal Ontario Museum (ROM), who also had knowledge of Meyer's report. Like Meyer, Montgomery was very impressed by the educational work of American museums and demanded that the ROM play a crucial role in popular education. He favored the principle developed in 1860 by Louis Agassiz of having a separate "exhibition collection for visitors and a scientific collection for investigators." The Museum of Comparative Zoology at Cambridge, which had been established by Agassiz, was the first to follow this principle. According to Montgomery,

> all new museums in the United States were similarly arranged from that time. In 1881 the National Museum at Washington adopted as of prime importance the general principle "to place no object on exhibition which had not some special educational value and which was not capable of attracting and instructing a large proportion of the visitors." . . . Consequently, the visitor to a museum is not tormented with endless series of like or similar objects, and he need not himself laboriously pick out from an excess of material the objects which are to him comprehensible, instructive, or entertaining. They are placed before him without any annoying and tiresome labor on his part.[71]

The financing scheme of the ROM closely followed the model of the Metropolitan Museum of Art and the American Museum of Natural History in New York. The museum building was financed by the provincial government of Ontario and the university using mainly tax money. The acquisition of collections and singular art objects depended on wealthy Torontonians. In contrast to the New York museums and even to the Art Gallery of Toronto, Walker and Charles T. Currelly (1876–1957) were not able to convince a large number of Torontonians to join a membership association. When in March 1922 Currelly proposed the creation of such an organization consisting of seven classes of members—annual members ($10 per annum), sustaining members ($25 per annum), fellows ($100 per annum), friends ($500 per annum), fellows for life ($1,000), fellows in perpetuity ($5,000), and benefactors ($10,000)—the success was limited. By the mid-1920s only seventy-eight Torontonians had signed up for a membership (fourteen longtime members and sixty-four annual members). The Toronto Art Gallery had nearly ten times as many members. The reasons for this lack of interest and financial support are not apparent.[72]

Toronto, with its museums, was part of a transatlantic network of urban communities and cultural life. Such a network provided the context for the establishment of museums in North American cities during the nineteenth and early twentieth centuries. Americans and Canadians relied on European models and observed how cultural institutions had been created and maintained in European cities. However, New York's organizers "translated" certain principles of museum organization and maintenance for application in North America. As the English translation of Meyer's investigation into European museums shows, American museum makers were, even after 1900, still intrigued by the ways their European counterparts created and maintained museums. When the board of trustees of the Museum of Fine Arts in Boston decided to construct a new building in 1902, it appointed a commission to collect information on architectural aspects of European museums. Samuel D. Warren, Edward Robinson, R. Clipston Sturgis, and Edmund M. Wheelwright spent three months (January 2, 1904, to April 2, 1904) on the continent "to study European museums, and, hopefully, discover excellencies of detail that might be anthologized in the future Boston design." The Boston Four did not have to search for new organizational models. The Boston Museum of Fine Art, like the New York Metropolitan

Museum, was connected to a membership organization that provided the necessary funding. The Bostonians simply searched for architectural ideas concerning how to arrange the collection, how to effectively light the exhibitions, and how to provide an entrance hall that invited visitors. They toured ninety-five museums in Italy, Germany, Switzerland, Holland, Belgium, and England, looking at the general character of museum architecture, exterior landscaping, lighting, the size of the galleries, the arrangement of paintings and sculptures, and even the technologies of heating and ventilation. However, the board of trustees was also concerned with the tasks and purposes of an art museum regarding the education of the general public and the provision of study collections. To discuss these issues, the board of trustees included in its four-volume report, *The Museum Commission in Europe*, articles and essays written by several European authorities on museums. This collection included an essay by Ernst Grosse, professor of the history of art at Freiburg University, on the aims and arrangements of German museums of fine arts and an article written by Alfred Lichtwark, director of the Kunsthalle in Hamburg, about the faults of existing museum buildings and his visions for future buildings.[73]

The Bostonian observers seemed to be very impressed by the New Grand Ducal Museum in Darmstadt: "In its general features it was found the most suggestive as embodying ideas that had been under consideration in the study of the proposed Boston building." Evaluating the Darmstadt museum, the Bostonian visitors remarked: "It would appear that the architect had here sought to give expression to the reasonable theories recently advanced by museum authorities, which are based upon the principle that the collections should be arranged upon a system which permits the public to see them with the least confusion of mind and the minimum of fatigue; to this end objects should be grouped in well-defined departments, and each class of objects should have the method of lighting suited to its best display." The organization of the Darmstadt museum into separate and autonomous departments impressed the visitors very much. "The Mediaeval and Renaissance Department is, in fact, a separate Historical Museum, a diminutive model of that at Zürich, and presents an interesting example of the historic-picturesque arrangement as opposed to the scientific dispositions of the older museums."[74]

The architectural plans for the new building of the Museum of Fine Arts followed this concept of departmentalization. The building was divided into "segments to contain departments structurally separate, each constituting a museum complete in itself, with a well-defined circuit for the visitor." This is captured in Samuel D. Warren's description of the museum: "The building may be described as a group of museums under one roof, the space in each devoted to collections compactly arranged and two rooms for study being approximately equal to the gallery space."[75] In the end, the trustees of the Boston Museum of Fine Arts received valuable information regarding nearly all architectural and technical aspects of a museum building. Furthermore, the reports printed and published by the Museum of Fine Arts provided an English translation of the newest German academic and artistic discussions on the purposes and aims of museums. These translations benefited not only the Boston enterprise but also museums in the United States in general.

The transatlantic transfer of cultural and intellectual concepts and ideas has never been a one-way street. Transfer always occurred in both directions and in some cases involved objects that have been repeatedly exchanged. In this process of multiple transfers, the origin of the objects became obscured and the object gained universality in its application. In 1913, Woldemar von Seidlitz, advisor to the Royal Art Museum in Dresden, published an essay in the German journal *Museumskunde* in which he provided an overview of Museumsvereine (museum patrons associations) in Germany, France, and Great Britain. These associations were, according to Seidlitz, phenomena of the late nineteenth century that originated with the Metropolitan Museum Art Association in 1870. Seidlitz's essay delivered a detailed description of the New York museum association and of subsequent associations in Lübeck (1880), Amsterdam (1883), Krefeld (1883), Berlin (1897), Paris (1897), Frankfurt am Main (1899), Celle (1900), London (1903), Munich (1905), Stuttgart (1906), Leipzig (1909), Breslau (1910), Dresden (1911), and Halle (1912). The existence of earlier versions of such museum associations in Germany and their influence on the emergence of similar institutions in New York was either disregarded by or unknown to Seidlitz. It is the irony of history that Seidlitz looked to the United States for ideas regarding the reorganization of Germany's museums and that he propounded the Metropolitan Museum Art Association as a model for Germans when in fact the New York art association had been inspired by earlier art associations in cities such as Leipzig.[76]

LENDING LIBRARIES IN A TRANSATLANTIC WORLD

Often social reformers champion foreign ideas and concepts on purpose. Reference to such alien ideas greatly enhances the possibility of change in the receiving society because the giving society is always portrayed as advanced and superior. The realization that these ideas might have originated in the receiving society would have proved counterproductive to the goals of the agents of transfer who wanted change. When Seidlitz suggested that museum associations were an American idea, either he was not aware of their German roots or he intended to distance himself from the earlier German manifestations of collective philanthropy.

According to standard accounts, the public library in Boston provided the model for subsequent public libraries within the United States and in Europe. Just a few years before Seidlitz championed the adoption of the American museum association, Constantin Nörrenberg advocated the American model of the free lending library for German cities. American scholars agree "that it was the establishment of the Boston Public Library which really heralded the beginnings of the public library movement." Two eminent scholars and Bostonians, George Ticknor (1791–1871) and Edward Everett (1794–1865), engaged in this project and convinced the city and wealthy peers to support this enterprise. However, as in the case of the Metropolitan Museum of Art, the foundation of the Boston Public Library would be unthinkable without European models and examples. George Ticknor, who spent several years in Germany, used his experience with the Royal Saxon Library in Dresden to organize the Boston Public Library. This aspect has been entirely overlooked not only by the author of Ticknor's biography but also by scholars exploring the history of the public library movement.[77]

Ticknor went to Europe several times, first between 1815 and 1819 to study at the University of Göttingen,[78] between 1835 and 1838 for research and enjoyment,

FIGURE 1.5. George Ticknor, ca. 1910. Courtesy of the Trustees of the Boston Public Library.

and again during the 1850s to purchase books for the library. In contrast to Comfort, Ticknor gave us a detailed account of his encounters in Germany in his extensive journals. Ticknor's European travel journals "consist of eighteen volumes, number-ing some 8,900 manuscript pages."[79] In 1815, he went with Everett from Liverpool and London to Göttingen, "the foremost university in Germany." He stayed there for more than two years studying literature, philosophy, history, and classics. During this time, Ticknor enjoyed using the university library, which had a collection of 200,000 volumes. This library was by far one of the largest in the German Confeder-ation; at his disposal were not only books he had ordered for use in Boston "at great expense from Europe, [but also] works he had known only by name, and volumes totally new to him."[80] The easy access to the library impressed Ticknor the most. He noted in his journal: "Every student can take out six separate works, and exchange them if he pleases, every day; and those of us, who come from a great distance and may, therefore, be supposed to be particularly anxious to use the library freely, are not restricted as to the number of books we may take out. I have received assurance

FIGURE 1.6. View into the stacks of the Royal Saxon Library. Watercolor by Edmund Oswald Pfennigwerth. Courtesy of the Sächsische Landesbibliothek—Staats- und Universitätsbibliothek Dresden (SLUB)/Abt. Deutsche Fotothek.

that I may call for them indefinitely. The mode of taking them out is simple and at the same time singular. You send in the name of the book you want on a slip of paper with your own name and the librarians look out [for] the book in the course of twenty-four hours" (August 6–8, 1815).

After having spent one year in Göttingen, Ticknor embarked with Everett on a trip through Leipzig, Dresden, Jena, Weimar, Halle, and Berlin. In Dresden, Ticknor was introduced to the royal family, and he visited Dresden's famous art gallery and the Royal Saxon Library, which he called a public library and described

FIGURE 1.7. The Japanese Palace in Dresden, which was home to the Royal Saxon Library from 1786 until 1945. Courtesy of the Kupferstich-Kabinett, Staatliche Kunstsammlungen Dresden.

as being "beyond praise."[81] This library housed about 200,000 books, 2,000 manu-scripts, 90,000 pamphlets, and 12,000 maps. Among its rarities were the first book printed in German from 1459, the first edition of the Vulgate Bible, a beautifully illustrated copy of the Koran, and a copy of a pre-Columbian Mexican book. This library was open to the public four hours each day. Comparing the Göttingen and Dresden libraries, Ticknor noted, "Each has its advantages—This has a greater number of old books and the Göttingen a greater number of recent ones—This is better managed on with shelves and more elegant—the Göttingen has a catalogue . . . and is a more practical library" (September 22–23, 1816).

The praise for the Dresden library was shared by many American visitors. For Henry E. Dwight, the author of the widely read *Travels in the North of Germany* (1829), the Dresden library was "one of the most valuable in Germany." The library occupied "the second story of the Japanese Palace, where it was removed to in the year 1788, and is arranged, according to the different subjects, in twenty-two of the saloons [*sic*] and rooms of this edifice. One is devoted to manuscripts, another to geography; one of the saloons and five of the rooms to history, the history of literature, &c. Oriental literature, works on the fine arts, romance, lexicography, medicine, &c., have each a separate apartment." Dwight judged that though "the library of Göttingen can boast of a more valuable historical collection, it is inferior to this in works on classical literature." Access to the library was, according to Dwight, open to every citizen: "Students, and many of the inhabitants, are allowed to take books to their houses, with almost the same freedom as from a circulat-ing library." Furthermore, the "library is open every day, except the Sabbath." The organization of the book collections was considered to be very convenient "and perfectly intelligible. Even a stranger would be able, in a very short period, to lay his hand on any work which is to be found on its shelves."[82]

In 1819 Ticknor returned to Boston to receive a professorship in French and Spanish languages and literatures at Harvard University. Having enjoyed the advantages of the libraries of Göttingen and Dresden, Ticknor was determined to enlarge Harvard's library and to create a new public library in Boston. According to the memoir prepared by his wife and oldest daughter, "the idea of a grand, free library, to supply similar resources in this country was talked of by him with a few of his friends, and was for a time uppermost in his thoughts."[83] During his second visit to Europe, Ticknor spent several months in Dresden (November 20, 1835, to May 12, 1836) in order to use the public library for his research. Ticknor noted in his journal: "I have sometimes had fifty or sixty volumes at my lodgings, and there is no limit on the time a stranger may keep them, unless somebody else asks for them. . . . I have books now, that I have had three months."[84] Given these excellent conditions, Ticknor felt more than ever the advantages of German libraries over anything similar in his home country.

When he returned to Boston, Ticknor "watched with interest every symptom of the awakening of public attention in America to this subject, and every prom-ise of opportunity for creating similar institutions."[85] The establishment of a great public library in New York by John Jacob Astor (1763–1848) prompted a number of Boston's Brahmins to agree that their city needed a public library or it would have to "yield to New York in letters and in commerce."[86] In July 1838, Astor pub-licly announced that he would leave a substantial amount of money to the city of

New York for the establishment of a public library. In his last will and testament of August 22, 1839, Astor "set aside four hundred thousand dollars as a bequest for the establishment of a public library 'to be accessible at all reasonable hours and times, for general use, free of expense to persons resorting thereto, subject only to such control and regulations as the trustees may from time to time exercise and establish for general convenience'; specifying the location as the corner of Lafayette Place and Art Street (now Astor Place), fixing the sum to be expended for books at one hundred and twenty thousand dollars." The money for this project would become available only after Astor's death, which occurred on March 29, 1848. The library building, stocked with nearly 90,000 volumes, was opened to the public in January 1854.[87]

It was Joseph Green Cogswell (1786–1871) who persuaded Astor to dedicate part of his fortune to the foundation of a public library in New York. Like so many young Americans, Cogswell spent four years in Europe (1816–20), where he studied with Ticknor and Everett at the University of Göttingen. Cogswell, Ticknor, and Everett traveled all over Europe and explored the cultural life in Berlin, Dresden, London, and Paris together. Like Ticknor, Cogswell taught at Harvard after he returned to his home country. Between 1820 and 1823, he also served as assistant librarian for Harvard's library. In 1836, Cogswell moved to New York and became a house teacher for the children of Samuel Ward, an eminent New York banker and friend of Astor. Ward introduced Cogswell to Astor, "who had given up active connection with business" and was searching for ideas on how he could leave some of his fortune for public purposes.[88] Cogswell, who frequently exchanged letters with George Ticknor, wrote to him on July 20, 1838:

> I must tell you a word of what I have been doing for some months past, or you may think I have been wasting time. Early in January Mr. Astor consulted me about an appropriation of some three or four hundred thousand dollars, which he intended to leave for public purposes, and I urged him to give it for a library, which I finally brought him to agree to do.[89]

One week later Cogswell traveled to Boston to meet Ticknor and to discuss this issue. Over the following years, Ticknor and Cogswell exchanged letters informing each other of the progress of the library question in New York and Boston. However, Cogswell did not share Ticknor's enthusiasm for a public lending library.[90] This issue was hotly debated between Ticknor and Everett during the founding of the Boston Public Library.

Following the example set by the Royal Saxon Library in Dresden, Ticknor favored a library that "should circulate its books freely—that is, citizens should be allowed to take books home rather than having to read them at the library."[91] Furthermore, Ticknor demanded that in such a library "any popular books, tending to moral and intellectual improvement, should be furnished in such numbers of copies that many persons, if they desired it, could be reading the same work at the same time." Ticknor also suggested establishing a department of consultation that would hold newspapers, encyclopedias, and dictionaries, which should never be taken out from the library building. Everett was very skeptical about the issue of allowing books to be taken out. In a letter to Ticknor, Everett pointed out that those "who have been connected with the administration of such libraries [i.e., lending libraries] are apt to get discouraged, by the loss and damage resulting from the loan of books. My present impressions are in favour of making the amplest provision in the library for the use of books here."[92]

In the end, Ticknor was able to convince the other Bostonians involved in the founding of the public library to allow free circulation of books.[93] The free lending library was for Ticknor a place of moral improvement of society. And there was no doubt in his mind that this moral education of the masses had to be guided by the well-educated well-off members of the Brahmin caste. Libraries and museums thus represent at least the attempt of a social class to impose its social norms and values on society at large.[94]

During the 1840s, some four or five thousand books and pamphlets had been collected by the city government and stocked in the attic of city hall. Ticknor felt that this collection of books was "entirely unsuited to stimulate either the popular taste for reading, or the disposition of the Common Council to make appropriations." Beginning in the 1850s, the city council provided $1,000 for the purposes of a public library, which was used for the purchase of some books. However, a public library did not yet exist. In this situation Ticknor wrote a report for the library trustees (a committee of wealthy Bostonians interested in the establishment of a public library), in which he developed his plan for the establishment of such an institution. This plan came to the attention of Joshua Bates (1788–1864), "a self-made banker who had grown up in Boston and who had become a partner in the London firm of Baring Brothers." Bates, who enjoyed reading, informed Ticknor in October 1852 that he would provide $50,000 for this future library if the city would finance a library building.[95]

Bates's donation was significantly smaller than the amount provided by Astor for the establishment of a public library in New York just a few years earlier. However, it was sufficient to realize Ticknor and Everett's dream of establishing a municipal library. Ticknor convinced Bates "that his donation should be funded, the income only to be applied to the purchase of books."[96] In this way, an annual income of $3,000 would be available for the acquisition of new books. Over the following years, Bates donated thousands of books to the new library, which received its own building in January 1858. Wealthy Bostonians joined Bates in donating books and money. By 1862 the Boston Public Library administered five funds with a total of $95,000 producing an annual income of $5,700 devoted to the purchase of books.[97] During the 1850s and 1860s, Ticknor made several trips to Göttingen, Leipzig, and Berlin to purchase books for the new library. In 1856, Ticknor traveled three times to Leipzig because of its recognized position in the German book trade.[98]

It was the Boston Public Library's policy on book circulation and not the financing scheme that made this institution the starting point of the public library movement in the United States. As the example of the Astor Library shows, early American libraries were mostly reference libraries with restricted access for members of the lower classes. In contrast to Astor, Ticknor insisted that the public library should serve as an educational institution for the common people and therefore books should be freely circulated and purchased in high numbers to allow a large number of readers to read the same book at the same time.[99] The library was thus seen as an institution for the betterment of the lower classes and their integration into society. This concept was adopted by many other American cities, paving the way for the later Carnegie libraries and finding admirers among German library reformers during the 1890s.[100]

In 1893, Constantin Nörrenberg, the chief librarian of the university library in Kiel, arrived to participate in the World's Congress of Librarians in Chicago.[101] During his stay, Nörrenberg collected material on the public library movement. He felt overwhelmed by its positive results and was convinced that the concept of the public library had to be imported to German cities. Back home, Nörrenberg called for a reform of the German libraries informed and guided by the experiences of the American movement. In 1895, he published a programmatic speech detailing the main goals and functions of a public library.[102] This led to the establishment of public libraries in all major German cities based on the American model—the circulatory library.[103] That the American public library movement, strictly speaking, had its forerunner in the Royal Saxon Library in Dresden was known neither to the people involved in the German public library moment nor to the scholars researching the history of the American public library movement.

Nevertheless, the model of the free public library brought (back) to Germany by Nörrenberg differed greatly from the Royal Saxon Library in Dresden. The latter was intended to be a collection of the most important and influential writings in several academic disciplines. As such, the Dresden library displayed the economic and cultural power of its owner, the King of Saxony, and was meant for use by scholars from all over the world and not only by average readers in Dresden. Ticknor was one of the eminent scholars of his time who profited from the use of this rich collection. The Boston library was not intended to be a scholarly library but to serve the greater community by providing books that were of interest to the average readers in that city. While the Royal Saxon Library in Dresden attempted to present a universal collection—buying books in every field of knowledge—the Boston Public Library limited its field of collection to books that would educate the readers morally and aesthetically. By providing multiple copies of much-demanded novels and short stories, the Boston Public Library appealed to a very different readership. It was this concept of popular education and social betterment which traveled back to Germany.[104]

CHAPTER TWO

Heavy Luggage: The Intercultural Transfer of Models for Social Housing Enterprises

I n the second half of the nineteenth century, the population of American cities increased significantly because of a new wave of European immigrants.[1] America's leisure class became concerned about the social, cultural, and political repercussions of the dreadful housing conditions of the poor. According to Anthony Jackson, the population of New York City at the outbreak of the Civil War was eight times the population at the end of the war of 1812.[2] Overcrowded tenement buildings with awful sanitary conditions were considered breeding grounds for immorality and moral decay. The housing of the poor was viewed in a broader context and conceptualized as a danger to all members of society. The anonymous author of *The Tenement Houses of New York City*, published in 1891, dealt with the housing problem as if it were an outbreak of the plague: "Healthful homes are required for the physical and moral welfare of the people, and unsanitary homes breed immorality as well as disease. Though these resulting evils affect directly only the residents of the tenement-houses, the remaining population of the city cannot escape. Through contact in crowded cars, in the streets, and other public places, the diseases generated in the tenement-houses spread through the entire community."[3]

The housing of the poor (immigrants) and emerging working class became a focal point of private social reform in the United States.[4] The family, as the perceived essential basic unit of society, needed protection to prevent society from dissolution. Providing healthy and affordable housing was increasingly seen as the basis for social and political stability. The author of *The Tenement Houses* further argues that it is well known "that an immoral people will in time become a lawless and corrupt people. Indifference to the condition of the tenement-house will show itself both in an increased death-rate and in the corruption of public affairs."[5] Housing reform was thus not simply a reform of one aspect of urban life; it was, at least for its instigators, a reform of the entire society.

Neither the problem of working-class housing nor the demands for a housing reform in the nineteenth century originated in the United States. All emerging capitalist societies faced similar challenges: immense urban growth, the birth of tenement housing, and the creation of densely populated working-class apartments that seemed to promote physical and physiological illnesses. Therefore, Americans such as Henry Ingersoll Bowditch and Alfred Treadway White, who were interested in social reform, did not limit their search for solutions to their hometowns but embarked on "research trips" to European cities that had experienced the same problems much earlier.[6]

Philanthropists and social reformers in London and Leipzig had developed—and were still working on—solutions for the housing problem of the lower classes at the time American social reformers and philanthropists became interested in this matter. As much as the creation of the cultural infrastructure in American and Canadian cities can be understood only within the framework of a transatlantic transfer of ideas, the establishment of social housing companies and foundations in the United States, Germany, and Great Britain can be understood within the same setting. Housing reformers and philanthropists in New York, Boston, Toronto, London, Leipzig, Hamburg, and Frankfurt were part of a transnational and transatlantic network that organized informal contacts and exchanges of ideas through travel and publication of observations in the form of letters, pamphlets, and books.[7] Based on their observations of social housing enterprises in London, Bowditch and White founded social housing companies in Boston and New York, respectively.[8] The publication of their observations and their practical realization of such projects attracted the attention of fellow American philanthropists and social reformers who considered following their example.[9] Boston and New York thus received the function of being the "transmission and translation laboratories" for housing reform inspired by English and German models.

The extent of the transatlantic transfer of models for social housing enterprises has long been underestimated and explored in only four essays over the last forty years. Furthermore, these essays are limited to the British-American connection, and they exclude the larger European-American transatlantic context. In 1965 Robert H. Bremner published his article on the integration of Octavia Hill's housing management system in American social housing enterprises during the 1880s in the *Social Service Review*.[10] More than twenty years later, Eugenie Ladner Birch and Deborah S. Gardner explored the transfer of limited dividend companies and Hill's housing management system from London to Boston, New York, and Washington in their article published in the *Journal of Urban History*.[11] Gerald Daly followed suit by investigating the British roots of the American public housing program.[12] However, American social reformers did not limit their search for models of social housing to Great Britain. Following a perceived "colonial tradition," they studied private social housing enterprises from all advanced capitalist societies. Germany occupied an essential position in this learning process. Building on Birch and Gardner's argumentation, this chapter will advance the discussion of the transatlantic transfer of social housing models and provide a comprehensive and interconnected study of the private provision of social housing in the nineteenth- and early twentieth-century transatlantic community. As William B. Cohen reminds us, "Emulation and borrowing were frequent in a world of welfare and philanthropy."[13] However, processes of cross-cultural and transatlantic borrowing, imitation, and adaptation do not attract the attention of most historians. "Historical scholarship," as Daniel T. Rodgers points out, "bends to the task of specifying each nation's distinctive culture," and not to the task of showing the interconnected and interrelated character of each country's history.[14] Leaving the cage of national history, Rodgers and Axel R. Schäfer have shown how European concepts of social welfare influenced American social policy.[15] However, both authors focus on the political level and are concerned with state policy. They neglect the level of individual and private contacts as well as the private philanthropic provision of social welfare in American and European cities.

The influence of British models in the establishment of social housing projects in German cities during the second half of the nineteenth century has not been explored. German historians have been reluctant to investigate instances of private social welfare in German states.[16] Recently, Jean H. Quartaert published her study of women's philanthropic associations and their contribution to the creation of German nationalism.[17] Despite a surge in civil society studies during the last ten years, the private provision of social housing, private financing schemes of hospitals, and private poor relief have remained a marginalized field in German studies, thus supporting the myth of Germany as a "Patron State" in which the "non-profit sector did not develop in antithesis to the State, but in interaction with it."[18] However, as Andrew Lees has pointed out, "German society during the Imperial period was marked by a far-flung network of charitable institutions, many of which were led and supported by people who hoped, through philanthropic activity, to contribute to the solution of social problems."[19]

The goal of this chapter is twofold: first, to explore the observation and perception of private social housing institutions in European cities by American and German social reformers and philanthropists; second, to analyze when and how a transfer of philanthropic models was instigated and how this transfer happened. By analyzing the process of observing the philanthropic provision of working-class housing by American and German social reformers and philanthropists, the complex and transatlantic character of the social question will become clear. Furthermore, one sees that the transfer of social housing models happened on an individual, nongovernmental level and depended on the activities of agents of intercultural transfer. Coming from wealthy families, these agents of transfer assumed this function in an attempt to justify social privilege and to live up to the new expectations of a society in which the value of individuals was measured against a Protestant work ethic.[20] Furthermore, these agents of intercultural transfer popularized their observations about the provision of social housing in other cities and countries and thereby created a public discourse about the value and opportunities of philanthropy in a society that witnessed the emergence of new social classes and conflicts over social domination. In this context, philanthropy offered unique ways of social and cultural domination. While economic success and marriage strategies certainly helped to create class coherence, they were not sufficient means for pacifying and dominating a modern society.

Discovering How the "Other Half" Lived

Before traveling abroad, all individuals involved in the housing reform in Boston, New York, and Leipzig needed to visit parts of their own city they had never seen—the slums and working-class districts. Collecting information about the actual living conditions of working-class families and then publishing it was the first step to solving the social question.[21] The wealthy were simply not familiar with the life-style and the housing conditions of the poor. Observers and social reformers often "compared themselves to explorers investigating foreign, 'savage,' and unchartered territory."[22] As a nineteenth-century German Conservative newspaper stated, "We were better acquainted with the condition of life of the half savage African tribes than with those of our own people."[23]

Therefore, Gustav de Liagre (1842–1904) and Herrmann Julius Meyer (1826–1909)—two key figures in the social housing reform of Leipzig—first volunteered as "friendly visitors" (*Armenpfleger*) who would visit working-class families in their homes and make decisions about granting financial assistance before they engaged in social housing projects. The communally organized but privately financed relief organization of Leipzig, which was founded in 1803, subdivided the city into districts and subsections headed by elected officials and volunteers. Liagre was elected district official in 1875, and Meyer became a "friendly visitor" in 1880 and a district official in 1881. The volunteers were responsible for twenty-five to thirty poor families. Their duties involved visiting families in their homes, assessing their needs, and deciding about the amount of financial and material relief granted.[24] It was this involvement in social work and the acquired knowledge about the living conditions of the lower-class families that persuaded many volunteers to engage in social housing projects. In fact, many of the Leipzig philanthropists who financed housing foundations and associations had been "friendly visitors" in the first place.

Some of the people involved in this practical work wanted to alert their contemporary citizens to the social problems they encountered. They gave talks about their encounters and published articles describing single tenements inhabited by working-class families and plans for the improvement of these housing conditions. In 1886/87, Dr. H. Mehner visited several Leipzig working-class tenements and published a detailed account of one family in Eutritzsch, just north of the old Leipzig downtown area in 1887. He described the husband's work experience (hours, income), expenses for food, clothing, and rent, and the housing conditions of the family of five. For an annual rent of 72 marks, this family occupied a tenement with one living room, a bedroom, an entrance hallway, and a storage room (for coal, wood, and food). The entire tenement was wet, the walls were mildewed, and the apartment was much too small to house five people. The bedroom that the parents and the three children shared had only about 16 cubic meters. According to Mehner, this was about 70 cubic meters short of what was considered necessary.[25]

Parallel to this impressionistic approach to the social questions, Ernst Hasse (1846–1908) began collecting empirical data concerning the housing of the Leipzig poor after the German-French War (1870–71).[26] Before his military service between 1866 and 1871, Hasse had studied economy and political sciences at the University of Leipzig. In 1873, he decided to continue his university education and joined the Seminar for Royal Prussian Statistics in Berlin. In April 1875, he was appointed director of the Statistical Office of the city of Leipzig and in 1886 professor for statistics at the University of Leipzig. During the 1870s and 1880s, Hasse began collecting data on housing conditions of the poor in all parts of Leipzig. As a result, he published his major study, *Die Wohnungsverhältnisse der ärmeren Volksklassen in*

Leipzig (The living conditions of the lower classes in Leipzig), in 1886. He provided extensive material regarding the limited availability of small single-family apartments, the increase in rent over fifteen years, a comparative analysis of incomes earned by workers and the rent for working-class apartments, etc. According to this analysis, working-class families with an income of less than 600 marks annually spent on average 29 percent of their income for rent in 1875. Families with an income of 600 to 1,200 marks spent only 21 percent of their annual income for rent. Hasse considered it to be deeply unjust that the social group with the lowest annual income had to pay the highest percentage of their income for rent. Furthermore, the number of tenements with one room—the typical tenement for a working-class family—grew disproportionally to the overall increase of working-class families in the city. At the same time, developers and construction firms provided a much larger number of apartments with more than two or three rooms, which were available for extremely high rents.[27] Since a single working-class family could not afford these apartments alone, many families arranged for renting such an apartment and subletting parts of it (a room or only a place to sleep) to single men and women who did not belong to this family. It was exactly this subletting practice that social reformers believed was leading to the destruction of the social and moral basis of society—the family. Housing reform thus became for Hasse a way to prevent the decay of society. In his conclusion, Hasse called for support from the state and municipal governments. His research quickly received acclaim within the German academic world and among social reformers.

Hasse's study of the housing of the lower classes in Leipzig was included in *Die Wohnungsnoth der ärmeren Klassen in deutschen Großstädten* (The shortage of tenements for the lower classes in German cities), which was published as volume 31 of the *Schriften des Vereins für Socialpolitik* (Publications of the Society for Social Policy) in 1886. This volume provided an empirical basis for any future steps of philanthropists and social reformers to solve the housing problem of the lower classes. Chapters on the living conditions of working-class families in Bochum, Chemnitz, Osnabrück, Krefeld, Dortmund, Essen, Berlin, Elberfeld, Breslau, and Leipzig offered insight into topics such as rent increases, hygienic standards, architectural structures, and population density. As Jan Palmowski rightly pointed out, "The importance of this investigation for housing reform throughout Germany can hardly be overestimated, for it ended over a decade of silence."[28] However, this volume did not cause state action.[29] Instead, it encouraged private engagement in the housing field. Housing foundations, limited dividend companies, and housing cooperatives sprouted all over Germany as a result of this initiative. Yet the articles compiled in this volume were written by social scientists and socially concerned civil servants, not by architects.

In 1902, the *Handbuch der Architektur* dedicated one volume to the construction of *Arbeiterwohnungen* (apartment buildings and houses for working-class families). This handbook became the standard work for German architects and historians of architecture. In more than thirty volumes, architects and city planners discussed every element of urban life, from the organization of waste disposal to the construction of sidewalks. Using various examples of already existing philanthropic housing foundations and companies as well as housing cooperatives and factory settlements, the authors of this particular volume discussed all aspects of housing the poor: size of the apartments, placing of the apartment buildings and houses in relation to the place of work and the cities, hygienic organization of the apartments, including different technologies for waste disposal and lavatories, etc. They used the existing social housing facilities to develop architectural models for working-class housing. They demanded that each apartment should be well ventilated. Influenced by American and English models, they further suggested integrating communally used bathrooms into apartment buildings. Lavatories were not considered essential parts of the apartments. They could be placed in separate buildings or, if necessary, in the staircases of the apartment building. Each apartment was to consist of a living room, a kitchen, and a bedroom as well as a hallway separated from the staircase. The closed off hallway integrated into the apartment was of very high importance for social reformers and architects because it prevented close social contacts between the different tenants of the apartment buildings; therefore, it was thought to stabilize the family and thus society.[30]

In the beginning, wealthy Americans were as unaware of the dreadful living conditions in the immigrant and working-class neighborhoods as their German counterparts. New York and Boston social reformers and philanthropists' first expedition was to tour the slums and collect data regarding the housing of the lower classes. In the 1870s, the newly founded Board of Health of the City of Boston took a lead in investigating the living conditions of the city's poor. In April 1873, the board began a large-scale inspection of tenement housing in Boston.[31] Already in early 1870, Henry Ingersoll Bowditch (1808–1892), an eminent physician, author, and abolitionist, after he was elected chairman of the Massachusetts State Board of Health, toured the slums of Boston. The tenements he saw left him appalled and resolved to achieve betterment. On December 1, 1870, he embarked on a second trip into Boston's slums. Bowditch reported this second encounter with lower-class housing in his published "Letter from the Chairman of the State Board of Health," hoping that wealthy Bostonians would feel compelled to engage in housing reform. To underline the importance of such reform, Bowditch included a graphic description of one particular Boston home:

> This cellar room is scarcely high enough for us to stand erect. One can easily almost touch each of the four sides while standing in the centre of it. The floor is dark, dirty and broken; apparently wet also, possibly from the tide oozing up. Two women are there, commonly, yet rather tawdrily dressed, and doing nothing but apparently waiting, spider-like, for some unlucky, erring insect to be caught in their dusty but strong meshes. Tubs, tables, bed-clothes and china ware are huddled incongruously together. Our guide strikes a match by the stove, and then opens a door into a so-called bed-room. It is a *box*, just large enough to hold a double bed. No window is in it, no means of ventilation, save through the common room up the cellar steps. The bed is of straw, covered only by a dirty blanket. Everywhere is the picture of loathsome filth. The stench, too, of the premises is horrible, owing to long accumulated dirt, and from the belching up of effluvia from solutions of dark mud, reeking with sewage water from the city drains and water-closets. It is difficult for us to breathe in the tainted atmosphere.[32]

This description gave a human face to the statistics provided by the state and city boards of health. Bowditch hoped that such an account of physical and moral decay would shock readers and force them to take action. By comparing the dreadful housing situation in Boston with the much higher standards of lower-class housing in London in the same report, Bowditch not only pointed to a problem but also provided the solution.

Many visitations by state officials and statistical accounts about the housing of the lower classes followed. The Bureau of Statistics of Labor of Massachusetts observed the housing situation since its establishment in 1869. State officials visited the slums regularly and reported on the improvements and deteriorations.[33] Other cities followed suit and published statistics and firsthand accounts of "friendly visitors." Already in 1843, reform-minded New Yorkers had founded the Association for Improving the Condition of the Poor (AICP). This organization, which closely followed the model set by private poor relief organizations in German cities, as for instance in Leipzig, championed the principle of "friendly and discriminating intercourse between the abodes of the charitable and those of the poor."[34] The city was divided into small sections, each with about twenty-five families who required support. Each section was assigned to a visitor who would have to visit the poor families in their homes and make decisions about financial and other assistance.[35] From the outset, the visitors of this organization faced overcrowded tenements that were "overstocked with inmates, and in many instances, very badly arranged: the sleeping rooms, for example, are frequently without means of ventilation, being dark, or having windows 18 inches square."[36] While the housing of the poor was not the reason this organization was founded, its members and supporters had to face this fact. In 1856, the AICP was able to take "a complete social, moral, and statistical census" of New York's Eleventh Ward. A few years earlier, in 1848, the board members of the AICP published and distributed "elaborated plans for tenement houses, which were lithographed" among investors and builders. And in 1855, it even organized the establishment of the Working Men's Home—a short-lived philanthropic enterprise that "was designed to show how much order, quiet, comfort, and neatness may be secured to the humblest in the community, by the erections of buildings properly adapted to tenant purposes." In 1878, the AICP established a Committee of Public Hygiene, "which through competent inspectors has ever since . . . maintained an unceasing investigation into the healthfulness of tenement houses."[37]

In 1890, in his book *How the Other Half Lives,* Jacob August Riis produced a moving account of what it meant to live in New York's slums. Riis pointed to the fact that New York's East Side had become "the most densely populated district in all the world." There are several tenement houses with a population of hundreds of people "that have a pro rata allotment of ground area scarcely equal to two square yards upon the city lot, court-yards and all included." In one particular case, Riis noted, five families "comprising twenty persons of both sexes and all ages" shared one room, twelve feet square, "with only two beds, without partition, screen, chair, or table."[38]

At the end of the nineteenth century, local statistics were accompanied by statewide statistics, which provided, for the first time, an overview of housing conditions in all major American cities. In 1893, Marcus T. Reynolds published his study of the housing of the poor in American cities, which had won the first prize of the American Economic Association.[39] Only two years later, Elgin R. L. Gould's study *The Housing of the Working People* was published as the Eighth Special Report of the Commissioner of Labor.[40] Both authors delivered an analysis of the housing of the poor in the United States and suggested looking to Europe for solutions.

FROM LIMITED DIVIDEND COMPANIES TO HOUSING COOPERATIVES

Since England had a head start in industrialization, it faced its social repercussions much earlier than the United States or Germany. In response to the emerging housing problem for the lower classes, a number of limited dividend housing companies were founded in London. These companies differed from other housing enterprises in that they limited the dividend paid to investors to 5 percent (Philanthropy and 5 Percent). The first such company, the Metropolitan Association for Improving the Dwellings of the Industrious Classes (MAIDIC), was created in 1841.

Common to all these companies was the desire to combine making a modest profit with providing healthy and affordable housing for working-class families. While making a profit with the construction of urban tenement buildings was not a novelty and certainly not philanthropic, the idea of providing affordable and hygienic tenements that satisfied basic standards for human housing was both new and philanthropic. London landlords had been accustomed to providing housing to working-class families that German observers such as Victor Aimé Huber (1800–1869) likened to the housing of animals in barns. Huber was even more

Table 2.1   Limited dividend housing companies in London

Limited dividend housing company	Year founded
Metropolitan Association for Improving the Dwellings of the Industrious Classes	1841
Society for Improving the Condition of the Labouring Classes	1844
Central London Dwellings Improvement Company	1861
Improved Industrial Dwellings Company	1863
Artizans', Labourers' and General Dwellings Company	1867
East End Dwellings Company	1884
Four Per Cent Industrial Dwellings Company	1885

SOURCES: Susannah Morris, "Private Profit and Public Interest: Model Dwellings Companies and the Housing of the Working Classes in London, 1840–1914," Ph.D. diss., Oxford University of Oxford, 1998, 24–38; John Nelson Tarn, *Five Per Cent Philanthropy: An Account of Housing in Urban Areas between 1840 and 1914* (Cambridge: Cambridge University Press, 1973), 15ff.

enraged by the very fact that London's landlords, ignoring the social and cultural repercussions of these living conditions, earned enormous profits by renting out these tenements.[41]

During his many visits to London, Huber witnessed the emergence of philanthropic housing companies and came into contact with its chief founders. In early 1847 he was introduced to Lord Ashley, the later Lord Shaftesbury (1801–1885), who had founded the Society for Improving the Condition of the Labouring Classes (SICLC) in 1844. Full of new ideas with regard to cooperation and shared responsibility, Huber approached Ashley with a text he had just written in which he argued that renters should be included in the financing schemes and administration of social housing associations. Although Ashley fundamentally disagreed with the young and idealistic Huber on that point, he still arranged for Huber to visit the new tenement buildings of his housing association.[42] And although Huber's nineteenth-century biographer, Rudolf Elvers, consistently denies any English influence on Huber's ideas, it seems clear that his English experience had an impact on his concept of "innere Colonisation" (internal colonization).[43] It would be wrong to assume, however, that Huber adopted English ideas in their original form. As it always happens, ideas traveling between places mutate in the process of transfer. In the case of Huber, two concepts merged and provided a new approach for the solution of the housing problem in cities such as Berlin. Huber, who saw the necessity for reform, advocated the combination of two modes of social action: philanthropic assistance by well-off citizens and noblemen combined with the self-help of the working people. For Huber, the improvement of the social conditions of the working classes had to begin with the improvement of their living conditions. However, the provision of healthy and affordable housing was just the beginning of the reform Huber envisioned. It had to be followed by a moral and intellectual transformation of the workers and their emancipation by the formation of associations (cooperatives).

In 1846, Huber published "Über innere Colonisation" ("About Internal Colonization"), in which he attacked earlier attempts at social reform and cooperation (Robert Owen) and advocated reform within the existing capitalist system in order to avoid class conflict. Based on his deep religious beliefs, Huber believed in the solidarity between men of all social classes and the possibility of cooperation between nobility, factory owners, and workers. However, the central point of his reform was to enable workers to gain a position of self-determination and self-reliance. Since he did not see a possibility for workers to achieve such a position on their own, Huber believed that the concept of self-help (association) was flawed. Therefore, Huber propagated the combination of social assistance and self-help. In order to raise the living conditions of working-class families, he further suggested the creation of factory villages outside big cities, which he identified with material and moral decay. These factory villages were to be built in close proximity to the workplace and connected to industrial areas as well as the city by trains and buses. They were to provide healthy and affordable housing and gardens for each family. Since workers could not finance the construction of these complexes, Huber believed that factory owners, noblemen, and the government should provide the necessary funding. From the beginning, Huber envisioned these settlements as profitable enterprises, which were to accrue a fair return of 5 percent on the invested sums. Renters were to be encouraged to form consumer associations in order to lower the costs for food and heating materials. Associations were considered a central part in Huber's reform concept, which ultimately was to lead to moral and social improvement of the working classes.[44]

Huber's article found an enthusiastic audience in Berlin, where a couple of reform-minded citizens deliberated the founding of a social housing company for some time.[45] Carl Wilhelm Hoffmann, the royal architect (Landbaumeister) in Berlin, published in February 1847 a call for the founding of a Berliner gemein-nützige Baugesellschaft.[46] This association, Hoffmann argued, was to follow the model of the MAIDIC. Hoffmann was convinced that Berlin needed a social housing company that would provide healthy and affordable housing for working-class families in order to stop the increasing speculation on the housing market that led to dreadful housing conditions and unreasonable profits. He convinced fifty-two like-minded individuals to create this social housing company as a limited dividend company in November 1847.[47] The founders read Huber's article on "inner colonization" and adopted some of its ideas for their housing enterprise and in fact invited Huber to take a position in its administration. Huber's pamphlet introduced the concept of renters associations and thus provided for the merging of the Philanthropy and 5 Percent model with the idea of self-administration and the idea that the renters should acquire their homes over time.

Following the model of London's limited dividend housing companies (here the SICLC and the MAIDIC), the Berliner gemeinnützige Baugesellschaft was founded as a stock company. Wealthy and reform-minded citizens purchased shares (100 Thaler each) to the total amount of about 200,000 Thaler.[48] The investors were promised a steady return of 4 percent. Huber compared this return with the return offered by several railway companies and argued that, in contrast to risky private stock companies, the housing association would offer a guaranteed protection of the invested sums even in case of default, since the land and buildings would not lose their value. And although the founders envisioned that the tenants would eventually own these tenements, Hoffmann, because of the high prices for the land, persuaded the board to construct apartment buildings with up to nineteen units in one house. In contrast to London's limited dividend companies, the Berlin enterprise included renters associations. These associations, founded at Huber's request, were supposed to establish reading rooms and kindergartens. They organized meetings for renters to discuss problems and the future of the enterprise on a regular basis. Trustees participated in these meetings and encouraged the participation of the renters in the administration of the housing association.

It is an irony of intercultural transfer that the modifications and mutations that occurred in this particular case proved to be unsuccessful. Huber's insistence on renters associations as well as the original plan of selling the tenements to its renters had to be abandoned in the 1850s.[49] With these changes, the Berlin housing company became a "pure" limited dividend company that barely showed any differences from its London predecessors. Further, it was the earliest attempt within German-speaking Central Europe to tackle the housing problem of working-class families.[50] Although the company failed to produce a large number of apartment buildings in and around Berlin, and therefore had only a limited effect on Berlin's housing market, it set an example that was followed later in cities such as Frankfurt am Main.[51] Furthermore, it paved the way for the integration of philanthropy and self-help in the German savings and building cooperatives.

In May 1860, five civic-minded members of Frankfurt's upper class published a call for the formation of a gemeinnützige Baugesellschaft.[52] Among these individuals was Johann Georg Varrentrapp (1809–66), who like Huber traveled extensively across Western Europe in search of ideas for improving various aspects of social life. He was interested in prison reform, the health care and hygiene movement, waste disposal, and housing conditions.[53] Varrentrapp was born into a wealthy and established Frankfurt family. He followed in his father's footsteps and became a physician. For about ten years he even assisted his father, Johann Conrad Varrentrapp, by working at the Heiligen Geist-Hospital (Holy Ghost Hospital). He was one of the first known German social reformers who traveled extensively across Europe to study prison systems, housing standards, and the provision of health care in urban societies. During the spring and summer of 1832, he embarked on his first trip to Stuttgart, Munich, Vienna, Prague, Dresden, Berlin, Halle, Leipzig, Hamburg, and Bremen to expand his knowledge of diseases—such as cholera—and the organization of hospitals. In 1838, Varrentrapp went on his 100-day voyage to the Netherlands, England, Ireland, Scotland, and Belgium to visit hospitals and institutions of welfare. Back in Frankfurt, he published his 678-page *Tagebuch einer medicinischen Reise* (Diary of a medical journey) in order to provide useful information to physicians and to appeal to the general public with his extensive descriptions of the nature, art, culture, and education in the countries he had visited.[54]

Following his 1838 voyage and several more visits to England, Varrentrapp engaged actively in prison reform (he favored the Pennsylvania system of solitary imprisonment), the hygiene movement, and the housing reform.[55] Discussions at the First International Congress on Public Hygiene in Brussels in 1852 sparked his interest in the housing question. Following the congress, Varrentrapp traveled repeatedly to England and France to study the early forms of private social housing companies. He was most likely the primary instigator of the Frankfurt limited dividend housing company and possibly the major author of the *Aufforderung zur Gründung einer gemeinnützigen Baugesellschaft in Frankfurt am Main* (Call for the creation of a social housing enterprise in Frankfurt am Main). In this call for support, the authors argued that a limited dividend company would constitute a philanthropic enterprise like many others that Frankfurt's citizens had already established (insane asylum, kindergarten, institute for the blind and deaf). However, in this case, instead of donating money, the participants were asked to buy shares that were to yield a 4 percent return. The main goal of the company was to limit speculation with housing property and thus the provision of healthy and affordable housing. Attached to the call for support were the bylaws and a text by Varrentrapp in which he surveyed the attempts at social housing in various European countries (England, France, Belgium) and cities (Amsterdam, Groningen, Copenhagen, Basel, Bremen, Berlin). England and London were first in his presentation, and Varrentrapp repeatedly pointed to the SICLC as a model for the Frankfurt social housing company.[56] Varrentrapp succeeded in convincing a large number of Frankfurt's well-to-do citizens to purchase its 4,000 shares for 425 marks each. According to the annual reports of 1868 to 1905, this housing association was very successful in keeping its promise to pay a 4 percent dividend each year and still accumulate enough capital to maintain and expand the building complexes. By 1909, the housing enterprise owned 524 apartments.[57]

The gemeinnützige Baugesellschaft in Frankfurt am Main followed its English predecessors closely from the onset and excluded the cooperative elements Huber had introduced to the Berlin company. It was, however, this combination of philanthropic support and self-help that would determine the production of social housing in Germany at the end of the nineteenth century. Although during the 1870s and 1880s a number of such limited dividend companies were founded all over Germany, the legal framework and economic conditions did not favor such enterprises and their widespread support. Instead, a new model of social housing—a hybrid between limited dividend company (philanthropy) and cooperative (self-help)— emerged as the dominant player in Germany's social housing sector.

After the German government introduced the principle of "limited liability" for all economic enterprises in 1889[58] and after the Spar- und Bauverein Hannover (Hanover savings and housing association, founded in 1885) had set an example of how to combine 5 Percent Philanthropy with self-help did the social housing movement gain strength. Before 1885, most housing cooperatives were based on the idea of transferring the homes into the private property of its members. The most important such cooperative was the Flensburger Arbeiterbauverein, founded in 1878. But these cooperatives, which were influenced by the model of the Kopenhagen Arbeiterverein, were not a suitable instrument for dealing with the housing problems of the lower classes.[59] Therefore, reform-minded citizens of the city of Hanover and workers who experienced the lack of affordable housing founded the Spar- und Bauverein. The founders of this new association turned their attention back to English models and attempted to integrate, as Huber had championed, the concepts of cooperative association (self-help) with philanthropic assistance. However, in contrast to Huber and Hoffmann's gemeinnützige Baugesellschaft in Berlin, the Hanover enterprise was founded on three innovative tenets: (1) it did not produce housing units that could be bought by its members over time; instead, the buildings were to remain in the possession of the cooperative indefinitely; (2) it combined self-help (each renter had to be a member of the cooperative and was expected to purchase at least one share of 300 marks) with financial assistance from wealthy citizens (who were allowed to purchase multiple shares) by merging the housing cooperative with a credit union; and (3) it adopted the legal provision of limited liability and thus limited the liability of shareholders to the amount of their shares (300 marks).[60]

The establishment of a credit union in conjunction with the housing cooperative provided for an economic solution in which individual wealthy citizens were encouraged to "invest" their money in social housing associations. The contributions of such wealthy individuals were significant for the economic well-being of such associations, as the example of the Hanover cooperative proves. In 1900 its members had purchased shares for 583,510.23 marks, while wealthy citizens had deposited 659,922.68 marks with the credit union of this association.[61] As A. Grävell points out in his history of the German cooperative movement, many cooperatives founded on the model of the Hanover housing cooperative allowed in their regulations for individuals to purchase multiple shares of 100 to 300 marks each. Such rules enabled private citizens to acquire shares of up to 40,000 marks at a guaranteed return of 4 percent, and it provided these housing cooperatives with sufficient funding for the production of affordable and healthy working-class housing.[62] It set an example for all German cities and soon sparked imitation in Berlin, Göttingen, Leipzig, and Dresden.[63] The number of housing cooperatives increased, according to Rudolf Albrecht, from 28 with about 2,000 members in 1888 to 764 with about 140,000 members in 1908. Those cooperatives owned property (land and buildings) valued at more than 200 million marks by 1908.[64] And in contrast to British and American limited dividend companies, these saving and housing associations were, at least until World War II, even more successful in guaranteeing a steady return of 4 percent.[65]

Until the early 1920s, the German housing cooperatives were dominated by wealthy burghers who run these associations and limited the influence of its members to an absolute minimum. Only after World War I, with the general democratization of German society, did these associations become institutions of self-help in which workers/tenants took over the administration of those associations and increasingly assumed financial responsibility for both the shares and the savings deposited with the credit unions.[66] Such emancipating goals were not part of the "Philanthropy and 5 Percent" inspired housing reform in England or in the United States.

The Philanthropic Trinity of London: George Peabody, Sydney Waterlow, and Octavia Hill

Neither philanthropic housing foundations nor limited dividend companies were invented in London. Housing foundations have existed in many European cities since the Middle Ages.[67] The most prominent foundation is the Fuggerei in Augsburg, which was founded in 1516 by Jacob Fugger (1459–1525). Between 1519 and 1523, Fugger financed the construction of fifty-three houses, each containing two tenements (about sixty square meters each). The tenements were to be given to poor Catholic citizens of Augsburg for a symbolic annual rent of one Rheinische gulden. Since this rent covered only one-third of the annual expenses of the foundation, Fugger added a foundation capital of about 25,000 Rheinische gulden, which was to be set aside in a trust fund. The interest on this amount was to be used for the maintenance of the apartment buildings.[68] Nineteenth-century philanthropists who set up housing foundations followed this model by financing the construction of apartment buildings and setting aside a certain amount of money as foundation capital. In contrast to their sixteenth- and seventeenth-century predecessors, however, they actually insisted on charging cost-effective rents that allowed for a return of 1–3 percent. This return was to be used for the maintenance of the buildings and, if possible, for the future expansion of the enterprise.

In the spring of 1853, several wealthy Bostonians concerned with lower-class housing in their city agreed to form the Model Lodging-House Association. With the goal of providing "healthy homes," the organizers proceeded to erect two brick five-story houses, each containing twenty apartments. The $46,000 needed to finance these buildings came from the bequest of Bostonian merchant Abbott Lawrence, who died in 1855 and left $50,000 "for the erection of dwellings for the poor." The rents for these apartments ran from $2 to $2.87 per week. "The total annual amount of rent received from each house is $2,353, which, after paying taxes, water-rates, gas-bills, and all other expenses, including all repairs necessary to keep the building in good order, leaves a full six per cent interest upon the sum invested."[69] The organizers of this limited dividend company wanted to show they could provide affordable healthy dwellings for the poor and at the same time produce a profit of 6 percent for the investors. However, the fact that most of the funds did not come from private investments but from the bequest of Lawrence seemed to prove that this early enterprise did not catch the eye of contemporaries and did not cause imitation or even recognition elsewhere.[70]

Even the concept of "friendly visiting" attributed later to Octavia Hill did not originate in London but was a product of earlier practices of providing welfare. It was a central element of private poor relief in many German cities from the end of the eighteenth century onwards. The Hamburg philanthropist Amalie Sieveking (1794–1859) was one of the first to suggest that "friendly visiting" should become an integral part of "moral supervision" in her housing foundation in 1837. In a letter from December 26, 1837, Sieveking argues in favor of establishing a housing foundation for poor people, since concentrating poor people in one place would allow for close moral supervision by people involved in this enterprise.[71]

Concepts of social housing provisions thus did not emerge within a vacuum but in a social space that transcended regional and national borders. Since all cities faced the same problems—industrialization and the housing of the working classes—it might not be a surprise that similar ideas emerged within the transatlantic world. These ideas were exchanged and improved before models emerged that were in turn studied and exchanged between the urban communities within the transatlantic world.

The identification of George Peabody, Sydney Waterlow, and Octavia Hill's housing projects as models for social housing can only be understood in the transnational and transcultural context of nineteenth-century social reform and the very nature of intercultural transfer. Peabody's housing foundation, Waterlow's Philanthropy and 5 Percent, and Hill's "friendly visiting" scheme quickly gained admiration and imitation in many European and North American cities. In contrast to earlier associations, they established sizable models at a time when the social question seemed to be so pressing that a large number of reform-minded philanthropists was susceptible to these solutions. Furthermore, Waterlow and Hill engaged in a campaign style of publicizing the successes of their enterprises. Observers and agents of intercultural transfer bought into the convincing arguments advanced by Waterlow and Hill. They returned to their hometowns filled with admiration for the London housing projects and often exaggerated the success of these enterprises in order to persuade fellow citizens to adopt similar strategies. In this process, London's housing enterprises attained the status of being models for social housing reform.

George Peabody (1795–1869), an American banker, who had lived in London since 1837 and had gained an immense fortune, entertained the idea of presenting a gift to the citizens of London that would be "a lasting memento of his gratitude." Looking for a specific purpose, first Peabody thought about financing the construction of "an elaborate scheme of drinking fountains" for which the "water would be centrally purified, then piped to a network of fountains to be erected in various parts of the city." After abandoning this idea, Peabody considered giving his donation to the Ragged Schools, which offered religious instruction for children of poor families. However, Lord Shaftesbury, who was consulted in this matter, suggested not supporting the Ragged Schools but rather donating the money for providing better housing for the poor. Pointing out the horrific housing conditions in London's slums, Shaftesbury hoped to persuade Peabody to contribute to his SICLC.[72]

Convinced by Shaftesbury that the housing question was of a much higher importance than pure water or religious education, Peabody donated £150,000 for the construction of model dwellings in London. To Shaftesbury's disappointment, Peabody insisted on establishing his own housing enterprise, the Peabody Trust.[73] He announced his gift in 1859, but it took three more years before the donation was officially made. The outbreak of the American Civil War and the support of the British for the Southern Confederation produced an awkward political climate for Peabody, who had to postpone his donation for some time. However, in January 1862, Peabody went ahead and made arrangements for the transfer of the amount promised. The founding letter was finally published in the *Times* and in all other major English newspapers on March 26, 1862. In this letter, addressed to the trustees, Charles Francis Adams, Edward George G. F. S. Stanley, the 14th Earl of Derby, Curtis Miranda Lampson, Sir James Emerson Tennent, and Junius Spencer Morgan, Peabody defined the purpose of his foundation as to provide relief for the poor and needy of London by establishing model dwellings. Only Londoners "by birth or residence" should benefit from this foundation. The "sole qualification for participation in the Fund was that the individual be poor, have moral character, and be a good member of society. No one should be excluded on grounds of religious belief or political bias." Since Peabody did not define exactly who was to be considered "poor," the trustees "decided to provide inexpensive dwellings, not for people requiring charity, but for workmen and their families who were in employment but had very low incomes." Bowditch wrote in his "Letter from the Chairman" in 1871 that "no tenant can enter the buildings if he receives more than thirty shillings weekly."[74]

Between 1862 and his death in 1869, Peabody raised the amount of his endowment to £500,000.[75] The trustees "decided that from the outset the trust should be self-perpetuating." The rent was expected to cover the maintenance and repair of the buildings and at the same time to provide for a modest return of up to 3 percent, which was to be used for the further expansion of the trust. The trustees moved quickly and purchased a site in Spitalfields in 1863. Within a year, the first housing block on Commercial Street was opened. It was four stories high and contained floors with sets of two-room units, which shared a common corridor, washing facilities, lavatories, and sculleries. This first apartment building was in its architectural style and arrangements merely an experiment and "was not really typical of the subsequent" building complexes. In the following years, four large estates—Peabody Square at Islington, Shadwell, Westminster, and Chelsea—were "scattered in various districts of the metropolis." The trustees always purchased very large sites "so that it was possible to build four detached blocks surrounding a central open space." Each of the four apartment blocks was four or five stories high "with a centrally placed staircase in each, leading to spine corridors on every floor

and off these opened the sets of rooms." According to Bowditch, the four building groups were "all erected in a rectangular form, with broad intervening spaces,
allowing free access of light, sun, and air and, at the same time, in the centre is a
playground for the children." John Nelson Tarn pointed to the deliberate seclusion
of these housing complexes. "The site itself was railed off from the surrounding
streets so that the Peabody community was in every sense separate, socially as well
as physically." When Bowditch visited London and studied the Peabody buildings,
he noted that the buildings were not only very neat but also had "an air of real
grandeur." Inside the building complex, "parties of laughing children are almost
always playing." However, the secluded and separated character of the building's
architecture extended even to the children. Bowditch remarked that "none from
the outside are allowed to enter."[76]

The Peabody Trust became, as David Owen remarked, one of the main pro-
viders of social housing in London. "Within six years they had erected four groups
of buildings to house a population of nearly two thousand individuals. Thirty-five
years later, with a capital outlay of over £1,250,000, the Trust was housing nearly
twenty thousand persons in over fifty-one hundred separate dwellings."[77] However,
Peabody, his motives, and his actions did not remain shielded against criticism.
Some contemporaries, like Benjamin Moran and Robert Winthrop, complained
about the idleness of Peabody and his self-glorification.[78] Others criticized the
economic structure of his trust, which was not really capitalist and was therefore
unlikely to spark imitation.[79] Peabody represented a strain of philanthropy that
was commonly referred to as "pure philanthropy" and that provided immediate
practical help but was criticized by contemporaries as shortsighted and marginal.
While the Peabody Trust accrued a net return of about 3 percent each year, this
return was not a profit distributed among investors. It was set aside for the expansion of the housing trust. Thus it did not attract investors.

The essential element of nineteenth-century philanthropy was the creation of a
model that could spark widespread imitation. This understanding of philanthropy
already recognized the large-scale character of the social question. Nineteenth-
century philanthropy was certainly, as Kathleen Woodroofe pointed out, an individualized answer to a perceived individual failure, but there is already a recognition of the danger for the entire society that resulted from the lack of affordable
and healthy housing of working-class families. The expectation that social housing
projects should not only provide space for a certain number of poor families in
need but also serve as models for bigger changes reflects a recognition of the extent
of the social question. It already points to a transformation of philanthropy from
an individualized solution to a general conceptualization of the social question
in terms of social and environmental causes.[80] Furthermore, Victorians viewed
philanthropy as being most effective only when both sides—giver and receiver—
would gain something from it. Receiving a limited return (maximum of 5 percent)
was seen as not only acceptable but honorable and "truly philanthropic." It was
assumed that this "true philanthropy" would provide the people who depended
on philanthropy with a certain degree of independence and self-respect. Philanthropy and 5 Percent thus was seen as more helpful than pure philanthropy. "Lord
Stanley described this system," according to Susannah Morris, "as a 'fair and equal
bargain between man and man' for 'there was no sacrifice of independence on

either side. They [the investors] got a fair return for their capital, and the workman got a better quality of lodging.'"[81]

Sydney Waterlow (1822–1906) and his Improved Industrial Dwellings Company (IIDC) have come to embody the concept of Philanthropy and 5 Percent. Waterlow was the son of a city stationer, and with his three brothers, he turned their small family business into a great printing house. Besides his economic success, Waterlow concerned himself with politics and the social problems of his day. In 1857, he was elected city councilor, and in 1863 he became an alderman. He was the sheriff of London in 1866–67 and Lord Mayor in 1872–73. In 1867 Waterlow was knighted.[82]

According to Bowditch, it was Matthew Allen who had the idea of construct-ing model tenements for working-class families that could be rented at an afford-able price and at the same time guarantee a return on the invested capital.[83] Allen was brought to Waterlow's attention when he worked for him as a mason. When Allen suggested building working-class apartment buildings, Waterlow listened "and with three other friends agreed to advance the means upon the plan sug-gested by Mr. Allen, provided, on its examination by an accomplished architect, it should be found to be according to strict legal and architectural principles, so as to give safety to every room and individual in it."[84] After an architect approved the plan, Waterlow and his friends provided £10,000 for the construction of four blocks of dwellings to accommodate eighty families on Mark Street. Waterlow chose the single staircase model and made it five floors in height. In contrast to the Peabody Buildings, these blocks were subdivided into self-contained tenements with separate sculleries and water closets. It was Waterlow and Allen' s intention "to produce a housing unit which could be easily built and let at a suitable rent to artisans, while at the same time showing a profit of five-per-cent for the owner."[85] This project proved to be so successful that within one year, Waterlow had attracted the interest of a sufficient number of potential investors that he created the IIDC in 1863. According to David Owen, Waterlow raised £25,000 from fourteen friends as founding capital of this company, which quickly rose to £500,000. Before World War I, the IIDC was the third largest philanthropic housing enterprise in London, owning about 5,510 dwellings.[86] This company established the model of a limited divided company that was replicated in German and American cities from the 1870s onwards.

The limited dividend company represents an intriguing combination of mar-ket mechanisms and the "provision of social welfare" which proved that the mar-ket, in fact, could provide social welfare if the dividends were limited. In the past many historians have simply disregarded this form of philanthropy, since it did not fit our modern-day understanding of philanthropy. Susannah Morris recently reminded us that historians need to develop a language and a terminology that captures past understandings of philanthropy. Based on the idea that philanthropy does not refer to an unchangeable and static social-cultural practice, Morris con-tends that Victorian philanthropists developed forms of social assistance that are no longer considered philanthropy.[87] However, even Morris argues that the differ-ences between a normal capitalist enterprise and a limited dividend company with regard to the dividend expectation were not as large as contemporary accounts implied. She suggests that the dividends offered by the limited dividend compa-nies "were comparable with those paid by other property companies and for most of the period the annual average realized returns offered were not markedly different from those paid to holders of other domestic assets."[88] If this were the case, why would it be possible then to consider this enterprise philanthropic?

The problem rests with the timeframe of Morris's investigation. She analyzed the dividends paid by different types of enterprises from 1887 to 1913 when, as a result of economic crisis and a slowing down of industrialization, dividends in general decreased. Morris neglected to consider that, based on previous profit margins, the investors of the IIDC had an expectation of higher dividends on their invested capital (more than 5 percent), and the IIDC in fact accrued an annual return of more than 5 percent.[89] George Smalley, in his biography of Waterlow, pointed out that the "usual return for house property" was not "5 but 7 or 10 per cent."[90] In his study of the development of German and English train companies and railroad systems during the industrialization, Volker Then noted that two-digit dividends were normal until the 1860s.[91] The decision of a capitalist to invest his money in a company that decided to pay him a maximum of 5 percent dividends indicates that he voluntarily gave up the claim to a potentially higher return.

While Peabody and Waterlow are credited with the development of philanthropic housing companies, which constructed thousands of healthy and affordable tenements, Octavia Hill (1838–1912) did not engage in the construction of new apartment buildings. Rather, she changed rent collecting and the rules of inhabiting apartment buildings.[92] Hill believed that the poor were incapable of appreciating the new homes provided by Waterlow and Peabody, and she was convinced "that they would only turn clean new homes into filthy new slums." According to Tarn, Hill believed "that this class of persons must first learn to live decently within their natural environment before they were fitted for a new home."[93] Therefore, Hill advocated cleaning up old tenement buildings and reeducating the tenants. She was deeply influenced by her maternal grandfather, Southwood Smith (1788–1861), a physician who was engaged in the public health movement of the 1840s and was the "main driving force" behind the creation of the Metropolitan Association for Improving the Dwellings of the Industrious Classes in 1841.[94] It was her fundamental conviction "that the poor needed example, tuition, inspiration and guidance in their everyday lives more than they needed charity."[95] However, Hill would never have been able to realize her ideas without the support of John Ruskin (1819–1900), who had been her employer and friend. Ruskin, a fierce critic of capitalism who felt "temperamentally unable to deal personally with poor people," encouraged Hill to develop her ideas about improving living conditions for poor families.[96] After Ruskin inherited a considerable amount of money from his father in 1864, he approved Hill's plan of purchasing three houses "in one of the worst courts of Marylebone."[97] While Hill prepared a plan to clean up these apartment buildings and to implement her system of friendly rent collecting and close supervision and education of the tenants, Ruskin concerned himself with the financial aspects of this undertaking. Perhaps following Waterlow's idea of combining philanthropy with market mechanisms, he convinced Hill that "it would be far more useful if it could be made to pay; that a working man ought to be able to pay for his own house; that the outlay upon it ought, therefore, to yield a fair percentage on the capital invested."[98] Hill agreed and went ahead to purchase the three houses in her immediate neighborhood for £750. The three houses were well built, but as she described in detail in one of her early articles, they were in terrible condition:

The plaster was dropping from the walls: on one staircase a pail was placed to catch the rain that fell through the roof. All the staircases were perfectly dark; the banisters were gone, having been burnt as firewood by tenants. The grates, with large holes in them, were falling forward into the rooms. The washhouse, full of lumber belonging to the landlord, was locked up; thus the inhabitants had to wash clothes, as well as to cook, eat and sleep, in their small rooms. The dust-bin, standing in the front of the houses, was accessible to the whole neighborhood, and boys often dragged from it quantities of unseemly objects and spread them over the court. The state of the drainage was in keeping with everything else. The pavement of the back-yard was all broken up, and great puddles stood in it, so that the damp crept up the outer walls. One large but dirty water-butt received the water laid on for the houses: it leaked, and for such as did not fill their jugs when the water came in, or who had no jugs to fill, there was no water.[99]

This condition of the buildings hurt not only the tenants who had to live in the dirty and dysfunctional tenements for which they had to pay very high rents. It also hurt the owner of the buildings, who confessed to Hill that most tenants owed "six, seven, or eight weeks' rent . . . and in some cases very much more."[100]

Since Hill believed in environmental conditioning and education, her first step was to clean up these tenements. Each room was to be

distempered and painted. The drains were put in order, a large slate cistern was fixed, the wash house was cleared of its lumber, and thrown open on stated days to each tenant in turn. The roof, the plaster, the woodwork were repaired; the staircase-walls were distempered; new grates were fixed; the layers of paper and rag (black with age) were torn from the windows, and glass was put in: out of 192 panes, only 8 were found unbroken. The yard and footpath were paved.[101]

However, Hill refused to add any new appliances because she wanted to see first if the tenants would react to the changes by changing themselves. Hill's approach seems to reflect the ideas of Robert Owen, who suggested that the character of an individual was a product of society. Owen concluded that a change in society would result in a change of the individual's character. According to Owen, the factory system as he had found it was to blame for all vices in society and not the individuals, whom he considered to be only a product of this system. Character, according to Owen, could and should be formed:

Any general character, from the best to the worst, from the most ignorant to the most enlightened, may be given to any community, even to the world at large, by the application of proper means; which means are to a great extent at the command and under the control of those who have influence in the affairs of men.[102]

To manage the tenements in the three houses, Hill set up a management system that included weekly visits and contacts with the tenants, insistence on punctual payment of rent, and strict standards of cleanliness for the communal parts of the houses and the tenements. In order to avoid overcrowding the apartments, Hill encouraged big families to rent two instead of just one room "and for these much less was charged than if let singly."[103] Subletting was strictly prohibited, and tenants were evicted if they did not follow Hill's instructions or destroyed parts of the tenements. In articles describing her housing reform, Hill included instances in which tenants who had previously engaged in violent quarrels with other tenants felt compelled to change their behavior because of personal advice given by Hill. She felt confirmed in her conviction that even minor changes in the outside world can and will cause changes in people's behavior. Furthermore, Hill was able to prove that all this was possible while producing a net return of 5 percent on the invested capital.[104] In fact, Hill criticized the Peabody Trust for its alleged ineffective and costly construction of healthy apartments. In an article published in the *Nineteenth Century* in December 1883, Hill wrote: "The Peabody Trustees have spent, we are told, 75 l. per room on buildings; while the Industrial Dwellings Co. have only required 51 l. a room, and a block has been to my knowledge built by others lately at under 50 l. per room. This reduces the cost by one-third, leaving a good margin for higher interest, or lower rental than 2s. 11d., whichever is deemed advisable."[105]

Hill, like Waterlow, was never interested in small-scale reform projects. She hoped to develop a model that could be followed by others and lead to a tremendous improvement in living conditions for London's poor. Hill began publishing articles in several English journals to propagate her ideas. The first article was published in the *Fortnightly Review* in November 1866, but was actually sent to this journal six month earlier—in May 1866 (only about one year after Hill had bought the three houses).[106] More articles followed in *Macmillan's Magazine* and the *Nineteenth Century*. These articles were later combined into the volume *Homes of the London Poor,* first published in London in 1875.[107] As a result of this publicity campaign, Hill found herself in charge of 5,000 to 6,000 houses after a couple of years. She had become an icon of housing reform, which attracted visitors from all of continental Europe and North America. Hill's articles were reprinted in the *Journal de St. Petersbourg*. Louisa Lee Schuyler, who had founded the State Charities Aid Association of New York (SCAA), organized the publication of Hill's *Homes of the London Poor* in New York in 1875. The SCAA sold the 78-page work for twenty-five cents each.[108] These publications offered an alternative avenue for intercultural transfer which had been connected so far to travel and firsthand observation. Publishing about her London housing projects in Great Britain and abroad, Hill reached an international audience on both sides of the Atlantic and even in South Africa.[109]

Octavia Hill, Sydney Waterlow, and George Peabody became famous and admired housing reformers who attracted visitors from many countries. Hill's writings were reprinted in the United States and translated into German and Russian. The reading of her accounts attracted much attention in Europe and North America. Well-off women from Germany, the United States, Sweden, and the Netherlands traveled to London to work and study with Hill.[110] Henry I. Bowditch, Marcus T. Reynolds, Wilhelm Ruprecht, and Paul Felix Aschrott went to London to study the social housing projects of Hill, Waterlow, and Peabody. Their published observations and travel reports transmitted the knowledge about their social housing models to a German and American reform-minded audience. While previous studies have already suggested that Hill's social housing enterprise inspired German and American housing reformers and philanthropists,[111] none of them have actually investigated how the London models of social philanthropy (Peabody, Waterlow, and Hill) were replicated in German and American cities and how they were integrated into a new and distinct social, economic, and cultural context. It will be shown that nineteenth-century philanthropy and social reform cannot be understood within a national framework, since the establishment of social housing enterprises was a local and transnational phenomenon at the same time.[112] It was local insofar as social housing enterprises were established within the setting of urban communities by wealthy philanthropists who acted independently of regional and state governments; it was transnational because these philanthropists looked not to their neighboring cities but to other regions within the transatlantic world for ideas. Wealthy Bostonians and Leipziger looked to London—not to New York and Berlin—for ideas about how to solve the housing problem of the lower classes. Travel reports and published accounts of study trips played a key function in the process of intercultural transfer. The knowledge provided therein became the intellectual basis for the creation of philanthropic housing enterprises in German and American cities from the 1870s onwards.[113] These reports, published in books, journals, and annual reports, helped to shape the understanding of philanthropy. The authors of these widely read reports claimed the power to present ultimate answers to burgeoning questions. For social reformers, these reports presented a unique chance for public recognition of their expertise and proof of their belonging to the educated and privileged circles of society.

THE FIRST WAVE: THE AMERICAN OBSERVERS

Henry Ingersoll Bowditch was a pioneer in this transatlantic transfer of social housing models. He belonged to an old Brahmin family from Massachusetts.[114] Like George Ticknor, Bowditch was born into a very exclusive caste of a wealthy, Harvard-educated elite of Puritan descent. The Brahmins looked to Europe's rich cultural, social, and intellectual life and sent their children to the famous universities of Paris, Göttingen, Leipzig, and Berlin. The Brahmin caste replicated as much as New York's Knickerbocker families aristocratic forms of behavior and established exclusive social circles in Europe. Although Frederic Cople Jaher suggested that "the Brahmins were not a completely closed class until the 1860s,"[115] it was not easy for an outsider to become a Brahmin. Like the European nobility, the majority of Brahmins were born as Brahmin. Brahmin families could trace their family trees back to British ancestors who had settled in New England during the first half of the seventeenth century. Bowditch's forebearers had arrived in this country in 1639. In this year, William Bowditch settled in Salem and founded the American branch of the Bowditch family. Nathaniel Bowditch (1773–1838), the father of Henry Ingersoll Bowditch, became famous for his work as a mathematician, astronomer, and navigator as well as for his translation of Laplace's *Mécanique céleste*.[116] Born in 1808, Bowditch graduated from Harvard College in 1828 and from Harvard Medical School in 1832. Upon graduation, he embarked on a three-year European tour, studying at the University of Paris. When he returned to Boston, he opened a private practice and served as a physician in the Massachusetts General Hospital (1838–64) and of the Boston City Hospital (1868–72). In addition, he held the Jackson professorship of clinical medicine at Harvard Medical School from 1859 to 1867.[117]

Driven by empathy for the poor and the belief, as well as the fear, that dreadful housing conditions cause epidemics and social decay, and convinced that only the wealthy were able to fight these evils, Bowditch grew concerned with housing reform.[118] He believed that "defective house accommodations produce disease, immorality, pauperism and crime, from generation to generation, until vice has become a second nature, and morality, virtue, truth and honesty are to human beings so debased, mere names."[119] Housing reform, guided by the wealthy and reform-minded citizens, was at the heart of preventing the destruction of society. Housing reform, public health, the crime rate, and social unrest were, at least in Bowditch's mind, interconnected. His "influence in stimulating the public health movement in the country was probably greater than that of any other man of his time."[120] He was a "potent influence" in the establishment of the Massachusetts State Board of Health in 1869 and served as chairman of this panel from its inception until 1879.[121]

After he was elected chairman of the State Board of Health, and after he had toured Boston's slums, Bowditch traveled to London, probably to visit the family of his wife, Olivia Yardley, the daughter of John Yardley of London, whom he had married in July 1838. During his six-month stay in the British capital in 1870, Bowditch "thought [he] could not serve Massachusetts better than by investigating, as thoroughly as [he] could in the short time at [his] disposal, the homes of the London poor, and some of the means now used to improve them, together with some other topics of similar importance." Bowditch visited the tenement buildings of Peabody, Waterlow, and Hill and met with Waterlow and Hill to discuss their experiences.[122] The result of these observations and encounters with them and the tenants living in these social housing projects became the subject of his 61-page "Letter from the Chairman of the State Board of Health Concerning Houses for the People, Convalescent Homes and the Sewage Questions." This letter was subdivided into several sections—a night stroll with a London policeman; observation of the Peabody and Waterlow Buildings; description of the "organized work among the poor" by Octavia Hill, etc.—and published in the *Second Annual Report of the State Board of Health of Massachusetts* in 1871. Bowditch dedicated five pages to a detailed description of Hill's work among the poor, thus providing the very first account of her approach to an American audience. This description was based on a statement that Hill had originally written "at the request of Mr. Wilkinson" and which she copied for Bowditch's use.[123]

While Bowditch praised the work of Hill and Waterlow, he remained skeptical of Peabody's housing foundation. Bowditch recognized the successes of the Peabody Trust in elevating the social and moral conditions of their tenants. He remarked that "the influence of these buildings for good upon the health, physical and moral, of the people residing therein is immense." However, since the Peabody buildings "are almost purely philanthropic," Bowditch doubted that they represented a potential way to solve the housing problem. "The percentage for rents on the original outlays is so small that no capitalist would desire to employ his surplus funds without greater gain." Bowditch believed that philanthropy was supposed to provide a net gain for both sides—the one who gives and the one who takes—and that the main function of model tenements was to spark imitation. He concluded that "we must look in other directions as for plans and successful experiments in which philanthropy and capital join hands." Disappointed about the perceived limited success of the Peabody endeavor, Bowditch quoted the critique of an anonymous London capitalist on the Peabody buildings: "Excellent as they are, how much more good would have been done, and how many more families would have been placed in healthful homes if instead of building these large and expensive tenements, the fund had, in part at least, been spent in the purchase of suitable sites which might have been let at such low ground-rent as to induce capitalists to build houses according to certain specifications to be laid down by the trustees."[124]

Rejecting the concept of a housing trust and "pure philanthropy," Bowditch found his perfect solution to the housing problem in Waterlow's IIDC. Although a similar undertaking had been organized in Boston during the 1850s, Bowditch remarked that "nothing has ever been carried out on so grand a scale as by the above named company in London."[125] With his written account (published in 1871) and his practical engagement in the housing reform, Bowditch can be regarded as the first American to popularize the concept of Philanthropy and 5 Percent within the United States. Waterlow's enterprise fulfilled all of Bowditch's expectations: it provided affordable and healthy housing for poor families; it allowed for a modest return on the invested capital and thus combined the provision of social welfare with market mechanism; by allowing for a limited return, it was suited to convince capitalists who were not primarily interested in providing social housing to invest their capital in such projects; and it promised to cause imitation by other reform-minded citizens in Boston and in other U.S. cities. After his return from London, Bowditch was convinced that just writing about London's philanthropic housing projects would not induce action. Therefore, he decided to prove practically that Waterlow and Hill's concepts were compatible with American social and economic conditions. In May 1871, Bowditch convinced a number of wealthy Bostonians to form the Boston Cooperative Building Company (BCBC), which was capitalized at $200,000 and limited to 7 percent dividends. Inspired by Bowditch and headed by Martin Brimmer (1829–1906), this social housing enterprise combined the Philanthropy and 5 Percent concept of Waterlow with the management system of Hill.[126] However, in contrast to Hill's insistence on rent collecting by volunteer lady visitors or landlords, the directors of the BCBC decided not to participate in rent collecting but hired a paid female agent. The *Third Annual Report* of the BCBC stated:

> Our objective was to try whether a "soulless" corporation, by means of well-selected paid agents, could gain the two objects which Miss Hill had so admirably succeeded in attaining, viz.: first, in making the investment of money a pecuniary success, and second, in improving and raising the whole tone of the building and of its occupants.[127]

The BCBC set an example for social housing projects in other American cities. According to the *Twenty-third Annual Report* of the company, housing reformers and philanthropists from "New York, Philadelphia, and Baltimore, and one even from Europe, who all commended the general plan and construction of our houses and the facilities they afford for housing the poor," visited and studied this enterprise.[128] After Bowditch and Schuyler publicized Hill's ideas in the United States, many well-to-do women enthusiastically embraced these ideas and embarked on visits to Octavia Hill in London to study and work with her. Ellen Chase of Philadelphia went to London in 1886. She stayed for several years and compiled her experiences in her book *Tenant Friends in Old Deptford.*[129] After her return to Philadelphia, she and Helen Parish campaigned for the creation of a social housing association based on the principle of friendly rent collecting. In 1896, Nathaniel B. Crenshaw, Hannah Fox, Mrs. William F. Jenks, Mrs. Thomas S. Kirkbride, Hector McIntosh, Helen L. Parrish, Mrs. William M. Lybrand, George Woodward, and C. H. Ludington Jr. founded "the most notable American application of the Octavia Hill system"—the Octavia Hill Association of Philadelphia.[130] The aim of this association was "to improve old houses and small properties" that were either owned or just managed by this association. In 1902, the Octavia Hill Association was in charge of seventy-seven houses—"sixty-five of which are small houses for separate families, and twelve are tenements of a medium size, averaging eleven or twelve rooms each." It was organized with a capital stock of $50,000 and paid yearly dividends of 4 to 4.5 percent. Paid and volunteer rent collectors were responsible for weekly visits with the tenants.[131]

Bowditch and the BCBC served as a conduit for the translation of Hill and Waterlow's concepts into the American social, cultural, and economic context. While the basic elements of both models remained unchanged, the limitation on the dividends was raised slightly to 7 percent and the rent collecting was not conducted by the directors of the housing company and volunteer friendly visitors but by paid agents. For Hill the direct contact between friendly visitors and tenants was at the center of her concept, since she believed in the necessity of molding the behavior of those tenants. American social reformers, in contrast, seemed to care more about the dividend of up to 7 percent than about the moral betterment of the renters. This modified concept of the limited dividend company and the friendly rent collecting system was copied in many American cities during the 1880s and 1890s. After Alfred Treadway White (1846–1921) had followed in Bowditch's footsteps and traveled to London in 1872, he established the Home Buildings in Brooklyn in 1877.[132] These buildings were in their architecture the "first literal translation of the Waterlow type."[133] Three years later, White, who has been considered "the undisputed evangelist of model-tenement gospel in the postwar period," was able to persuade fellow wealthy New Yorkers, such as Cornelius Vanderbilt, to found the Improved Dwellings Association as a limited dividend company.[134] In 1896, White finally initiated the establishment of another limited dividend company—the City and Suburban Homes Company (CSHC). Headed by Elgin R. L. Gould, this company "was destined to become the largest builder of model tenements in the country."[135] It built fifteen housing projects within the city of New York between 1896 and 1938. These included "11 apartment projects containing 4,300 dwellings, 1 hotel accommodating 350 business women, a garage development, and 2 suburban projects with more than 300 single family and row houses." The company succeeded in producing low rent housing while paying an average annual dividend of 4.2 percent since 1898.[136] Philanthropists and housing reformers in Washington and Cincinnati created similar housing enterprises that were based on the Americanized version of Hill and Waterlow's projects.[137]

The Second Wave: Alice and Her Translation of Octavia Hill

Even though Huber and Varrentrapp had already published accounts of London's philanthropic housing projects, German housing reformers maintained a preference for firsthand observation and study. London thus continued to attract American and German pilgrims who sought answers to the pressing question of how best to house the rising numbers of urban lower-class families. In this context, traveling to London became a ritual for social reformers, and it provided a cloud of authority to the traveler who could boast to have seen social housing reform in action.

In contrast to the shipment of philanthropic models via the Atlantic, German social reformers and philanthropists not only had a much shorter distance to overcome but also enjoyed the help of a British royal who assumed the function of an agent of intercultural transfer. In July 1862, Alice (1843–78), the second daughter of Queen Victoria, married Duke Ludwig of Hesse and moved from London to the provincial city of Darmstadt. Very soon Alice, "who had hardly ever been away from her family before, was homesick and bewildered." She felt alienated and rejected by Darmstadt's higher society. "Within a week of arrival she had met all the members of the government and found them almost impossible to talk to. They stood waiting to be spoken to and were wholly unresponsive to her desperate efforts to make polite and suitable conversation." Furthermore, the new social environment did not offer her a role in public life that could have fulfilled her expectations. Reinhard Carl Friedrich von Dalwigk, the grand duke's principal minister, implied "that the young Princess could do nothing more than imitate her sister's example in Berlin. By this he was implying that Alice was and should remain a mere cypher."[138] Gillian Darley even contended in his biography of Hill that Alice was not only "unhappy" in Darmstadt but that she "hated life in a provincial German city."[139] While Gerard Noel and Gillian Darley's assumption about the unhappy marriage of Alice has been repudiated by Eckhardt G. Franz, it is clear that she longed for a purposeful task within Darmstadt's society.[140]

Beginning in 1863, Alice began visiting "hospitals at Mayence, Offenbach, and Giessen, and had many consultations with the heads of these various hospitals with a view to possible improvements." Influenced by Florence Nightingale, Alice founded the Hülfsverein (Committee of Aid) and the Alice Society for Aid to the Sick and Wounded. It was her goal to establish a network of aid associations run by women for the entire Duchy of Hesse-Darmstadt after the blueprint of Baden, Bavaria, and Prussia. These organizations were to provide care for the wounded and sick independently of the churches. When the Alice Society was officially founded in December 1869, it united thirty-three local organizations with about 2,500 members. In addition to her engagement in the field of medical care, Alice considered the education and professional training of women an essential part of her reform agenda. Influenced by Luise Büchner (1821–77), Alice created the Alice Society for the Education and Employment of Women. In 1874, Alice and Büchner founded the Alice Lyceum to educate women of the higher classes. Students were introduced to English and German literature, art history, German history, and natural history.[141]

In 1872, Alice invited representatives of women's organizations from more than twenty German cities and several guests of honor from Great Britain, the Netherlands, and Switzerland to attend a general meeting, which soon was called the Women's Parliament, in Darmstadt. Among the participants were eminent leaders of the German women's movement such as Johanna Goldschmidt (Hamburg), Lina Morgenstern and Jenny Hirsch (Berlin), Anna Simson (Breslau), and Luise Büchner (Darmstadt). Mary Carpenter, Florence Hill, and Susanna and Catherine Winkworth joined these meetings to present papers on various aspects of social work performed by women. According to a letter written by Alice on October 13, Mary Carpenter spoke "on all relating to women's work in England. . . . Her account of the Queen's Institute at Dublin was most interesting. Miss Hill . . . about the boarding-out system for orphans. Miss C. Winkworth, about higher education in England." In the same letter Alice proudly wrote about the focus and scope of this meeting: "The meeting went off well, was very large, the subjects discussed were to the purpose and important, and not a word of the emancipated political side of the questions was touched upon by any one. Schools (those of the lower, middle, and higher classes) for girls was the principal theme; the employment of women for post and telegraph offices, etc.; the improvement necessary in the education of nursery-maids, and the knowledge of mothers in the treatment of little children; the question of nurses and nursing institutes."[142]

Alice was not interested in a women's movement based on political radicalism. She shared Carpenter and Hill's desire to improve the "women's status in terms of education, ownership of property and professional training and work opportunities," but she did not favor a battle for universal suffrage.[143]

Over the next couple of years, Alice's focus on social reform shifted from education to the housing conditions of the poor. During an 1876 visit to London, Alice arranged to meet Octavia Hill and took an incognito tour of the social housing projects administered by Hill. Alice described her impressions from such a visit in a letter to her daughter:

> With a charming excellent lady Miss Octavia Hill . . . I have been this morning in some of the very poor courts in London, garrets and streets . . . such quantities of little children and so many living in one dirty room. It was sad to see them—on one way, but beautiful to see how these ladies worked amongst them, knew them, did business with them. I have been trying to see as much and learn as much as possible of what is done for the poor in every way and have heard of such good and unselfish noble people.[144]

Impressed by Hill's housing management system, Alice entered into an exchange of letters with Hill to learn more about her concepts. In late 1876, Alice asked Hill for permission to translate her book *The Homes of the London Poor* into German. Hill responded enthusiastically and even suggested that Alice should write an introduction to the translation. With the arrangement for the translation of this book, Alice virtually occupied the position of translator for Hill's methods into a German environment. In 1878, this text appeared in Wiesbaden under the title *Aus der Londoner Armenpflege* and became quickly the most influential book on housing reform in Germany.[145] Housing reformers such as Wilhelm Schwab (Darmstadt) and Gustav de Liagre (Leipzig) used the German translation as a guidebook in their attempts to establish social housing enterprises following Hill's model.[146]

Inspired by Hill's successful London endeavors, Liagre and eleven friends purchased two buildings with 240 rooms in Leipzig in 1883.[147] Liagre came from a European transnational merchant family that had originated in Brussels (Austrian Netherlands) and dispersed over the cities of the Holy Roman Empire and, after 1806, the German states. The first to settle in Leipzig was Charles Benoit François de Liagre (1789–1855), a merchant who specialized in linens and French batistes. In 1832 he married Ottilie Küstner (1811–92), the daughter of Heinrich Küstner, the consul-general of Saxony-Weimar in Leipzig. In 1846 he opened his trade company in Leipzig. His business was engaged in trade with Odessa, Brody, Gotha, Weimar, Valparaiso, Hamburg, and Bucharest. Soon after his arrival in Leipzig, de Liagre was elected head of the small Catholic community in the overwhelmingly Protestant city. He held onto this position until his death and is remembered for his many philanthropic foundations for the Catholic community of Leipzig. At the time of his death, his trading company was worth about 24,066 taler. That was little more than twice the amount of his wife's dowry (10,000 taler). In his last will, de Liagre asked that his wife, Ottilie, be put in charge of the company, since his two sons, Albert de Liagre (1833–1908) and Gustav de Liagre (1842–1904), were still too young to shoulder this responsibility.[148]

Giving in to social pressure and his desire for social integration, Gustav de Liagre decided in 1873 to convert to Protestantism because "of his disbelief in the infallibility of the Catholic Church and his doubts over the doctrine of transubstantiation," which he claimed to have had since his very early youth.[149] However, this conversion can be seen in context with his desire to integrate into a predominantly Protestant society and the upper class of Leipzig. Since he engaged, first as an apprentice, later as a co-owner, in business with Hermann Samson, the head of the Jewish community between 1847 and 1856, Liagre had even more reasons to display a very conformist behavior if he wanted to be included in Leipzig's High Society. Only after the death of Samson in 1865, after he and his brother, Albert de Liagre, took over the firm of Samson, was he invited to join the Gesellschaft Harmonie, one of the most socially exclusive societies in Leipzig.[150] This longing for integration is important for understanding Liagre's engagement in housing reform, since philanthropy provided an excellent tool for social integration. Economic success certainly provided a necessary precondition for integration into the leading circles of society. It was in itself not sufficient for social acceptance, however. Marrying into old families could help in overcoming the barriers between old and new money, but not everyone who wanted to be included in the leading circles of society could take advantage of this possibility. Another way was to comply with the behavioral patterns of the old elites such as their civic engagement for public purposes and institutions. Showing an interest in social problems and working toward the creation of public funds and institutions that would secure the status quo of society was a clever strategy to impress the guardians of the old elites and to prove oneself worthy of acknowledgment and inclusion.

Like Hill, Liagre did not construct new buildings but purchased rundown buildings close to the inner city of Leipzig. He convinced eight men and three women to each contribute 5,000 marks to this enterprise by promising them a 4 percent return on their invested capital. Liagre chose a building he was already acquainted with from his time as a "friendly visitor" (Armenpfleger) during the 1870s. After acquiring these tenement houses, Liagre insisted, like Hill, on basic improvements but did not add any new appliances. His goal was to provide healthy and affordable small tenements for poor families who had shared much larger apartments with other families before they entered Liagre's housing complex. He insisted on weekly rent collection by lady visitors, compliance to certain cleanliness standards among the tenants, and the ban on subletting parts of these tenements. Liagre's enterprise received much attention among housing reformers in Leipzig and in other German cities. The social housing projects of Emma Hasse, Therese Rossbach, and Herrmann Julius Meyer in Leipzig were inspired by Liagre's success.[151] Moreover, the influence of this model reached far beyond Leipzig. In his history of the Verein zur Verbesserung der kleinen Wohnungen in Berlin (Association for the Improvement of Small Tenements in Berlin), Paul Felix Aschrott pointed out that it influenced housing reforms in Berlin.[152] Liagre (Leipzig) and Schwab (Darmstadt) were among the first German housing reformers to replicate Hill's management system in Germany. In contrast to Schwab, however, Liagre gave public talks in many German cities and published accounts of his enterprise. He was able to show that it was possible to integrate Hill's method into the German social and economic environment.[153] Therefore, Liagre—not Schwab—was regarded as the expert on Hill's concepts. Whereas Alice remained anonymous—she signed the introduction to the German translation of Octavia Hill's book just with A—Liagre became a public figure who gained extensive influence among philanthropists and housing reformers alike.

THE PROFESSIONALIZATION OF INTERCULTURAL TRANSFER

Interest in housing reform and practical steps to solve the housing problem of the lower classes increased during the 1880s and 1890s because of the accelerated urbanization in the German Empire. Leipzig's population, for instance, increased from 106,925 in 1871 to 170,342 in 1885 and 386,363 in 1895.[154] Social reformers were therefore even more interested in learning about the social housing projects in London, especially the Peabody and Waterlow endeavors. Travel and first-hand encounters remained the most important methods of intercultural transfer. Even though the number of published articles and books about housing reform increased significantly, seeing the London housing projects seemed to be essential for German housing reformers. In contrast to earlier instances of intercultural transfer (Huber, Varrentrapp, Bowditch, and White), the next generation of travelers/observers took a professional interest in social reform. They were trained in subjects such as statistics, political economy/political science (Ruprecht, Aschrott, Gould), and architecture/engineering (Reynolds, Albrecht). They even held doctoral degrees in areas related to social reform (Ruprecht), or they made housing reform their profession (Albrecht). They published their observations in book form and went on lecture tours.

In 1884, Wilhelm Ruprecht (1858–1943) published the first German scholarly account of housing reform in London, *Die Wohnungen der arbeitenden Klassen in London* (The tenements of the working classes in London). Ruprecht was born into a wealthy Göttingen publisher family in 1858. His father was the owner of the prestigious Vandenhoeck & Ruprecht Press, who expected his third-born son to take over the business after he had finished his education. Ruprecht had little interest in either school or a publisher's career. Yet he complied with his father's wishes after being promised that he could participate in military training while attending the university. His inner desire was to enter the army and have an officer's career. When he turned eighteen, Ruprecht entered the University of Leipzig to study political economy and related sciences with Wilhelm Roscher. He continued his studies with the Kathedersozialisten (socialist of the chair) Gustav von Schönberg and Neumann at the University of Tübingen. After one year of military and two years of university training, he received his doctoral degree from the University of Tübingen for his thesis *Die Erbpacht: Ein Beitrag zur Geschichte und Reform derselben insbesondere in Deutschland* (Hereditary lease: A contribution to history and reform of hereditary lease in Germany). With this thesis, which was published by his father's publishing house in 1882, Ruprecht entered the national discourse on housing reform. Erbpacht was one of the most discussed solutions to the housing question in the last two decades of the nineteenth century. German municipalities traditionally owned large plots of land within the city limits. To encourage the production of improved apartment buildings that could be rented out at low prices, social reformers asked city governments to lease out their land for extremely low fees to housing cooperatives and limited dividend companies, which were to provide affordable and hygienic housing for lower-class families on this land.[155] Using the example of Leipzig, Johann Heinrich Andreas Hermann Albrecht, Graf von Bernstorff, provided the American public with an excellent explanation of this Erbpacht system in his printed baccalaureate address on social reforms in Germany delivered at the University of Wisconsin in Madison on June 19, 1910:

> Leipzig is one of the cities—and there are many of them—which have devoted a portion of their real estate to the housing of the working classes. The municipality there has leased for 100 years at a low rent to a philanthropic building society a large piece of communal land in the environs for the erection of cheap houses. The majority of the houses have to contain three and some of them more than four rooms. This society cannot transfer its leasehold rights to third parties without the consent of the municipality, and in the event of doing so, both the offending contract and the lease itself may be cancelled. The municipality undertook the initial construction of all squares, roads, and footpaths and went further in undertaking to advance money for the mortgage for building purposes should the building societies' revenues prove inadequate, with the provision that the society must refund the loan by regular repayments in such a manner that on termination of the lease the mortgage will be redeemed. The municipality will then take over the land and the dwellings built upon it without compensation.[156]

In January 1882, Ruprecht began his apprenticeship as publisher in his father's publishing house and half a year later in the publishing house of Max Niemeyer in Halle. Throughout the year, he refreshed his English and prepared for a yearlong stay in London. An old friend of his father, Nikolaus Trübner, offered to employ Ruprecht for a year in the oriental department of his London publishing house. In October 1883, he left for London. However, after just a few weeks, Ruprecht was bored by the monotonous work in this enterprise. He chose to dedicate much of his time to studying the housing conditions of London's working class instead. The result of this research became his second book, again published by his family's publishing house. The book was positively received by fellow social reformers, and it led directly to the formation of the Göttinger Spar- und Bauverein (Göttinger Building and Savings Society), which dominated social housing in that city after 1900.[157]

Based on his research trip to London in 1883/84, personal interviews with individuals who were involved in the housing reform, the analysis of government reports and laws, as well as books such as *The Homes of the London Poor* and newspaper and journal articles from the *Nineteenth Century, Times, Pall Mall Gazette,* and the *Contemporary Review,* Ruprecht provided an exhaustive overview over the housing problem in Great Britain's capital, the English laws concerning working-class housing, and the steps taken by Peabody, Waterlow, and Hill to change this situation. Writing for a German public, Ruprecht hoped that his descriptions of housing reform would convince politicians and philanthropists alike to tackle this social problem back home. Arguing that there were many parallels between London's and Berlin's problems with regard to the housing of the urban poor, he intended to provide an account of possible solutions that had already withstood the test of time.[158]

Ruprecht called for close collaboration between state and philanthropists— the state was expected to provide the legal framework that would set up certain standards of housing (regulation regarding overcrowding, architectural standards, etc.), and the philanthropists were expected to follow in Peabody, Waterlow, and Hill's footsteps by financing affordable and hygienic apartment buildings. Rejecting the idea of self-help via housing cooperatives, Ruprecht argued in favor of philanthropic help for the poor. He further rejected the provision of housing by employers, since not all of the urban poor worked in factories. The absence of factory housing in London confirmed his suspicion that factory villages could be created only in a rural setting and not in highly urbanized industrial centers.[159] Subsequently, Ruprecht felt that the Peabody Foundation, Waterlow's limited dividend company, and Hill's housing management system represented the best solutions.

By describing these three approaches, Ruprecht highlighted the economic aspects of these enterprises, their architectural specifications, the intentions of the founders, and the outcome of these projects. Wilhelm Ruprecht and later Paul Felix Aschrott were interested in the Philanthropy and 5 Percent concept and attempted to prove to their German readers that it actually worked. It is interesting to note that while Susannah Morris recently argued that London's limited dividend companies rarely reached the promised 5 percent dividend, German nineteenth-century observers insisted that these companies reached their intended goal of guaranteeing a 5 percent annual return.[160] The picture created in these accounts depicted Peabody, Waterlow, and Hill's enterprises as shinning examples of what could be done if wealthy burghers would be willing to tackle the housing problem. While Ruprecht admired the quantitative success of the Peabody Trust—24 million marks capital, about 4,400 tenements, and 18,000 inhabitants by 1883—he shared Bowditch's doubts and favored the Waterlow Company. However, his admiration was not unlimited, since he pointed out that most of the people living in both the Peabody Trust and the Waterlow Company did not belong to the lower parts of the working class. He credited Hill with accomplishing exactly what Peabody and Waterlow's enterprises did not achieve. In his eyes, only the combination of all three forms of philanthropy, with a dominance of the investment philanthropy model, would provide a viable social system to end the housing crisis of modern urban society. Like Bowditch, Ruprecht argued that causing imitation was to be the main task of philanthropic housing enterprises. Offering a limited annual return of about 5 percent seemed to provide an incentive that potentially would attract German investor-philanthropists to participate in such enterprises. It should be noted that Ruprecht did not advocate state action for solving the housing problem. He called for private action by reform-minded wealthy burghers based on the model of investment philanthropy and hoped that in the long run these enterprises would attract investors who were not primarily interested in providing social welfare.[161]

Initially, he did not see a role for housing cooperatives in solving the housing problem, since the cooperatives he had encountered in England were based on the idea that the members of the cooperative would buy their homes. Ruprecht realized that working-class families would not have the necessary financial means to do so.[162] After his return to Germany, however, he discovered a very innovative model that mixed cooperation with Philanthropy and 5 Percent. Intrigued by the combination of both principles in the Hannover Spar- and Bauverein, Ruprecht published two texts explaining and advertising the basic principles of this enterprise. In 1896, Ruprecht contributed a chapter, "Gesunde Wohnungen" (Healthy apartments), to the journal *Göttinger Arbeiterbibliothek* (Göttinger Workers' Library), edited by the eminent social politician Friedrich Naumann.[163] In this chapter, Ruprecht described in detail the economic and financial aspects of the Hanover housing enterprise.

Advocating the imitation of this savings and housing association, Ruprecht insisted that the state should play only a very limited role in housing reform. Arguing against Paul Lechler's suggestion of large-scale state support for the creation of housing cooperatives, Ruprecht felt that the solution could not be achieved by simply providing a large number of apartments.[164] Negating the idea that the housing question was only an economic issue, Ruprecht argued that it had a social and cultural dimension. Of course, workers had to be in a position to afford the apartments built for them. These workers also needed education and guidance in how to maintain the apartments. In his view, many workers seemed not to care for keeping the apartments in good shape and therefore could not be entrusted with improved housing conditions. These ideas closely reflect Octavia Hill's opinion on working-class housing. Only after working-class families were trained to maintain a certain level of cleanliness and care did Hill consider them deserving of better housing. Both Ruprecht and Hill saw the housing question as a financial and educational project that could be accomplished only over a longer period of time.

In the same year that Wilhelm Ruprecht's book *Die Wohnungen der arbeitenden Klassen in London* (1884) was published, Paul Felix Aschrott (1856–1927) embarked on one of his study tours to London to collect information on the topic of housing reform in the British metropolis. Aschrott was born in Kassel in 1856 to a wealthy German-Jewish family. His father, Sigmund Aschrott, who made his fortune in the textile industry, was one of the richest men in Germany around 1900. His fortune was estimated at 20 million marks.[165] After attending law school in Heidelberg, Leipzig, and Berlin (1874–77), Aschrott received a doctoral degree in law and started a career in the Prussian civil service. In December 1877, he entered the legal profession as an articled clerk (Referendar) at the court of Cöpenick. In 1878 he was drafted into the one-year obligatory military service, but received a leave of absence after six months of service to reenter the university. He studied political economy and political science with J. A. R. Helferich and Wilhelm Heinrich Riehl in Munich and with Gustav Schmoller and Georg Friedrich Knapp in Straßburg. When he was appointed to the court of Berlin in 1880, Aschrott continued attending lectures at the University of Berlin, and for half a year he was even an assistant at the Department for Statistics, directed by Ernst Engel, a founder of the Verein für Sozialpolitik (Association for Social Policy) and was instrumental in establishing statistics as a science in Germany. Since 1861, Engel had been head of the Statistical Bureau of the Kingdom of Prussia and held a professorship of statistics at the University of Berlin.[166] In a May 1883 letter to the president of the Royal Chamber Court, Aschrott voiced a desire to continue his academic education in national economy and social policy. Probably influenced by Engel, Aschrott grew increasingly more interested in the reform of working-class housing. He applied for an unpaid leave of absence from his duties for an entire year in June 1884 to study the social housing projects in London. After the Prussian minister of justice, Heinrich von Friedberg, granted his request, Aschrott embarked on his journey on July 1, 1884. He returned from London on July 23, 1885.[167]

The result of this research trip was "Die Arbeiterwohnungsfrage in England" (The question about how to house the working class in England), which was included in the already discussed volume *Die Wohnungsnoth der ärmeren Klassen in deutschen Großstädten und Vorschläge zu deren Abhülfe* published by the Verein für Socialpolitik in 1886. In 53 pages, Aschrott described the horrible living conditions of the London poor, focusing on overcrowding, the existence of basement tenements, and the percentage of workers' incomes spend for rent. Using statistical methods, Aschrott pointed out that 46 percent of all tenants paid between 25 and 50 percent of their wages for rent. He continued to analyze the causes for the crisis in working-class housing and the reactions of parliament and government. Discussing the Labouring Classes Lodging-Houses Act (1851), the Artizans' and Labourers' Dwellings Act (1868), and the Artizans' and Labourers' Dwellings Improvement Acts from 1875, 1879, and 1882, Aschrott pointed to the inherent flaws, especially in the last two legislations, which actually encouraged landlords to worsen the living conditions in their tenement buildings instead of improving them. Positively mentioned are the government loans for building societies that provide healthy tenements for working-class families and the introduction of trains to transport workers from the suburbs into the city for affordable fares, thus exporting the problem of housing the poor from the city to the suburbs (Cheap Trains Act of 1883).[168]

After briefly discussing building societies that enabled members to purchase the house in which they lived, Aschrott focused on the Peabody Trust, the MAIDIC, the IIDC, and the renting practice of Hill. His description of the Peabody Trust includes important observations of the paternalistic regime over its tenants. The majority of tenants were, according to Aschrott, trained workers and artisans who had steady jobs and a secure income. However, applicants with a weekly income of more than 30 shillings were not accepted as tenants. The families living in the Peabody Buildings were forbidden to sublet rooms and had to comply with a certain set of rules. Every night at 11, the gaslight would be turned off and the entrance gate to the building complex closed. Tenants possessed their own house keys, but they had to enter the building through one main entrance and thus were spotted, controlled, and noted by the doorman. Showing up drunk after 11 PM during the week and even on weekends resulted in immediate cancellation of the rental contract.[169]

After the Peabody Trust, Aschrott went on to discuss what he called the Baugesellschaften mit humanitärem Charakter (building societies with humanitarian character). These building societies, the MAIDIC and the IIDC, differed from the Peabody Trust in that they expected an annual dividend of 4–5 percent. Aschrott, however, considered them to be of humanitarian character because they were founded to improve the living conditions of the working poor, and the dividend for the investors was limited. He concluded his article by suggesting that German housing reformers should consider the English experiences. He also pointed out that housing reform was the necessary basis for any other far-reaching social reform, thus mirroring the common assumption about the family as the basic cell of society and the home as the place where every social change has to begin.[170] After his return from London, Aschrott attempted to combine a career as lawyer and later judge with his activities as social reformer. Between 1884 and 1903, Aschrott was appointed as judge at various courts in Berlin and Landsberg. In 1903 he was made a judge at the Landgericht Elberfeld. He retired in 1905 at the age of 49 to fully dedicate his energy toward social reform projects.

In 1886, Aschrott was asked to contribute his report on the housing conditions of the London poor to the volume *Die Wohnungsnoth der ärmeren Klassen*. He was awarded a doctoral degree from the University of Leipzig in the same year. Several books about various aspects of social reform followed quickly: in 1886 Aschrott published his detailed study, *Das englische Armenwesen in seiner historischen Entwicklung und in seiner heutigen Gestalt* (The English poor law system, past and present, translated into English and published in 1888), in 1887 his masterful work on the English criminal institutions with the title *Strafensystem und Gefängniswesen in England* (Penal system and prison organization in England), and in the same year he also published *Das Universitätsstudium und insbesondere die Ausbildung der Juristen in England* (The university education and the education of lawyers in England). However, Aschrott was not only a prolific writer who resorted to theoretical discussions of what could be done; he was also a passionate practitioner who engaged in housing reform. In June 1888 Aschrott, together with the architect Alfred Messel and the banker Valentin Weisbach, founded the Verein zur Verbesserung der kleinen Wohnungen in Berlin (Society for the Improvement of Small Tenements in Berlin). This housing society closely followed Waterlow's limited dividend company, since the bylaws stated that investors should receive a maximum annual return of 4 percent on their invested capital. Beginning in 1891, a number of High Society women joined the society and, following the example of Hill, took over the responsibility of weekly rent collecting and friendly visiting.[171]

In 1891, Heinrich Albrecht (1856–1931) joined Ruprecht and Aschrott in their call for a housing reform that was informed and influenced by British models. Albrecht was born in Rastede, Oldenburg, to a middle-class family. He entered the Technical University Hanover in 1875 to become an engineer. After his graduation in 1880, he returned to academia in 1884 when he entered the University of Berlin to pursue a doctoral degree in political science and studied with Gustav Schmoller and Adolph Wagner.[172] In 1891, Albrecht published his first book on the housing problem in German cities. *Die Wohnungsnot in den Großstädten und die Mittel zu ihrer Abhülfe* (The lack of affordable housing in big cities and suggestions for a reform) was based on a series of articles Albrecht had published in one of Germany's leading periodicals, *Deutsche Rundschau*, in 1890.[173]

In contrast to Ruprecht and Aschrott, who both had traveled to London to receive firsthand information about the housing reform, Albrecht relied on newspapers, journals, and books. It was no longer necessary to travel to London, since the number of publications on the topic of housing reform increased significantly and even included many firsthand observations of London's philanthropic enterprises. Besides Hill's *Homes of the London Poor*, he used articles from the *National Review, Fortnightly Review*, the *Daily News*, and the *Pall Mall Gazette*. He also utilized Ruprecht and Aschrott's publications. Albrecht was convinced that housing reform was at the heart of a reform of the entire society. He considered good, clean housing as the precondition for happy people who would live together in harmony. However, Albrecht refused to acknowledge a connection between income and rent. Higher wages for workers, he was convinced, would not lead to better housing conditions. Albrecht further assumed that private individuals and employers as well as the state and municipalities had an interest in solving the housing problem. Thus only collaboration of all these agencies could guarantee improved housing conditions and a society without social tensions and class struggle. Yet his later engagement in the cooperative movement seems to suggest that Albrecht considered self-help, supported by state and municipalities, to be an important element of the housing reform.[174]

Looking at English, German, French, and Belgian examples, Albrecht provided detailed accounts of how the housing of the working classes could be improved. His discussion focused on the legislation with regard to British working-class housing; the provision of housing by employers (for example, the famous Krupp settlements in Essen); the self-help of workers (cooperatives in Copenhagen, Berlin, etc.); the provision of working-class housing by single individuals (Peabody Trust and Herrmann Julius Meyer's Housing Foundation in Leipzig); and the limited dividend companies (which in the end is an exclusive discussion of Hill's house management system and its application in several German cities). Although Albrecht's book included legal and organizational principles, he was, as an engineer, much more interested in the architectural and financial aspects of these enterprises. He reiterated the essential characteristics of the three London models, and his argumentation does not differ much from Ruprecht and Aschrott's suggestions. However, since he wrote in the 1890s, he could already include a description of housing companies in German cities that had been inspired by London's housing companies. Albrecht gave, for instance, a detailed account of Gustav de Liagre's Leipzig enterprise and showed how Liagre subsequently influenced housing projects in Leipzig and Dresden.[175] He also pointed to the mutations that Hill's concept underwent in the intercultural transfer of social housing models from London to various German cities.

The Dresdner Mietzinssparkasse (rent-credit union) was one such mutation. Influenced by Hill's demand for weekly rent payment (at the time, rent was collected in monthly or even trimonthly periods), Victor Böhmert (1829–1918),[176] a university professor at the Technical Institute in Dresden and co-editor of the journal *Der Arbeiterfreund* (Worker's Friend), founded a Mietzinssparkasse in 1880. Since the city's private homeowners were not willing to change their policy on rent collection, Böhmert established a credit union for the sole purpose of allowing working-class families to deposit their rent in weekly intervals with the credit union, which would pay the rent at the due date (in monthly or trimonthly intervals). More than 1,000 tenants whose annual rent was less than 240 marks participated in this project and received a dividend of 4–10 percent on their rent accounts.[177]

Albrecht was convinced that purely philanthropic housing enterprises such as the Peabody Trust were unsuitable to improve the housing conditions of the poor. He argued that only private building companies that were subject to market laws could effectively improve housing conditions in big cities. Albrecht suggested that limited dividend companies with a fixed return of 4 percent on invested capital would be the only possible way to improve living conditions. However, he also suggested essential architectural standards. He pointed out a general need for more two-room apartments consisting of a living room and a kitchen and maybe an additional room for children. Following Meyer and his architect Max Pommer's concept of separated staircases and entrances, Albrecht considered the separation of hallways essential. Every family was to have a closed hallway, which was to be part of the apartment. Furthermore, staircases were to be integrated into the house structure in such a way that no more than six to eight apartments shared one staircase and no more than two apartments shared one landing. Reflecting on contemporary German debates about the connection between social segregation and social tensions, Albrecht strongly recommended desegregation by providing different types of apartments in the same house, thus attracting families of different social standing to live under the same roof.[178]

In 1896, Albrecht published his second book, *Das Arbeiterwohnhaus* (The apartment building for workers), focusing nearly exclusively on the architectural side of housing reform.[179] Reiterating some of his earlier statements and descriptions of Hill and Peabody's enterprises, Albrecht, with help from Alfred Messel, provided detailed guidelines for building affordable and healthy apartment complexes for working-class families. Twenty-four pages were dedicated to the architectural-technical side and seven pages to the financial side of such endeavors. The book was accompanied by sample contracts and bylaws of already existing German social housing enterprises and several drawings of model tenements. In 1902, Albrecht included a chapter on social housing in his *Handbuch der Sozialen Wohlfahrtspflege* (Handbook of social welfare).[180] Within sixty-two pages, he offered an overview of ways to provide housing. This account reflected the different approaches of German housing reformers in the nineteenth and early twentieth centuries and included housing provided by employers (Krupp), philanthropic foundations, philanthropic building societies, and housing cooperatives (Ostheim in Stuttgart, Meyer's Housing Foundation in Leipzig, Berliner Spar- und Bauverein [Berlin Savings and Buildings Society]). While Albrecht did not practically engage in providing housing for working-class families, he became the most important pioneer for building societies and cooperatives in Germany. He was appointed assistant at the Zentralstelle für Volkswohlfahrt (Central Office for Communal

Welfare) in 1892, became its director in 1907, and edited its journal, *Concordia*, until 1920, propagating housing reform and the creation of social housing companies. In 1897, Albrecht created the first unified national organization of housing cooperatives—the Verband der auf der Grundlage des gemeinschaftlichen Eigentums stehenden Baugenossenschaften. And in 1902 he founded the journal *Zeitschrift für Wohnungsreform* (Journal for Housing Reform).[181]

Around 1900 American social reformers caught up with their German counterparts. Facing the increased need for affordable and healthy housing for lower-class families, American scholars such as Marcus T. Reynolds and Elgin Ralston Lovell Gould were sent to Europe to study social housing provision and report their findings. Reynolds and Gould followed in the footsteps of Bowditch and White and could build upon earlier transatlantic webs of cultural exchange. It may have been true that American social reformers, as Daniel T. Rodgers suggests, "had no automatic access to the networks and discussions taking shape in Europe." The Atlantic may have kept "them at arm's length, . . . both physical and cultural," but intellectually and morally American social reformers were closely connected with the way their European counterparts thought.[182] Private action was still considered essential in solving the housing problem of the lower classes. In contrast to the first wave of socially concerned Americans, who limited their investigation to London, Reynolds and Gould were able to study the London projects and attempts to re-create these projects in different social and cultural settings all over Europe. They could thus study the transferability of social housing concepts from one country to another. After London, Leipzig became a laboratory of social housing and the transferability and compatibility of philanthropic models. Furthermore, Reynolds and Gould could rely on a large number of publications written by German, French, and British social reformers. Although these publications provided detailed descriptions of the philanthropic housing projects in London, little had been published on the attempts to create similar institutions in other European cities. Thus travel proved essential for a study of the transfer of social housing concepts.

In 1887 Elgin Ralston Lovell Gould (1860–1915) traveled to Europe as head of a commission of six officers from the bureau of labor to study various aspects of economic life such as wages, housing conditions, and family budgets. He had been assigned to study the housing conditions of the lower classes by Carroll Davidson Wright (1840–1909), commissioner of labor from 1884 to 1905, for whom he worked as an expert assistant while he pursued graduate work in history and economics at Johns Hopkins University. Gould documented his observations in *The Housing of the Working People*, which Jacob A. Riis regarded as the standard work on the subject.[183]

Like Hasse, Wright considered the collection of statistical data a necessary precondition and an integral part of social reform. From his appointment as chief of the bureau of labor for Massachusetts, Wright engaged in large-scale sociological studies focusing first on Massachusetts, later on the United States, and finally on a comparative level with European societies. The scope of his sociological investigations included the education and employment of the young, the conditions of workingmen's families, illiteracy, profits and wages, the relation of intemperance to pauperism and crime, divorce, cooperation and profit sharing, prices and cost of living, and factory legislation. No such statistical work had existed before, and his studies were used as textbooks in colleges "and attracted attention in Europe."[184] While the reports, prepared under his supervision, did not convince American lawmakers to intervene on behalf of the lower classes, they provided conscientious Americans with the necessary knowledge about how to begin a private social reform.[185]

Gould based his 443-page study mostly on his own observations of social housing enterprises in Europe. Inspired by the desire that this investigation would "stimulate undertakings in the direction of improving the dwellings of the people," Gould dedicated two chapters (roughly two-thirds of the book) to an in-depth analysis of housing companies in the United States, Great Britain, France, Germany, Holland, Sweden, Belgium, and Denmark. Chapter 9 was dedicated to model block buildings in Great Britain (60 pages), the United States (37 pages), Germany (30 pages), France (9 pages), Sweden (3 pages), and the Netherlands (2 pages). Looking at the page numbers, it becomes clear that British and German housing reform and philanthropic housing enterprises were closely studied by American social reformers. Like his predecessors, Gould described Peabody's housing foundation (7 pages) and related housing foundations as well as Waterlow's IIDC (8 pages) and several other limited dividend companies. From the outset, Gould made it very clear that the lesson American social reformers could learn from their European counterparts was "that proper housing of the great masses of working people can be furnished on a satisfactory commercial basis."[186] Evaluating the undertaking of Sydney Waterlow, Gould concluded:

> The Improved Industrial Dwellings Company is a purely commercial organization. It has done nothing directly for the sake of philanthropy, though indirectly the most important philanthropic results have been reached. The aim of the president, Sir Sydney Waterlow, a veteran in this field of social labor, has been to pay a 5 per cent dividend annually and to carry a sufficiently large sum to the reserve account. The company caters to the artisan rather than to the laborer, but in the view of Sir Sydney Waterlow and Mr. Moore, the secretary, this is not only a perfectly legitimate but useful thing to do, in that those who are capable of paying higher rentals, when induced to leave their old surroundings and come into model, self-contained dwellings, leave their former residences for the class below them. Beginning at the top results in improvement, both sanitary and ethical, all along the line. The prime feature of the enterprise has been to secure the independence and isolation of the individual family to as great a degree as possible. With this end in view, two living apartments only are entered from the same landing.[187]

Within the chapter on Germany, Leipzig occupies a prominent position. Gould dedicated three pages, plus five illustrations, to a detailed account of Herrmann Julius Meyer's housing foundation that included an analysis of its architectural, urban planning, and economic aspects. By discussing the economic setup of this enterprise, Gould pointed out that Meyer fixed "the rent on the basis of 3 per cent net on his investment, and spending the net income each year in extending the work. In this plan, he has followed the conceptions underlying the Peabody trust." Gould repeatedly pointed to the transfers of philanthropic models showing how London's models of social housing had been successfully imported by German social reformers and philanthropists. Not only did Peabody's concept make it across the British Channel but Octavia Hill's house management system could be

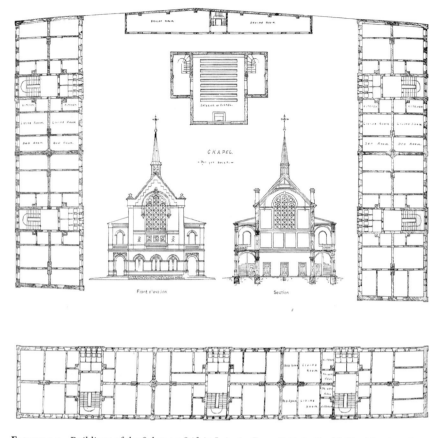

FIGURE 2.1. Buildings of the Salomon Stift in Leipzig. From E. R. L. Gould, *The Housing of the Working People* (Washington, D.C.: Government Printing Office, 1895).

found in Emma Hasse's model tenements on the Goldene Höhe in Leipzig.[188] These examples of cultural exchange made it clear that a transfer of philanthropic models was possible and thus set a further example for American social reformers.

Like Bowditch and Aschrott, Gould decided he wanted to prove that the ideas on social reform, especially the concept of the limited dividend company, were feasible and could be replicated in an American social and cultural environment. In 1896, therefore, Gould and AICP president Robert Fulton Cutting persuaded wealthy New Yorkers to found the City & Suburban Homes Company (CSHC) following the model set by Sydney Waterlow. Out of the 410 shareholders who had bought the $10 shares of this housing enterprise, 300 owned 50 shares or less, while 185 individuals bought 10 shares or less. Its goal was "to offer to capital what is believed to be a safe and permanent five per cent. investment, while furnishing wage-earners wholesome homes at current rates."[189]

However, Gould seemed to turn Waterlow's concept of balancing capitalist desire for profit with caring for the common good even more capitalistic by putting the assurance of a 5 percent profit before the objective of producing healthy

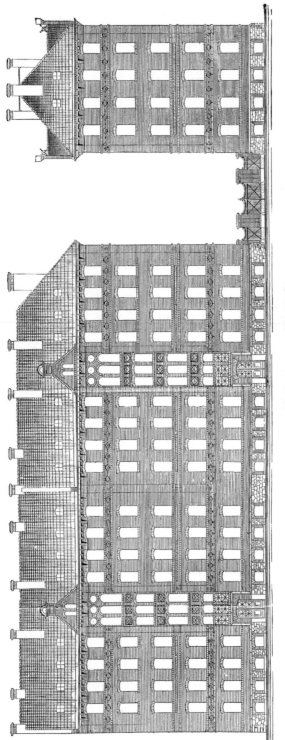

FIGURE 2.2. Buildings of the Salomon Stift in Leipzig. From E. R. L. Gould, *The Housing of the Working People* (Washington, D.C.: Government Printing Office, 1895).

and affordable housing. Philanthropy and 5 Percent became 5 Percent and Philanthropy. Over the years, Gould's company appeared to be very successful. In 1942, it owned 3,894 apartments and reported a net income of more than $300,000. According to its fiftieth annual report, shareholders had been paid semiannual dividends at the average rate of 4.6 percent since 1898. Gould thus proved that Waterlow's concept of limited dividend companies, if not to the fullest extent, could work in American society. He also reintroduced Hill's house management system to American social reformers. Women of social distinction periodically visited the renters in order to collect rent and to observe the "living conditions with a view to offering suggestions to occupants on any feature of housekeeping which might make for more happiness and contentment at home."[190] Gould remained president of that company until his death in 1915.

Marcus Tullius Reynolds (1869–1937), who entered the debate on social housing with his study *The Housing of the Poor in American Cities*, did not have to travel to London but relied on the available publications. Based on German, French, and English publications from the 1870s and 1880s, which included statistical studies of the housing conditions and the lack of affordable and healthy housing for the lower classes, descriptions of social housing enterprises, annual reports of philanthropic housing enterprises, and legal literature, Reynolds developed suggestions for the housing of the urban poor that were mostly inspired by London's philanthropic housing projects.

Reynolds was born in Barrington, Massachusetts, where he grew up in the house of his aunt, a widow of Bayard Van Rensselaer. Because of this family connection, Reynolds was introduced into New York's most exclusive social circles. According to Eugene J. Johnson, "Reynolds was a social creature, a bachelor who dined abroad in Albany's best houses, who lunched with his buddies at the Fort Orange Club, who played a lot of poker, who spent his weekends golfing at the Albany Country Club or traveling around to visit friends at their country places." It was from these social circles that he would later draw the bulk of his clients. After graduating from Williams College in 1890, he entered the architecture school at Columbia University and became an independent architect. It is not clear why Reynolds decided to write a study on the topic of housing for lower-class families. Johnson suggested that perhaps "he was simply ambitious to make a name for himself quickly." Even though his obituary states that this topic "remained a lifelong interest," Johnson could not find any evidence in Reynolds's diaries to support such a claim.[191] In the context of the interpretation of philanthropy put forward in this book, it might have been Reynolds's way of showing his social consciousness and thus his realization that he bore a responsibility for the greater good because of his standing in New York society. This awareness, and the example set by many of his friends and family members, who were involved in one or the other social and cultural philanthropic association, may have sparked his interest in this matter, which was closer to his expertise as an architect than—for instance—the support for existing museums and hospitals.

Beginning in 1888, the American Economic Association organized essay competitions on social questions such as immigration, child labor, and taxation.[192] When in 1891 a group of philanthropists, including Andrew Carnegie, offered a first prize of $300 for an essay on the topic of "The Housing of the Poor in American Cities," Reynolds decided to participate in this competition. Some suggest he was influenced in this choice by Riis's *How the Other Half Lives* (1890), but there is no proof to support such a claim. In 1892 Reynolds won the prize for best essay with his 132-page treatise on the housing of the poor. Reynolds's study *The Housing of the Poor in American Cities* was subsequently published by the American Economic Association in its March and May proceedings of 1893.

Relying heavily on firsthand accounts, Reynolds provided a condensed account of several philanthropic models in London and in American cities. He began by stating: "England tried the experiment and set us the example thirty years ago; but it was not followed in this country for fully fifteen years, and even now we are far behind in the number of model tenements." Brushing off earlier attempts at housing reform during the 1870s as insignificant, Reynolds's basic assumption was that housing reform in the United States was still in its infancy and that American social reformers should learn from their English colleagues. Like his predecessors, Reynolds praised the philanthropic models established by Peabody, Waterlow, and Hill by arguing that these enterprises provided for an environment in which the death rate of the renters decreased tremendously. The death rate was, according to Reynolds, the most significant marker of a successful housing reform. Since Reynolds was a staunch Knickerbocker, he argued in his book that the "movement to secure better and cheaper homes for our poor by building large, well-appointed tenements took substance in America first in Brooklyn." It is here that the limits of Reynolds's knowledge on the topic become obvious. Alfred T. White is wrongly credited with having established the first model tenements. Bowditch is not mentioned at all; his BCBC appears far back in the book and out of chronological order. However, Reynolds points out that White's housing project was indebted to its London predecessors. This assumption was followed by an architectural and economic analysis of successive philanthropic housing enterprises in New York City, Boston, and Philadelphia.[193]

At the end of his text, Reynolds clearly stated that the adoption of limited dividend companies were the only acceptable solution to the housing problem of the poor. Arguing from an economic point of view, he remarked that wealthy citizens could be persuaded to invest their money in such housing enterprises only "if it is clearly demonstrated that a dividend of at least five per cent. will be forthcoming." Housing reform, in Reynolds interpretation, was not about charity but about the provision of healthy and affordable living space for a fair rent that would allow for a limited return on the invested capital. The guarantee of a 5 percent return would set an example and attract other wealthy citizens to participate in these enterprises or set up their own social housing projects. Such thinking closely mirrors that of German housing reformers who saw social housing enterprises as models that were to spark imitation by fellow citizens.[194]

THE CANADIAN WAY: AN ATTEMPT AT CO-PARTNERSHIP

The housing of the poor in eastern Canadian cities, such as Montreal and Toronto, became a topic of public discourse on philanthropy only around 1900 when industrialization and immigration had produced social tensions similar to those in Boston and New York during the 1870s. Social reformers, conservative and progressive alike, no longer viewed poverty as a "result of personal improvidence," and they considered unsanitary housing conditions as breeding grounds for disease and crime.[195] Canadians such as Herbert Brown Ames, Goldwin Smith, and George Frank Beer admired the models for social housing developed in London. Ames was born to wealthy American parents, Caroline Brown of New York City and Evan Fisher Ames of Massachusetts, living in Montreal. They could afford to educate their son in Canada, the United States (Amherst College), and France, where he was trained in French language and literature. After he returned from Europe, Ames joined his father's firm, the Ames-Holden Limited, a very successful boot and shoe company. He inherited the directorship of his father's company and entered business in a way that required little personal effort. P. F. W. Rutherford suspected that Ames "found his directorships a bit boring."[196] It might be for this reason that he retired from business in 1894 and dedicated his life to social and political reform. After conducting an extensive sociological survey of Saint-Antoine, Montreal's working-class district, in autumn and early winter 1896, Ames published *The City below the Hill* in 1897. It was the first comprehensive survey of working-class families' incomes, rental costs, and housing density in Montreal. Following in Gould's footsteps, Ames compared the housing conditions in Montreal with the housing of the urban poor in American and European cities such as Philadelphia, Baltimore, New York, Chicago, Birmingham, and Glasgow. He further suggested that out of the forty-nine limited dividend companies in Europe described by Gould in *The Housing of the Working People,* 88 percent were financially successful.[197] Ames shared the positive view of limited dividend companies that can also be found in the writings of his German and American counterparts. Just like Reynolds, Ames relied heavily on printed reports about philanthropic housing enterprises in Europe and Gould's study in particular. Thus Ames saw the European housing reform through American eyes.

Ames called for a housing reform in Montreal that was guided by the Philanthropy and 5 Percent concept. He suggested that businessmen should build dwellings for working-class families that responded to a certain set of norms with regard to space, aeration, and the number of occupants. Inspired by the activities of the CSHC, Ames demanded that such housing companies needed to guarantee a profit of about 5 percent. To set an example, he founded his own limited dividend company, which in 1897 began construction of thirty-nine tenement buildings. Diamond Court provided housing for lower-class families at a rate that allowed for a 6 percent return on the invested capital. In the eyes of the eminent municipal reformer William Dow Lighthall (1857–1954), Ames's housing project proved "beyond doubt that very considerable building can be safely, effectively, and also profitably done upon similar lines, and that, therefore, a good work lies before any capitalist who leans towards service to humanity." In his article on "Rehousing in Canada," Lighthall suggested replicating Octavia Hill's management system in Canadian social housing enterprises. After he had learned about Hill's management system from John Sutton Nettlefold's account of Hill's undertakings, Lighthall publicized her basic principles. For Lighthall the housing problem depended "more than anything else upon the relationship between landlord and tenant." Hill's greatest achievement, in his opinion, was that she treated "tenants as human beings, and not as mere rent-producing animals." In addition, her work proved to

Lighthall "that landlords who recognize their responsibilities, do in the long run, benefit financially from their consideration for others. The owners of property managed by Miss Hill always get a steady 4 per cent. and sometimes 5 per cent. on their investment, which is far better business than to get 20 or 30 per cent. for a few years followed by a closing or demolition order."[198] In general, Canadian social reformers admired British models of investment philanthropy.

In 1904, the Toronto Associated Charities sent its secretary, Frank J. Walsh, and J. A. Macdonald of the *Toronto News* to England and Ireland, "to report on methods of better housing for the poor."[199] They returned advocating Philanthropy and 5 Percent. In September 1904, Goldwin Smith (1823–1910), an affluent citizen of the municipality whom we already know from the founding of the Toronto Art Gallery, suggested to the board of the Associated Charities the formation of a limited dividend company to be called the Artisans Dwellings Company. The report of the Associated Charities, as well as his friendship with James Mavor, may have influenced Smith's decision to engage in housing reform. Before coming to Toronto, Mavor had participated in the Glasgow Working Man's Dwelling Company, a limited dividend company based on Philanthropy and 5 Percent. He was also involved in the Kyrle Society, which adopted Hill's management system. After his appointment as professor of economics at the University of Toronto in 1892, Mavor quickly befriended Smith, and they met regularly to discuss political and social topics. For many years they sponsored a "roundtable" at the Grange, Smith's home. The two would invite eminent Torontonians to dinner and to discuss important topics during the winter months.[200]

In November 1904, Smith purchased a plot of land within the city limits with the intention of erecting tenement buildings for working-class families. He planned to endow the company with this plot of land. This idea deviated from the British model of limited dividend companies and mixed it with the concept of a housing trust. It reminds one of the critique of an anonymous London capitalist on the Peabody buildings reported in Bowditch's "Letter from the Chairman." The capitalist suggested that Peabody would have accomplished much more if he had simply bought land for housing construction and donated it to limited dividend companies. It is, however, not clear whether Smith was aware of this criticism and the inherent suggestion. Nevertheless, he did exactly what the capitalist proposed. The Artisans Dwellings Company was to be a joint stock company with a basic capital of CAD$100,000 divided into $10 shares. The investors were to be guaranteed a 5 percent return on their capital. However, very few wealthy Torontonians were willing to invest in this enterprise. Furthermore, one member of the board of the Associated Charities, H. P. Dwight, had actively opposed Smith's plan and encouraged wealthy Torontonians to abstain from it. Dwight did not recognize the necessity for social assistance in the housing sector, arguing that he doubted there was "another city in Canada or on this continent [which is] in a more prosperous condition, or where more people of all classes own their own homes or are independent or where there is less of actual poverty."[201] In the evaluation of Lorna F. Hurl, "Toronto's charitable elite were not ready for such an idea."[202] The Associated Charities abandoned the project in June 1905. Yet three events revived Smith's plan within ten years.

On April 10, 1907, the *Weekly Sun* published an article by Mavor entitled "Increase in the Cost of Living in Toronto: Causes and Extent of the Change Which

Has Taken Place since 1897." This study was based on a survey of forty-three Toron-tonian lower-class families conducted by Ella M. Keys. One of the major findings was that rent increased by nearly 95 percent between 1897 and 1906. Based on this evidence, Mavor suggested the founding of limited dividend companies fol-lowing the model of the City and Suburban Homes Company in New York and of the Artisans Dwellings Company in Glasgow.[203] On July 5, 1911, Charles Hast-ings submitted his "Report of the Medical Health Officer Dealing with the Recent Investigations of Slum Conditions in Toronto Embodying Recommendations for the Amelioration of the Same" to the local board of health. Hastings, physician of Grace Hospital, became involved in social reform in the 1880s. He engaged in the fight against consumption, emerged as the head of the campaign for pure milk in 1908, and finally was appointed medical health officer in 1910. Providing extensive statistics about the unsanitary, overcrowded, badly ventilated tenements for working-class families, Hastings made it clear that "there are few conditions found in the slums of European cities, or in the greater American cities, that have been revealed in Toronto, the difference being only one of degree."[204] George Frank Beer, the later founder of the Toronto Housing Company, commented: "This report was so convincing that we found it impossible to satisfy ourselves by sympathetic resolutions passed at public meetings or by letters expressing our deep distress published in the daily press."[205]

Both reports indicated that immediate action was needed. In this situation, Henry Vivian, a Liberal MP in Great Britain, active trade unionist, and cham-pion of garden suburbs and co-ownership for tenants, toured Canada. Vivian had founded the very first British co-partnership housing scheme, Ealing Tenants Ltd., in West London in 1901.[206] Afterwards he helped establish several co-partnership companies in the style of garden suburbs (garden city concept) in which the ten-ants who were living in the houses owned by the housing enterprise were share-holders of that company. Shares could be purchased by tenants as well as outsiders with dividends limited to 5 percent. This model represented a synthesis of the Phi-lanthropy and 5 Percent model and the cooperative model, a fact overlooked by Paul Adolphus Bator and Lorna F. Hurl in their respective studies of the Toronto Housing Company. Both mistakenly label this synthesis simply Philanthropy and 5 Percent, hiding the distinct character of this concept. Bator goes so far as to sug-gest that Vivian's model was "based on outdated experiments already discarded in Great Britain and the United States as incapable of solving the problem of hous-ing for poor workers."[207] He based his argument on a study published by Percy E. Nobbs, professor at McGill University in Montreal, in 1912. Nobbs argued that it was impossible for a social housing company to produce a profit over 1 percent in Canada.[208] Dismissing or ignoring contemporary studies on the success of invest-ment philanthropy in Great Britain, Germany, and the United States, both Nobbs and Bator suggest that limited dividend companies were not suitable to solve the housing question. In their opinion, only municipal housing could be considered as an adequate way to provide housing for working-class families.

There is a difference with regard to the origin of the agents of intercultural transfer within the realm of social housing between Germany and the United States, on the one hand, and Canada, on the other. In the case of Germany and the United States, agents of intercultural transfer almost always belonged to the receiving society. The only notable exception in the case of Germany was Alice. In the case of Canada, it was not a Canadian but a British housing reformer, Vivian, who initiated the intercultural transfer. He came to Toronto in 1910 to propagate co-partnership and garden suburbs. He was invited to give three speeches on October 13: the first at a Canadian Club luncheon, in the afternoon to the City Council Civic Improvement Committee, and in the evening at the University of Toronto. For his third talk Vivian was introduced by Sir Edmund Walker, the central figure of Toronto philanthropy. These talks were of uttermost importance for social reform in Canada. Shirley Campbell Spragge called Vivian "John-the-Baptist" for the Toronto Housing Company. For Beer, Vivian's visit to Toronto "was the starting point for reform." Twenty years later, Noulan Cauchon, who was the director of the Ottawa Planning Commission, told the British Town Planning Institute that "the function of town planning, as indispensable to housing, was brought home to us by your Mr. Henry Vivian in his addresses on co-partnership housing during his tour of Canada in 1910."[209]

In February 1912, representatives of Toronto's Civic Guild, the Toronto Branch of the Canadian Manufacturers' Association, the Board of Trade, the University Settlement, the national Council of Women, and the City Council announced their intention to create a limited dividend company to solve the housing problem. This company was to be founded on the principles of Philanthropy and 5 Percent as well as cooperation. Furthermore, it was expected that the municipality would provide some support for this private company. George Frank Beer prepared the incorporation of the Toronto Housing Company in 1912/13. Born in 1864, Beer entered the family dry goods business at age 22. In 1901, he relocated to Toronto, where he served as treasurer of the Eclipse Whitewear Company. He advanced quickly in the Canadian Manufacturers' Association, becoming vice chairman of the Toronto branch in 1911 and Toronto chairman and member of the national Finance Committee in 1912. After his retirement from business in 1913, Beer engaged in social reform, including housing, tax reform, minimum wages, restrictive immigration, and financial provision for unemployment, sickness, accidents, and old age. Motivated by religion, idealism, a conviction that capitalism and social reform could go hand in hand, and a firm belief in country and empire, Beer, according to Hurl, considered social reform a necessity.[210]

In early 1913, he announced the founding of the Toronto Housing Company (THC). It was his goal to set "an example to private enterprise that such projects were economically feasible." The company was to build settlements inside the city limits but close to industrial centers. The apartments were to be rented to tenants who "would own a minimum of five shares (at $50 per share)." Following the example of Vivian's Ealing Tenants Ltd., outsiders were invited to purchase shares. The dividends were limited to 6 percent. The initial plan of selling shares to tenants on a co-partnership basis distinguished the Toronto Housing Company from philanthropic housing companies in American cities, but brought them closer to European models of social housing in both Great Britain and Germany. While many of the British and German housing cooperatives were in fact financed by tenants and outside investors alike, no such enterprises emerged in Boston, New York, or Philadelphia. However, the co-partnership/co-ownership idea was abandoned before construction of the first apartment buildings began. Shirley Campbell Spragge considers the quick dismissal of this innovative concept puzzling, but points to the criticism voiced by the District Labour Council (DLC) in March 1912. The DLC condemned "the project as useless to workers because few could pay the $250 down payment required."[211]

However, like Waterlow in London, Meyer in Leipzig, and Bowditch in Boston, Beer never intended "to house all workmen in the city, or indeed any large part of them," but to demonstrate "how a workman may be decently housed at an annual rental rate that is not going to eat up a third to a half of his annual income."[212] Following Waterlow, Beer differentiated between different strata within the working class. He maintained that there existed three "classes" of people that social workers dealt with: those with "physical and mental deficiencies," the "boarder-land" men and women who were generally self-sufficient except in times of economic depression, and the "financially independent" whose offspring were nevertheless susceptible to moral degeneration, that is, they could easily fall into the first two classes and therefore needed general guidance and social enrichment.[213] Only the latter were the preferred tenants of the THC, which restricted access on two conditions: the rent was payable in advance and a damage deposit was required. With his classification of the working class, Beer followed Waterlow's theory to the letter. Waterlow contended that the working class consisted of various levels (the upper, the lower, and the middle strata) and "it would not have been right to build down to the lowest class, because in so doing his company would have been obliged to construct a class of tenements which, it is to be hoped, no one at the end of a few years would be satisfied with."[214] Not everybody, however, shared this view. Gould especially rejected this part of Waterlow's concept. He stated that this "dissimilarity of outlook reflected the difference between the comparatively closed society of Britain, gradually raising standards of its poorest citizens through a century of evolutionary reforms, and the open, immigrant society of the United States continuously absorbing the indigent of Europe. The former could assume a constant rate of improvement that would render a low-standard building obsolete long before the end of its normal life. The latter envisaged a constant high level of need by a recurring influx of similar groups."[215]

After the idea of co-ownership was abandoned, Beer and his supporters engaged in a fund-raising campaign to secure CAD$100,000 before incorporation of the THC. One important supporter in this "Better Housing Campaign" was Lady Gibson, the wife of Lieutenant Governor Sir John Gibson. She organized a "large meeting of ladies" to advertise and sell the shares. Within a short time $104,000 had been subscribed by 170 individuals and companies. All of the shareholders came from Toronto's most exclusive social circles. As Hurl pointed out, "The efforts of the promotion committee attracted a high caliber of supporters. The prominence of shareholders, by Beer's own admission, was such that a list of their names might almost be taken as a copy of *Who's Who* in Toronto."[216] Among its directors and company advisors were Alexander Laird (banker), Thomas Roden (manufacturer), Edward Kylie (professor of history at the University of Toronto), Sir Edmund Osler (president of the Dominion Bank of Canada), Joseph Flavelle (manufacturer), and Zebulon Lash (lawyer). The THC, however, was still in need of financial support to finance its construction program.

Beer's opposition to state intervention seemed to rule out the possibility of financial assistance from the government of Ontario. In an article for the *Gar-*

den Cities and Town Planning Magazine, Beer stated that "while town planning is essentially a matter for the action of governments, housing by its nature is a field in which private initiative should be most influential." He demanded that "governments should remove obstacles to development, should direct aid and supervise but should not enter into competition in a matter which is so largely of individual choice and requirement."[217] However, while Beer opposed state-run social housing projects, he did not exclude the possibility of financial support from the state for philanthropic housing companies. Therefore, he asked Lash to develop a bill that would guarantee financial support of the THC by the Ontario government. This draft "proposed that the provincial government should issue bonds to supply eighty per cent of the company's financial needs." This bill, unfortunately, did not win the support of the Conservative premier, Sir James Whitney, and was rejected. In April 1913, the Ontario legislature passed the Act to Encourage Housing Accommodation in Cities and Towns, Hanna Act named after Provincial Secretary William J. Hanna. The Hanna Act enabled companies incorporated to provide housing for the lower classes at moderate fees to petition municipal councils to guarantee its bonds up to 85 percent. If such a company would receive this support, it was obliged to allow the city council to appoint one board director. Furthermore, the city council would have to be consulted in the selection of land and the construction plans. The dividends of such a company had to be limited to 6 percent.[218]

After passage of the law, Beer petitioned the Toronto City Council for financial support. By 1913, the THC had sold a little over 2,000 shares and accumulated about $104,000. This made the THC eligible for $550,000 worth of bonds from the city of Toronto. In 1913, the city council "guaranteed $550,000 of THC five per cent gold mortgage bonds, redeemable in forty years."[219] This move enabled the company to begin construction of its first project, Spruce Court. The Hanna Act, which followed a similar provision enacted in Nova Scotia, set Toronto apart from both its European and American counterparts, where a municipal guarantee of bonds was unknown until World War I.[220] The decision of Toronto philanthropists to ask for municipal financial support and the willingness of Toronto's city council to grant such support distinguishes Toronto's social philanthropy from the transatlantic world of philanthropy. While it was common that city councils before 1900 granted financial assistance for the establishment of museums, art galleries, and libraries, it was inconceivable that the same would have happened within the field of social housing.

The Toronto case, however, symbolized the transition of social housing from being a private task to becoming a publicly funded function of municipal and then state government. As Susannah Morris points out, historians tended to describe this transition as necessary and inevitable. Newer research, however, suggests that this transition was caused by a changing perception of how social welfare was to be provided rather than by purely economic considerations.

PART 2

CHAPTER THREE

How to Become a Gentleman:
Philanthropy and Social Climbing

T he intensive intercultural transfer across the Atlantic resulted in the creation of a tight network of cultural and social philanthropic institutions
within urban centers of the transatlantic community. Philanthropists—
women, men, Catholics, Protestants, and Jews—organized and financed the museums, libraries, hospitals, and social housing enterprises that became essential
elements of urban culture. The creation of these public institutions reflected two
interrelated developments. First, established elites of merchants and landowners
faced an increasingly affluent and assertive group of industrialists and capitalists.
Both groups competed for social, cultural, and political dominance in city affairs.
Members of both groups engaged in the founding of institutions of culture and
learning to prove their superiority and to claim cultural hegemony. Second, both
groups competed in the realm of private social welfare for the lower classes for
dominance and influence. Both the cultural and the social institutions of the nineteenth century are evidence of a contested urban culture and a "civil war" between
different factions of the leisure class.

In this context, philanthropy was a powerful strategy employed by members of
both factions to claim dominance over public urban spaces. Philanthropy contributed to the creation of an urban cultural and social infrastructure that mirrored, at
least initially, the fault lines between the old and new groups within the leisure class.
Even though museums were in dire need of financial support, it would be misleading to assume that those in charge of museum associations "had no intention of
limiting the base of their support,"[1] as Daniel M. Fox suggested. The membership
of New York's museum associations were initially as closely guarded against social
climbers as the membership lists of the city's social clubs. Within the context of the
civil war between the two factions of the leisure class, philanthropy was an instrument and a visible sign of social exclusion and inclusion.[2] Since the focus of this
study is the creation of the urban cultural and social infrastructure, it seems necessary to limit the discussion to those social groups which supported museums and
social housing enterprises. As Peter Dobkin Hall has reminded us, by the 1850s
American elites had "largely overcome their suspicion of voluntary associations
and private charity." They turned increasingly "to philanthropy and associational
activity as alternatives to electoral politics."[3] Even though philanthropic practices

were never an exclusive privilege of the wealthy, nineteenth-century elite philanthropy contributed significantly to the shape of modern cities and the definition of
social and cultural urban society.

Since there was no direct connection between economic success and social
recognition and since wealth did not guarantee immediate integration into the
exclusive social circles of any urban community,[4] the newly rich industrialists and
capitalists had to find other ways outside the realm of economics to gain recognition
from the established social elites, such as marrying up, traveling to Europe, building impressive mansions, and philanthropy. However, the most important aspect
of attracting favorable attention from the established social leaders was nuance.
According to Judith Martin, the difference between old and new money was not the
financial resources they could rely on but the presence or absence "of the graces that
should go with it."[5] For the New York journalist and publicist Junius Henri Browne
(1833–1902), the Knickerbockers were an odd bunch, "often the narrowest and dull-
est people on the Island," who insisted that the first place in society belonged to
them. The newly rich, in contrast, "have the most imposing edifices on the Avenue,
the most striking liveries, the most expensive jewelry, the most gorgeous furniture,
the worst manners, and the most barbarous English." Browne felt, nevertheless, that
"after two or three generations, even the new rich will become tolerable; will learn to
use their forks instead of their knives in transferring their food to their mouths; will
fathom the subtle secret that impudence is not ease, and that assumption and good
breeding are diametrically opposed."[6]

Frederic Cople Jaher and David Hammack argue that since American society
lacked a clear hierarchical social structure, expressed in titles and social ranks,
"American social elites and their historians must rely on such 'intangible' symbols
of social prestige as 'the multiplication of family ties, of inheritances, of memberships in patrician organizations,' and the like."[7] Martin suggests that the conflict
between old and new elites was fought out not using money but using taste. "You
would be ranked not by how rich you were but on how you behaved and what you
enjoyed or pretended to enjoy. You could build a palace, fill it with Old Masters
and a bejeweled mistress of the house, feed and entertain everyone in town, and
still lose on the grounds of being vulgar."[8] By focusing on manners and taste, old
families felt safe from the intrusions of social newcomers, since neither could be
bought with the riches these self-made men amassed in the new industries. However, nouveaux riches recognized that manners and taste could be learned and
that a longer stay in one of Europe's cultural centers was time well spent, since
it promised recognition as "men of culture" back home. Subsequently, American
colonies sprang up all over the German countries, and American visitors stayed
there for several months.[9] Those who followed in these footsteps and organized
their lives according to the standards and norms of the old elites could expect to
receive an invitation to the "leading circles of society."[10] Nowhere else was this
system of exclusion/inclusion so formalized as in New York, where Mrs. John Jay
established her "dinner and supper list" containing the names of 160 men and later
Mrs. William Astor and Ward McAllister drew up her famous List of the 400 to
protect Knickerbocker society from unwanted newcomers.[11]

Religious, ethnic, and social prejudices on the side of the established elites frequently resulted in the creation of obstacles and hurdles for the aspiring new elites,

who were kept at arm's length until they conformed to expectations, as it happened in Boston, Toronto, and Leipzig, or until the new elites grew so strong that they successfully challenged the existing social structure, as it happened in New York. In both models, however, new social elites accepted established behavioral patterns of old elites and followed in their path by, for instance, traveling to Europe to accumulate culture and education and by engaging in philanthropy that allowed them to prove that they possessed a feeling of responsibility for the common good.[12]

The following analysis is based on a historical-sociological analysis of the membership associations for museums, art galleries, and shareholder organizations and associations for social housing enterprises and hospitals in Leipzig, Boston, New York, and Toronto from the early nineteenth century to the early twentieth century.

Based on the membership records of these philanthropic institutions and associations, biographical databases have been created containing key information with regard to gender, social and economic status, family history (including arrival of the families in the respective cities), religion, club memberships, and overall engagement in philanthropy. These databases provide the basis for a historical-analytical study of "the giving class" in a transatlantic setting. It is the goal of this study to provide a collective biography of the philanthropists involved in the creation and maintenance of public cultural and social institutions in Boston, Leipzig, New York, and Toronto. Since a historical-statistical analysis has its clear limits, this study relies extensively on exemplary biographies of philanthropists, which will give a face to the otherwise abstract conclusions drawn from the databases. While this study derived much inspiration from Francie Ostrower's social-structural approach, which was based on interviews she conducted with ninety-nine wealthy donors in New York City,[13] my study is the first to investigate philanthropy from a historical social-structural perspective in a comparative and transatlantic setting.

Since all of the individuals under study are long dead, this study has had to rely on recorded biographical information as it can be found in *Famous Families of New York* and *Prominent Families of New York,* to name just two examples.[14] However, these encyclopedias cannot be considered absolutely reliable sources, since some of them seem to contain fictional elements, especially when it comes to ancestry. New York, in particular, was famous for having genealogists who made their living by providing social newcomers with invented family trees and coats of arms. In *The Great Metropolis,* Browne provided a vivid description of an office of heraldry on Broadway that guaranteed "the socially ambitious and the pecuniarily prosperous . . . for a certain consideration, documentation of the past glories of the family." This heraldry office was frequented by people "aspiring to a recognized position, who have more money than ancestors, and wish to exchange a little of the former for a good deal of the latter." For $100, New York families received a genealogical history stretching back to the Norman or Saxon times including counts, dukes, and kings. The historians of this office twisted "the name of any of their patrons into some form that figures in history, or is known in the peerage, and give lineage therefrom. Muggins is made De Mogyns; Jones is made John or Jean and derived from King John of France or England; Thompson is made Temps fils, the son of Temps, a powerful baron, and so on to the last limit of absurdity."[15]

Such interest in genealogical research and the invention of family (hi)stories stretching back to the early Middle Ages was certainly not unique to New York City.

Table 3.1 Philanthropic associations selected for this study

City	Membership association/ shareholder company	Year founded	Members
Boston	Massachusetts General Hospital	1811	274 (1828–43)
	Co-operative Housing Company	1871	163 (1872)
	Museum of Fine Arts	1870	370 (1876) 1,183 (1895)
New York	New York Hospital	1771	1,122 (1771–1913)
	Metropolitan Museum of Art	1870	320 (1876) 512 (1895)
	American Museum of Natural History	1869	52 (1871) 410 (1895)
	City and Suburban Homes Company	1896	410 (1896)
	Association for Improving the Condition of the Poor	1893	202 (1893)
Leipzig	Art Museum (Kunstmuseum)	1836	567 (1857) 731 (1897)
	Applied Arts Museum (Kunstgewerbe-Museum)	1865	719 (1897)
	Verein Ostheim	1898	115 (1904)
Toronto	Toronto General Hospital	1820	283 (1861–1906)
	Toronto Housing Company	1913	151 (1913)
	Toronto Art Gallery	1913	822 (1926)
	Royal Ontario Museum	1912	263 (1911–26)

SOURCES: Derived from various annual reports of these associations.

Wealthy families in Boston and Toronto wanted to see their lineage collected in bio-graphical encyclopedias, and they even financed the publication of individual books detailing the history of particular families, such as the Cawthras.[16] In the case of Leipzig, the city was chosen as the headquarters of the Verein für Deutsche Per-sonen- und Familiengeschichte (Association for the History of German Individuals and Families). Although a national organization, this genealogical research institu-tion was backed by a significant number of well-off Leipzigers who exchanged finan-cial support for publications of biographical encyclopedias and company histories.[17]

Johannes Hohlfeld, the director of this institute, published the monumental three-volume encyclopedia *Leipziger Geschlechter* (Leipzig dynasties), which included photographs, family trees, and short histories of eminent Leipzig families. He was also author of the Festschrift published for the centennial of the Bibliographisches Institut, the well-known German publishing house owned by the sons of Herrmann Julius Meyer, the founder of Leipzig's largest housing trust.[18]

On both sides of the Atlantic, wealthy families (old and new money) discovered their love for publishable or at least displayable family trees and coats of arms. Encyclopedias included these coats of arms and often provided a detailed explanation of their meaning. Autobiographical and semiautobiographical collections and books prominently displayed coats of arms on their cover. While some of the old families could claim legitimate coats of arms because of royal edicts and prominent forebears, new families "were forced" to make up for this lack of feudal tradition by inventing their own. Since older families in New York, such as the Livingstons, Schuylers, and Schermerhorns, possessed colorful and impressive crests, new families were eager to create similar or even more colorful ones.

Handbooks about heraldry, such as *A Hand-book of Heraldry* published by T. W. Gwilt Mapleson Esq. (printed in color), became the basis for creating such symbols. Mapleson published his guidebook in 1851 because he was concerned with the new interest of New York's wealthy in heraldry and the "misuse" of the heraldic art. In the introduction to his work, the author pointed out:

> Until recently, the use of arms on plate, carriages, &c., seemed to have been discontinued in this country, but of late years it has been revived, with a painful disregard, however, for correctness and authenticity. In fact, I have observed that the owners of carriages cause arms to be painted on them to which they have no right (whereas it is likely that by a proper search they might discover those they have a right to wear), and that they sometimes quarter the arms of families improperly, that is to say, on account of some alliance, instead of descent from an heiress, without which no one has a right to quarter the arms of any family—excepting by a special grant from the Herald's College, with the sign manual, in pursuance of the requisition of some person by will.[19]

Mapleson thus provided his audience with the necessary know-how regarding how to "properly" create one's own coat of arms. His book contained a short introduction to heraldic terminology: he discusses the difference between a crest and arms as well as between baron and femme. He also provided instructions about where to attach arms and crests and which materials to use. At the same time, Mapleson pointed out that only those listed in the second volume of *Berry's Heraldry* are entitled to bear arms.[20] It seems as if the author wrote this book in defense of those Knickerbockers who were entitled to bear arms and to ridicule those who imitated them but lacked a proper pedigree and tradition. Mapleson dedicated his book to the Anson family, who belonged to the earliest settlers, although of Scottish origin, and arrived in the New World around 1674. The book's publication was financed by subscription: 125 copies were paid for before publication by New York's illustrious Knickerbocker elite. Several members of the Livingston family pledged to acquire eighteen copies alone. Among the other subscribers were Van Rensselaer, De Peyster, Schuyler, and even the Stuyvesant family.[21]

New and old elites shared the desire to possess glorious family histories and impressive coats of arms. Since older families with legitimate claims to nobility and family crests did not hesitate to display these symbols publicly, new families could not resist the temptation to invent and create their own insignia. These constructed identities found their way into several biographical dictionaries and became more or less accepted by contemporaries. Ward McAllister has been noted for his complaints about New York's "aspiring mothers," who visited him to ask that their daughters be invited to the Family Circle Dancing Class, a small and intimate gathering of the younger members of New York's High Society. In his memoirs, McAllister noted that "the family always went back to King John, or in some cases to William the Conqueror."[22] One of the older Knickerbocker families, the Carletons, set the tone by boasting that their family "dates from the time of the Norman Conquest in 1066. The name was originally a title of nobility, and its first bearer was a Carleton-Baldwin de Carleton."[23]

The creation of impressive family trees and coats of arms was just one facet of the competition between the two factions of New York's leisure class. Another consisted of transatlantic marriages between the daughters of social newcomers and poor European noblemen, thus endowing American nouveaux riches with aristocratic titles and European noblemen with much-needed funds. By 1915 no less than 454 American women had married into European aristocratic families. Wealthy American families could boast of having produced 42 princesses, 17 duchesses, 19 viscountesses, 33 marchionesses, 46 ladies (wives of knights or baronets), 64 baronesses, and 136 countesses.[24] These marriages were the result of purely economic and social calculations—New York's nouveaux riches promised financial support to impoverished European aristocrats in exchange for social honor. Incidental in its beginning, the transatlantic marriage business quickly received structure and organization. Publications such as *Titled Americans: A List of American Ladies Who Have Married Foreigners of Rank,* published quarterly and revised annually for a subscription price of one dollar, included "A Carefully Compiled List of Peers Who Are Supposed to Be Eager to Lay Their Coronets and Incidentally Their Hearts, at the Feet of the All-Conquering American Girl."[25] Such publications and numerous personal ads in New York's newspapers became the basis for many unions between new American money and old European nobility. One such transatlantic marriage was the union of Consuela Vanderbilt, the 19-year-old daughter of William Vanderbilt, with the Duke of Marlborough, who agreed to this marriage in 1895 for a $2.5 million settlement. Maureen E. Montgomery has shown that the vast majority of American women married to European aristocrats between 1870 and 1914 were "members of the new rich." She suggested that their interest in these transatlantic marriages was sparked by "the attempt to create a more exclusive elite with a formalized structure." Montgomery further asserts that those families which had been "unable to secure entry into Mrs. Astor's circle bypassed New York and attempted to establish a foothold in European society instead."[26] Transatlantic marriages thus seemed to offer a much faster alternative road to social recognition. Those families excluded from the established social circles of old New York were able to circumvent New York society by finding inroads into a much more exclusive social group—the European nobility.

The ways and strategies of the nouveaux riches to fit into the High Society of New York, Boston, Toronto, and Leipzig were not so dissimilar. Newcomers hoped that they would find an inroad into High Society by conforming to the set of established norms and standards of the old elites. However, resistance of the old elite was sometimes fierce. It was the duration and disruptive power of confrontation between old and new money as well as its solution that set cities apart. While historians have investigated the economic power of old and new elites as well as marriage strategies, club memberships, associations with elite institutions such as Harvard College, leisure and travel, and the public display of wealth by constructing impressive mansions, the field of philanthropy in relation to the conflict between new and old money has not been a subject of historical inquiry.[27] Yet nouveau riche families, Catholic and Jewish families, and women recognized the value of philanthropic engagement for integration into the leading circles of society and actively sought to employ philanthropy for their social advancement. Philanthropy offered opportunities to industrialists and entrepreneurs to enter the leading circles of society. It further allowed women to become active players in the public sphere. And it opened the doors to Protestant-dominated society for Jews and Catholics. However, as the example of Boston's Irish and Toronto's Jewish communities will show (see chapter 5), philanthropy also served to exclude unwanted citizens from participation in high culture and thus from domination of urban society. In the end, philanthropy played an important role in the diversification or unification of different social strata (old and new money, ethnically and religiously defined groups) within the transatlantic world.

Although the majority of individuals who were involved in philanthropy abstained from political careers, philanthropic power has never been entirely disconnected from political control.[28] Robert Dalzell and Kathleen McCarthy note that philanthropy offered an alternative way of exercising power. Dalzell speaks of setting standards and norms; McCarthy argues that museum and charity boards represented a countergovernment that empowered women long before they received the right to vote.[29] Social capital and power gained by philanthropic engagement extended far beyond the times of individual philanthropists. The financial support for public social, cultural, and educational institutions allowed them to leave their visual imprint on the cityscape, since financial support almost always resulted in the attachment of the philanthropists and their family name to hospital and museum wings, paintings, apartment buildings of social housing companies, and so forth. From the records of museums, art galleries, hospitals, and social housing enterprises, it becomes clear that most donations came from individuals and not from businesses and associations. Furthermore, the overwhelming majority of donations for these institutions did not come from anonymous donors but were clearly identified and publicized on paper and/or in stone.[30]

Women and men who pursued philanthropy were thus able to immortalize their legacy. They made sure that even decades after their death, new generations of citizens would still talk about the names they could find engraved in the entrance hall of the Metropolitan Museum of Art or on the outside walls of the Toronto General Hospital and wonder about the significance of these individuals for the existence of these institutions. Philanthropists achieved fame beyond their graves and thus assured the perpetuation of their family's fame. Future generations lived off the accumulated "cultural interest" of the social capital their grandparents and great-grandparents had amassed.

Table 3.2 Ratio of anonymous to identified contributions

Institution	Year(s)	Total members	Anony-mous contri-butions	Members representing corpora-tions and associations	Donations in form of bequests and trusts
Museums					
American Museum of Natural History, New York	1895	410	0	1	0
Applied Art Museum, Leipzig	1897	719	0	6	0
Art Museum, Leipzig	1899	731	0	3	0
Metropolitan Museum of Art, New York	1895	512	0	0	0
Museum of Fine Arts, Boston	1895	1,183	0	8	0
Royal Ontario Museum, Toronto	1911–26	263	0	8	11
Toronto Art Gallery	1926	822	0	1	2
Social housing enterprises					
Boston Cooperative Building Company	1872	163	0	0	2
Toronto Housing Company	1913	151	0	0	1
Verein Ostheim, Leipzig	1904	115	0	6	4
Hospitals					
Massachusetts General Hospital	1828–43	274	1	29	1
Toronto General Hospital	1861–1906	283	0	2	3
New York Hospital	1771–1913	1,122	0	0	0

SOURCES: Derived from various annual reports of the associations.

PHILANTHROPY AND POWER

When around 1870 New York City received simultaneously two major museums—the Metropolitan Museum of Art (MMA) and the American Museum of Natural History (AMNH)—it was not the inevitable outcome of the expansion of urban culture but the deliberate decision of two competing groups—the Knickerbockers and the nouveaux riches—to create public institutions that were to highlight each group's economic power and cultural aspirations.[31] Museums, perhaps the most important cultural invention of the nineteenth century, were founded by educated and wealthy activists as the "official repositories of history's treasures, guardians of traditional values, and sites of scholarly research." In an age of colonialism, rapid industrialization, and urbanization, museums played an important role in the formation of identity and authority. Linking museums to the new scholarly discipline of history, James Sheehan suggests that both were to provide "bridges linking the present to the past" and thus legitimacy for political authority.[32]

According to Eileen Mak, museums were also "places in which knowledge was created through the collection, classification, and organization of the natural and manufactured world." By its public display, knowledge represented in these collections of art and artifacts appeared to the visitors as "truth." Museums with archaeological and ethnological collections, in particular, contributed to the definition of European superiority over other peoples and cultures. In the case of Germany, ethnographic museums were, as H. Glenn Penny suggests, not based on a racist or imperialist message from their inception but were forced to alter their displays and visions under pressure from the audience and the market. It was these museum collections that set non-European people and cultures apart from the European and North American visitor, and "in displaying exotic artifacts, curiosities, and the art of other cultures, i.e., in showing what the citizens of European nations were not, museums defined the nation within which they existed."[33]

Neil Harris argues that museums were an element of social policy. Museum makers, curators, donors, and organizers of exhibitions decided which art and artifacts were put on display. They were, for instance, in a position to make public their wish for which artistic tradition was supposed to be revered by an audience. Museums, from their inception, shared the social mission of schools, libraries, and universities, but as Harris reminds us, the later ones "were, in a sense, far less authoritarian." While one could argue in a classroom if one disagreed with the professor's opinion and while one was free in the selection of books to choose from the library, "the ordinary museum-goer was hostage, in a sense, to the taste, standards, and goals of the specialists organizing the display."[34] However, displays could be changed and visitors could voice their concerns about collections and displays. Looking at major German ethnographic museums, Penny highlights the role that visitors played in initiating "changes in both ethnologists' collecting practices and the nature of their displays." Complaints from museum patrons about boring ethnographical collections forced museum directors to instruct ethnologists to change their collecting strategies and to provide museums with artifacts that caught the eye of the visitors. In some cases audiences successfully protested the removal of certain collections and the organizational principles of museum displays. When the Leipzig ethnographic museum, for instance, moved into its new building in 1896, "its ethnologists received local criticism for neglecting to include Europe in its displays and for banishing European prehistory and German Ur-Volkskunde" to the basement. Since the protest of the visitors did not stop, the museum board decided to create a "temporary exhibition" of European material culture, which seemed to satisfy the expectations of this museum's audience.[35] Although Penny provides an important counterpoint to Harris's interpretation of museums, Penny fails to clearly identify the sources of protest and to distinguish between museum patrons and museum visitors. It is not absolutely clear whether this protest, which seems to stem from highly educated and well-off Leipzig burghers, does support the claim that it was audiences that had an impact on museums or whether it was simply the group of patrons who supported the museums financially who made their voices heard. Museums are always a product of a community. It would be wrong, however, to assume that the audience was this community alone. The community constituted patrons, museum officials, museum workers, and the museum visitors who all gave structure and shape to the museum in its architecture, its contents, and its displays.

Visiting the museum was certainly an educational experience, but did it also allow its makers to exercise social control over the visiting audience? Low entrance fees, the introduction of "free days" (in the case of the MMA, Mondays and Thursdays were made free days in 1875; the AMNH introduced free admission every day in 1907 and the Museum of Fine Arts in Boston in 1918), extended evening hours, and the opening of the museums on Sundays (Boston's Museum of Fine Arts admitted the public on Sundays from its opening in 1876 and the MMA was opened on Sunday afternoons after 1891) helped in turning these museums into educational institutions that attracted the attention of lower-class visitors.[36] These visitors were initially eyed with some suspicion by museum boards, and their behavior was monitored and regulated. Some visitors brought their lunch or appeared in "dirty clothing" in New York and Leipzig. Reflecting on these challenges, Louis P. di Cesnola, the director of the MMA, was able to report by the end of 1891 that the decision to open the museum on Sunday afternoons from 1 PM until sunset had been a great success.

> At first a certain element of turbulence and disorder was noticeable in the attendance. Many visitors took the liberty of handling every object within reach; some went to the length of marring, scratching and breaking articles unprotected by glass; a few proved to be pickpockets, and others brought with them peculiar habits which were repulsive and unclean. With the beginning of August, however, these disorders in a large measure ceased, and toward the end of the year the change in the character of visitors on Sunday afternoons was as marked as it was gratifying. The attendance is now respectable, law-abiding and intelligent.[37]

Sunday afternoons quickly emerged as the day of the laboring classes in the MMA. Young people, in particular, were drawn to its collections. In 1893 the MMA had 659,267 visitors, with 214,203 arriving on Sunday afternoons.[38] In the first five months of 1909, when the museum was still located in Copley Square, the MFA in Boston attracted 63,406 visitors who took advantage of the free admission on Saturdays and Sundays. A few years later, in 1912, the museum, then in its new location on Huntington Avenue, admitted 194,682 visitors free of charge.[39] After Leipzig's elites opened the doors of their cultural institutions to workers, it was not only the social establishment that seemed to be concerned with the workers' behavior in these places. When workers were allowed to enter Leipzig's concert hall for the first time to listen to a concert, "the carpets had been rolled up, the seats had been covered, and only half the usual lighting was used."[40] The Arbeiterbildungsinstitut Leipzig, a Social Democratic institution for the organization of cultural entertainment and continuing education for workers, continuously published for its working-class readership instructions about how to behave in theaters and concert halls: for example, dress appropriately and do not bring sandwiches.[41]

Museums, art galleries, and concert halls seemed to have played a role in disciplining urban crowds. In his book *The Artist in American Society,* Neil Harris suggested that American travelers in Europe learned to appreciate the use of art as a means to gain social control over the masses. Referring to the observations of several Americans who had traveled to France, Spain, and Italy during the 1830s, Harris noted that these Americans were surprised to see European crowds that were "orderly and restrained" while American crowds always appeared to be "dangerous and unruly." The reason for this appeared to be that "European governments, despotic as they were, nonetheless interested themselves in the sensory welfare of their populations, supplying them with parks, galleries, and museums. The French were governable, said John Durbin, precisely because their senses were gratified with shows, gardens, theaters, and music."[42] Visiting museums was certainly not only a practice of the middle classes, as Nick Prior suggested, but rather a socially differentiating practice that was part of the integration of workers into society.[43] Museums, libraries, theaters, and concert halls offered new and in some cases even free ways of educating young workers who sought cultural and social advancement and who took advantage of the many avenues of leisure offered in an urban setting. Representatives of the philanthropic and political establishment, such as Boston's mayor Samuel Cobb, did not hide their expectation that "all classes of people will derive benefit and pleasure from barely looking upon objects that appeal to the sense of the beautiful. Even the least favored and least cultivated person cannot fail to derive some refining and elevating influences from the sight of beautiful things."[44] Cobb's hopes that the MFA would contribute to the aesthetic and moral improvement of Boston's population closely reflects John Stuart Mill's "trickle down" concept of cultural and moral advancement. Believing that contact with art has an enormous impact on the upbringing of children, Mill advocated a significant improvement of higher education, which would produce a small elite group of "persons of the highest degree of cultivation. . . . From such persons, civilization would rain down its influences upon the remainder of society, and the higher faculties having been highly cultivated in the most advanced part of the public, would give forth products and create an atmosphere, that would produce a high average of the same faculties in a people so well prepared, in point of general intelligence, as the people of the United States."[45]

Museums and their exhibitions created an environment of admiration for the objects on display and potentially led to the acceptance of norms and standards established by the display of these objects. It was expected that visitors would admire exhibited objects that had been chosen by museum workers and collectors/benefactors. Admiration for the art object, however, also included admiration for its donor, who was always clearly identified. Thus museums fulfilled a function in the much larger project of legitimizing and enforcing elites' hegemony. Refusing a simplified Foucauldian interpretation of museums as places of producing knowledge and power, Steven Conn reminds us that "museums stand with department stores as institutional embodiments of Veblen's culture of conspicuous consumption."[46] Old and new elites possessed immense financial resources, which they disposed of by purchasing furniture and objects of arts, traveling extensively, and building mansions. Buying these "products" was, however, closely related to social status and, for new social elites in particular, to aspirations to move up the social ladder.

As Miles Orvell reminds us, "Individuals sought an elevation of status through the purchase and display of goods whose appearance counted more than their substance."[47] Most gifts to museums and art galleries came with strings attached. When in 1891 Edward C. Moore, the president of Tiffany & Company, died, the MMA received his art collection: Greek, Roman, and Etruscan vases, Tanagra groups and figures, glass, jewelry, porcelain, metalwork, and other objects of art, together with a reference library of many hundred valuable illustrated works. This donation was made with the understanding that these "objects were to be kept together and preserved as a separate collection."[48] Museums thus were intended not only as educational institutions but also as memorials to its founders and supporters. Philanthropists who provided material and financial support for museums, art galleries, and libraries considered these public institutions their own private property. They kept an eye on their donations even after they had given them to a museum. For them the museum and its collections remained their private property, although open to the public and defined as public institutions that were to educate the masses.[49] Penny tells us the story of H. Göring, who had given a collection of Chinese and Javanese objects to the ethnographic museum in Leipzig. When he realized that his donation had not been "labeled to his satisfaction," he complained to the museum director and reminded him bluntly, "I was promised, that every single piece would be properly labeled as belonging to me."[50] Providing endowments and art collections to museums gave these patrons the opportunity "to make themselves remembered."[51] Cesnola, the president of the MMA, bitterly complained about New York's millionaires, "who did not like to give endowment funds" to the museums. "They will give money for buying collections, and for building purposes, because both remain visible monuments to their generosity . . . while endowment funds are invisible and remain unknown to the general public."[52] In the case of the AMNH, according to John Michael Kennedy, the trustees "preferred to buy spectacular objects that would exhibit well, giant moa bones rather than insect collections. They also liked to buy rarities, or natural history collections that were famous, and that other museums were seeking. 'The trustees,' Albert Bickmore wrote a friend, 'like to be sure they are getting value for their money.'"[53]

While museums and art galleries allowed philanthropists to impose their artistic taste on larger segments of the urban population, social housing enterprises accorded philanthropists even greater power. They found themselves in a position to define social structures such as the family.[54] Guided by the belief that the family is at the very heart of society and that a stabilization of society cannot succeed without a stabilization of the family, philanthropists who engaged in social housing projects alone or in the company of fellow philanthropists dedicated much time to the planning of apartment buildings. The idea of a closed and separate tenement dominated the nineteenth-century discourse on social housing on both sides of the Atlantic. In these debates, philanthropists advocated the creation of self-contained apartments that included a kitchen, one to three bedrooms, and a hallway. Only washrooms and lavatories were removed from the apartment and placed in communally used staircases or hallways because of hygienic standards and architectural-technical difficulties. Max Pommer, the architect of the Meyersche Stiftung in Leipzig, further demanded that not more than two apartments should have access from the staircase at the same floor, thus further isolating the families living inside these apartments.[55]

Social reformers and philanthropists invested much time and money in the planning and construction of such apartment buildings because they believed that intermingling of neighbors in an apartment house caused a breakdown of social rules and standards and was to blame for the outbreak of infectious diseases. These philanthropists considered the open structure of families and flats as a threat to the state. "We have learned by experience," stated the *Third Annual Report of the Boston Co-operative Building Company*, "that such tenements as this which has common corridors, common water rooms, and, above all, common privies, are a disgrace to modern civilization, and public nuisances, inasmuch as they encroach upon the family relations, tend to make them impure, and thereby sap the very foundations of the State."[56] The intermixing of family members with neighbors and friends led, in the eyes of English social reformers, inevitably to the corruption of the city youth. Living in overcrowded tenements, young women and men were exposed to sexual promiscuity and subsequently succumbed to crime and poverty.[57]

For contemporary housing reformers and philanthropists, there were basically only two ways to intervene: (1) social control and supervision or (2) separation of the families in independent apartment units. The decision to build apartment buildings with isolated units resulted from the recognition that social control of working-class families in houses with communal facilities proved to be ineffective. Therefore philanthropists, guided by the concept of the nuclear family, began in the second half of the nineteenth century to produce apartment buildings with clearly defined private and public spaces. The apartment was to be closed with a locked entrance door. Only those individuals who possessed a key handed out by the housing authorities were allowed to enter the apartment. The hallway prevented the outside visitor, who would knock on the entrance door, from looking directly into any of the rooms. Entrance and hallway thus provided a much higher degree of often "unwanted" privacy.[58]

By making decisions about the architectural structure of apartment buildings, philanthropists and their architects were in a position to define the concept of "family." Housing reform was thus more than just the provision of affordable housing; it was the attempt to create "domesticity, or the family's awareness of itself as a precious emotional unit that must be protected with privacy and isolation from outside intrusion."[59] Social housing enterprises offered apartments with a specific number of rooms, thus determining how many members a family occupying such an apartment was allowed to have. Herrmann Julius Meyer, for instance, insisted that his housing trust should provide apartments only for families with three to five members.[60] Therese Rossbach, a fellow Leipzig housing reformer, was certainly the exception among nineteenth-century philanthropists for allowing families with up to ten children in the apartment buildings of the Verein Ostheim.[61] As a rule, nineteenth-century philanthropists sought to encourage families to produce not more than two or three children. By providing a certain architectural structure, these philanthropists hoped to influence the social relations between their tenants. Separate apartments, so it was hoped, would infuse families with a heightened sense of privacy and isolation from their neighbors. The intention of social reformers and philanthropists was not to encourage inhabitants of their housing projects to form deep social bonds but to accept the separation of their familial spaces. The apartment structure thus helped to seal off families from their "traditional interaction with the surrounding world." Fathers and mothers were to spend more time at home and to create a culture of domesticity and solidarity with the other members of the family. Parents and children were expected to develop a higher degree of mutual understanding and companionship for each other than for members of their own age and sex peer groups.

By limiting the number of adjacent apartments on one floor to two or three, the possibilities of meeting other people during the evening and over the weekend were already limited. To make sure that the tenants understood the expectations of their landlords, management systems such as Octavia Hill's system of friendly visiting brought well-off ladies into the apartments to supervise and instruct the tenants. Published regulations reminded the renters that they were not supposed to spend too much time in the hallways because their place was at "home" in the circle of their family.[62] In the case of Meyer's housing trust in Leipzig, women who were reported chatting extensively with neighbors outside their apartments were reprimanded and in rare cases even dismissed from the apartments.[63]

The architectural structure of apartment buildings built by social housing enterprises and housing trusts reveal the thinking of their creators with regard to their concepts of social organization. Compared with the influence and power that philanthropists exercised in museums and art galleries, philanthropists who created social housing projects were in a much stronger position to realize their visions. While museums, art galleries, and even libraries could suggest a certain artistic standard or a specific literary taste, social housing projects were the places where the museum-goers had to live after they returned from the museum. Although it was still left to the individuals living in these apartments to change the structures according to their own intentions, walls and entrance doors set definitive limits. And even if entrance doors were left open, social housing projects, such as Peabody's and Meyer's housing trusts, were gated communities with walls and gates surrounding the settlements and thus keeping outsiders out.[64]

DIVIDED PHILANTHROPIC CULTURE

Beginning in the 1860s, new and old elites competed for participation and domination in museum associations and social housing companies.[65] This competition resulted in either a divided philanthropic culture (New York and Leipzig) or a unified philanthropic culture (Boston and Toronto).

Divisions in philanthropic practice always reflect divisions within the urban leisure class. While in Boston the Brahmin elite succeeded in integrating a relatively small number of Protestant and Jewish newcomers, New York's emerging elite proved to be too large to be absorbed into the Knickerbocker elite without irreversibly changing the nature of the latter.[66] The distinction between the new and the old elites is of central importance for our discussion of philanthropy in New York. Here as elsewhere, tradition and status mattered in the assessment of one's social and cultural prestige.

First Mrs. John Jay, in the years following the American Revolution, and then Mrs. Caroline Schermerhorn Astor took the lead in the Knickerbocker-dominated High Society of New York and guarded it well from intrusion by new-comers.[67] Both women created exclusive guest lists for balls and dinners that hosted New York's High Society. Jay's "dinner-and-supper list" included the names of 160 respectable men, "but the husbands, wives, sons, and daughters connected to those listed raised the number to an approximately 300."[68] In the 1850s, Caroline Astor's invitation list contained the names of 400 New Yorkers (the number that could fit into her ballroom).[69] Inclusion into the famous 400 "could not simply be procured by the possession of great wealth," as the nouveau riche families could attest. For Ward McAllister, the days had passed "when great wealth admitted men to exclusive society."

> Twenty or thirty years ago it was otherwise. But now with the rapid growth of riches, millionaires are too common to receive much deference; a fortune of a million is only respectable poverty. So we have to draw social boundaries on another basis: old connections, gentle breeding, perfection in all the requisite accomplishments of a gentleman, elegant leisure and an unstained private reputation count for more than newly gotten riches.[70]

Since most members of the newly rich families were continuously excluded from the guest lists of Jay and Astor, prevented from acquiring a box in the prestigious and exclusive Academy of Music, not invited to participate in the creation of the MMA, and largely excluded from New York's social clubs, the city's nouveaux riches grew so frustrated that they gave up their attempts at integration into the established Knickerbocker society and created their own philanthropic sphere.[71] It was not the competition between new and old elites that set New York apart from other cities but rather the old elites' prolonged attempt to prevent the new from entering High Society. Although this attempt finally failed, it took decades before the Knickerbockers' social clubs and philanthropic establishments opened up to members of the new elites.

New York's social clubs were among the most exclusive social clubs in the trans-atlantic world, probably surpassed only by those of London. According to Edward Pessen, the social clubs of New York, "consisting as they did almost entirely of the social and economic elite, provided their members with a recognizable status in a society lacking in official emblems of social hierarchy."[72] In order to belong to one of these clubs, one had to possess "the clubbable disposition," which appeared "to run in families, if not to be, in some respects, subject to the ordinary laws of hereditary descent." An "examination and careful comparison of the lists of the great leading associations proved," according to Francis Gerry Fairfield, "that one-half of the club-men of the city are descended from less than a score of the old families."[73] Membership in the Union Club, the St. Nicholas Society, or the Mayflower Association was more than just a social experience. It "became a matter of prestige, of social and of business importance. It became the badge of social rank."[74] The mentioning of one's membership in the St. Nicholas Society, for instance, made clear to the audience that one's ancestors had come to the United States before 1785.[75] And while the St. Andrew's Society accepted only Scotsmen,[76] the Union Club instituted even stricter rules with regards to its membership requirements.

The Union Club was the "representative organization of the old families. Livingstons, Clasons, Dunhams, Griswolds, Van Cortlandts, Paines, Centers, Vandervoorts, Van Rensselaers, Irelands, Stuyvesants, Suydams, and other names of Knickerbocker fame filled its list of membership with a sort of aristocratic monotony of that Knickerbockerism which has since, in solemn and silent Second Avenue (the faubourg St. Germain of the city), earned the epithet of the Bourbons of New York."[77] Founded in 1836, its membership was limited to 400 of the most distinguished citizens. Each candidate for admission had to be proposed by one member and seconded by another. The entrance fee was $100, and the yearly dues were $20. While some of its members were physicians, educators, and politicians, quite a few have been described as "gentlemen of leisure." Following the example of London's social clubs, the Union Club was established with the single purpose of promoting "social intercourse amongst its members." Belonging to the Union Club was synonymous with belonging to the leading circles of New York society.[78]

When the Union Club somewhat relaxed its admission standards after the Civil War and allowed for 1,000 members, some felt that "the venerable Union had become a little lax in its admission standards."[79] In 1871, after their request to restrict its membership to gentlemen of Knickerbocker descent was rejected by the governing committee, about 200 gentlemen founded the Knickerbocker Club.[80] Each candidate for membership had to "be proposed and seconded by two members of the Club" before all members were invited to participate in a ballot.[81] However, although its membership was limited to 300 gentlemen, the constitution of this new club did not stipulate that only descendants of Knickerbocker families were eligible. It was, therefore, not as "blue-blooded" as it was intended to be. While one could find among its members many representatives of the old Dutch and English Knickerbocker elite, such as S. van Rensselaer Cruger, John Jay, Robert J. Livingston, and Frederick W. Rhinelander, there were also representatives of a middle generation of New York's leisure class who had come to North America during the eighteenth century (John J. Astor and Adrian Iselin). Finally, even the Knickerbocker Club admitted newcomers, such as August Belmont, who had arrived in New York only in 1837.[82]

In late December 1868, a small group of predominantly nouveau riches claimed their share of New York's urban culture by petitioning the commissioner of Central Park for help in establishing "a great Museum of Natural History." The nineteen petitioners were mostly self-made men and industrialists such as Adrian Iselin, James Brown, and Robert L. Stuart, who were considered "architects of their own fortunes." The hardware store owner John David Wolfe, whose grandfather had emigrated from Saxony early in the eighteenth century, was elected the first president of the AMNH. Robert L. Stuart, whose family arrived in America only in 1798, and William A. Haines were selected as vice presidents to assist Wolfe. While New York's elitist social clubs and the Union League Club in particular played a dominant role in founding the MMA, none of these clubs took an interest in the project of a natural history museum. Only eight of the nineteen museum makers belonged to the Union Club, and while the first meeting of New Yorkers interested in the founding of the MMA was held in the theater of the Union League Club, the first meeting for the people interested in creating a natural history museum occurred in the private residence of Benjamin H. Field.[83] Although never officially excluding the competing group, the MMA relied predominantly on the Knickerbocker elite (in 1876 about 66 percent of its supporters belonged to the Knickerbocker elite and 34 percent could be classified as nouveaux riches) while the AMNH received most of its support from the nouveaux riches (in 1871 about 70 percent of its supporters came from new families). The natural history museum project offered these new families an opportunity to demonstrate their economic success, and it strengthened their social position in New York society. It further signaled that the nouveaux riches no longer limited their attempts at integration into New York's High Society to acquiring memberships and shares in existing clubs and associations. The AMNH was the first sign of an attempt to create institutions independently of the old Knickerbocker elites. By establishing such a museum, the new elites also laid claim to their share of the cultural cityscape. By naming it the American Museum of Natural History and not the New York Museum of Natural History, its founders expected that it "would have the same stature in the United States as the British Museum had in England." For the new elites it became clear that this museum not only offered them an opportunity to define their place within New York's cultural infrastructure but also "reinforced the claims of the city's elite to the status of a metropolitan gentry."[84]

Not to be outdone by new money, the old Knickerbocker elite pursued the project of the Metropolitan Museum of Art. It received significant support from the Union League Club, the New York Historical Society, the Century, and the Manhattan Club.[85] Among the fifty gentleman who were appointed to the organizing committee of the MMA were Samuel Latham Barlow Mitchell, whose English ancestors arrived in the New World in 1620, Benjamin H. Field, whose family had come to North America from England in 1630 and who was married to Catharine M. Van Cortlandt de Peyster, and Rutherfurd Stuyvesant, who descended from several great colonial ancestors of New England. Stuyvesant could claim among his ancestors Governor Peter Stuyvesant of New Amsterdam, Governor John Winthrop of Massachusetts, Governor Joseph Dudley of Connecticut, and Lewis Morris, chief justice of New York and first governor of New Jersey. His family tree also included Robert Livingston, Balthazar Bayard, Walter Rutherfurd, and Lewis Morris, the signer of the Declaration of Independence.[86] There was, however, some overlap between the Committee of Fifty and the Nineteen New Yorkers who had signed the petition that led to the establishment of the AMNH. Seven men representing both new and old money (William T. Blodgett, Benjamin H. Field, Howard Potter, Marshall O. Roberts, Alexander T. Stewart, D. Jackson Steward, and Robert L. Stuart) joined both groups and thus potentially provided a bridge between both philanthropic institutions and both factions of the leisure class.

However, even in 1895, about 68 percent of the art museum's supporters were of Knickerbocker descent. Names such as Beekman, Rhinelander, Stuyvesant, Tiffany, Townsend, Whittredge, Winthrop, and Worthington still dominated the membership lists, and family stories such as the one of Levi P. Morton, who could claim to be a descendant of George Morton, the financial agent of the *Mayflower* Puritans, were still the norm.[87] Newer families found inroads into New York's philanthropic establishment, however. The 1895 membership list of the museum association shows that seven members of the Vanderbilt family who had been cast out of New York's cultural life for so long had bought memberships in this association. Another name in this list that represents the new elites is John Stuart Kennedy (1830–1909), who had immigrated to New York from Glasgow in 1850 and become one of the foremost financiers in the United States. Kennedy acquired a philanthropic reputation by distributing vast amounts of money to various charities. In 1884 he became president of the Presbyterian Hospital, to which he donated $1 million in 1908. He gave the money in order to erect the United Charities Building on Fourth Avenue, which furnished the headquarters for the Charity Organizations Society and the Association for Improving the Condition of the Poor. In 1907 he gave $500,000 to Columbia University. In addition to being the vice president of the MMA, he was also appointed trustee of Columbia University and the New York Public Library (having been president of the Lenox Library before its consolidation).[88] His will, under which he left an estate of over $67 million, set aside nearly half of it for the welfare of the public.[89]

Kennedy's various interests make it clear that philanthropists rarely limited their engagement to one field. Irrespective of the time they dedicated to philanthropic pursuits (full-time career or part-time engagement), most philanthropists lent their support to social and cultural institutions. As in the case of the AMNH, the Presbyterian Hospital owes its existence to the engagement of a group of philanthropists. In early 1868 James Lennox approached thirty-two wealthy New Yorkers and convinced them that New York, although it already possessed several hospitals "under the control of nationalities and religious denominations" such as the Jewish hospital, the German hospital, and St. Luke's Hospital (Episcopalian), needed a similar institution for Presbyterians. Lennox provided the necessary land and about $250,000. "Next to Mr. Lennox, the largest donors were the brothers Robert L. and Alexander Stuart, men of ample means but of still broader generosity and public spirit."[90] Many of the philanthropists involved in the founding of this hospital were also engaged in the founding of the AMNH (James Brown, Robert L. Stuart, and Morris K. Jesup) and the MMA (William E. Dodge, John Taylor Johnston, and Jonathan Sturges).

The same holds true for the New York Hospital (NYH), which much earlier had attracted the attention of New York's Knickerbocker families. Founded in 1771, the hospital received support from all factions of New York's elite: the old Dutch families (Stuyvesant, Duyckinck, Beekham, etc.) were joined by Huguenot (Goelet, de Peyster, etc.) and English families (Livingston, Morris, etc.). The various religious groups, with the exception of Jews, were almost equally represented.[91] Over the following 140 years, Knickerbocker families dominated the membership association of the NYH. Between 1771 and 1913, about 76 percent of all its philanthropists could claim that their families had arrived in British North America before 1700. About 20 percent derived from families who had arrived in the New World between 1700 and 1800. And only about 4 percent had immigrated to the United States between 1800 and 1900. Many of the names in the membership list of the NYH reappear in the membership lists of the MMA (Astor, Bishop, Bliss, Dodge, Field, Johnston, Stuyvesant) and to a lesser degree in the membership lists of the AMNH (Aspinwell, Cadwalader, Isham, Vanderbilt). In contrast to the socially selective membership organization of the NYH, the Association for Improving the Condition of the Poor, founded in 1843, seemed to have provided newer families with an outlet for philanthropic activity for social projects at least at the end of the nineteenth century. Among the members of this association, one could find, in 1893, families with ancestors who arrived in the New World during the eighteenth century together with newcomers from the nineteenth century. Germans such as Oswald Otten-dorfer, the editor of the *New Yorker Staats-Zeitung*, Jews such as Jefferson Seligman (first-generation American), who was a partner in the firm of J. & W. Seligman & Co., and nouveaux riches such as John D. Rockefeller joined with members of the Knickerbocker elite and with those citizens, such as Astor, who occupied a middle position in New York's hierarchical social order.[92]

Although a significant overlap developed between the MMA and the AMNH, both the Knickerbocker elite and the nouveaux riches remained very much apart. In 1880 about 36 percent of all members of the AMNH also held memberships in the MMA. By 1895, however, this overlap declined to 28 percent. And although the percentage of members of the AMNH who came from Knickerbocker back-ground (the most prominent families being Church, Schermerhorn, and Stuyve-sant) had slightly increased from about 30 percent (in 1871) to about 45 percent (in 1895), the museum was still controlled by the new elites.

Following the path set out by the organizers of the MMA, the organizers of the AMNH created a highly hierarchical membership organization with several classes of membership depending on the financial contribution of the members. In the case of the MMA, the museum makers had established a membership organization with three classes of membership: one could become a patron for $1,000, a fellow in per-petuity for $500, or a fellow for life for $200.[93] The founding fathers of the AMNH basically copied this system but changed the financial contributions necessary to become a patron ($2,500), a fellow in perpetuity ($1,000), or a fellow for life ($500).[94] The creation of such a hierarchical membership structure could be interpreted in two ways. First, it made very clear the financial needs of the new institution and provided guidance to prospective donors by suggesting levels of financial commit-ment. Second, this system seems to confirm that New York's wealthy longed for some kind of visible social hierarchy in a society that did not allow for social distinctions based on birth. Membership in exclusive social clubs, which could be listed on busi-ness cards, the social prestige that came with one's "elevation" to the patronage of a museum, and finally the inclusion into the *New York Social Register,* published since 1887 and modeled after the *Almanach de Gotha* and *Burke's Peerage,* allowed for a level of social distinction comparable to European nobility.

The years between 1869 and 1885 saw a heated competition between old and new social elites, which led to the creation of two museums, whose organizers insisted on an equally important place in the cityscape for their creation (east and west of Central Park), the building of the Metropolitan Opera House (entirely funded by the new elites), and the passing of social leadership from Caroline Schermerhorn Astor to Alva Smith Vanderbilt.[95] At the end, New York's old Knickerbocker families ceded defeat by closing the Academy of Music and acquiring boxes in the new Metropoli-tan Opera House. "It represented," according to Lloyd Morris, "the passing of social power into new hands, the final defeat of the city's aristocracy by the great capitalists who were masters of banks, railroads, vast industries."[96] New York's nouveaux riches did not integrate into the existing High Society as it happened to the nouveaux riches in Boston and Toronto. New York's newcomers created their own philanthropic cul-ture and their own cultural institutions. During the 1890s, old families enjoyed the opera in the new Metropolitan Opera House and attended social gatherings of the new social leader, Alva Smith Vanderbilt. This might suggest an integration of the old elites into the infrastructure created by the new elites. In the field of museums, however, the division between old and new money remained high. Although a significant number of nouveaux riches were integrated into the MMA and although a comparably high number of old families supported the AMNH, both institutions remained distinctly defined as museums of the old versus the new elites.

While not as divided and separated as New Yorkers, Leipzig's old and new elites—the merchants and the industrialists—faced a similar situation. As in the case of New York, both groups embarked on competing museum projects and jostled for their share in social housing companies and trusts. This competition resulted in the creation of three museums—the art museum and the ethnographic museum controlled by the old mercantile elites and the applied arts museum controlled by the new industrial elites. In the realm of social philanthropy, old and new elites created separate housing trusts but interacted continuously and influenced the organizational and architectural structures of their projects.

The Leipziger Kunstverein (Leipzig Art Association) was founded by representatives of the old commercial elites with the goal of establishing an art museum in 1836. The merchant Carl V. Lampe and the publisher Hermann Härtel invited several wealthy citizens of Leipzig in November 1836 to discuss the founding of an art association. Among the invitees were merchants (such as Gustav M. Clauss and Wilhelm Gerhard), book publishers and book traders (such as Heinrich Brockhaus), bankers (such as Gustav Harkort), lawyers, professors, and noblemen (such as Max von Speck-Sternburg).[97] Margaret Menninger, who provides a social analysis of the Leipzig Art Association, shows that the majority of its members lived within Leipzig (73 percent). Refuting traditional American perceptions about art patronage in German cities during the nineteenth century, she also shows that only 21 out of 580 members belonged to the nobility.[98] It was the mercantile elite (trade and commerce, especially book trade) that instigated the founding of this association and that provided most of the funding for this project. Menninger categorized about 44 percent of its members as belonging to the mercantile elite while only 7 percent belonged to the industrial elite. Its leadership was closely aligned with Leipzig's other elite-defining institutions. According to Menninger's analysis, 11 out of the 15 members of the Kunstverein board belonged to the Gesellschaft Harmonie and 4 of the 15 also belonged to the very exclusive society Die Vertrauten.[99]

The Gesellschaft Harmonie was founded during the winter of 1775–76 by merchants, professors, civil servants, and artists as a social club that would provide a place of social intercourse for Leipzig's elites as well as an organization that promised help to misfortunate individuals who fell on hard times (Personen die unverschuldet in Armut geraten sind). The membership was limited to 100 men and was divided into two classes of equal standing: (1) the class of educated individuals (professors, civil servants, artists) and men of leisure, and (2) the class of merchants. As in the case of some New York clubs, new members had to be nominated, and the entire membership was to participate in the election of new members.[100]

Die Vertrauten was established in 1680 as a reaction of wealthy Leipzigers to the outbreak of the plague. Initially conceived of as a mutual aid society, it soon developed into a highly selective social club that permitted each of the city's leading families to be represented by one member. Between 1680 and 1880, Die Vertrauten consisted of only 152 individuals. Membership was passed from father to

FIGURE 3.1. Share certificate for the shareholders of the Leipzig Art Association (1862). Courtesy of the Stadtarchiv Leipzig.

son, and many of its members were interrelated by marriage. Merchants dominated this association for most of the eighteenth and nineteenth centuries.[101]

As in the case of the AMNH, it was the industrial elite that pushed for the creation of the Applied Arts Museum in 1868. Although the mercantile elites still represented, according to Menninger, about 19 percent of the applied arts' association membership, the industrial elite was the strongest group with about 27 percent. The remaining members were civil servants, lawyers and doctors, architects and engineers, artists, artists for applied arts, and artisans. From its inception, the project of a museum of applied arts was closely tied to the commercial and industrial interests of Leipzig's new industrial elite, which saw the creation of such a museum as central to Saxony's economic success on the world market. The museum was intended to serve as a mediating place between art and industry, "where the development of taste could be influenced, and where models 'from the best artistic times' would be available to those creating the crafts themselves." Although the mercantile elite was still the second largest group among the members of the applied arts museum association, its influence appeared to be weakened. However, one could also be tempted to argue that the mercantile elite simply had less interest in this museum and therefore abstained from the new project. The project of an applied arts museum in Leipzig and of a natural history museum in New York clearly appealed to new elites because it gave them an opportunity to promote industry and science, the foundations of their economic success. The old elites continued to patronize institutions that were dedicated to the celebration of past aesthetic artifacts and art. Since old families in New York and Leipzig considered history (family histories and family trees) an integral part of defining their identity and justifying their claim to social dominance, art collections and art

museums were part of the old elites' strategy to establish social and cultural superiority. When just a few years later, in 1873, a group of wealthy Leipzig professors,
merchants, and publishers met to create an ethnographic museum, the mercantile
elite proved to be, as in the case of the art museum, the strongest group among the
members of this new association. According to Menninger, roughly 68 percent of
its members belonged to the city's commercial elite, and not a single member of
this association belonged to the industrial elite. By 1900, the share of the industrial
elite had increased to barely 5 percent of the association's membership, while the
share of the mercantile elites still remained at a very high level (48 percent).[102]

Leipzig's ethnographic museum, however, received substantial financial and
material support from one of the city's new families—the family of Herrmann
Julius Meyer (1826–1909), owner of one of Germany's most important publishing houses, the Bibliographisches Institut. Meyer's two sons, Hans (1858–1929)
and Herrmann (1869–1932), who were engaged in overseas and colonial exploration as well as German migration projects, provided the museum with extensive collections of artifacts and financial support. The success and fame of the
Bibliographisches Institut rests with its publication of the 55-volume encyclopedia
Meyers Konversationslexikon and *Meyers Groschenbibliothek,* a collection of texts
written by classic German poets (Goethe, Schiller, etc.) that was affordable for
the masses. Herrmann Julius Meyer, who took charge of the publishing house in
1856, decided in 1874 to relocate his business from Gotha to Reudnitz, an eastern
suburb that was incorporated into Leipzig in 1889.[103] At this point Leipzig had
already been established as a city of book production and book trade and was
home to many famous German publishing houses (Reclam, Brockhaus, etc.).[104]
Newly arrived in Leipzig, the Meyer family engaged heavily in philanthropy and
financed social housing projects, gave money to Leipzig's art museum and university, and provided financial and material support to the ethnographic museum and
the Museum of Regional Geography. Since they were new to Leipzig, Meyer and
his sons, although they had very different opinions about the purpose of philanthropy, seemed to have recognized its value for social integration.

In 1884 Meyer made the decision to spend a great deal of money for the creation of affordable housing for working-class families. His volunteering as a friendly
visitor and the general fear of social unrest and revolution started by a rebellious
working class caused him to become involved in social reform.[105] (Leipzig was the
headquarters of Germany's Social Democratic movement, and Leipzig's working
class has always been portrayed as very radicalized.)[106] In this respect, Meyer's
motives were not different from the concerns of Henry I. Bowditch and Elgin R. L.
Gould, who worried about the survival of the existing socioeconomic order. New
York's elites engaged in social philanthropy in response to the growing social problems in immigrant and working-class neighborhoods.[107] The specter of revolution
and the news about the Paris Commune contributed to the willingness of wealthy
Leipzigers, New Yorkers, and Bostonians to provide funds for improving the living
conditions of working-class families.

In 1886, Meyer bought land in Lindenau, a suburb to the west of Leipzig, with
the goal of erecting apartment buildings for working-class families. Two years
later, construction began under the supervision of Max Pommer, who became the
leading architect of Meyer's housing trust and a member of its board.[108] Between

Table 3.3 Expansion of the Meyersche Stiftung

Part of Leipzig	Period of construction	Buildings and apartments	Construction costs in marks (including money for the acquisition of the land)
Lindenau	1888–98	52 apartment buildings with 501 apartments (plus a daycare center, a washing facility, 202 garden plots)	2,625,992
Eutritzsch	1899–1901	39 apartment buildings with 344 apartments (plus a daycare center and a bathing facility)	2,248,998
Reudnitz	1903–1908	56 apartment buildings with 447 apartments	2,754,800
Kleinzschocher	1907–37	139 apartment buildings with 1,404 apartments (plus communal facilities)	11,207,504

SOURCES: Annual reports and newspaper articles in the Meyersche Stiftung archive; Marta Doehler and Iris Reuther, *Die Meyer'schen Häuser in Leipzig: Bezahlbares Wohnen* (Leipzig: Stiftung Meyer'sche Häuser, 1995).

1888 and 1937, Meyer's housing trust built four large settlement projects in various parts of Leipzig at a total cost of 18,837,294 marks.[109]

In 1888 Meyer had founded the Verein zur Erbauung billiger Wohnungen (Association for the Construction of Affordable Apartments) as the legal owner of these housing projects. Since his sons Hans and Herrmann repeatedly rejected their father's notion of social philanthropy, Meyer created the Stiftung für Erbauung billiger Wohnungen in Leipzig (Foundation for the Construction of Affordable Apartments in Leipzig) in 1900. This legal move prevented his sons from exercising any influence over these housing projects. Instead of charging his sons with the administration of this housing trust, Meyer put Pommer and his son-in-law, Paul Georg Otto Schlobach, in charge. While his two sons considered Meyer's philanthropic engagement to be worthless and threatening to the financial stability of their publishing company, Meyer's housing trust put his family right at the center of Leipzig's philanthropic establishment and led to the inclusion of his sons into Leipzig's social establishment (both sons were invited to join the Gesellschaft Harmonie). Furthermore, his housing trust became a matter of national and international interest and positioned Leipzig within the transnational discourse on social housing.[110] However, Meyer and his sons' interest in philanthropy was guided by very different goals and ideas. While Meyer's engagement was limited to the community of Leipzig, his sons thought in colonial dimensions, dedicating much of their available resources for philanthropic purposes to this end.

Hans Meyer donated 150,000 marks to the University of Leipzig in 1911. This financial support was intended to establish research institutes for universal history, ethnology, and psychology of a people. Just one year later, he created an endowment of 150,000 marks at the University of Berlin for the establishment of a chair in colonial geography. This was the first such chair established in Wilhelmine Germany. Further donations of books, collections, and smaller endowments followed. In 1888, for his contributions to Leipzig's ethnographic museum (he donated his collections from his travels around the world in 1881–82 to the museum), Meyer was rewarded with the title "patron" of the museum. In 1890 he entered the board of the museum and participated actively in the expansion of its collections and the organization of its displays. After the turn of the century, he donated collections from Germany's colony in East Africa, the famous Benin Collection, and collections from New Guinea, New Zealand, the Salomon Islands, the Bismarck Archipelago, Japan, and Ecuador.[111]

Hans's brother, Herrmann, who engaged in German settlement projects in southern Brazil (Rio Grande do Sul), joined Hans in his support for the ethnographic museum in Leipzig. He donated 11,000 marks to buy the Calchaqui collection, 10,000 marks to purchase statues from the Buddhist Pantheon in Japan, and the necessary funds for the acquisition of Central American artifacts. In addition, he gave to the museum his valuable Xingú collection (about 1,900 objects), his notes from his South American expeditions, a collection of photos from these expeditions, and the two ethnological collections from Borneo and British New Guinea. With his brother, Meyer contributed financial support on several occasions for the purchase of collections from Africa.[112]

Philanthropy for Hans and Herrmann Meyer was to improve Imperial Germany's prestige and standing in the world. While Hans Meyer used his financial resources to support German explorers in Africa and South America, to bring ethnographic collections to Germany, and to fund colonial geography as an academic subject, Herrmann Meyer also supported the creation of German settlement colonies in southern Brazil.[113] The meaning and purpose of philanthropy for the Meyer family thus moved from a concern for the social problems of capitalist society to a colonial project in which knowledge and artifacts from Africa and South America were brought to German museums and German settlers were exported to South America in an attempt to spread German culture and German virtue. The case of the Meyer family makes clear how easily philanthropy could be transformed from an internal force that targeted domestic issues to an external force that dealt with transatlantic issues such as exploration and migration. This transformation of philanthropy within two generations was conditioned by political circumstances and the shift of Imperial Germany's focus from social reform (during the 1880s) to overseas exploration and conquest (during the 1890s).

Unified Philanthropic Culture

While in New York and Leipzig old and new elites created parallel philanthropic spheres, Boston and Toronto's old elites succeeded in absorbing socially ambitious and economically powerful new men and integrating them into the existing philanthropic culture. In both cities, handpicked social climbers were invited to participate in the financing of cultural and social public institutions. Toronto and Boston differed from New York and Leipzig in the size and character of the potential challengers to the established philanthropic networks. Boston's Irish population did not possess the financial resources to create their own philanthropic counter-culture. Therefore, they focused on the conquest of political power and thus access to tax-funded institutions. Toronto's social newcomers were too few and too iso-lated from each other. Furthermore, even the old elites were not numerous enough and financially strong enough to organize and finance their own museums. They depended on financial infusions from social newcomers. Fortunately for Toronto, its High Society could count on Sir Edmund Walker, who negotiated the integra-tion of old and new money into one unified philanthropic culture.

Over the course of the entire nineteenth century, Boston's Brahmins succeeded in dominating the city's philanthropic institutions.[114] From the founding of the Mas-sachusetts General Hospital (MGH) to the establishment of the Museum of Fine Arts (MFA), Brahmin families instigated, organized, financed, and ran the social and cultural public institutions that were essential to Boston's cityscape.[115] When James Jackson and John C. Warren authored in August 1810 a letter "addressed to several of our wealthiest and most influential citizens, for the purpose of awakening in their minds an interest" in the establishment of a general hospital, both authors expected Boston's old merchant families to provide the necessary funding. This cir-cular letter resulted in the creation of an association for the purpose of finding a suit-able plot of land and building a general hospital on it. A board of trustees was put in charge of fund-raising and establishing a membership organization. Between 1811 and 1818, this association received the support of 1,047 subscribers from Boston, Salem, Plymouth, Charlestown, Hingham, and Chelsea; 245 subscribers gave $100 or more and thus became members of the corporation. According to an analysis by Nathaniel I. Bowditch, the brother of the physician and housing reformer Henry Ingersoll Bowditch, the hospital association received $146,992.57 by July 1843. The highest single subscription was about $20,000 and came from William Phillips, whose father had instigated the hospital project by bequeathing the sum of $5,000 to the town of Boston for such a purpose in 1797. Twenty-six subscribers donated between $1,000 and $5,000, 15 donated between $500 and $1,000, 252 gave between $100 and $500, and 895 donated up to $100. The list of the members and trustees of this association reads like a *Who's Who* of Brahmin society.[116] The overwhelming majority of its subscribers claimed to come from old colonial stock. Their ancestors belonged, with few exceptions, to the English Puritans who were forced to leave England in the 1620s and 1630s. Only a handful of subscribers were identified as self-made men who did not inherit wealth from their forebearers. Among its sub-scribers one could find Amos (1786–1852) and Abbott Lawrence (1792–1855), the two brothers who invested in cotton manufacturing and made their fortunes in the manufactures of Lowell and later in the Pacific Mills, located in Lawrence. Both men quickly entered the group of Boston's wealthiest people. In 1846, Amos Lawrence's wealth was assessed to be $1 million and Abbott Lawrence's wealth was estimated at $2 million. The unknown author of "*Our First Men*" wrote, "Perhaps no family in N. England has acquired property with greater rapidity or more uniform good fortune, than the Lawrences."[117]

The two Lawrence brothers were joined by several members of the Amory (3), Appleton (4), Coolidge (2), Jackson (3), Lowell (3), and Lyman (3) families in their support of the MGH. These interrelated families were all of Brahmin heritage, but they adapted to the new industrial age and thus, according to Frederic Cople Jaher, "mastered the first challenge to its community leadership and ensured predominance for the next two generations." These families engaged in cotton manufacturing and provided the necessary funding for the establishment of the nation's largest manufacturing center in Lowell in the first half of the nineteenth century. "They became," as Jaher pointed out, "the new economic core of blueblood Boston."[118]

When, more than five decades later, Henry I. Bowditch and Martin Brimmer called on their fellow citizens to support the project of a social housing company and of an art museum, the same families which had supported the hospital project rallied again around these projects. The overwhelming majority of the stockholders of the Boston Co-operative Building Company (BCBC) could trace their family trees back to English Puritans who arrived in the New World before 1650. One-third were engaged in manufacturing (James L. Little, Arthur Theodore Lyman), railroad construction (Edwin Hale Abbott, William Endicott Jr.), and financing/banking (Henry Purkitt Kidder). About 43 percent of them belonged to the free professions (Henry Ingersoll Bowditch, George Otis Shattuck), and about 25 percent were engaged in trade (John Lowell Gardner). The lines between these different fields of economic engagement were, however, not so clearly drawn, since many of these stockholders had moved from a merchant career to manufacturing and/or financing/banking. Arthur Theodore Lyman (1832–1915), for instance, entered the East India trade as a merchant upon graduation from Harvard College in 1853. After some years in this field, Lyman became interested in the manufacture of cotton. In 1860 he was made treasurer of the Hamilton Manufacturing Company and in 1861 of the Appleton Company at Lowell.

Many stockholders of the BCBC were involved in the association of the MGH and in the establishment of the MFA. William Endicott Jr. was instrumental in the establishment of the MFA. He was one of its incorporators, a trustee from its incorporation in 1870 until his resignation in 1907, and president of the museum association for five years. In addition, Endicott was a trustee of the MGH for twenty-two years. As an analysis of the membership lists of various philanthropic institutions in Boston shows, engagement in philanthropy had been a tradition that was handed down from parents to their sons and daughters throughout the nineteenth century. There was only one individual among the 163 stockholders who could claim Irish ancestry. Richard Sullivan was the son of James Sullivan (1744–1808), the governor of Massachusetts (1807–1808). He had nothing in common with the poor Irish who arrived in Boston during the nineteenth century. Sullivan was active in the real estate business, and his net worth was estimated in 1851 at $100,000 by Forbes and Green. According to the city of Boston's tax documents from the same year, his real estate was valued at $11,500 and his personal wealth at $12,000. Forbes and Green mention that in addition to his real estate possessions in the city of Boston, Sullivan also owned "large quantities of valuable vacant lands in Charlestown and Somerville, which are rapidly coming into the market at high prices."[119] Sullivan had also supported the MGH by serving as a trustee from 1813 to 1823.[120]

Timothy Bigelow Lawrence (1826–69), the son of Abbot Lawrence (1792–1855), bequeathed "to the Athenæum a very valuable collection of armor and arms" and thus sparked the plans for an art museum in Boston. The Athenæum, founded in 1807, was both a library and an art gallery which, until the opening of the MFA, had "provided the only permanent public collection of works in Boston." However, the ever-growing "demands of its library and reading-room had diminished the space given to the fine arts, and it had become evident for some time that another building would be required for that department."[121] In this situation Lawrence made his bequest, "for which no proper room within the building could be found." The construction of a new building had become an inevitable necessity. Lawrence's wife, after learning of these developments, immediately "offered to give the sum of $25,000 for this purpose." The bequest of Lawrence and his wife's offer to contribute to the construction fund for a new building triggered the creation of the MFA.[122]

In contrast to New York, Leipzig, and Toronto, Boston's Brahmins seemed to have envisioned the need for a large art museum for some time and engaged in long-term planning that set Boston apart from similar projects in other cities. According to the 1876 MFA annual report, a few gentlemen "who foresaw the demand for such a museum" had persuaded the Boston Water Power Company

> to convey to the city a lot of land on the corner of St. James Avenue and Dartmouth Street, containing 91,000 square feet, and surrounded by streets on every side, to be used for an Institute of Fine Arts or for an open square; and the City Council, aware that the former purpose was the one intended to be carried out if practicable, granted this land to the Trustees for this object upon condition that a building of the value of $100,000 should be erected upon it within three years, a term afterwards extended to six years, and that the museum should be open free of charge four days in each month.[123]

On February 3, 1871, at a public meeting in Boston's Music Hall, a large committee was formed "by those to whom we habitually look for counsel and encouragement" to solicit funds for the construction of this museum building from its fellow citizens. "Smaller meetings in private houses added much to the interest in the scheme; and the committee performed its task with such energy and success that before the summer of 1871 about $250,000 had been promised." Contributions were received from 301 wealthy individuals and 69 corporations. The three largest contributions came from Mrs. T. B. Lawrence ($25,000), Thomas Gold Appleton ($15,000), and Nathaniel Thayer ($10,000). Thirteen individuals each contributed $5,000, 6 individuals donated $2,000, 65 individuals and corporations $1,000, 45 individuals and corporations $500, 12 individuals and corporations $300, 13 individuals $250, 35 individuals and corporations $200, and 178 individuals and corporations $100.[124]

As in the case of the BCBC, the overwhelming majority of philanthropists who supported the museum project were able to trace their ancestry to Europeans who had arrived in the New World during the 1620s and 1630s. More than 90 percent of the museum supporters claimed ancestors who had arrived in Massachusetts before 1650. Only a handful of these philanthropists had ancestors who had arrived between 1650 and 1750. Among the latter was Martin Brimmer, whose family had come from the northwestern part of the Holy Roman Empire (Hamburg area) to Boston sometimes after 1700. The Brimmers intermarried with old

Brahmin families. In 1742 Martin Brimmer II (1742–1804) married Sarah Watson, who claimed as an ancestor George Watson, "who came from England to Plymouth, Mass., about the year 1632." Their son, Martin Brimmer III (1793–1847), entered the store of Theodore Lyman Sr. and thus laid the foundation for the Brimmer merchant firm.[125]

As the case of Brimmer shows, not all of these philanthropists were of Puritan English descent. Two individuals claimed German-Huguenot (Martin Brimmer) and Scottish (John Cummings) ancestry. Four who gave money to this museum project could be classified as self-made men, including Enoch Redington Mudge and Erastus Brigham Bigelow. Bigelow (1814–79) was born into a poor family of farmers or cotton weavers (the biographical information about his background offers both). The *Biographical Encyclopædie of Massachusetts* simply refers to his father as "a man of small means." Therefore, Bigelow was forced to care for himself at age 10 when he began working on a neighboring farm. At 14, he invented "an automatic machine for the manufacture of piping-cord." The money earned from this invention allowed him to attend Leicester Academy. After he had finished his formal education, Bigelow relocated to Boston, where he found employment in a dry goods store. In 1838 he invented a power-loom for weaving knotted counterpanes. A few years later, Bigelow and his brother Horatio established a gingham mill at Leicester and formed the Clinton Company in 1841. Between 1845 and 1851, Bigelow worked on the invention of a power-loom for the manufacture of Brussels and Wilton carpets. At the end of his life, Bigelow owned about fifty patents. He had "invented and put into operation the first successful power-loom known in the history of industrial art for weaving coach-lace, wire-cloth, ingrain carpets, tapestry carpets, Brussels and Wilton carpets, and silk brocatel."[126]

While in New York the division between old and new elites was not only social but also economic (real estate/trade/free professions versus industry), Boston's Brahmin families succeeded in adapting to new economic trends by investing in textile industry and by establishing manufacturing centers such as Lowell and Clinton. At the same time, Brahmin society was able and, in stark contrast to the Knickerbocker elite in New York, willing to integrate newcomers and self-made men of various geographical (German and Scottish), religious (Jewish and Huguenot), and social (farmers) backgrounds. It was this flexibility and limited exclusivity that ensured the survival of the Brahmin families as the dominating social and cultural elite, even after they had lost political power.[127]

Toronto seemed to have followed along a very similar path. Aware of the structural weakness of Toronto's leisure class, Sir Edmund Walker knew that it could not afford a division into parallel philanthropic networks. For this reason, he worked restlessly on the integration of potential philanthropists into one unified philanthropic culture that produced the Toronto Art Gallery (TAG), the Royal Ontario Museum (ROM), the Toronto Housing Company (THC), and the Toronto General Hospital (TGH). Walker was instrumental in founding the TAG and the ROM; he was a trustee of the TGH and a shareholder of the THC. His position as president of the Canadian Bank of Commerce gave him the economic security and the freedom to devote himself to these cultural and charitable philanthropies.[128]

Byron Edmund Walker was born on a farm near the village of Caledonia, Ontario, in 1848. This farm was carved out from the woods by his grandfather,

FIGURE 3.2. Sir Edmund Walker. Courtesy of Wentworth Walker.

Thomas Walker, a skilled watchcase maker from London, in the early 1830s. One of Thomas's sons, Alfred, married Fanny Murton in 1845. Three years later Edmund was born. "Through both parents he was of English lineage, thus standing out as an exception among the bankers of Canada, most of whom have been Scots by origin."[129]

A few years later Alfred Walker moved with his family to Hamilton, where Edmund spent his childhood. At age 4 he started school, which was run by his grandmother, Mrs. William Murton. When he was ready for the Normal School in Toronto, a physician forbade it and recommended to the family that Byron should get a little flesh on his bones before continuing with his schooling. In August 1861, when he was 12, Walker entered the exchange office of his uncle, J. W. Murton, in Hamilton, "really as an experiment in health."[130]

For the next seven years, Walker was a successful apprentice in the banking profession. The first opportunity to prove his abilities came in September 1866 when the Bank of Upper Canada, where his uncle had a sizeable account, went bankrupt. At the time, his uncle was in Europe, so Walker had been placed in charge of the office. At a jubilee marking fifty years of service with the Canadian Bank of Commerce, Walker recalled that the bank suspended payment in Toronto at 10 AM. A telegram announced the fact in Hamilton, but the office there had not closed, and I made it my business in the remaining time to withdraw five or six thousand dollars of my uncle's. The bank in Hamilton suspended payment at one o'clock on the same day. I was then 18 years of age, and I walked out of that office with pride consistent with eighteen years.[131]

Walker had managed to save his uncle a significant loss by not hesitating to act quickly and without waiting for his uncle's directions.

In July 1868, at the age of 20, he entered the service of the newly established Canadian Bank of Commerce as a discount clerk. In 1873 he was sent to New York as a junior agent, a time when Europe and America was undergoing a deep economic and financial crisis. Walker had the opportunity to "gain experience of a first-class panic first hand."[132] Successively he filled the positions of manager in London (Ontario), inspector at head office, and manager in Hamilton. In 1886 he was appointed general manager and in 1906 elected a director. His career with the Canadian Bank of Commerce culminated in his election to the presidency of the bank in 1907, "which has caused him to be recognized in public life as one of the most eminent of Canadians." In 1908 Edward VII made him a Commander of the Victorian Order, and George V knighted him in 1910.[133]

Banking, to Walker, provided the necessary financial means to make a living and to finance his real passion: art and learning. As soon as Walker had secured a stable position in his business life, he dedicated all his energy to the establishment of the ROM and the TAG. Eleanor Creighton tells us that Toronto is "almost wholly indebted to Sir Edmund Walker" for the ROM. It was Walker who supported Charles Trick Currelly in his desire to create a museum in the city. Walker opened his house to fund-raising events, lobbied the provincial government (with Sir Edmund Osler) for funding for the construction of a suitable building, and created with the "Ten Friends of Art" a financial scheme to sustain the museum. His engagement in philanthropy for cultural institutions and for the University of Toronto seems to be a reflection of his lack of extensive formal education. Once when he was asked about his education, Walker replied: "I hadn't any education; my father chiefly grounded me in the rudiments, and practically all that I know I have gained through reading."[134] If the circumstances and his health had been better, he would have inevitably studied at the university. Walker invested more than CAD$100,000 in the founding of Appleby Boys School between 1909 and 1912. He became a trustee of the University of Toronto in 1892 and a senator in 1893. From 1910 until his death in 1924, Walker served as chairman of the board of governors of the University of Toronto.[135]

Walker was not a banker by choice. Within his family "he used to say that he ought never to have been a banker." He "knew the value of money, and its lack of value," and he had no real interest in money "after he had made decent and proper provision for the comfort of his family."[136]

When the bank sent Walker to Windsor, he took up geology. He began to accumulate a large collection of fossils, which he eventually donated, together with a comprehensive library of books on paleontology, to the University of Toronto. This collection formed the nucleus of the Museum of Paleontology, which had been incorporated into the Royal Ontario Museum. He used his two appointments in New York to broaden his cultural experiences. "In fact, we have his own word for it that with the first money he could spare after entering the bank he went to New York to see A. T. Stewart's collection of pictures." He and his wife, Mary Alexander, whom he had married in 1874, spent most of their free time visiting the Metropolitan Museum of Art. Both were lovers of good pictures as well as of good concerts and plays. The climate at the home of the Walker family was characterized by discussions about flowers, music, fossils, science, and literature.[137] Colby points out that Walker "had a broader knowledge of English literature than a well qualified university professor of the subject need have, and a broader knowledge of paleontology than most professors of geology."[138] Even though this remark may be highly exaggerated, it is clear that Walker was very interested in science and humanities. Because he had no opportunity to study paleontology or literature in depth, he tried to compensate by financing educational and art institutions.

Exhibitions of paintings in the TAG and of fossils in the ROM were the culmination of his interests. It would be inaccurate, as Colby points out, to call these collateral pursuits avocations. "Considered in their totality it is not too much to say that cultural beneficence was Walker's vocation whereas banking was simply his avocation."[139] However, the banking profession enabled Walker to support cultural and charitable philanthropies in Toronto. Although his financial contributions remained limited, Walker was well connected with a very large number of wealthy Torontonians. He brought together the Torontonians who had the money and the intellectuals who had the ideas. This happened in two ways: (1) in the case of the TAG, it was his frequent meetings with Goldwin Smith that paved the way for the establishment of the art gallery; (2) in the case of the ROM, it was his fundraising dinners that brought together the individuals who possessed the necessary financial means to support such a museum. In addition, Walker was able to use his business connections through the Canadian Bank of Commerce to entice potential donors to support these two projects.

In contrast to New York, Boston, and Leipzig, where wealthy citizens initiated the establishment of art galleries/art museums by forming associations that had the sole goal of collecting funds for the construction of a museum building and the acquisition of museum collections, in Toronto it was the artists themselves who founded the Ontario Society of Artists (OSA) with the intention of establishing an art museum. OSA was founded in 1872 at about the time when similar projects were under way in Boston and New York. However, at this point Toronto did not have a sufficient number of wealthy citizens who could have funded an art museum. For nearly thirty years nothing happened. When the president of the OSA, George A. Reid, persuaded Sir Edmund Walker to chair a committee with the purpose of establishing a Toronto art museum in 1900, the idea became feasible because of the advanced industrialization of the city and the emergence of a financially potent leisure class that had accumulated enormous wealth.[140] At the first meeting of interested Torontonians on December 7, 1900, Walker was able to announce CAD$26,000 subscriptions—CAD$5,000 each by Messrs. Joseph W. Flavelle, Hon. George A. Cox, William Mackenzie, the estate of H. O. Massey, and Frederic Nicholls and CAD$1,000 from Walker himself. In January 1901, a roll of annual members was started. Four classes of membership were established. One could become a founder for CAD$5,000, a benefactor for CAD$500, a life member for CAD$100, and an annual member for an annual fee of CAD$10 for a layman and CAD$5 for any member of a recognized art body. Within the next twenty-five years the membership list included 35 founders, 87 benefactors, 254 life members, and 557 annual members (including 130 artist members). The financial support of the first three classes of membership amounted to nearly $244,000.[141]

The art museum project received the backing of Toronto's leading families of English, Scottish, and Ulster origin. About 65 percent of all members of Toronto's art association claimed English origin; 31 percent were of Scottish background, and about 10 percent could trace their ancestry back to English and Scottish settlers in Northern Ireland. In only three cases (1.6 percent) did members claim "true" Irish-Catholic ancestry. Less than 2 percent were able to trace their ancestry back to Germany, Sweden, and France. This dominance of English families was not limited to the TAG. An analysis of the membership associations of the TGH and the THC produced a similar picture: 57 percent of all members of the association for the TGH and 60 percent of all stockholders of the THC derived from English backgrounds. In both cases, Scottish and English-Irish ancestry ranked second and third. Less than 4 percent of members of the TGH claimed non-English-speaking ancestry (Dutch, German, Italian, and Danish). This seems to be in stark contrast to the ethnic structure of Toronto society. Beginning in the 1860s, Toronto experienced an enormous growth of its Irish population. During the 1850s, the Irish even outnumbered the British in this city. And although between the 1860s and 1900 more English than Irish immigrants arrived in Toronto, the Irish still represented the second-largest segment of Toronto society. Yet, as in the case of Boston, Toronto's philanthropic establishment was predominantly Protestant and English.[142]

Among the philanthropists one could find representatives of Toronto's oldest families such as the Cawthra, Gooderham, and Worts families (all of English descent), the Eatons (Ulster origin), and the Macdonalds (Scottish). These families arrived early in the nineteenth century and dominated Toronto's economic and social life for much of the nineteenth century. They successfully invested in real estate, trade, banking, manufacturing, and railway construction.[143] The Cawthras, for instance, left Yorkshire, England, sometimes after 1800. After a short stay in New York, they moved to York (later renamed Toronto) in 1802. Joseph Cawthra received a 400-acre tract of undeveloped land from the Crown under the condition that he would build a house on it within four years. This real estate and his apothecary shop became the basis for his family's enormous wealth, which was invested in several business ventures and real estate.[144]

Although the English elite clearly dominated Toronto philanthropy, many of the philanthropists were newcomers to the city (Flavelle, Warren) and had made their money in the new industries.[145] In the case of the TAG, only 23 percent of its supporters were born within the city of Toronto while about 45 percent were born somewhere in the Province of Ontario. An analysis of the membership of the THC and TGH produced a similar picture with significant numbers of its supporters born outside of Toronto. While these numbers might not come as a surprise, since Toronto experienced a significant economic and social transformation in the last third of the nineteenth century, the information with regard to the educational levels of cultural philanthropists offers us some insight into the motivation for their philanthropic engagement. More than one-third of those who provided funding for the art gallery had only a grammar or public school education. Like Sir Edmund Walker and Sigmund Samuel, they had entered business at a young age and did not have an opportunity for higher education. The lack of this formal training at universities and colleges proved to be an important motivation for these philanthropists to engage in philanthropy for cultural and educational institutions. In the eyes of these individuals, providing funding for institutions of higher learning brought them into close contact with educated people and elevated their intellectual status.[146]

As in the case of New York, Boston, and Leipzig, the first task of the art museum association was to secure a building. Coincidentally at this time Harriet Elizabeth Mann Dixon, the spouse of Goldwin Smith, thought about bequeathing her home, the Grange, for some public purpose. The architect D'Arcy Boulton had erected this building in 1820, "and the records state that it was one of the pioneer dwellings which ushered in the 'brick period' of York's history."[147] Harriet, the widow of William Henry Boulton, married Goldwin Smith in 1875. She was two years younger than Smith and, as Elisabeth Wallace remarks, "completely devoid of any intellectual interests."[148]

Although Walker and Mavor were often guests at the Grange, neither were true friends of Goldwin Smith. Mavor noted that he received no intellectual stimulus from Smith and that Smith had no interest or knowledge of art. Walker, though loyal to the British Empire, was a staunch Canadian. As such he did not have much in common with Smith, who not only believed in the superiority of the Anglo-Saxon race but went so far as to demand the incorporation of Canada into the United States.[149] Nevertheless, in 1903, Walker persuaded Mrs. Smith to bequeath the Grange to the Art Museum of Toronto. He used the next seven years to acquire quietly much of the property surrounding the Grange.[150] After Goldwin Smith died in June 1910, the museum council was able to take possession of the Grange. The TAG signed an agreement with the city council under which the grounds became a public park. In return for the city government's promise to contribute $5,000 annually to the maintenance of the gallery, the museum trustees agreed that one day each week admission to the gallery would be free of charge. The city council agreed to buy the land surrounding the Grange from Walker.[151] As in the case of New York and Boston, the city government supported the philanthropists in the establishment of an art gallery by providing land for the building. However, the New York municipal government also financed the museum building. This was not the case in Toronto. On the other side of the Atlantic, the city government of Leipzig provided the philanthropists with neither the land nor the building.[152]

While Walker's involvement in the creation of the art museum went beyond organizing and involved financial contributions, his engagement in the creation of the ROM was focused on raising the necessary funds from individual philanthropists and the provincial government. He acquired a reputation for organizing dinners during which he would talk attendees into offering financial support to one of his pet philanthropic projects. It seems that Joseph W. Flavelle, chairman of the board of trustees of the TGH, introduced Walker to this fund-raising tactic. Flavelle felt forced into more aggressive fund-raising tactics when he discovered that his goal of erecting a new building for the TGH on University Avenue could only be fulfilled if he could raise CAD$2.6 million. Although he managed to persuade the university and the city government to contribute significant funds (CAD $600,000 from the university and CAD$400,000 from the city), he still needed $1.6 million from Toronto's leisure class. Deeply concerned about his ability to raise such an amount, Flavelle developed a special plan for acquiring this support. He decided to ask five well-known and very wealthy philanthropists—George Cox, Timothy Eaton, Chester Massey, Edmund B. Osler, and William Mackenzie—for donations of CAD$50,000 to CAD$75,000 each. He offered "to name sections or wings of the hospital after each large donor to establish a basis for similar future gifts." Flavelle and Walker organized a special meeting with these prominent philanthropists, "enabling the hospital board to proclaim that more than a quarter of a million dollars had been raised in two and a half hours."[153]

In Toronto society it became known that dinner invitations by Sir Edmund Walker were often "expensive evenings," since Walker would take the opportunity to introduce his guests to his favorite projects, hoping that these guests would share his enthusiasm and provide the necessary funding.[154] Charles Trick Currelly seemed to have been fully aware of Walker's interest in cultural philanthropy. Currelly, who was engaged in excavations in Egypt under the supervision of Flinders Petrie, returned to Toronto to visit his family in the autumn of 1905. Because of his long friendship with Edmund Walker Jr., he had no difficulties in gaining access to Walker Sr. Invited to his house, Currelly disclosed his dream of building a museum in Toronto. He found a comrade-in-arms in Walker, who had had the same dream for more than twenty years. Walker, who was involved in the establishment of the art gallery at this time, had been deeply impressed by the museums and the cultural philanthropy of New York City.[155]

In December 1905, Currelly was appointed to collect Egyptian artifacts for a possible museum at the University of Toronto. He used the next four years to buy a large number of artifacts at the expense of the provincial government, the University of Toronto, and private subscriptions. His accumulations in these years were impressive. "It was a museum of archaeology; all it required was a building." In January 1909 Currelly organized an exhibition that "was sensational both in the scope of the collection it revealed and in the individual artefacts, many of them as striking and unusual as those to be seen in the great museums of London and New York." This exhibition impressed the premier of Ontario, Sir James Whitney, the members of his cabinet, and the university board of governors. When Walker received a letter from William Arthur Parks, a professor of geology, pointing out that the university collections of geology and mineralogy needed new space, he took action. In February 1909 he asked the university to approve the building of the first section of the museum. Estimating the construction costs for the museum to be CAD$400,000, Walker proposed, perhaps influenced by the collaboration between city government and private philanthropists in New York City, "that the Ontario government and the university should each provide half of the capital and half of the cost of maintenance."[156]

Walker and Sir Edmund Osler were convinced that this would be a good time to bring the matter of the museum building before the Ontario government. Currelly described Osler as "one of the leading members of the Conservative Party, one of the shrewdest business men in Canada, and the man on whose advice the party leaned a great deal." His support was necessary for the realization of a government-supported museum because the Conservative Party had the majority in the Ontario Parliament. Whitney listened attentively to the proposal of Walker and Osler "and then explained that he was much interested, but he couldn't tell what the House would say when it met in February." Osler replied: "That's all right, Whitney; you give it to us, and if there's any objection from the House, I'll pay it out of my own pocket."[157] Osler's assurance convinced Whitney that there would be no resistance in the legislature. He authorized the payments, and construction began before the bill was passed in parliament.[158]

Since construction of the museum building amounted to about CAD$350,000, that left CAD$50,000 for equipment. The new museum was actually a complex of five museums—Archaeology, Geology, Mineralogy, Paleontology, and Zoology—each with its own director and collections. The provincial government and the university agreed to share the annual maintenance costs, which quickly rose from CAD$30,000 in 1912/13 to CAD$75,000 in 1924. However, acquisitions and special exhibitions depended on wealthy philanthropists who either presented new objects to the museum or donated money for purchasing. Sir Edmund Walker and Mrs. H. D. Warren held key positions in the philanthropic network that secured the existence of the ROM. Walker continuously looked for new financial resources for this museum project and worked hard on the integration of new philanthropists (such as the Mond brothers and Sigmund Samuel) into the financial safety net for the ROM. Walker opened, in the name of the ROM, an account at the branch of the Canadian Bank of Commerce in London with a limited overdraft that Currelly was able to use for his purchases for the museum.[159] To ensure that Currelly's expenses were repaid, in 1917 Walker organized the "Twenty Friends of Art," a small group of patrons who each agreed to contribute CAD$500 annually to this museum purchasing fund. All subscriptions were transferred to the museum account in London and were used to offset the overdraft incurred by Currelly. Recognizing the limited attraction of such a fund, which did not guarantee its members that their name would explicitly and eternally be linked to a specific piece exhibited in the ROM, Walker changed the group's name in 1924 to the "Ten Friends of Art." Between 1917 and 1924 a sum of more than $24,000 was donated to this fund by the following philanthropists:

Sir Edmund Osler	3,000.00
David Alexander Dunlap	3,000.00
Sigmund Samuel	3,000.00
Colonel R. W. Leonard	3,000.00
Mrs. H. D. Warren	2,500.00
Chester D. Massey	3,000.00
Sir Edmund Walker	2,500.00
W. C. Edwards	2,500.00
Zebulon Aiton Lash	1,000.00
Sir Alfred Mond, 2 payments, one being	
paid direct to C. T. Currelly	928.98
Interest	153.76
Total	24,582.74[160]

In addition to this fund, the ROM received gifts and donations on a fairly regular basis. Between 1911 and 1926, the ROM received gifts from 263 men and women of predominantly English background. In contrast to the TAG, a much higher number of patrons had a university or college degree, and a significant number of its supporters occupied legal and academic professions. The patrons of the ROM could make their support a full- or part-time occupation. Financial and material support poured in from all age groups. It would be wrong to assume that philanthropy was left to a late stage in one's life. Toronto's philanthropists came from all age groups, although half were over 50. The philanthropists who invested money in charities were older than philanthropists who invested money in cultural institutions: 85 percent of philanthropists of the TAG and more than 62 percent of the philanthropists of the ROM were born after 1860. In contrast, 54 percent of the philanthropists who supported the TGH and 44 percent of the philanthropists who supported the THC were born before 1860. The reason for this may be the different amounts invested in charitable and cultural philanthropies. While much higher amounts were necessary for the building of the TGH, donations to the ROM or the AGT were much smaller. Younger Torontonians seemed to have been able to afford to give smaller amounts to museums and art galleries while building their careers. Giving to hospitals, however, demanded the funds of a successful and well-established person who had already made his or her fortune. Although this was occasionally the case (for instance, Cawthra Mulock enjoyed the good fortune of inheriting a small fortune at a young age), it was much more likely late in life.

Although the ROM received the support of a significant part of Toronto's leisure class, Walker and Currelly's plan to establish a museum association similar to that of the TAG ultimately failed. After Currelly suggested the creation of one unified membership association for the ROM in March 1922, the directors of the other four museums of the ROM recommended that "each of the constituent Museums should have a separate membership, issuing its own membership cards and deciding what privileges should be accorded to members but that the scale of subscriptions and donations should be the same for each":

Annual members	˙ CAD$10 per annum
Sustaining members	CAD$25 per annum
Fellows	CAD$100 per annum
Friends	CAD$500 per annum
Fellows for life	CAD$1,000.00
Fellows in perpetuity	CAD$5,000.00
Benefactors	CAD$10,000.00[161]

After the recommendations were approved by the board of trustees, Currelly started to build a membership organization for the Museum of Archaeology with only limited success. Only 78 Torontonians—14 longtime members and 64 annual members—were willing to support it in the mid-1920s. The TAG had nearly ten times as many members (383 permanent members and 439 annual members). In December 1924 the balance in the membership account was meager:

CAD\$3,455.[162] This result makes very clear the economic limitations of Toronto's philanthropic culture. In contrast to Boston, New York, and Leipzig, Toronto's leisure class did not possess the financial potential to create two strong membership associations supporting two museums. For Walker, the only way of financing both institutions was to integrate as many prospective philanthropists as possible into the existing philanthropic network. Any division of economic and financial power would have resulted in the demise of one of the two existing museums.

CHAPTER FOUR

Bountiful Ladies: Philanthropy
and Women's Place in Society

The phrase "women's nature and mission"[1] dominated the nineteenth-century discourse on the place of women in bourgeois society. Because of assumptions about their "natural role," women were stereotyped as care-givers who "could only" find fulfillment in the management of their household and family. Well-off women were expected to supervise servants, to present a picture of a harmonious family to the outside world, and to arrange social events (dinners, balls, etc.). They were excluded from the public sphere and far removed from the world of commerce and paid labor.[2] Free from the necessity of providing for the economic well-being of their families, well-off women were charged with taking care of their families and homes. Such a description is, according to Ute Frevert, much too simplistic and one-dimensional. "It is clear that women too were part and parcel of the emergence of social associations, a process which had begun in the late eighteenth century and made a decisive impact on the political structure of Imperial Germany."[3]

Based on Jürgen Habermas's model of private and public spheres, many historians have described European associational life in the nineteenth century as male-dominated. Stefan-Ludwig Hoffmann even goes so far as to suggest that the most striking characteristic of European associations during the nineteenth century was the exclusion of women. Focusing on social clubs and societies, he claims that there was a clean break between the male associational world and the female home. According to Hoffmann, women began only around 1900 to establish their own associations for philanthropic and charitable purposes. He is able to reach such a conclusion, however, only by excluding a large variety of social, charitable, and philanthropic associations that emerged between Paris and St. Petersburg during the eighteenth and nineteenth centuries.[4]

If one includes such associations, our picture of associational life and the place of women in nineteenth-century society changes dramatically.[5] Benjamin Maria Baader, for instance, shows that German-Jewish women created independent voluntary societies at the end of the eighteenth century. "Between 1745 and 1870, Jewish women in German lands founded more than 150 sick-care, charitable, and other benevolent societies and directed most of them for decades." These female benevolent organizations predated non-Jewish women's associations and "ran counter to the exclusion of women from a public arena that was conceived of as male both in its symbolic construction and in its social realization."[6] During the Anti-Napoleonic Wars, patriotic women's associations, "which tended to wounded soldiers and looked after war widows and orphans," were founded all over the German states.[7] These associations fulfilled, as Jean H. Quataert argues, a central role in state-building and the creation of regional and national identities. For women, these associations provided avenues for leaving the confinement of the home. They "acquired a civic identity through the public roles and activities that were named 'patriotic' by the dynasty."[8] In the United States, women had engaged in the creation of asylums and charities since the 1790s. The first female-controlled charities emerged in New York, Boston, and Philadelphia. According to Kathleen D. McCarthy, these "women's charities created a political and economic space for female enterprise," challenged "misogynistic stereotypes," and forged "a feminized version of the republican credo of public service, personal self-sacrifice, and individual virtues."[9]

From its very beginning, philanthropy played an important role in the integration of women into the public sphere. Since women were considered to be caregivers, it seemed to be acceptable for wealthy men to allow their wives and daughters to engage in charitable and philanthropic activities. As Frank Prochaska points out, "Whether casual or institutional, charitable work was relatively free from the restraints and prejudices associated with women in paid employments."[10] According to Anne M. Boylan, women could attribute their motivation to perform charitable work "to their sex's special capacity for religion or nurturance."[11] Religion taught Christians that women "had a rightful and important place in the charitable world."[12] Either believing in this predestination or exploiting gender stereotypes to their advantage, women were applauded for their engagement in public societies, which offered assistance to the poor. However, by creating charitable organizations, women not only engaged in social work and thus fulfilled an expectation of their paternalistic society; they also claimed a specific social space of society for themselves. This remained not entirely unnoticed by contemporaries who recognized that the philanthropic involvement of women went potentially against nineteenth-century assumptions about women's roles in society. Henry I. Bowditch, the Boston philanthropist who admired Octavia Hill's engagement in philanthropic housing projects, felt compelled to remark in his "Letter from the Chairman of the State Board of Health" that "what she has undertaken and has accomplished, most people would say was entirely out of woman's sphere."[13] Although such criticism was not an isolated incidence, it did not stop the expansion of female-dominated charities and associations within the transatlantic world.[14] Furthermore, many observers considered women's involvement in philanthropic projects as valuable contributions to the solution of the social question. In 1898 writing about Toronto's charities, John James Maclaren remarked, "I know of no place where there are so many charitable organizations in proportion to its population as in Toronto, and an unusual number of the boards are composed of women. The difference between such boards and those managed by men is, as I have noticed it, that they make the money intrusted to them go farther than the men can do."[15]

Involvement in social philanthropy allowed women to break free from their everyday routine. It could be seen as a "leisured woman's most obvious outlet for self-expression,"[16] as an undisputed way out of the household, and subsequently as an attempt at emancipation. Philanthropy thus was just the first step toward women's integration into the public sphere. By looking at the Russian example, Richard Stites suggested that charity provided

> experience in leadership, nurtured a feeling of self-respect, and aroused a consciousness of women's ability to function in public life. Most important, these efforts brought together many women of similar backgrounds in new situations that transcended the salons and the other established forms of social intercourse that prevailed among ladies. Philanthropy blended easily into feminism, and in a short time their efforts were pointed in the direction of helping other women to live, to study, and to work.[17]

Following this interpretation, philanthropy and female engagement in philanthropic activities could be regarded as a school for emancipation. "Clubs, charities, and colleges all served, according to the American temperance leader and reformer Frances Willard, as 'schools for women in which they might learn how to take their place alongside men in the great work assigned to useful human beings.'"[18] For Eugenie Ladner Birch and Deborah S. Gardner, "the work of women such as Edith Elmer Wood and Catherine Bauer brought women from the social-worker tradition of the philanthropists to new roles as policy makers, planners, designers, and administrators."[19] Emancipation thus appears to have been a multistep project that began with the integration of women into the public sphere through social work. In her study of German aristocratic women's involvement in philanthropy, Quataert suggested that this involvement gave meaning and purpose to women's lives. It further "forged bonds among women through time spent together but linked them inextricably to like-minded men, with whom they collaborated, socialized, corresponded, and traveled."[20] In the first half of the nineteenth century, women engaged in social philanthropy by visiting poor families, distributing charities, and providing guidance.[21] In the second half of the nineteenth century, women joined men in founding social housing enterprises. And although women left the directorship of these enterprises initially to men, they quickly learned how to run and to finance them. Later, they engaged in cultural philanthropy by joining membership organizations for museums and art galleries.

Around and after 1900, the share of women among social and cultural philanthropic organizations rose dramatically, and women began to achieve leadership positions. About 25 percent of all supporters of the Toronto Housing Company and about 30 percent of all donors to the Royal Ontario Museum in Toronto were women. In the case of the Ostheim in Leipzig, women even contributed most of the necessary funds.[22] After 1900, women's engagement in philanthropy was not limited to working with poor families; women created, financed, and ran social housing trusts, museums, and art galleries. Frank Prochaska finds that British women "contributed vast sums to nineteenth-century societies." Furthermore, a sample of 100 wills from the 1840s shows that women left on average twice as much to charities than men.[23]

In the antebellum United States, legal provisions made it nearly impossible for women to become patrons of social work and art. Before the Married Women's Property Act (1861), married women "could neither own nor alienate money," thus leaving them only with their household skills as possible contributions to philanthropic organizations. During the 1840s and 1850s, Chicago's benevolent ladies turned increasingly to asylum work, which "allowed them to escape the narrow confines of the home without openly challenging the dictates of the cult of domesticity." As Kathleen McCarthy pointed out in her masterful study of social and cultural philanthropy in Chicago between 1849 and 1929, these women defy an easy categorization. "Some were feminists, some bluestockings, while some were sincerely pious women who had dedicated their lives to furthering Christian aims." However, the Civil War combined with the legal changes regarding married women's rights to property and the improvement of the economy changed the influence and position of women in Chicago's philanthropic world tremendously. While "antebellum women were expected to participate, not as donors but as volunteers," postbellum women "began to donate sums of an ever-increasing scale, inspired by the example of outstanding feminine philanthropists like Britain's Baroness Angela Burdett-Coutts." During the 1880s, women donated about $700,000 to philanthropic health organizations, $32,000 to asylums, and $18,000 to cultural institutions. The largest gift provided by a woman was the 1884 bequest of $625,000 for a Home for Incurables by Clarissa Peck.[24]

Nevertheless, there are few studies on the involvement of women in philanthropy in American, Canadian, British, and German history. Although German historians published a large number of local and regional studies in the last fifteen years, women are rarely mentioned. Only in 2002 did a special issue of *Ariadne,* the leading German journal for women's and gender history, call attention to this deficit.[25] This negligence seems to be based on an unspoken assumption that even when women donated money for philanthropic causes, it was still the money inherited from their fathers or money received from their husbands. In other words, nineteenth-century women (married and unmarried) are still considered economically dependent, and their donations are subsequently not viewed as a product of their own productive activity. The same argument, however, could be made for nineteenth-century men.[26]

In 1903, when Joseph Flavelle engaged in a major fund-raising campaign for the construction of the Toronto General Hospital, he was approached by a very wealthy man. Sir William Mulock's son, Cawthra, was about to turn 21, and Mulock told Flavelle, " I am very anxious he should make something out of his life. He has enough money to spoil him if he does not have some serious work to do, and I think if he were to go into the Hospital, and you could get him to go to work, it might be of benefit."[27] Cawthra Mulock was the sole heir to the Mulock family fortune and was expected to inherit CAD$8 million dollars. Flavelle immediately agreed, and the younger Mulock contributed CAD$100,000 to the hospital construction. In turn he was made a member of the board of trustees.[28] This incident highlights two aspects of our discussion: First, the donations made by male and female philanthropists were not always the result of their own economic activity but, as both Edward Pessen and Frederic Cople Jaher have shown, often came from inheritances from their fathers or grandfathers.[29] As such, it should not matter from which source (inheritance or independent economic activity) the financial contribution derived. Or, at least, a double standard between women who used their inheritance for philanthropic purposes should not be derided for the same practice praised when employed by men who donated parts of their inheritance. Cawthra Mulock, or at least his father for him, was searching for a meaningful position in society as much as every woman who contributed to social and cultural philanthropies. Second, philanthropy provided social and economic positions to members of the leisure class who wanted to be useful but who did not have to work. Many philanthropists retired early from their business life after they had amassed riches; others like Mulock and William H. Vanderbilt came to be rich because of their father's fortunes. They took the opportunities offered by a career in philanthropic institutions to invest their money and at the same time to influence social and cultural trends of society.

Participation and even dominance in the philanthropic world provided women with a public voice even before they gained the right to vote.[30] Diana Pedersen suggests that "denied the opportunity to participate directly in the political life of the city, middle-class women used the voluntary association as a channel for their interests and ambitions, playing a prominent part in the Progressive movement for the reform of North American cities in the early decades of this century." These women strived, according to Pedersen, to impress their ideas about morality and virtues upon urban life. She considers women's engagement in philanthropy as the attempt to transform the character of urban communities according to the "cult of domesticity." By domesticating the city, urban culture was to "conform to the demands of an ideal home environment."[31] Expanding this cultural argument into a political one, McCarthy argues that women successfully influenced "local, state, and national legislative debates, as well as the distribution of charitable resources," by donating money to charitable institutions which they also administered. Treating the philanthropic organizations as a "parallel power structure" to the established and male-dominated local, state, and federal governments, McCarthy contends that women participated in politics, although they did not have the right to vote before World War I. She suggests "that women rather than men were the primary architects of the American welfare state."[32] A similar argument could be made for Germany where the wives of German dynastic rulers advanced to the status of the *Landesmutter* (Mother of the People) during the Anti-Napoleonic Wars. Representing the well-being of the community and responsible for the care of the people in need, aristocratic women assumed a new importance in the dynastic system of government. They took responsibility for the wounded soldiers, the veterans, and their families. During the 1820s and 1830s, a vast network of philanthropic societies emerged that were largely run and staffed by aristocratic women.[33]

The following investigation of women's involvement in philanthropy in German and North American urban society follows McCarthy's suggestion that philanthropic institutions offered women opportunities to shape the emerging public sphere in their cities. Women employed their involvement in funding and running philanthropic associations and institutions (here social housing enterprises and museums) to claim their place in the public sphere. Philanthropy is thus seen as a tool of sociocultural domination that allowed women to leave their mark on urban society without having to enter politics. The distance of the state on the local and regional levels in nineteenth-century German, Canadian, and American society allowed philanthropists—male and female—to occupy important places in the public sphere of urban societies and to define these spaces according to their own views. Philanthropists decided which museums to build and what would be put on display in these museums. They further decided the architectural structures of social housing projects and thus had their hands in the definition of what constituted family.

This chapter will provide a comparative historical-sociological investigation of women's involvement in social and cultural philanthropy during the second half of the nineteenth and first half of the twentieth centuries in Boston, New York, Toronto, and Leipzig. Furthering the argument developed in the first two chapters of this book, the following analysis will contrast and compare female philanthropy on both sides of the Atlantic. It will be shown that financing social and cultural institutions allowed women to claim an important place in nineteenth-century public life. These philanthropic institutions could provide the first step in women's emancipation. However, not all women considered philanthropy as a stepping-stone to female liberation and independence. Mrs. H. D. Warren, for instance, seemed to have considered philanthropy as a means to improve the social standing of her family rather than as a tool to claim her independence. Using extensive statistical data on women's involvement in financing social housing enterprises and museums[34] as well as the case studies of five women—Mrs. H. D. Warren, Adelheid Gräfin Ponińska, Emma Hasse, Hedwig von Holstein, and Therese Rossbach—it will be shown that philanthropy empowered women but that these women did not use the power won through philanthropic activity for claiming equal rights (especially the right to vote), since they considered philanthropy to be a powerful force in itself. Some well-off women thus seemed to have developed a different model of civil society and emancipation. While, for Alexis de Tocqueville, associations were the precondition and training ground for civil society, some female philanthropists at the end of the nineteenth century seem not to have seen it the same way. For Mrs. H. D. Warren, philanthropic engagement did not lead necessarily to political activity. It appeared to offer a power structure parallel to the political sphere. For women who had been actively involved in philanthropy and who occupied board positions, the right to vote did not seem to offer more influence in society.[35]

FEMALE PHILANTHROPY AND MUSEUMS

Wealthy women in Leipzig, Boston, New York, and Toronto financed social housing enterprises as well as museums and art galleries. In fact, the same women who gave money to social housing enterprises also invested in art galleries, natural history museums, and design and applied arts museums. The number of women who bought memberships in museum associations is generally comparable to the number of women who acquired shares in social housing companies, although there seem to be distinct German and North American patterns. In Toronto, Boston, and New York, women played a much larger role in cultural philanthropy than in Leipzig. From a financial point of view, one would expect that museum associations attracted more women than social housing enterprises, since the financial threshold was much lower for becoming a patron of such museums and art galleries than purchasing shares in social housing companies and hospitals. However, it was not economics that determined women's choices of philanthropic associations and

Table 4.1   Share of women in museum associations

Association	Total members	Female members
Art Museum of Leipzig	567 (1857)	52 (9.2%)
	731 (1897)	58 (7.9%)
Applied Arts Museum, Leipzig	719 (1897)	55 (7.6%)
American Museum of Natural History, New York	52 (1871)	0
	172 (1880)	5 (2.9%)
	410 (1895)	23 (5.6%)
Metropolitan Museum of Art, New York	320 (1876)	10 (3.1%)
	512 (1895)	89 (17.4%)
Museum of Fine Arts, Boston	370 (1876)	42 (11.4%)
	1,183 (1895)	408 (34.5%)
Toronto Art Gallery	375 (1926)	62 (16.5%)
Royal Ontario Museum	263 (1911–26)	77 (29.3%)

SOURCES: *Adressbuch des Vereins Kunstgewerbe-Museum zu Leipzig Erster Jahrgang 1897* (Selbst-verlag des Vereins Kunstgewerbe-Museum zu Leipzig), 54–79; *Bericht des Leipziger Kunstvereins 1857* (Leipzig: Breitkopf & Härtel, 1857), 14–22; *Bericht des Leipziger Kunstvereins 1900* (Leipzig: Breitkopf & Härtel, 1900), 19–36; Margaret Eleanor Menninger, "Art and Civic Patronage in Leipzig, 1848–1914," Ph.D. diss., Harvard University, 1998, 121; Anett Müller, *Der Leipziger Kunstverein und das Museum der bildenden Künste: Materialien einer Geschichte (1836–1886/87)* (Leipzig: Nouvelle Alliance, 1995), 51; *The First Annual Report of the American Museum of Natural History January, 1870* (New York: Major & Knapp Engraving, Mfg. & Lithographic Co., 1870), 30; *The Second Annual Report of the American Museum of Natural History January, 1871* (New York: George F. Nesbitt, 1871), 31–32; *The Eleventh Annual Report of the American Museum of Natural History, Central Park, New York, February 10th, 1880* (New York: Thitchener & Glastaeter, 1880), 27–28; *The American Museum of Natural History Central Park, New York City. Annual Report of the President, Act of Incorporation, Contract with the Department of Public Parks, Constitution, By-Laws, and List of Members for the Year 1895* (New York: Printed for the Museum, 1895), 87–97; *Report of the Trustees—Metropolitan Museum of Art 1870/71–1894*, 86–90, 623–30; *Proceedings at the Opening of the Museum of Fine Arts: With the Reports for 1876, a List of Dona-tions, the Act of Incorporation, By-Laws, etc.* (Boston: Alfred Mudge & Son, 1876), 21–32; *Trustees of the Museum of Fine Arts: Twentieth Annual Report, for the Year Ending Dec. 31, 1895* (Boston: Alfred Mudge & Son, 1896), 34–46; Minutes of the Board of Trustees of the Royal Ontario Museum, vol. 1 (1911–20) and vol. 2 (1921–26), ROM archive; *Catalogue of Inaugural Exhibition January 29th to February 28th Nineteen Hundred and Twenty-Six* (Toronto: Art Gallery of Toronto, 1926), 68–71.

projects but social expectations and moral standards of a male-dominated society. In the intellectual framework of nineteenth-century men, women's involvement in social philanthropies was expected and tolerated, but women's involvement in cultural and educational philanthropy was still a matter of debate.

In Leipzig two museum projects—the art museum and the Kunstgewerbe-museum (applied arts museum)—attracted the attention and support of the city's affluent and wealthy families. However, women represented only a very small fraction of the overall membership in both museum associations. This level of women's involvement in museum associations, although not limited to these two Leipzig museums, as the example of the American Museum of Natural History in New York shows, was unusually low if compared to other major museums in New York, Boston, and Toronto. In contrast to these museum projects, the American

Museum of Natural History was the only one that was founded exclusively by men. Only after the establishment of its membership association did a few women gain access to this organization.

As table 4.1 shows, women participated in the founding of the Metropolitan Museum of Art in New York (MMA), Boston's Museum of Fine Arts (MFA), the Royal Ontario Museum (ROM), and the Toronto Art Gallery (TAG), and they continually supported these museums by paying dues as well as making financial and material donations. In the process, the share of women among the members of these museum associations grew continuously.

The financial and material contributions of women to these museum projects were not small either. Miss Catharine Lorillard Wolfe (1828–87) was one of the benefactors who supported both the MMA and the American Museum of Natural History (AMNH). Her grandfather had emigrated from Saxony to America before 1729. Her father, John David Wolfe (1792–1872), was a successful merchant who had made a fortune in New York's real estate market. Long before he turned 50, Wolfe was rated among New York's wealthiest merchants. He was one of the founders of the AMNH and became its first president. Following in the footsteps of her father, Catherine L. Wolfe gave money to several philanthropic institutions including the Union College in Schenectady, St. Luke's Hospital in New York City, the American School of Classical Studies at Athens, and the Home for Incurables at Fordham. She presented her collections of paintings to the MMA and provided the museum with an endowment of $200,000.[36]

There can be no doubt that women played a major role in the establishment of philanthropic networks in nineteenth-century cities. It is, however, not entirely clear how we should interpret the statistical evidence. What were the motives of these women to contribute time and energy as well as material and financial resources to museums and art galleries? By giving paintings and endowments to such institutions, women and men ensured that their names, or the names of their families, would be attached to collections and buildings, which were part of the public urban space. Philanthropy provided donors with an opportunity to showcase one's cultural education and taste. As cultivated citizens, philanthropists could claim a leading role in society, since they possessed the appropriate cultural training and since they also had the financial means to enlighten and educate society. By engaging in philanthropy, these individuals not only claimed a certain space and fame but also made sure that this claim would outlive them. Paintings in the MMA and in Boston's MFA still carry the names of their donors. Wings in museums and art galleries are still named after the individuals who provided the necessary funding to accomplish the construction of these building projects decades ago. Philanthropy thus potentially paved the way for a long-term recognition of a family and its philanthropic deeds by generations to come.

Did men and women differ with regard to philanthropic acts? Does philanthropy have a gendered dimension?[37] The women involved in museum associations were in many cases the wives and daughters of men who had purchased memberships or shares in the same institution. In some cases, these women were the unmarried daughters of fathers who had founded these museums or the widows of men who had been involved with these cultural institutions and therefore felt obliged to further support these museums in order to carry on a family tradition. According to the customs of the times, they were normally identified by their husband's name. In many cases we do not even have their first name. The eminent Toronto philanthropist Sarah Trumbull van Lennep, who had married Harry Dorman Warren, to give one example, was subsequently listed as Mrs. H. D. Warren. Biographical information for these women can be found only in exceptional cases. The sources of the financial and material support that they extended to the museums are often not identified. Did these women inherit money from their parents? Did they have their own professional careers (such as the Toronto entrepreneur Mrs. H. D. Warren and the Leipzig physician Anna Kuhnow)? Did the financial support they offered to social and cultural institutions originate from their husbands? And what would this mean for an evaluation of female philanthropy and the position of women in nineteenth-century bourgeois society? Such questions are certainly important. They are, however, rarely asked about male philanthropists. In many cases, male philanthropists involved in museum associations (for instance, William Henry Vanderbilt)[38] actually did not acquire their financial wealth through their own work but by inheriting fortunes from their parents. How is the financial and economic position of these men then different from those of women?

Of greater importance is the question of why these women engaged in philanthropy. Did they consider it a way to claim their space in the public sphere? Did they see philanthropy, as Prochaska contends, as a socially accepted way out of the home?[39] Did it, as Stites argues, serve as a precondition in the larger project of emancipation?[40] Or did the participation of women in philanthropic projects just serve to enhance the influence of their husbands and families? Were these women just extensions of their husbands, who increased their control over philanthropic institutions by involving as many family members as possible? A look at the career of Mrs. H. D. Warren might help in sorting out some of these issues.

In the first half of the twentieth century, Warren occupied an eminent position in the philanthropic art world of Toronto. Together with Sigmund Samuel and Alfred Mond, she provided a financial "safety net" for the intellectual driving force behind the ROM, Charles Trick Currelly, and often helped the ROM in situations when purchases were not approved by the board or funding was not available. In addition, she was one of the founding members of the TAG; she became one of the Ten Friends of the Arts (for the ROM); and she had been appointed to the board of trustees of the ROM.

Sarah T. van Lennep was born in Orange, New Jersey, in 1862. She came from an old colonial family of Dutch descent, which intermingled and intermarried with European nobility. Her grandmother, Adèle Marie von Heidenstam, was the daughter of Gerhard Balthazar von Heidenstam, who served as Swedish ambassador at Constantinople, and Countess Catherine Anne de Hochefried. On her mother's side, she was a descendant of Jonathan Trumbull, who was governor of Connecticut from 1769 to 1784. He had been the only colonial governor who continued his career as state governor when the United States achieved independence. Trumbull was a close friend of George Washington and became famous for his role in feeding Washington's armies. He was also a descendant of John Alden, who was one of the 102 pilgrims who crossed the Atlantic on the *Mayflower* in 1620. The van Lenneps were an established family in New England long before American independence. They claimed Dutch ancestry that reached back to 1330 and produced several politicians, artists, and businessmen who dominated life in New Jersey, Connecticut, and New

York.[41] However, Sarah was not raised by her parents. Her mother died shortly after giving birth to a daughter in March 1865. Her father, Augustus Oscar van Lennep, proved to be incapable, financially and emotionally, of raising his six children. For this reason, Sarah grew up with her aunt in Montclair, New Jersey. Here she received a private education. Her father died in 1883, two years before Sarah married Harry Dorman Warren. They most likely met when Warren studied at Princeton University, from which he graduated in 1878.[42]

Harry D. Warren was just two years older than his wife. He came from a New England family that, in keeping up with its peers, employed genealogists to prove that they too had prominent ancestors. According to the family tree, the Warren family was among the first settlers in Massachusetts. Its first known ancestor in America was Arthur Warren, who was born in Nottingham, England, in 1616 and emigrated to Weymouth, Massachusetts, before 1638. His soon-to-be wife, Mary, was born in Massachusetts in 1617. According to colonial documents, Arthur Warren died in Weymouth in 1658. Genealogical creative research did not stop here, however. The Warren family claimed that it could trace its roots back to Norman times and that the family was related to the ruling houses of both France and England. According to family tradition, ancestors of the Warren family fought in the Battle at Hastings in 1066. "In this conflict one of Duke William's most trusted lieutenants was Comte de Guaren, or the 2nd Earl Warren."[43]

Although his own lineage could not rival her ancestry, he was a very successful businessman. He had been a manager for the Gutta-Percha & Rubber Manufacturing Company in Brooklyn. This firm quickly became a leading producer of all goods made from gutta-percha, a natural plastic extracted from trees in Southeast Asia. It produced industrial belts for machines (conveyer belts), tires for bicycles and automobiles (first solid rubber tires and later pneumatic tires), rubber-lined cotton fire hoses and protective clothing for firemen, shoes, and gloves. During World War I, it manufactured parts for guns and gas masks as well as hospital supplies (rubber gloves, catheters, tubing, and water bottles). It competed with Goodyear Tire & Rubber Co. (founded in 1898) and the Firestone Tire & Rubber Co. (founded in 1900).[44]

Shortly after Sarah married Warren in 1885, they moved to Toronto, where he was put in charge of a new branch.[45] After he discovered that this branch was losing money, he decided to buy the Toronto enterprise with help from his father. Warren quickly transformed the business into "one of the most successful firms in the Canadian tire and rubber business."[46] By 1900 he was one of eleven millionaires in Canada. Conscious of his status as a newcomer to Toronto society, Warren sought integration into its established social circles. Sir Edmund Walker paved the way for his engagement in Toronto's cultural philanthropy, and Warren supported the creation of the ROM.[47] His wife, who has been characterized as a "very liberated woman," shared responsibility for the business with her husband. She was involved in major decisions and thus was prepared to take the helm when her husband died of cancer in March 1909. Her daughter characterized her as "a very feminine executive" who led "gently" and "never pushed."[48] Warren became one of the stockholder-members of the Toronto Housing Company (THC), contributed to the TAG, and dedicated much time and money to the ROM. She supported the Ten Friends of the Arts and bought artifacts for the archaeological collections (among them parts of the Chinese collection, a collection of 300 pieces of rare lace, and a collection of prehistoric bronzes). Currelly said, "Mrs. Warren has been fairy godmother to this museum from the first."[49] Although quieter in her giving than, for instance, Samuel, Warren faced similar problems. She was the only women among the Ten Friends of the Arts, and she was the only woman on the board of trustees for the ROM and the TAG. Her financial support was nevertheless essential to secure the survival of the ROM, and several times she saved the position of Currelly, who had made purchases without the board's approval or who had made promises to buy artifacts without having sufficient funds.

Warren's interest in the ROM was conditioned by her husband's earlier interest in museum philanthropy. She saw her engagement in cultural philanthropy as fulfilling the wishes of her husband. One is tempted to interpret her philanthropic activities as an attempt to enhance her family's social position and not as her own claim to female emancipation. Yet we should remember the description of her as a "strong woman" who knew what she wanted and who was capable of leading a great Canadian company. A look into Warren's social activities might illuminate her social, political, and cultural expectations of women.

Museums were not her only passion. Since she strongly believed in the necessity of educating women, she engaged in the Canadian Girl Guides movement, an outgrowth of the Boy Scout movement. Warren was one of the statutory incorporators of the Canadian Council of the Girl Guides Association. In the early 1920s, this organization boasted 30,000 members. When the first chief commissioner, Lady Pellatt of Casa Loma, died in 1922, Warren took over. She remained chief commissioner for almost twenty years. For her, this organization was to prepare girls for the modern world.[50] For this reason, she insisted, "Health of body and mind is emphasized, and woodcraft is studied by all members of the force. The outdoors life is a boon to all, and the campcraft is extremely useful. Cooking, of course, is studied and practiced thoroughly. In fact, a member of the Girl Guides is a wholesome and helpful woman, neither an angel, nor a vampire, just a lovable, friendly girl—a chum to all the world." Warren proclaimed that she was "in favor of the modern girl's freedom" but was "aware that we must be on our guard, lest it degenerate into licence."[51] As these statements make clear, Warren was no feminist. Although she believed in women's education and in the improvement of women's position in society, she did not advocate granting the right to vote to women.

While she had achieved an extraordinary position of influence in both the economic and social sphere, Warren believed that women did not need direct influence in the political sphere. Women, in her opinion, did not need the right to vote in order to have influence on the political life.[52] Subsequently, Warren founded the Association Opposed to Women's Suffrage in Canada and became its president in June 1914. In defense of her position Warren is said to have argued "that she feels that women will gain nothing in influence by having a vote, while she will gradually lose in some things. Her knowledge of Suffrage States has not demonstrated so far that conditions for the better have been in any way changed by having a vote, in which case, why withdraw women's strength and vitality from the direction in which it is so much needed. Mrs. Warren believes that women will more and more exert influence for good on the life of the country without sacrificing any of their special qualifications, to the physically trying machinery of politics." Her organization was characterized as a small but earnest body of workers who propagated the principle of limited suffrage guided by the idea that "the influence of women in public life brings no signal advantages with it."[53] When women gained the right to vote in Ontario in 1917, however, Warren was the first to embrace it, although she considered it a "casualty of the war."[54]

Warren's thinking on philanthropy and women's right to vote puts into question assumptions that female engagement in charitable and philanthropic projects led to demands for equality between men and women. For Warren, philanthropy offered potentially powerful positions in Toronto's philanthropic elite that provided women with opportunities to exercise power outside the political sphere and to claim dominating positions in the public sphere. Warren left her mark on Toronto's art life as much as contemporary male philanthropists. The financial support for Toronto's major cultural institutions and her board membership provided Warren with a sense of achievement that seemed to be a value in itself. Participation in politics did not offer much to her. Therefore, it might be appropriate to use caution in evaluating the engagement of women in philanthropic projects. One might even be tempted to view women's engagement in philanthropy as an alternative model to feminism. Kathleen McCarthy is certainly right when she claims that museum and charity boards created a countergovernment that gave women power over certain aspects of public life at a time when they were excluded from political life.[55] It is also correct that these institutions provided training grounds for women who later took over political offices.[56] It would, however, be wrong to reduce philanthropic engagement to a stepping-stone in the one-dimensional story of emancipation.

WOMEN AND THE STUDY OF HOUSING REFORM

In 1874, before Ernst Hasse and other housing reformers published their accounts of the dreadful living conditions in German cities (1886), and before Octavia Hill's *Homes of the London Poor* was translated into German (*Aus der Londoner Armenpflege*, 1878), a nearly forgotten female social reformer published the pathbreaking and influential treatise *Die Großstädte in ihrer Wohnungsnoth und die Grundlagen einer durchgreifenden Abhilfe* (The housing crisis in big cities and the basic elements for a solution) in Leipzig.[57] This was the first major book on housing reform published in Germany. It is also an important document in the history of city planning because the author, Arminius, was the first to point out the necessity of "green belts" surrounding city centers. Before the population of German cities exploded and new city quarters changed the cityscapes,[58] Arminius discussed the problems of urban planning, the mixing of socially diverse city populations, and different ways of providing affordable and healthy apartments for working-class families.[59] Arminius's book seems also to be the first German publication that discussed the concept of Philanthropy and 5 Percent and ways in which city governments and the state could participate in the construction of low-income housing. Arminius was the pseudonym chosen by Adelheid Gräfin Ponińska to publish the book she had written by about 1857, nearly twenty years before she found a publisher.[60] It is not absolutely clear what sparked her interest in the housing question. Werner Hegemann and Maja Binder claim that it was the architectural competition for the expansion of Vienna in 1857 that inspired Ponińska to work on a major treatment on the topic of housing reform in German cities.[61]

Adelheid Gräfin zu Dohna-Schlodien was born in 1804 in Kotzenau (Silesia) to an old and noble Silesian family that produced several reform-minded and liberal politicians in the nineteenth century. Both of her brothers, Hermann Dohna (1809–72) and Bernhard Dohna (1817–93), engaged in social reform. Hermann, the heir of the family estate in Kotzenau, was a national-liberal member of the North German and later German parliament from 1867 to 1872 for the district of Liegnitz, Silesia.[62] He developed an interest in the living and working conditions of the working class. In 1847, he published his first book on this topic, *Die freien Arbeiter im Preußischen Staate* (The free workers in the state of Prussia), followed in 1855 by *Das Einkommen des Arbeiters vom nationalökonomischen Standpunkte* (The income of workers from a national-economic point of view). His engagement for the improvement of the conditions of the working class caused his enemies to call him "the red count."[63] One year later, Bernhard Dohna published his *Analyse der socialen Noth* (Analysis of social crisis) in Berlin.[64]

In 1841 Adelheid married Adolph Graf Ponińska (1801–1878), who had inherited from his first marriage two landholdings, Kobilanz and Hreherow, both in Galicia (the Austrian part of Poland). His father, Ignaz Graf Ponińska, was a member of the regional government of Prussian Silesia (Regierungsvizepräsident). He also had landholdings in Siebeneichen and Kreibau. Since Adelheid was already 37, the marriage remained without children. Her husband appears to have supported his wife's interest in social reform, which might explain in part her extensive travels. According to Hegemann, she lived for several years in Vienna and London. In London, she met the leading social reformer of noble background, Lord Shaftesbury, who in 1844 instigated the founding of the Society for Improving the Condition of the Labouring Classes.[65] She was also familiar with the writings and ideas of Victor Aimé Huber, who visited London at about the same time. In 1866, she moved with her husband to Leipzig, where she was listed as an alien subject (Fremder) until 1876. There she put the finishing touches on her manuscript and searched for a publisher. With Duncker & Humblot she found a very well respected publishing house with a reputation in the fields of philosophy, history, and social reform.

In order to be taken seriously, Ponińska asked Theodor Freiherr von der Goltz to write an introduction to her book. He was a famous professor of agricultural policy at the University of Königsberg and a social reformer who was interested in the conditions of rural laborers. He had made a name for himself when he was asked to evaluate an inquiry into the situation of the laboring classes in 1872. Based on the results of this inquiry, Goltz published *Die ländliche Arbeitsfrage und ihre Lösung* (The land laborers crisis and suggestions to its solution), which instantly became a standard work.[66] Although a conservative, Goltz championed the creation of agricultural cooperatives and the establishment of vocational training schools.[67]

In her book, Ponińska discussed the appropriate size and location of housing complexes for working-class families and ways in which to finance healthy and affordable housing. She displayed a comprehensive knowledge of various models of working-class housing in England (Freehold Land Societies, especially the one organized by James Taylor in Birmingham) and France (Société industrielle, organized by Jean Dollfuß). She clearly favored the formation of cooperatives funded by industrialists and the state. Influenced by the working-class housing complex (Arbeiterhäuser) built by the Cité ouvrière in Mühlhausen, Ponińska preferred small houses with attached gardens. Yet she also realized that very few workers would be able to afford such houses and gardens. Therefore, she suggested building working-class settlements outside the big cities. These settlements would be close enough to public transportation lines so that its inhabitants would have easy access to the city and its industrial quarters. Ponińska demanded that city governments should become involved in the housing question on several levels. First, city officials were to collect data on the housing situation of the working classes. Based on this data, they were expected to announce a city planning and architectural competition in order to produce a comprehensive plan for expansion. Based on these plans, city governments would sell land to philanthropic housing companies under the condition that these companies would build affordable and healthy apartment buildings and that they would not increase the rent for their apartments for a certain number of years.[68]

Furthermore, Ponińska advocated that city governments should financially support philanthropic housing companies. She assumed that philanthropic housing companies could pay between 4 and 5 percent interest on invested capital. She suggested that the city government should provide funds equal to 2 percent interest on the invested capital to cover the maintenance costs of these buildings and that it should introduce a luxury tax on the construction of villas and mansions. Financial support for philanthropic housing companies, however, was expected not only from city governments but also from the Prussian state. The state was to provide funding by means of subsidies and interest-free loans as well as by granting exemptions from property taxes. As in the case of the municipal funding, Ponińska suggested introducing a special tax on stockholder companies and a tax on city house and property owners. The latter demand was directed against house owners who had unscrupulously increased the rent for their apartments during the 1840s well above market values (sometimes increasing the rent by as much as 50 percent over the course of several years) and taking advantage of the housing shortage. Ponińska suggested imposing a 25 percent tax on the difference between the original (true market value) rent price and the inflated price later demanded.[69]

In her chapter on philanthropic housing enterprises, Ponińska propagated the Philanthropy and 5 Percent model. She assumed that such housing companies could be expected to pay interest on the invested capital of 4–5 percent. Further, big cities should establish committees and spread the word about the necessity of providing affordable and healthy housing for low-income families. These committees, Ponińska suggested, should publish lists with the names of all wealthy citizens who provided funding to such companies. This publication of names was meant to induce other citizens to follow suit and become involved in the financing of philanthropic housing enterprises.[70]

FEMALE PHILANTHROPY IN SOCIAL HOUSING

Adelheid Gräfin Ponińska's call on wealthy men and women to create philanthropic housing associations echoed similar calls by Carl Wilhelm Hoffmann (Berlin, 1847) and Johann Georg Varrentrapp (Frankfurt, 1860). Her book publication, even though delayed, makes clear that housing reform was not left to men alone. However, the fact that she delayed the publication and that she published it under a very nationalistic pseudonym also reminds us of the limitations imposed on women in the philanthropic world. Women, nevertheless, played a decisive part in the founding and financing of philanthropic housing enterprises on both sides of the Atlantic. Octavia Hill's model of house management included the idea of friendly visits to the tenants by ladies of higher social standing. Following this idea, philanthropic housing projects in the United States and Germany were often administered by "female visitors" who were in charge of rent collection, surveillance of the tenants, and influencing tenants' behavior as well as arranging and canceling rental contracts. However, women not only run such enterprises founded by men like Henry I. Bowditch and Herrmann Julius Meyer; they also founded their own housing trusts and limited dividend companies in which they invited women and men to participate. By 1912, Bernard Newman, the secretary of the Philadelphia Housing Association, found "that women were intimately involved with all aspects of contemporary housing activities: management, research, and lobbying. In the *American City Magazine,* an influential journal of municipal affairs, Newman observed, 'So numerous and so regular are the reports of their work, that the conviction that women are playing an important part in this movement for social betterment is a legitimate one.'" Based on this observation, Birch and Gardner conclude: "Women's activities were no longer limited to teaching domestic skills or to investing in limited dividend companies. Instead, as the years passed, the work of women such as Edith Elmer Wood and Catherine Bauer brought women from the social-worker tradition of the philanthropists to new roles as policy makers, planners, designers, and administrators."[71] Limited dividend housing companies in particular allowed for a larger number of women to participate, since the financial contribution was limited and the companies required the participation of a large number of philanthropists.

As table 4.2 shows, women represented between a quarter and half of the stockholders of social housing companies. These women were not token members but

Table 4.2   Share of women in social housing associations

Housing company	Total stockholders	Female stockholders
Boston Co-operative Building Company	163	58 (35.6%)
City and Suburban Homes Company in New York	410	? (about 50%)[a]
Toronto Housing Company	151	38 (25.2%)
Verein Ostheim (Leipzig)	115	39 (33.9%)

SOURCES: "The Ontario Plan," first annual report of the Toronto Housing Company, Limited, 1913, 23–24, City of Toronto Archives, Better Housing in Canada; Stadtarchiv Leipzig Kap. 35 Nr. 748, Geschäftsbericht des Vereins Ostheim Leipzig für das Jahr 1904 (Leipzig 1905), 3–6; *The First Annual Report of the Boston Co-operative Building Company with the Act of Incorporation and By-Laws* (Boston, 1872), 3–4, 10, 16–17; Eugenie Ladner Birch and Deborah S. Gardner, "The Seven-Percent Solution: A Review of Philanthropic Housing, 1870–1910," *Journal of Urban History* 7, no. 4 (August 1981): 422; *First Annual Report of the City and Suburban Homes Company* (New York, May 17, 1897), 1; Riis, *The Battle with the Slum,* 128–29.

[a] Based on Birch and Gardner, "The Seven-Percent Solution," 422. A list of stockholders of this company could not be found.

FIGURE 4.1. Therese Rossbach, from the 1931 booklet
*Erinnerungen an die Entstehung und Schicksale
von Arvedshof.* Courtesy of Ortrud Woerner-Heil.

occupied important positions within these enterprises. In the Act of Incorporation
of the Boston Co-operative Building Company (BCBC), for instance, the company
was represented by two men (William Gray and Henry B. Rogers) and two women
(Abby W. May and Anna Cabot Lodge). Gray was chosen as president of the BCBC,
but nine of the nineteen directors were female, and women held the positions of
secretary and treasurer.[72] Wealthy Bostonian women, independent of their marital
status, not only financially supported this social housing company; they also ran it.

This Boston company was certainly not an exception. The Toronto Housing
Company and the Leipzig social housing association Ostheim had an equally high
share of female stockholders. The Ostheim board of directors included seven women
and nine men. The Ostheim owed its existence to one woman: Therese Rossbach,
who donated the land needed for the housing project.[73] Further, women proved
essential for the financial support of this institution. The Ostheim was funded in
three ways: (1) an annual contribution of at least 20 marks, (2) a donation of at
least 1,000 marks, or (3) the purchase of a share for 2,000 marks. While nineteen

women bought shares or made donations totaling 201,000 marks, twenty-seven men contributed together only 189,000 marks. Simply, women played a larger role in the financing of the Ostheim than men. The largest contribution, 100,000 marks, was made by Therese Rossbach, whereas the largest contribution by a man was only 40,000 marks. Of equal importance, the three-tiered financing scheme was linked to voting privileges among the members: (1) those who contributed an annual amount of at least 20 marks were entitled to one vote; (2) those who chose to donate money were given one vote for every 1,000 marks donated, up to a maximum of ten votes; (3) and those who bought shares for 2,000 marks were given a vote for each share, up to a maximum of ten votes. This meant that the women involved (in 1904) had 72 votes, while men had 125 votes. Given the higher financial involvement of women (over 50 percent of donations and shares sold), this voting system was unjust (37 percent representation for ca. 52 percent financial contributions). However, it did give women a slightly higher representation within the ranks of the association than would have been accorded if voting privileges had been based on a purely democratic scheme of one vote per person (37 percent compared with 30 percent).[74]

Women were extremely active in Leipzig's philanthropic housing projects between the 1880s and World War I. Three out of seven Leipzig philanthropic housing enterprises were founded and to a large degree financed by women.[75] Many more women participated in the social housing projects of Gustav de Liagre and Therese Rossbach. After her involvement with the social housing project of Gustav de Liagre, Emma Hasse established her own housing enterprise, which closely followed Octavia Hill's enterprise in London.

Emma Hasse, née Gottschald, was born in 1852 into a wealthy merchant family. Her father, Julius Gottschald, was one of Leipzig's eminent merchants, and he owned a summer mansion in Gohlis, a pleasant and exclusive neighborhood to the north of the old Leipzig city center. In September 1875, Emma, who had just turned 23, married Ernst Hasse, 29, who was appointed director of the statistical office of the city of Leipzig in April of the same year. In short succession, Emma gave birth to three children.[76] Encouraged by her husband, who was a major force in the social discourse on housing reform, she participated in 1883 in Gustav de Liagre's social housing project, which was inspired by Octavia Hill's ideas regarding the housing of the lower classes. When her father died in May 1884, she and her husband moved out of Leipzig to live in his summer mansion. Gottschald had left a small fortune to his daughter, who intended to use part of it to provide social housing in her new hometown of Gohlis.[77]

In early 1888, Ernst Hasse wrote to the Gohlis city council, announcing that his wife intended to found a social housing enterprise either on her own or (following in the footsteps of Liagre) in collaboration with a group of philanthropists. Emma Hasse envisioned this project not as a business venture but as a *gemeinnütziges Unternehmen* (an enterprise for the common good) that would provide affordable small apartments for widows and poor families. The renters would not be permitted to sublet rooms of their apartments, and the rent was to be collected on a weekly basis.[78] In a second letter, Hasse said that the rent was to guarantee a certain limited return on the capital invested in this housing enterprise. However, he did not expect that this return would be paid to the investor(s) but used for the maintenance and expansion of this enterprise. Inspired by Herrmann Julius Meyer and Max Pommer's plan for the Lindenau settlement of Meyer's housing trust, each tenant would also have a small garden plot.[79] When Elgin Gould visited Leipzig, two of the three buildings had been built and 109 gardens had been laid out. The rent for the apartments varied from 96 to 220 marks ($22.85 to $52.36) per year plus 5 to 15 marks ($1.19 to $3.57) for the garden. Emma Hasse and some lady visitors were in charge of collecting the rent and giving advice to the renters with regard to the maintenance of the apartment and social life.[80]

While Emma Hasse's housing enterprise was, because of its character as a limited dividend company, of limited existence,[81] Hedwig von Holstein intended to create a housing trust for perpetuity. As the daughter of Julius Salomon (1779–1851), a wealthy and influential merchant and landholder in Leipzig as well as an eminent member of the city government, Hedwig grew up in a very privileged environment. She learned French and English and took piano lessons. She attended concerts at the Gewandhaus and at her sister's musical salon and thereby became friends with a fellow piano student, Franz von Holstein (1826–78). Holstein came from an old noble family with a long tradition of military service. Although he followed the wishes of his father and entered the military academy in Braunschweig in 1841, he studied music and even composed an opera. Eventually he was able to convince his father that he belonged not in the army but in the concert hall. After some soul-searching, his father allowed him to enter the famous Conservatory of Leipzig. However, the stipend that he gave Franz was small. Hedwig asked her mother to provide the necessary fellowship for Franz to finish his education. In September 1855, Hedwig and Franz married. This union provided Franz with sufficient funding for a career as a composer, but he died of stomach cancer in 1878 at age 52.[82]

The death of her husband caused Hedwig von Holstein to consider her place in life and her engagement in Leipzig's society. The death of her parents a few years earlier had also put her in a situation of possessing wealth beyond her needs. Her mother and her husband, however, had both charged her with the task of creating social foundations. Franz encouraged her to create a foundation that would provide boarding and fellowships annually to seven poor and talented students of the conservatory (Holsteinstift). Hedwig created a home for seven students in a new house in her backyard. The conservatory waved the tuition for all seven students, and the Holstein trust provided a fellowship of 600 marks to each student. One year after her husband had died, in February 1879, Hedwig welcomed the first seven fellows (she called them the "seven ravens," and she considered herself their "raven mother").[83]

Her mother, who had died in 1876, had created a foundation for the poor but left it to her daughter to decide the specifics.[84] When her sister died in September 1888, Hedwig was put in charge of arranging for the philanthropic use of her sister's money. Part was to go to the communal office for poor relief in Leipzig (about 12,000 marks), another part was to be used for the construction of a hospital in Alt-Aussee, and the last part was a financial contribution (bonds and shares) that went to the Holsteinstift and the Salomon Stift.[85] She then decided to create a housing trust like the Fuggerei in Augsburg that would last for centuries and produce a sufficient amount of capital to expand over time.[86] In 1877, she had bought property in Reudnitz, a suburb to the east of Leipzig. Here she had financed the construction of three small buildings that provided apartments for fifteen families and a small number of single women. In addition, each renter received a small garden plot. In 1889, now in the possession of larger financial means, Holstein decided to transform this settlement project into a housing trust. She appointed a board of trustees (six men) and registered the trust fund with the authorities. She named the trust Salomon Stift in honor of her father.[87] Among the trustees were the eminent architect Arwed Rossbach (1844–1902) and the Protestant theologian Georg Rietschel.

Rossbach's involvement with this social housing enterprise as trustee and as architect points to the interconnected nature of local philanthropic cultures. After the construction of Holstein's housing trust was finished, Rossbach's wife (with her husband as chief architect) founded the Ostheim. One of the annual donors to the Ostheim was the architect Max Pommer, who was responsible for the construction of Meyer's housing trust, which preceded Hedwig von Holstein's project and may have influenced her decision how best to serve the needs of the poor.

In 1890 Rossbach applied for a building permit with the city council of Leipzig. In his letter to the city council, Rossbach outlined the goals and principles of Holstein's housing trust, which was to provide hygienic and affordable apartments for people who fell on hard times without having been responsible for it ("unverschuldet in mißliche Verhältnisse gerathene Familien und einzelne Personen"). In addition, inspired by Hill's house management system, Holstein and her support staff (friendly lady visitors) were to provide moral support and guidance for these individuals. Although the rent for each apartment was to be as low as possible, it was still expected that it would provide a certain return on the invested capital that was to be used for the maintenance and future expansion of the trust. Rossbach's plan envisioned the construction of five buildings (three apartment buildings, one chapel, and one laundry building). Each building was to be built five stories high and contain four apartments on each level. The apartments consisted of one hallway, one kitchen, and two rooms. The five buildings were to be built around an open green space.[88] The apartments were built between 1891 and 1900 and offered space for about 140 families.[89] Holstein's hope that her foundation would last for centuries was not fulfilled, although it survived the inflation and the Nazi dictatorship and even continued as an independent housing enterprise until 1979—after private enterprises had been nationalized in the early 1970s by East Germany's communist government.[90]

FEMALE PHILANTHROPY AND NATIONALISM

On June 1, 1898, Therese Rossbach informed the city council of Leipzig that she had purchased a plot of land in the eastern suburb of Leipzig, Sellerhausen, to provide affordable and hygienic apartments for lower-class families. Since the construction costs were estimated at 300,000 marks and Rossbach was able to contribute about 100,000 marks, she planned to establish a limited dividend company that would guarantee a 3 percent return on the invested capital. She also hoped that the city government would provide some additional funding toward the preparation of the surroundings of this new settlement. Rossbach asked specifically that the city cover the costs for sewage, street, and sidewalk construction.[91] The reaction of the city government is not preserved in the city's archive. However, on August 3, 1898, Arwed Rossbach petitioned the city again for a building permit. Between June 1 and August 3, Therese Rossbach founded the Verein Ostheim, which attracted a large number of wealthy Leipzigers who were interested in housing reform and wanted to contribute smaller amounts. In his letter to the city council, Arwed Rossbach now posed as the director of this association. His petition was quickly approved, and the construction of the first apartment buildings began in September 1898.[92]

It is possible that the first letter of Therese Rossbach did not receive the attention of the city council because it was written by a woman. It is tempting to interpret the existence of these two letters by Therese and Arwed Rossbach as a sign of sexual discrimination. In the case of the social housing enterprise of Emma Hasse, the petition to the city council was signed by her husband (first line), Professor Ernst Hasse, and herself (second line).[93] Most of the official correspondence bears the signature of Ernst Hasse and not that of his wife. However, in the case of Hasse, at least both seemed to be interested in housing reform. Hasse made a name for himself through his many publications on the housing problem of the lower classes. Arwed Rossbach, although involved in the construction of the apartment buildings for the Salomon Stift and the Verein Ostheim, did not write any text on social housing. In contrast to Max Pommer, the architect of Meyer's housing trust, Rossbach was not involved in the discussions of the financial and social setup of the Salomon Stift and the Ostheim settlement. Furthermore, Rossbach's career as an architect was focused not on social housing but on administrative, commercial, and religious buildings. Social housing, to Rossbach, was just a secondary outcome of his architectural work.[94]

Therese Rossbach was born into a well-off civil servant family in Berlin in 1861.[95] Her parents lived comfortably and engaged in charity. Since Therese was their only daughter, Johanna Sembritzky decided to open her home to fourteen orphans. Sembritzky insisted on educating girls and demanded that every woman should receive at least one year of training in homemaking and child care. She also advocated free access to all professions and university training for talented women. And she fought for equality between women and men, the consultation of women in all social, economic, and political decisions, and the right for women to vote. Johanna Sembritzky championed a reform of how women dressed, opposing the corset because it endangered women's health. She also advocated vegetarianism. When she died in 1884, she left six orphans, ages 2 to 8, for Therese to rear.[96] In 1891, Therese married Arwed Rossbach, who had lost his first wife four years earlier.[97]

Therese Rossbach was 30 when she got married and was incapable of having her own children. She lived as a Prussian among Saxons in a city entirely alien to her and longed for a vocation after her adopted children finally left home. She soon discovered Hill's *Aus der Londoner Armenpflege* and decided that she wanted to engage in housing reform. Endowed with sufficient financial support from her parents, Therese Rossbach bought the necessary land for the construction of working-class homes, provided 100,000 marks, and, probably under the influence of Gustav de Liagre's housing enterprise, created the Verein Ostheim in 1898.

Her engagement in philanthropy filled a void in her life and provided a means of integration into a new urban environment and into Leipzig's leisure class. Moving from Berlin to Leipzig was not simply a change of place. Over the centuries,

Prussia and Saxony had emerged as rival states with different lifestyles, worldviews, and cultures. Their people were separated by language and attitudes.[98] One can only imagine what it must have meant for Therese Rossbach to move from the capital of Prussia and Germany to the more regional but multicultural setting of Leipzig. Because of its semiannual fairs, Leipzig had emerged as an international center of commerce at the heart of Europe. Twice a year, the city would be transformed into a meeting place of buyers and sellers from all over the world. The Leipzig fairs made the city a world renowned metropolis and left a mark on its people.[99]

The Verein Ostheim was formed as a limited dividend company with the goal of providing affordable and hygienic apartments for working-class families with many children. This enterprise quickly received the support of the "first families" of Leipzig's High Society. Leipzig's publishers were represented by Hans Heinrich Reclam and Fritz Baedecker, the university by Hermann Bernhard Arthur Prüfer (professor of music), Rudolf Sohn (professor of law), and Julius Cohnheim (professor of medicine), the Reichsgericht (Imperial Court) by Senatspräsident Georg Otto Freiesleben and Reichsgerichtsrat Braunbehrens, and the banking sector by Oskar Meyer and Friedrich Nachod. While the majority of the Ostheim members and trustees certainly came from the city's Lutheran-Protestant establishment, there was also a small but significant number of members who belonged to the Jewish community (Cohnheim, Nachod, and Meyer) and the Reformed Church (publishers Georg Theodor Salomon Hirzel and Arnold Hirt).

Friedrich Nachod (1853–1911), whose father was the head of Leipzig's Jewish community, supported the Verein Ostheim from its inception and was even chosen as the director of its board. It was his responsibility to represent the Verein Ostheim in negotiations with the city government and other businesses. After Arwed Rossbach's death and after Therese Rossbach had left Leipzig, Nachod took over full responsibility for this enterprise.[100] His father, Jacob Nachod (1784–1882), was in charge of the Leipzig bank and trade company Knauth, Nachod & Kühne, which was involved in the export and import business with North America and functioned as an international bank that extended credit to American and German merchants. In 1844 Nachod created the Gesellschaft der Freunde (Society of Friends) as the precursor to the Jewish community of Leipzig, which was founded in 1846. From 1877 onwards, Jacob Nachod served as the head of Leipzig's Jewish community. His wealth—estimated at 2 million marks—enabled him to create several intrareligious foundations and charities.[101] After Jews in Saxony gained the right to vote in 1849, Nachod became Leipzig's first Jewish member of the city parliament in 1853.[102]

Friedrich Nachod, Oskar Meyer, and Mrs. Julius Cohnheim served on the board of the Verein Ostheim. Like Nachod, Meyer (1849–1925) was the co-owner of a traditional Leipzig banking house, Meyer & Co. He was elected member of city parliament from 1897 to 1906 and a member of the city council from 1906 to 1925. In contrast to Nachod, however, Meyer had been invited to become a member of the exclusive Gesellschaft Harmonie in 1872. Marta Cohnheim, née Lewald, was the wife of the eminent pathologist Julius Cohnheim (1839–84), who died at the age of 45 in Leipzig. These three Jewish members of the board were accompanied by one board member who belonged to the Reformed Church, a Protestant sect that had been founded by Huldrych Zwingli and Johannes Calvin in Switzerland. Georg Theodor Salomon Hirzel (1867–?) came from a family of Reformed immigrants from Switzerland. His father, Salomon Hirzel, had founded the Hirzel publishing house in Leipzig in 1853. This means that four of the seventeen board members belonged to religious minorities.

In 1912, Charles de Liagre (1862–?), a Catholic, joined the board of the Verein Ostheim and thus expanded its religious diversity. He was the nephew of the Leipzig housing reformer Gustav de Liagre. His father, Albert de Liagre, had been the head of Leipzig's Catholic community and one of the founders of the Vincentius Verein, a charitable Catholic association. He was elected to be the treasurer of this association in 1855 and continued to serve in this function until 1888. One year later, Charles replaced him as treasurer.[103] His mother was Anna Marie Samson, the daughter of Hermann Samson (1804–65), who was the head of the Jewish community between 1847 and 1856.[104] Before she married in October 1858, she converted to Catholicism.[105]

Therese Rossbach was not the only one new to Leipzig's High Society. Several of the members who donated 1,000 marks or more were not born in Leipzig but had moved to this city mostly for professional reasons. There were the members of the Reichsgericht such as Freiesleben who was born in Dresden, publishers such as Hirt who came from Breslau and Baedecker who was from Koblenz, and law professor Rudolf Sohn who grew up in Rostock. It should not be forgotten that this was a time of great regional mobility and urbanization. These newcomers intermingled with old Leipzigers such as Hans Heinrich Reclam, Hermann Bernhard Arthur Prüfer, and Heinrich Schomburgk. Probably because of the reputation of Arwed Rossbach, the Verein Ostheim became a place of social contact and intermingling between newcomers and established families.

Arwed Rossbach was born in Plauen, but advanced quickly to a respected position among Leipzig's first families as an architect. He was responsible for the construction of several villas for Leipzig's rich and several buildings for the city's university, which received praise beyond local and regional borders. In 1892, Rossbach was even made city councilor.[106] The twenty-seven male members of the Verein Ostheim, who donated more than 1,000 marks each, belonged to the same generation as Rossbach, who was born in 1844. Nearly all of these men were born during the 1830s and 1840s. Half of them held memberships in the Gesellschaft Harmonie, one of the most prominent associations for Leipzig's mercantile and educated elites. Founded in the winter of 1775–76, this society dominated Leipzig's public life. Its members were to be found in all of the city's social and cultural endeavors. Being accepted as a member in this socially exclusive society represented the first step toward integration into Leipzig's leisure class.[107]

In addition, the reputation of her husband as a leading architect and Therese Rossbach's plans for housing reform brought recognition and approval from Leipzig's social reformer caste. Gustav de Liagre, who introduced Hill's ideas to Leipzig, Emma Hasse, who had founded her own social housing enterprise, and Pommer, the architect of Meyer's housing trust could be found among the members of the Ostheim.[108] Although their financial contribution (20 marks annually) was marginal, their symbolic membership was of much higher importance because it represented their support publicly. With this gesture, Rossbach received the "seal of approval" from Leipzig's philanthropic elite.

The members of the Ostheim contributed about 400,000 marks to the construction of nineteen apartment buildings with sixteen to twenty apartments each. It has already been pointed out that more than half of this amount derived from female philanthropists, with Therese Rossbach contributing 100,000 marks and the necessary plot of land. In addition to the provision of affordable housing for working-class families, Therese Rossbach insisted on the establishment of a credit union and the provision of child care for the tenants (Kindergarten). In contrast to Meyer's housing trust, for which it was decreed that only families with less than three children would be admitted as tenants, Therese Rossbach insisted that the Ostheim would provide apartments for families with larger numbers of children. In 1905, 336 families were living in the Ostheim. Among the 2,060 tenants were 455 children under the age of 6, 707 children between the age of 6 and 14, and 226 children who had finished school but still lived with their parents. On average, each family had four children. In her autobiographical notes, Therese Rossbach mentioned, however, that there was even one couple with thirteen children living in the Ostheim.[109]

The Ostheim was created according to the concept of Philanthropy and 5 Percent and employed Hill's house management system. Inspired by the idea of friendly visiting, Therese Rossbach assigned each house to one lady of higher social standing. Many, but not all, had contributed money to the enterprise. They were the wives and daughters of judges at the Reichsgericht and university professors. These women collected the rent each Monday and used this opportunity to evaluate the maintenance of the apartments.[110] The Ostheim was a form of collective philanthropy like its counterparts in London (Improved Industrial Dwellings Company) and New York (City and Suburban Homes Company). However, the financing scheme of the Ostheim deviated significantly from these stock companies. While all these limited dividend companies were founded with the idea of guaranteeing a steady return (in the case of the Ostheim 3 percent) on the invested capital, the financial contributions to the Ostheim could not be considered shares. Philanthropists were invited to contribute annually at least 20 marks or donate at least 1,000 marks or purchase a share for 2,000 marks. Shareholders could neither sell their shares nor withdraw their stake in this enterprise.[111] While this provision provided absolute financial security for the Ostheim, the shareholders received an annual profit on their invested capital. The Ostheim thus provides another Germanized version of the Philanthropy and 5 Percent concept, which limited market forces even further by restricting access to the invested capital.

However, as the example of the Boston Co-operative Building Company (BCBC) shows, philanthropists who invested their capital in limited dividend companies rarely sold or withdrew their stocks. Often these shares were handed down from one generation to the next. The shareholders of the BCBC were originally promised a 7 percent return on their investment. This came true only between 1871 and 1875. Between 1876 and 1889, dividends were stopped or reduced to 3 percent and earnings were invested. In the 1890s, dividends reached between 5 and 6 percent.[112] It is telling that despite these lower returns the investors maintained their involvement. Obviously, making money was not their main concern. This point is confirmed by the fact that unlike a truly capitalist and free-market company, the stockholders in this philanthropic company never sold their shares.

In the case of the BCBC, shares were transferable but not available for purchase or sale.[113] Further, there is clear evidence that 44 percent of the shares were passed on from the original stockholder to trustees (through last wills and testaments).[114] There was a tacit agreement (and in the case of the Ostheim, a written contract) that the shareholder agreed never to withdraw their support, regardless of the financial success of the venture.

Limited dividend companies were founded with the intent of proving that the provision of social welfare—affordable and hygienic housing—could be achieved with limited but nevertheless market mechanisms. These companies were to set an example for how philanthropy could be aligned with profit. Waterlow, Bowditch, Liagre, and other housing reformers saw their enterprises as models that were to induce imitation and attract businessmen who would invest money not because they were necessarily interested in philanthropy but because they recognized that the limited dividend companies offered a steady return. Philanthropy and 5 Percent was intended to bridge the business world and the philanthropic world. However, as we have already seen, shares were bought mostly by philanthropists who were more interested in helping the poor and less in making a profit. The decision of wealthy men and women who had purchased shares in limited dividend companies to hold onto these shares regardless of the return was in clear contradiction to the original intention of the housing companies' founders. The shareholders transformed these limited dividend companies into much more philanthropic institutions than their founders intended. By considering their shares to be donations and not profitable investments, the shareholders prevented the limited dividend companies from becoming viable capitalist projects that would spark imitation among capitalists. One is tempted to argue that they defeated their own purpose because they were successful only among a limited group of men and women already engaged in philanthropy.

After her husband died in 1902, Therese Rossbach pulled back from the Verein Ostheim. Although she remained on its board, she did not take over the position of director. Instead, Nachod followed Arwed Rossbach as director and represented the Ostheim in all matters. Because of the loss of her husband, the only reason why she had moved to Leipzig just ten years earlier, Rossbach lost interest in the Verein Ostheim. According to the statutes of the Ostheim, land and property were to be transferred to the city in the event that the association was dissolved by its members. In 1918, Rossbach decided to transfer her housing enterprise into municipal ownership. Seven years later, in May 1925, the city of Leipzig assumed the legal ownership of this housing project.[115] In the meantime, Rossbach searched for a new occupation within the field of social work and became interested in poor orphans and illegitimate children living on Leipzig's streets. In this context, she learned about Dr. Thomas John Barnardo's work among poor children in London.

During the 1870s and 1880s, Barnardo had created several homes for poor girls and boys in London, Ilford, and Baby-Castle. Barnardo's Village Home for Girls, founded in 1870, was the most impressive of his settlements. Around 1900, it contained forty to fifty cottages, a church, a school, and several buildings for the professional training of girls (shops and craftsmen shops). About twenty children between the age of 4 and 18 lived together with a female caretaker ("mother") in one of the cottages. In 1902, there were more than 1,000 girls living in this

complex. The younger girls attended the schools, and the older girls were introduced to home economy, since all girls living in this village were trained to become
servants. When Rossbach learned about Barnardo's work, she immediately wrote
him a letter asking his permission to study his projects and to work with his staff.
Barnardo invited her to join his enterprise, and Therese Rossbach went to London, where she lived for some time with a Mrs. Soltau, who was one of Barnardo's
secretaries. During this time, Rossbach was introduced to the different parts of
Barnardo's youth project, of which she gives a detailed account in her unpublished
autobiography written around 1920.[116] While in London, Rossbach also visited
horticultural schools for girls.

Rossbach considered establishing a similar institution for girls in Germany.
She learned about Ida von Kortzfleisch's concept of women education in the rural
setting (wirtschaftliche Frauen-Hochschule).[117] Rossbach visited Kortzfleisch at her
women's school in Reifenstein and was immensely impressed by this undertaking
and by Kortzfleisch. She discussed her own ideas with Kortzfleisch who strongly
recommended that she try to establish a similar school in Saxony. In 1904, Rossbach
purchased an estate in Elbisbach for 140,000 marks. There she established a girls'
school modeled after the Reifensteiner school. This estate, renamed Arvedshof after
Rossbach's husband, was opened in 1906. The school's purpose was to train girls
and women between the ages of 18 and 40 for one year in home economics and in
agricultural practices. Yet the one-year training program also included chemistry,
physics, health care education, botany, and bookkeeping. After one year of training,
the students were able to either work as teachers of home and agricultural economics
or as servants in households or on agricultural estates.[118]

FIGURE 4.2. Arvedshof. Courtesy of Ortrud Woerner-Heil.

In 1913, Rossbach added a home for babies and small children, giving her students the opportunity to receive child care training. In 1924, she finally decided to sell her school to the state of Saxony. Already in 1918, Rossbach had bought property in Sellin on the island of Rügen, where she opened an asylum for home-less children (Villa Heimkehr) that she headed for several decades before she died in 1953.[119]

Philanthropy dominated Therese Rossbach's entire life. Introduced to social work and the fight for women's rights by her mother, Rossbach engaged in dif-ferent fields and different forms of philanthropy. She was involved in the care of orphans, and she organized a limited dividend housing company, a school of house and agricultural economics for girls, and an asylum for homeless children. In the case of Therese Rossbach, philanthropy worked as a means of integration on very different levels. First, it helped her to find a place in society when she moved from Berlin to Leipzig. Second, her philanthropy helped women and children to find their own places in society. She provided homes for children, and she organized female education so that women could claim their rightful places beside and not behind men. Born in the Wilhelmine Empire and raised in a male-dominated soci-ety, Rossbach considered raising children and doing housework important female tasks. She recognized, however, the necessity of education for women, and her school in Arvedshof provided more than just home economics. Her philanthropic engagement spanned several political regimes: from the Wilhelmine Empire to the German Democratic Republic. The tenets of Rossbach's philanthropic credo included helping the poor, encouraging and empowering women, and providing adequate care and education for children.

In an interview given in 1915 to the journal *Die Gutsfrau,* Rossbach reflected upon her philanthropic work and spoke about her future plans. She considered the Ostheim and the school in Arvedshof just steps toward her life-defining achieve-ment. Rossbach was convinced that education and betterment of individuals could happen only outside the big cities. She envisioned the creation of homes for small children in rural areas where children would grow up under her guidance, pro-tected from the negative influences of modern society. From an early age, these children were to learn how to work the land and how to take care of animals. Older children were expected to care for the younger ones so that they would develop a feeling of community. Rossbach wanted to provide an environment similar to the family, in which she would play the role of "mother." Since there was a shortage on seasonal workers in the rural areas of Prussia and Saxony, Rossbach hoped to train "her" children to become agricultural workers. These workers were to replace Pol-ish seasonal workers who came to help German farmers in times of planting and harvest. Rossbach was concerned about this influx of "alien forcers." She contended that there were "German streets" in some Polish villages that were labeled "Ger-man" because they had been built with German money earned by Polish *Schnitter* (workers who helped in the harvest) in Germany. Rossbach suggested that this money should remain inside Germany and be used to pay the wages of German agricultural workers. During the winter, when there was no work available for agricultural workers, the young men and women were to return to the homes cre-ated by Rossbach where they would be employed as linecrafts- and tradespeople. Basket weaving, carpentry, and masonry were to provide sufficient opportunities to make a living during these months. Young couples would be encouraged to marry and to build their own homes during the winter months.[120]

Jean Quartaert has already shown how female philanthropy became intertwined with patriotism and the creation of national identities. The case of Therese Rossbach highlights another aspect of the close relationship between philanthropy and national identity. Rossbach envisioned philanthropy as the basis for the creation of a better and "purer" German society. Philanthropy, in this case, was limited to German children and thus served to delineate German nationals from Polish nationals. One is tempted to see in Rossbach's vision a reflection of racial thinking and a foreshadowing of Nazi racial thinking. Her support and encouragement for families with more than three children runs counter to the mind-set of other social reformers of her time. Having one to three children was seen as desirable among social housing reformers. In the case of Meyer's housing trust, having "too many children" was even a cause for losing one's apartment. Does her emphasis on families with large numbers of children preempt Nazi population policies? Rossbach expected philanthropy to provide the basis for the transformation of Germany's economic and social system. Facing a constant decline of the birthrate for economic, social, and military reasons, Rossbach joined the group of conservative intellectuals who considered the increase of the birthrate and family size necessary for the survival of German society.[121] Nevertheless, Rossbach also shared ideas about the reform of education that had their roots in the late eighteenth century. According to her belief, a true and moral education of future generations of Germans could happen only far away from the morally destructive influences of modern society. Education, in her opinion, was to provide the basis for a renewed Germany.

CHAPTER FIVE

Giving for Good:
Philanthropy and Religion

The concept of charity is as old as human civilization and has become a mainstay of all three major monotheistic religions. As Kathleen Woodroofe has pointed out, however, "Ideas of philanthropy have varied at different times, for although the giving a man does is personal, it is influenced, not only by the size of his pocket, but by the gods he worships, the tribe to which he belongs, and the form of government under which he lives."[1] While the religious foundation of charity cannot be doubted, its repercussions for the nineteenth-century practice of dispersing social welfare as well as its function for the self-definition and formation of elite groups have still to be investigated. Reflecting on the German experience, Derek Penslar has pointed out that "traditionally, the churches and communities were the pillars of philanthropic activity." This resulted in the creation of separate religiously defined spheres of social welfare, in which Jewish welfare organizations provided welfare to the Jewish poor and needy, while Catholic social welfare organizations provided welfare to the Catholic poor and needy.[2] For the case of Toronto, Stephen A. Speisman contended:

> Torontonians in the early decades of the nineteenth century desired to fulfill their responsibilities toward their unfortunate fellow citizens and to do so as a religious community. In fact, prior to 1900, the very religious character of Toronto militated against the assumption of social welfare responsibilities by the city government. For one thing, the dispensing of "charity" was considered a purely religious function, and so the absence of a strong church-state connection in Upper Canada freed government at all levels from this task.[3]

Since Toronto was home to several religious communities (Catholics and Jews among the dominant Methodists), each of these groups created its own welfare service system, thus duplicating charitable and philanthropic institutions. Jewish philanthropic associations, for instance, were founded between 1850 and 1880 and centered around the synagogue. The founding of the Toronto Hebrew Ladies' Sick and Benevolent Society gave Jewish philanthropy a better organized and expanded form.[4] This duplication of philanthropic structures served not to integrate different religious groups into society but to keep them apart and thus strengthened religious and ethnic boundaries as well as social segregation. Comparing Jewish welfare in Manchester and Hamburg in the second half of the nineteenth century, Rainer Liedtke concluded that the existence of a separate Jewish welfare system, which "both in quantity and quality . . . had no equivalent in what other denominations offered 'their poor,'" represented a major factor in the "preservation and re-definition of a post-emancipation Jewish identity." Facing the challenge of an increasingly secularized society, Liedtke, whose interpretation reflects David Sorkin's concept of Jewish identity and a German-Jewish subculture, shows that "non-religious associations assumed the prime role in the preservation of Jewishness."[5] For his part, Penslar suggested that philanthropic activity "did not merely affirm Jewish identity but actually defined it." He further suggests that "Jewish welfare work, then, was more than the latest manifestation of the Jewish charitable tradition or the assertion of Jewish identity through social action. It was also a response to what was perceived as a very real problem, a uniquely Jewish variant of the 'social problem' that so worried the citizens of Imperial Germany."[6]

Comparing nineteenth-century Jewish philanthropy in the United States and Germany, Tobias Brinkmann showed that although Jewish philanthropy defined the Jewish community in both countries, it "did not lead to separation but rather increasing integration" in the United States because of the collaboration between members of different religions. Chicago's Jewish hospital, for instance, was financed by Jews and Christians. And although Jewish businessmen provided most of the necessary funding, German associations with a predominantly Christian membership contributed their share. While Brinkmann does not clearly identify how much of the total construction costs of $25,286 came from Christian supporters and how much from Jewish donors, he concludes that "almost all Jewish philanthropy projects in Chicago were explicitly supra-religious and thus accessible to non-Jews."[7] In contrast, Jacob Rader Marcus, pointing to the case of the Christian Hospital in Kansas City, observed that although a Jew was elected vice president of the new hospital and although Jewish philanthropists contributed large amounts to this project, "at the dedication no Son of Israel was invited to participate and for many years no Jewish physicians were tolerated on its staff."[8] Clearly, even in the case of the United States, religious fault lines emerged between various philanthropic establishments. These fault lines went through philanthropic activities and associational life.[9]

The creation of religiously defined and limited social welfare systems kept apart the philanthropists as well as the recipients of aid. Further, elites were divided not only along the lines of economic success and social status but also along religious and ethnic lines. The conflict between various factions of the leisure class thus also includes conflicts between Protestants, Catholics, and Jews over recognition from and admission to the leading circles of society. Participation in major philanthropic projects was hotly contested among potential philanthropists. Not everyone was invited to contribute to museums and art galleries. Wealthy Jews in Toronto, for instance, were excluded from philanthropic projects of Toronto's leisure class such as the Toronto Art Gallery, the Toronto General Hospital, and the Royal Ontario Museum until World War I. And even during the 1920s, only a handful of Jewish philanthropists were invited to participate in these projects.[10] And while Boston's Irish-Catholic population succeeded in claiming political dominance during the 1880s, it remained completely excluded from Boston's philanthropic establishment, which seemed to envision its philanthropic institutions as a form of cultural countergovernment. To nineteenth-century philanthropists, philanthropy meant more than just giving to social and cultural public institutions; it was seen as a socioeconomic tool that empowered individuals to claim power in the public sphere and to participate in the domination of urban societies.[11]

Boston and Toronto's philanthropic experience seems to provide a stark contrast to Brinkman's depiction of Chicago. Established Protestant elites in both cities guarded their philanthropic projects jealously against unwanted intruders—Jews in Toronto and Catholics in Boston—and either did not allow their integration or limited it to an absolute minimum. Philanthropy was always more than the mere provision of resources for charitable, educational, and cultural projects; it provided the mechanisms for exclusion and inclusion of individuals into the respected circles of local communities. Economic potential and individual willingness were not sufficient to engage in trans-ethnic and trans-religious philanthropic projects. Up until World War I, an invitation from the side of the established philanthropic elites was even more important than the availability of financial means and the willingness to distribute them for the good of the community. Although offered on several occasions, Sigmund Samuel's money was not accepted for some time by the Methodist philanthropic establishment of Toronto because he was Jewish. Eventually he succeeded in finding his place alongside Protestant philanthropists and became one of the most important supporters of the Royal Ontario Museum and the University of Toronto, but Samuel remained an exception. Leaving the Jewish community behind him and at arm's length, he was only slowly and reluctantly recognized by the Methodist establishment. The prize for his recognition by Toronto's philanthropic establishment was his alienation from the Jewish community. Although he never left the Jewish community, Samuel limited his contacts with other Jews and sought out closer ties to Christian society.

In Leipzig and New York, in contrast, members of the Jewish, Catholic, and Reformed communities found inroads into the philanthropic establishments. When New York City's leisure class embarked on a campaign for a general hospital in 1881, one-fourth of the necessary funding came from its Jewish fellow citizens, and Jewish philanthropists contributed largely to the city's museums.[12] As an examination of the relationship between philanthropy and religion will show, philanthropy was a field contested by members of various religious denominations. Receiving an invitation to participate in a major philanthropic project was synonymous with that individual's inclusion into High Society.

To be clear, this chapter is not concerned with philanthropy within a specific religious group (charitable support of Jews for Jews); it will discuss the philanthropic engagement of members of religious minorities for the larger community. Museums, universities, communal charitable institutions, and hospitals became the battlefields in which Jewish, Catholic, and Protestant elites competed for participation, integration, and dominance within urban society. In the case of Jewish philanthropy, anti-Semitic prejudice has been seen by some historians as a driving force for philanthropic engagement for general public projects.[13] Julius Hammerslough, the leader of the Jewish community in Springfield, Illinois, demanded of his coreligionists that "Jews must contribute generously to prove to the world that they are dedicated to liberty; through their giving they will moderate anti-Jewish prejudice."[14] Influenced by Hammerslough, Julius Rosenwald, the most eminent Jewish-American philanthropist, established the Rosenwald Fund dedicated to the "well-being of mankind" in 1917.[15] Philanthropy and its potential to transcend or to strengthen religious barriers as well as its importance for social, cultural, and economic integration or exclusion of religious minorities into/from High Society will be the main focus of the following discussion. Consequently, this chapter will discuss the exclusion of Catholics and Jews from the Protestant philanthropic establishment in Boston and Toronto as well as the attempts of individuals such as Sigmund Samuel and Alfred Mond to integrate into the majority culture.

DEFENDING SOCIAL STATUS AND POWER: THE BRAHMINS OF BOSTON

In the second half of the nineteenth century, Boston's upper class—the Brahmins—faced an outright challenge to their political, cultural, and social domination by the newly arrived Irish Catholic immigrants. In the struggle for control over the city, the Brahmin caste sought to employ philanthropy for the preservation of its claim to power—albeit social and cultural power—even after they lost political control. The Brahmins were an elite with "a coherent sense of identity and a proud past" who admired and imitated European aristocratic life.[16] Brahmin families prided themselves on family trees that stretched back to the 1620s and 1630s with ancestors who had played important roles in the colonial past of North America. Beginning in 1796, they bought up land on Beacon Hill where they built their family mansions. Harvard College played an important role in the education and reproduction of the Brahmin elite, since it "had been attended, supported, directed, and often staffed" by the Brahmin families as of colonial times. A mercantile elite in origin, the Brahmins were able to adapt to industrialization. In the second half of the nineteenth century, Brahmins invested in the textile industry and railroads. They were also prominent in trade and the legal, medical, and educational professions.[17]

Nineteenth-century society saw the founding of several social and cultural philanthropic institutions, including the Massachusetts General Hospital, the Boston Co-operative Building Company, the Athenæum, the Boston Public Library, the Museum of Fine Arts, and the Boston Symphony Orchestra. Founded almost exclusively by Boston Brahmins, these institutions were considered essential to the Brahmins' hold on power.[18] The creation of these institutions not only signified the emergence of a powerful leisure class but also represented this class's claim to social and cultural dominance. As Betty G. Farrell rightfully points out, "The museum and the symphony were not simply the inevitable products of an expanding urban culture, but organizations specifically planned, directed, staffed, and attended by members of—and those with aspirations to membership among—the upper class."[19] Turning on its head Kathleen McCarthy's argument about the empowering function of philanthropy for women, it will be argued here that Boston's Brahmins created a parallel power structure through a network of philanthropic institutions to secure their economic and political influence.[20] Philanthropy was thus not only the first step on the road toward political empowerment; it was also, at least in the case of Boston Brahmins, the last step on the road to obscurity.

Facing urban decay and the emergence of slums, Martin Brimmer and Henry Ingersoll Bowditch recruited 163 individuals for their Boston Co-operative Building Company (BCBC)—all of them from old colonial families whose ancestors had arrived in the New World sometimes between 1620 and 1650. Many of them could trace their ancestors back to signers of the Declaration of Independence (e.g., R. T. Paine Jr.) and famous governors from early colonial times (e.g., William Endicott Jr.). The Massachusetts General Hospital (MGH) relied on 312 subscribers for the period 1828–43, the BCBC relied on 163 shareholders, and the Museum of Fine Arts (MFA) counted 370 original subscribers in 1876, which increased to 1,183 subscribers in 1895. Only a very small number of shareholders/subscribers chose to remain anonymous (none of the 312 original subscribers to the MGH; none of the shareholders of the BCBC; and only 9 out of 370 original subscribers to the MFA). Most made sure that their names were made public and published in annual reports. They certainly did not share "a passion for anonymity," which Cleveland Amory claimed as characteristic for the philanthropic nature of "Proper Bostonians."[21]

Shareholder corporations, in which each interested individual would buy shares with a limited dividend or subscribe to a certain annual membership fee without any prospect of receiving a dividend, provided the Brahmin class with the perfect business model for running philanthropic institutions.[22] This model had the important advantage that the boards of trustees were filled with philanthropists "who were committed either to providing financial support or to soliciting it from their peers." It further ensured the independence of museums, hospitals, and social housing projects "from the pressures of the market" and from the interference of other social groups and classes as well as from the state.[23]

Robert Dalzell has suggested that Boston's philanthropic projects "were regularly designed to involve as many people as possible."[24] But his argument needs modification, since the number of individuals engaged in Boston's philanthropic institutions throughout the nineteenth century was almost always limited to philanthropists of the right family background and socioeconomic standing. Most of the male BCBC stockholders (44 out of 57 for whom we have biographical information) had graduated from Harvard College and pursued careers as lawyers (Sidney Bartlett, John Lathrop), physicians (Henry Ingersoll Bowditch), merchants (John Lowell Gardner), bankers (Henry Purkitt Kidder), and industrialists (Arthur Theodore Lyman and James L. Little [Pacific Mills]; Edwin Hale Abbot [Wisconsin Central Railroad]). They were born in Boston or its surrounding townships. They or their parents had contributed to the construction of the MGH and the Boston Public Library (BPL), and they had bought subscriptions to the MFA. In fact, it was the same group of individuals who had just one year earlier joined together to create the MFA. It is not a surprise, then, that the BCBC and the MFA boards shared the same president for many years: Martin Brimmer (1829–96).

Brimmer was the son of a former Boston mayor of the same name who came from a very well connected Boston family. After he graduated from Harvard in 1849, Brimmer became a lawyer. He supported Henry Ingersoll Bowditch in his plan to provide healthy and affordable apartments for working-class families and became a driving force behind the founding of the MFA. Brimmer subsequently served as president of the MFA from 1870 and as president of the BCBC from 1872 until his death.[25] The first board of trustees and even the general subscription list to the MFA reads as a *Who's Who* of Boston's exclusive Brahmin caste. Among the trustees were Harvard president Charles William Elliot, Massachusetts Institute of Technology founder William Barton Rogers, Henry P. Kidder, and William Endicott Jr. Both Kidder and Endicott were to ensure the "financial probity of the enterprise," since both were well-connected businessmen. Endicott (1826–1914) had left school at age 14 in order to work as a clerk in his father's store in Beverly. He became an influential merchant and banker, a member of the investment committee of the Suffolk Savings Bank for nearly forty years and its president for seventeen. Endicott was also was president of several western railroads, the most important one being the Burlington & Missouri River Railroad in Nebraska. When this railroad was consolidated with the Chicago, Burlington & Quincy Railroad in 1880, Endicott became the director of this new company and held this position for twenty-two years. Kidder (1823–86) had left school at 15 to begin his career in various enterprises related to railroad construction and banking. After a short period in the office of the Boston and Worcester Railroad, he entered the banking house of John E. Thayer & Brother. In 1858 he was made partner in that enterprise. Later on in life, he presided over the investment firm of Kidder, Peabody and Co.

A look at the list of general subscriptions to the MFA shows that Brahmin families took the lead in founding the museum.[26] The list contains 370 donations ranging from $100 to $25,000. The largest single amount, incidentally, came from Mrs. T. B. Lawrence ($25,000). The majority of contributors (178) gave $100. Among the subscribers were manufacturers, lawyers, merchants, professors, bankers, and physicians. Half had graduated from Harvard College. They derived from "old colonial stock" families who had arrived in North America during the 1620s and 1630s. Not much changed in the structure of the group of philanthropists who contributed regularly to the funds for the MFA. By 1895, more than two-thirds of the museum association members claimed an ancestry that reached back to the 1620s and 1630s. Their pedigree has been described variously as "old colonial stock" and "unmixed New England ancestry." Clearly, family history mattered to the Brahmins and set them even further apart from the Irish, who did not display a comparable interest in family trees and coats of arms.

Irish Catholics and Unitarian Brahmins were separated not only by their economic inequality but also by their very different value systems. The original subscribers ensured their further dominance over this organization by acquiring memberships for their wives, sons, and daughters. Some families (e.g., Bowditch, Bradlee, Brimmer, Endicott, Kidder, Peabody, Warren, and Woodbury) were represented by three to ten members. While the number of philanthropists increased tremendously between 1876 and 1895, from 370 to 1,183, and although the sociopolitical structure of Boston society was turned upside down due to the large influx of Irish immigrants and the passing of political power from the old Brahmin families to the new Irish politicians, only one person with some Irish background could be found among the members of this museum association: businessman George E. McQuesten. However, he was not one of the recent poor Irish newcomers. His father, William McQuesten, had emigrated from Scotland to Northern Ireland only shortly before 1700. They were Scotch Presbyterian. When in 1719 they became dissatisfied with conditions in Coleraine, William McQuesten considered immigrating to Great Britain's North American colonies. Sometime between 1735 and 1744 McQuesten settled in Litchfield, New Hampshire. His son received his collegiate training from the Massachusetts Institute of Technology before he entered McQuesten's enterprise and became one of the pioneers in the development of automobiles. George's integration into Brahmin society and its philanthropic projects was certainly helped by his marriage to Emma S. Sawyer, who came from an old Brahmin family that claimed ancestors among the earliest English settlers in Massachusetts.[27] However, economic success, marrying into the right families, and philanthropic engagement were part and precondition for his successful integration into the Brahmin caste.

The exclusion of Irish Catholics was not unique to the MFA. One could only rarely find Irish Catholic philanthropists among the supporters of the BCBC and the MGH. While Irish Catholics seemed to have been nearly entirely excluded from the philanthropic circle that ensured the financial well-being of these philanthropic projects, recent Scottish and German (Jewish) immigrants found their way into the philanthropic establishment much faster.[28] There were at least three Germans who had come to the United States after 1840, achieved economic success, and been accepted among the exclusive group of donors for the MFA. One of them was the German Jew Abraham Shuman, who was born in Schneidemühl (Western Prussia) in May 1839 and came to the United States with his parents when he was still a child. After having attended school in Newburg, New York, Shuman relocated to Boston in 1859 where he set up his own business. In 1869 he entered into partnership with John Phillips and founded a wholesale business in boys' clothing, which was the first American enterprise that specialized in the manufacture and wholesale of children's clothing. This business venture made him the "wealthiest Jewish clothing manufacturer and retailer in Boston in the nineteenth century."[29] In 1876 Shuman's business was probably worth more than a quarter of a million dollars. Shuman was not the only Jewish philanthropist accepted into the MFA membership organization, however.

In 1895, Mrs. Louis D. Brandeis, the wife of the successful Boston lawyer, could be found among its members. Her membership is even more surprising because her husband has been considered "isolated from Brahmin life" by historians and contemporaries alike.[30] Brandeis, who was born in Louisville, Kentucky, came from a German-speaking family from Prague that emigrated to the United States after the failed 1848 revolution. Educated in Dresden and at Harvard College, Brandeis graduated from law school in 1877 and became one of the first Jewish attorneys in Boston and, in 1916, the first Jewish member of the U.S. Supreme Court. Up until 1900, only about 1 percent of the 1,700 lawyers practicing in Boston were Jewish. While most of the old Brahmin families shied away from engaging in business with Brandeis, Boston's leading Jewish merchants became his clients and made him almost a millionaire by 1905.

The integration of Jews into the philanthropic establishment at a time when Irish Catholics were virtually excluded from these social circles seems even more surprising if one considers the proportion of the population that belonged to the Jewish religion. In 1845, it was estimated that between 40 and 100 Jewish families lived in Boston. Around that time, in 1842, Boston's overall population was 84,401. By 1895, Boston's Jewish population had grown to approximately 20,000 members, whereas Boston's total population in 1892 had risen to 448,477. Both Ellen Smith and William Braverman, however, argue that Boston's Jews advanced economically and socially faster than any other ethnic or religious group. Braverman suggests that this was due to the geographical-economic origins of Boston's Jews. "Coming from urban settings and used to living in a capitalistic economy, the Jews' adjustment to Boston was difficult but not nearly as traumatic as for the Irish or Italians who were almost all agricultural workers." Furthermore, Jews entered those sectors of the Boston economy (textile, boots, and shoe industries) "that held future promise."[31]

The Brahmin's overwhelming dominance in philanthropy was contrasted by their declining social, political, and economic dominance in Boston. Until the middle of the nineteenth century, the Brahmin families' hold on power remained unchallenged. With the steady and increasing flow of Irish immigrants after 1845, Boston's population not only increased significantly but also shifted in favor of the new arrivals. Of the 2.5 million Irish who left their country between 1835 and 1865, a very large number went to Boston. In 1847 alone, about 37,000 Irish arrived in Boston. As a result the city's population grew from 76,475 in 1842 to 133,563 in 1862. As early as 1850, Irish immigrants constituted more than a third of the city's population. For the old Brahmin Unitarian families, this influx of poor Irish Catholic immigrants contributed, as Martin Green points out, to an immense economic growth and great prosperity for the old elites, but it also meant "the decay of the communal hopes of earlier times" for "a city of small tradesmen and craftsmen, with an upper class of merchant princes," a city without slums and crime.[32]

After 1845, slums emerged in the city, and diseases such as smallpox and cholera returned. Drunkenness, crime, and prostitution spread. In the eyes of the old Brahmin families, the poor Irish farmers represented an enormous social, cultural, religious, and political threat to the status quo. Although the Puritans' dislike for Catholics had disappeared by the beginning of the nineteenth century, religious intolerance, according to Oscar Handlin, quickly reemerged in Boston in the 1840s and 1850s: "The economic, physical, and intellectual development of the town accentuated the division between the Irish and the rest of the population and engendered fear of a foreign group whose appalling slums had already destroyed the beauty of a fine city and whose appalling ideas threatened the fondest conceptions of universal progress, of grand reform, and a regenerated mankind."[33] While immigration was a general phenomenon of American society, "the Irish erupted on the scene in the 1840s in large numbers, and for the next forty years they were the only alien, immigrant group in Boston's midst."[34]

The arrival of the Irish challenged the dominant position of the Brahmins, and they reacted to this challenge in various ways.[35] Facing the emergence of an urban working class that as early as 1850 was predominantly Irish (about 45 percent),[36] Brahmins broadened their philanthropic activities to include charitable, welfare, and social housing projects. Between 1810 and 1840, about thirty benevolent institutions were founded—the most important institution being the MGH (1821). Over the years, Brahmins would make sure that they had an exclusive and absolute control over their hospital.[37] Several of the subscribers' names or their sons and daughters' names reappear among the members of the BCBC and the MFA. The Brahmins' control of the hospital extended, as Green shows, even beyond financial aspects. "Five families, the Warrens, the Jacksons, the Bigelows, the Shattucks, and the Cabots, have supplied the majority of the physicians and surgeons, have transmitted a corporate responsibility for the hospital, a genuine family vocation, from generation to generation." Dr. Shattuck and Dr. Warren, who were on staff at the hospital in 1947, represented "the fifth and sixth generations of their respective families."[38]

Besides providing social welfare to the new immigrants, the Brahmin class employed economic and political strategies to counter the growing Irish influence. Historians have argued that the decline of Boston's Brahmins began with the trust fund.[39] Sometime after 1830, "older families began to sterilize their capital by tying it up in trust funds, which tended to prolong these families in power because their wealth was less easily dissipated." Instead of trusting their heirs, Boston merchants put their entire fortunes into such trust funds, thus ensuring that their sons could not spend or risk the entire inheritance. They were condemned to live off the interest rate accumulated and to abstain from risky investments. This resulted in an economic situation in which subsequent Brahmin generations lived off the economic success of their forebears and became Back Bay gentlemen who reinvested their dividends and lived off the income from this reinvested capital. Although this was not a uniquely Bostonian development, William Shannon argues that in the case of Boston "it was also a response to and an insulating vacuum against the pressures of the ever-growing numbers of Irish who threatened the old values and old ways."[40]

From the founding of the MGH to the creation of the MFA, Brahmins moved away from close collaboration with the city government, which had been controlled by the Brahmin class up to the 1880s. The founding of the MGH and the BPL occurred in collaboration with the city council and private philanthropy. In the case of the hospital, private subscriptions between 1811 and 1843 amounted to $150,000 and the city provided the necessary land (valued at $40,000) for the side of the building.[41] In the case of the library, it was the donation of $50,000 by Joshua Bates in 1852 that sparked close private-public collaboration.[42] Already in 1848 the Massachusetts General Court, according to John Koren, passed "an enabling act, authorizing the city to establish and maintain a public library for the use of the inhabitants, but with the proviso 'that no appropriation for the library shall exceed the sum of $5,000 in any one year.'" Two years later, in August 1850, the library received its first financial gift ($1,000), which was raised by citizens as a testimonial gift to the former mayor of Boston, Josiah Quincy Jr. In January 1851, the city council appropriated another $1,000 for library purposes. Koren reminds us that this court decision constituted "the first statute ever passed authorizing the establishment and maintenance of a public library as a municipal institution supported by taxation."[43]

In contrast to the way the hospital (1821) and the library (1852) had been founded, Brahmins created the BCBC (1871) and the MFA (1870) without any support from the city government. Although the museum was conceived of as a public institution open to the general population (the museum was to be open free of charge at least four times a month), the museum board did not ask for financial support from the city government, nor did it receive municipal funding. The emerging divide between city government and private philanthropy seems to suggest that during the 1870s the Brahmin class grew skeptical that they could continue to dominate the city government. It also proves that the Brahmin class was still economically strong enough to finance a tight network of social, educational, and cultural public institutions without recourse to city and state government. Although the MFA went through twenty meager years in which it was not able to acquire new art, it could rely on bequests and an organization of annual subscribers.[44]

The Brahmins' retreat from political power was not as voluntary nor as easy as Paul Dimaggio and Ronald Story lead us to believe, though. Before the Brahmins were willing to relinquish their hold on political power, they considered other options such as restrictions on the right to vote. Brahmin families had successfully dominated Boston's political life up until the 1860s. They served as mayors, aldermen, common councilors, and overseers of the poor.[45] They remained indifferent to the Irish immigrants as long as the latter did not present a political danger. As Handlin pointed out, Irish voters were a small minority and "politically impotent" before 1845. "In 1834 the Irish claimed no more than 200 voters in all Suffolk County, and in 1839, no more than 500, while in 1845 less than one-sixth of the adult male foreigners in Boston were citizens."[46] This changed dramatically with the increase of Irish voters and their determination to play a role in Boston's politics. In the mid-1850s, ideas about the exclusion of paupers from voting and a literacy requirement were discussed. Even after Massachusetts had abolished all property qualifications connected with voting rights in 1820, it still kept a provision (third amendment) according to which every male citizen who had reached the age of 21 was eligible to vote in municipal and state election unless they were "paupers and persons under guardianship." In 1857 the Massachusetts legislature passed a further amendment according to which "No person should [have the right to vote, or] be eligible to office under the constitution of this commonwealth, who shall not be able to read the constitution in the English language, and write his name."[47]

In 1859, another amendment prevented foreigners from voting for two years after their naturalization. Although this legislation affected all foreigners, it was absolutely clear, as Handlin argues, that it "was directed primarily against the Irish,"[48] given that the Irish were the single largest group of immigrants. Probably influenced by the public discourse in New York City about limiting the right to participate in municipal elections to citizens of some financial means and the growing number of Irish Catholic immigrants in the second half of the nineteenth century, the idea of further restricting the right to vote was heatedly discussed in the Massachusetts legislature in the late 1870s.[49] It was already a common practice that municipal administrations engaged in "omitting from the voting-lists the names of all persons" who received public assistance. The legislators, however, wanted to go a step further. In 1878, the state legislature discussed a law that would have obliged boards of registration to submit a list of all men over 21 who had received public aid within the past year to the mayors and aldermen of said town so that they could effectively be excluded from participating in local elections.[50]

Only after all these political options were exhausted did the Brahmins decide to leave the political power to the Irish and retreat to the already existing sphere of their philanthropic organizations. Philanthropy allowed them to establish a "countergovernment" in the city and to "maintain some control over the community even as they lost their command of its political institutions."[51] By the time Hugh O'Brien became the city's first Irish mayor in 1884, the Brahmin class had made peace with their loss of control of city hall and consoled themselves with the knowledge that they continued to maintain control over the boards of nearly all philanthropic institutions.[52] Sitting on the boards of the MFA, they decided which art was to be displayed and employed in the education of the masses. The control over the BCBC allowed them to define who was eligible to live in social housing, and by controlling the construction of social housing apartments they even had their hands in the definition of what constituted a family. Although one has to be careful in evaluating the real power of such boards, which included ten to twenty trustees who represented 100 to more than 1,000 subscribers/shareholders with individual visions for their city and the communal life, one should not underestimate the power of these social-cultural institutions. By keeping the housing company and museum disconnected from the city government, its boards had exclusive control over the institutions, the artistic directions, and the treatment of visitors.[53] As Robert Dalzell reminds us, control over philanthropic institutions gave the Brahmins "the power to set standards."[54]

Frederic Cople Jaher's assessment that the Brahmins "were not exclusively a political elite" but that their political hegemony was only one "facet of the comprehensive leadership that the group exerted in Boston"[55] needs to be revised. The Brahmins were certainly an economic, political, social, and philanthropic elite, but they were first an economic elite that claimed political power in Boston and thereafter transformed itself into a social elite that invested part of its fortune in philanthropy. After the Brahmins lost economic dominance, they could hold onto political power until they were challenged by the Irish majority. This challenge transformed the Brahmin elite into a philanthropic class that exchanged political for cultural dominance. Boston thus represents a conservative model of philanthropy. Whereas in cities such as New York and Leipzig, new elites successfully employed philanthropy on a large scale to claim membership in the established elites, Boston's Brahmins successfully used philanthropy to prevent the integration of specific newcomers (here Irish Catholics).[56] Philanthropy fulfilled the function of preserving old social structures, to prevent intermingling of social groups, and thus to allow the Brahmins to cling to whatever power was left to them.[57] In contrast to New York, Toronto, and Leipzig, however, ethnic, religious, and class lines in Boston were almost congruent. The Irish majority, "who had the political power," as William Shannon points out, "felt themselves distinctly separated from the minority who had the economic power, and the separation was not only along economic lines, as it would be elsewhere, but also along nationality, religious, and cultural lines."[58]

The virtual absence of Irish among Boston's philanthropic establishment could be explained in two ways. One could argue that the Irish did not have the necessary financial means to become active in philanthropic pursuits. Both Shannon and Stephan Thernstrom show that Boston's Irish moved slowly into the middle and upper classes. According to Thernstrom, only 40 percent of American-born children of Irish immigrants in Boston ever reached middle-class positions. Political power did not bring equal economic opportunities for the Irish majority. One-quarter of Yankee youths but two-thirds of the Irish were employed as manual laborers. Furthermore, second-generation Irish were, as Thernstrom demonstrates, "less successful than other second-generation newcomers from groups that were politically much weaker. Eleven in 20 of the native-born sons of immigrants of British or West European (predominantly German and Scandinavian) descent ended their career in middle-class occupations, but fewer than 8 in 20 of the Irish."[59] And Handlin observes that the "mass of Irishmen continued to occupy the low places in society they had earlier held."[60] This economic disadvantage could be seen even at the level of political leadership. Investigating the economic background of Boston's city council members, Ernest S. Griffith observed, "In 1875 all of the aldermen owned property, the total assessed value of which was $769,600, and sixty-one out of the seventy-four members of the common council owned property totaling $1,530,800. In 1892 sixty-two out of eighty-seven councilmen owned no visible property. By 1904 the total assessed valuation of property owned by both aldermen and councilmen totalled only $87,000."[61] Nevertheless, a few Irishmen were economically successful. These individuals could have participated in the philanthropic network. Their absence could be credited to the refusal of Brahmins to open their ranks to the Irish newcomers as well as to the failure of the Irish to recognize the potential of philanthropy for integration or simply their disinterest in Brahmin society and its institutions.[62] However small the economic progress of Irishmen was, it did not result in Irish participation in Boston's philanthropic establishment or in the creation of a counter-philanthropic establishment.

Making Inroads into Toronto's Christian Establishment

Boston's High Society displayed an incredible ability to absorb different religious minorities as long as these minorities were not Irish Catholics. When it came to Irish Catholics, Boston Brahmins displayed an intolerance that was similar to Toronto leading social circles' zeal in excluding Jews from participation in philanthropic activities. The majority of Toronto's philanthropists belonged to the three major religious denominations of the city: Anglican, Methodist, and Presbyterian. About 85 percent of all philanthropists who were involved with the Royal Ontario Museum (ROM), the Toronto Art Gallery (TAG), the Toronto Housing Company (THC), and the Toronto General Hospital (TGH) belonged to one of these three churches or, later, to the United Church of Canada, which emerged from the union of the Methodist Church of Canada, the Congregational Union of Canada, and a large section of the Presbyterian Church of Canada in 1925. The Anglicans were, of course, the largest group with about 30 percent among the supporters of the THC, 41 percent among the supporters of the TGH, 40 percent among the supporters of the TAG, and 36 percent among the supporters of the ROM. Next were the Presbyterians and Methodists with an equally strong representation. This distribution of religious groups among the philanthropists is almost proportional to the percentage these religious groups occupied in the overall population of the city. In 1901, 30 percent of the 208,040 Torontonians were Anglican, 23 percent were Methodist, and 20 percent were Presbyterians. Baptists, who represented 6 percent of Toronto's population, could claim an equally high share of 6 percent among Toronto's philanthropists. Catholics, who represented roughly 14 percent of Toronto's population, were strongly underrepresented; less than 3 percent of the supporters of the ROM, the TAG, the THC, and the TGH were Catholic. Jews, who represented about 1.5 percent of the city's total population, were equally underrepresented. There were only six Jews among those who supported the ROM, the TAG, the THC, and the TGH. If one looks only at this statistic, one would have to conclude that this would have been almost proportional to the percentage of the Jewish segment of Toronto's total population. However, four of the six Jews (Sigmund Samuel, Robert Mond and his wife, and Sir Alfred Mond) did not even have their permanent residence in Toronto and were therefore not listed as members of Toronto's Jewish community. The two Jews permanently living in Toronto were Jacob Singer, who owned a real estate business, and Edmund Scheuer, who was an important jewelry merchant.[63]

The following discussion will follow the path of Sigmund Samuel and focus on his integration into Toronto's philanthropic establishment. It will be suggested that, first, the ability and willingness to engage in philanthropy was not a sufficient precondition for philanthropy and, second, that the cultural practice of philanthropy provided an important tool to achieve social integration into the majority culture.[64] By the end of the 1920s, Samuel had become one of the most influential members of Toronto's philanthropic establishment. Together with Sir Edmund Walker, Mrs. H. D. Warren, and Alfred and Robert Mond, Samuel pledged his support to the university, the museums, and the hospitals of his hometown. The Sigmund Samuel Library of the University of Toronto, the Royal Ontario Museum, and the Toronto Western Hospital are important pieces of Toronto's modern-day cityscape and remind us of his legacy. The path to such recognition, however, was not without obstacles for the Jewish businessman.

Although Sigmund Samuel was one of Toronto's richest residents, Toronto's Anglican-dominated and Anglophile leisure class prevented his integration into social clubs and social circles as well as his participation in philanthropic projects. In his autobiography Samuel reflected indirectly on his exclusion from philanthropic projects by stating that "as soon as it became possible to engage in philanthropy I began to do so, never restricting gifts to a specific segment of the population but trying instead to serve the greatest number."[65] Only over time and with the help of Sir Edmund Walker, who was in dire need of supporters for his pet projects (especially the ROM), was Samuel invited to participate in the philanthropic practices of Christian Toronto. His path exemplifies the exchange of economic capital for social and cultural capital. Based on Pierre Bourdieu's concept of different types of capital, social capital will be understood here as the integration into social circles of wealthy and influential men of Toronto's leisure class.[66] Often economic potential was insufficient for economic success, since one needed social connections to receive certain contracts. Marriage strategies, membership in social clubs, and invitations to the right social events influenced the economic success of an enterprise as much as pure economic strategy. The friendship with Walker and the subsequent integration of Samuel into the York Club had a positive impact on Samuel's social and economic future. Clubs such as the York Club were meeting places outside the public eyes, where businessmen could meet for lunch and dinner and talk about their social life and, of course, their business. It was a place where friendships were formed that influenced business and family relations. Being a member of this club was significant for one's economic and social advancement.[67]

Sigmund Samuel was born in 1867 into an orthodox Jewish family of English and German origin. His mother, Kate Seckelman, had left Sulzbach, Bavaria, for New York City around 1850. Related by marriage to the famous Seligman family in New York, she attracted the attention of Lewis Samuel, who met her at a dinner party in Syracuse. Although neither understood the language of the other, they were married two weeks later.[68] Relocating to Toronto for business reasons in July 1854 (he and his brother Mark established the company of M. & L. Samuel, commission and wholesale merchants in metal and hardware), Lewis Samuel became the driving force behind the Toronto Hebrew Congregation. This congregation was founded in 1856 and consisted of recently arrived Jews who had not joined the older Hebrew Congregation, founded in 1849, which included established Jewish families who prided themselves on their integration into non-Jewish circles.[69]

When Samuel arrived in Toronto, only a handful of Jewish families lived in the city. There was no synagogue and no weekly service. At Samuel's insistence, the Toronto Hebrew Congregation "hired a man from New York to oversee the killing of animals in the Orthodox fashion, to conduct services on Friday nights, Saturdays, and holidays, to teach, and to perform other necessary offices." Lewis Samuel and his wife were very active members of Toronto's Jewish community. Although he dedicated time and effort to the Toronto Mechanics Institute, an early institution of continuing education for adults, Salomon's main interest was Toronto's Hebrew Congregation (Holy Blossom). He and Kate were instrumental in organizing a campaign to build the Holy Blossom Synagogue between 1874 and 1876 on Richmond Street. "It was largely through their personal efforts that by the time the building was opened donations amounted to $6,000, of which one-quarter came from Toronto Christians and the rest from Jews as far away as New York and New England." Lewis Samuel served as president of this synagogue almost continuously from 1862 to 1885.[70]

Born and raised in Toronto, Sigmund Samuel attended first Upper Canada College and then Toronto's Model School, which was, in contrast to Upper Canada College, founded to train the next generation of businessmen and merchants. After school, he would study Hebrew and prepare for his bar mitzvah. He developed an interest in the history and geography of Canada as well as stamp collecting. Unlike most of his school friends, however, Samuel held onto his interest in philately beyond his childhood. It was this experience, he claims, that "proved valuable in all subsequent collecting, no matter what the later interest happened to be."[71]

After Samuel had completed two years at the Model School, his father decided that it was time for him to begin practical business-oriented training. In 1881, at age 14, Samuel entered his father's business. He regretted that he was not allowed to finish the Model School and to enter the University of Toronto. It was this lack of a formal higher education as well as his interest in intellectual matters that led him to engage in philanthropy for educational and cultural institutions. Samuel sought to counterbalance this lack of formal education by reading books, engaging in conversations with academics, supporting educational/intellectual projects that brought him in close contact with intellectuals, and traveling abroad. At the end of his life, Samuel wrote that he had "managed to win one or two honorary degrees of my own."[72] The picture of Sigmund Samuel used in his autobiography and several other brochures about him show him not in a suit but in a graduation robe.

From an early point in his life, Samuel was concerned with fitting into Toronto's High Society. After leaving school, Samuel joined the Mutual Improvement Society (MIS), a group of eleven boys who lived in the same neighborhood and attended either the Model School or Jarvis Street Collegiate Institute. This small group, which had "originated in a theatrical group for young men and women at the Metropolitan Church," met every week to organize trips and to discuss history and natural sciences. Samuel was the only Jew in this group, which was dominated by Methodists. Reflecting on his relationship to Jewish friends, Samuel wrote in his autobiography: "I did have some close Jewish friends whom I saw frequently, but in general the association with the M.I.S. was most attractive, more congenial than confining myself only to persons of my own faith." This socializing practice included several compromises with regards to his religious beliefs and his lifestyle. Although raised in an orthodox family, in which his mother insisted on keeping her kitchen kosher, Samuel accepted invitations to dinner from two of his friends, Will and Harry Mason, after they informed him that their mother had "decided not to serve pork at the table any more, so that you can stop with us for dinner whenever you want." After the outbreak of World War I, Samuel further decided to break with family and religious tradition by keeping his enterprise open on the Sabbath.[73]

In 1897, during a visit to London, Samuel met Leah May Mandelson, who was living with her uncle.[74] She had been born in Australia into the family of wealthy English settlers who had engaged in trade and sheep ranching. Since "her father had never stopped thinking of England as home," he returned with his entire family to London after he had reached an age and a position that allowed him to retire. At the time that Samuel met May Mandelson, both of her parents had died and May, as the oldest daughter, was put in charge of raising her younger siblings. Married in July 1898 in the New West End Synagogue in London, Samuel and his wife entered a typical nineteenth-century relationship, as he described in his autobiography: "From the first, my wife and I had an understanding that she would have complete charge of the household, its furnishing and operation. I would provide the necessary funds but then, without conflict, could devote myself entirely to business."[75]

This marriage strengthened Samuel's interest in English culture and the English way of life. Naturally, his wife had many friends and relatives living in London and wished to be close to her siblings. She "was very well connected socially in London" because she was the niece of Sir Louis Cohen, Lord Mayor of Liverpool, and her name was inscribed "on the social list of the Royal Family." Consequently, "she was frequently a guest at the Royal Garden Parties."[76] It did not take much convincing for Sigmund Samuel to find a place to live in the British metropolis. His desire to become an English gentleman was, of course, part of his overall strategy at integration into Toronto's social elite, which was dominated by socialites of English origin. The first essential step was the acquisition of a house in London at Porchester Terrace, "a pleasant West End Street leading directly into Kensington Gardens and Hyde Park." It was a "good-sized solid Georgian house with a broad frontage, a courtyard at the front and in the rear a garden and tennis court."[77] Beginning in 1914, Samuel divided his time equally between Toronto and London, living for six months at a time in each city.

The most important turning point in Samuel's life was his acquaintance with Sir Edmund Walker, the kingpin of Toronto philanthropy. Samuel and Walker shared a common admiration for art and education. They had met before 1914, probably at a lecture series organized by the Royal Canadian Institute that was held every Saturday night at the University of Toronto. In both cases, their school time had been cut short in favor of an early start in business life. Both had achieved

tremendous economic success, and both were interested in bolstering their economic success with the acquisition of social and cultural recognition by the members of Toronto's High Society. Walker, however, had an easier way into the leading
circles of Toronto society because he was of the right religion—Presbyterian. He
was instrumental in helping Samuel overcome religious prejudice in the interest of
advancing Toronto's philanthropic culture.

Walker was a member of the board of the Mond Nickel Company, which had
opened an account with the Canadian Bank of Commerce. In 1917, Samuel met
Sir Robert Mond, who was an avid amateur Egyptologist. One year later, at a dinner at Walker's home, Samuel made the acquaintance of Sir Alfred Mond (the later
Lord Melchett). Like Samuel, the Mond brothers were Jews with roots in Germany,
and all three were united in their attempts at integration into Britain's social elite.

Robert (1867–1938) and Alfred (1868–1930) were the sons of Ludwig (1839–
1909) and Frida Mond (neé Löwenthal, 1847–1923). Ludwig had been born and
raised in Kassel before he entered the University of Marburg to study chemistry
with Hermann Kolbe, an authority in organic chemistry. In his second year he
enrolled at the University of Heidelberg to work with Robert Bunsen, the leading
scholar in organic chemistry. Mond entered the electroplating business of his
uncle in Cologne, then moved on to work in different chemical enterprises. He
finally made a fortune in England with the development of his sulphur-recovery
process and his ammonia-soda patent.[78]

After Ludwig Mond and Frida Löwenthal were married in October 1866, they
relocated to Farnworth in England in July 1867. Although both had been raised in
the Jewish faith, they did not join a synagogue, and lighting candles for Hanuk-
kah became a faint memory of their childhood.[79] Their experience was not entirely
unusual, since voluntarism was the only organizing principle of British religious life.
Jews were not forced to join the Jewish community, which in turn could not monitor
the social behavior of its members. In contrast to Central and Eastern European societies, which imposed large numbers of restrictions and limitations on Jews and Jewish communities, England in the eighteenth and early nineteenth centuries provided
such "an extraordinary degree of personal freedom" that Jews "rearranged their personal priorities in such a manner that their Jewishness came to occupy only a segment of their personal identity."[80] Loneliness and social isolation were side effects of
this unlimited religious freedom and the patriarchal organization of society. Writing
to her mother-in-law, Frida Mond complained, "The English say, 'My house is my
castle,' but they ought to add 'and I am locked up in it.'"[81] Having relinquished any
ties to religion, and never having attended synagogue services in their new home,
Frida Mond was condemned to a life in social isolation. This isolation was broken
only by the arrival of Henriette Hertz (1846–1913), a girlhood friend, who agreed to
live with Frida and Ludwig Mond for many years.[82]

Hertz's presence in Mond's house, one could argue, strengthened the family's
isolation, since German became the language of the house and the hiring of a German governess to raise the children secured the continued exclusion of the family
from public English life. Their first son, Robert Ludwig, was born just two months
after their arrival in Farnworth. The second son followed a year later. Ludwig and
Frida raised their children in the German culture and language. They decided to
ban the Bible from their household "because its cruel stories and allegories were
considered unsuitable reading." Both boys were raised at home until they reached

the age of 13 and their parents enrolled them in Cheltenham College. Alfred, in particular, "was immediately attracted to the more casual, understated British life-style. . . . He found a world of which he desperately longed to be a part, but from which he seemed to be excluded because of his guttural accent and his German upbringing." His marriage to the devout Christian Violet Goetze, the daughter of the painter Sigismund Goetze, who produced the mural *Britannia Pacificatrix* in the Foreign and Commonwealth Office during World War I, strengthened his desire to integrate into British society. Although her family did not possess finan-cial riches, Violet "had social ambitions." She was able to fulfill these ambitions by marrying into the Mond family.[83]

Shortly after his marriage, Alfred and his brother joined their father in the for-mation of the Mond Nickel Company after Ludwig Mond had discovered an inex-pensive and easy way of extracting nickel from ore. After an experimental nickel extraction plant at Smethwick near Birmingham ran to the satisfaction of Ludwig Mond, additional extraction sites in Wales at Clydach and Ontario near Sudbury were opened.[84] Their involvement in this enterprise provided Alfred and Robert with sufficient financial means to accomplish very successful social, political, and profes-sional careers and "to pursue their own ways." According to J. M. Cohen, they were too ambitious to limit their activities just to these enterprises.[85] The Nickel Company, however, brought them into contact with individuals such as Sir Edmund Walker of Toronto who provided them with opportunities to pursue their interests in culture and history as well as with avenues to social and cultural advancement. Their father had become famous for his extremely progressive social welfare programs for his workers. Alfred and Robert directed their philanthropy toward cultural and colo-nial projects (Egyptology and the Royal Ontario Museum) and purposes that helped enhance their social standing.

In 1905, Alfred Mond entered politics and run as a Liberal in the conservative stronghold of Chester. He won his seat in Parliament with a razor-thin majority.[86] Although his aspiration to high political offices (prime minister) remained unful-filled, he was made a baronet in 1910 and became Baron Melchett in 1928.[87] Mond created his own coat of arms that displayed a doctor of science of the University of Oxford holding in the exterior hand a chemical measure glass, on the sinister a laborer holding in the exterior hand a pick resting on the shoulder.[88] Soon after, he purchased a country estate in Hampshire with a Victorian house, a large farm, and extensive parkland. His immense wealth allowed him to transform this ugly estate into one of the most fashionable homes in England. Surrounded by an artfully arranged Italian garden with fountains, a rose garden, and greenhouses for orchids, the mansion provided an impressive setting for Mond's art collection (Roman and Greek sculptures and bronzes as well as paintings). His political career, his title, and the acquisition of this property in the countryside were all part of becoming integrated into the British aristocracy. The renovation of the house turned it into an attractive meeting place for eminent and influential members of British society (Lloyd George, for instance, became a frequent guest).[89]

Alfred Mond's attempts to integrate into British Christian society even included celebrating Christmas. "On Christmas Eve, presents were handed out in accordance with the German custom, carollers sang round the giant tree and the guests listened to the band which had been engaged by Ludwig." Nevertheless, Mond refused to "embrace Violet's religion which was a very strong force in her life. . . . But he was a man of obdurately independent judgement and, although not a practicing Jew, he never regarded himself as other than a Jew and was always conscious of his Semitic roots." Yet it remains open what exactly it meant to him to be Jewish. He was not raised in the Jewish religion: his father decided not to circumcise him because he "thought it irrational for an agnostic to insist on a religion for his children," and Alfred did not have a bar mitzvah. To regard himself as Jewish points less to a religious affiliation and more to the realization to be the "other." It also seems to suggest that his lifelong passion "to be accepted as British" remained unfulfilled.[90]

Mond's feeling of being a Jew thus was a reflection of his status as an outsider who was considered Jewish by his fellow citizens, who increasingly saw Jews as a race and not as a religious group. It was the anti-Semitism and anti-Germanism that Alfred Mond and his family had to face before and during World War I that made him defend his religious roots and increase his attempts at integration into British society. His son, Henry, was frequently confronted with anti-Semitic remarks at school (he was called a "dirty Jew" by fellow students), and Alfred Mond faced anti-Semitic comments from Lord Winterton while Mond gave speeches to Parliament. The outbreak of war in 1914 made it clear to Mond that he was further from his goal of being accepted as British and a member of the aristocracy than he had made himself believe. Immediately after Great Britain declared war on Germany, Mond was accused in person and in the newspapers of being a "German Jewish traitor." Newspaper articles pointed out that his second name was "Moritz" and that his father had made several bequests to his hometown in Germany, and a neighbor accused him of being a German spy who kept carrier pigeons in his London home. Many Englishmen of German origin withdrew from public life, but Mond chose to do the opposite. He turned his estate at Melchett into a military hospital, and he directed his factories entirely to producing armaments. His enterprises produced TNT, the first British gas masks, as well as gas and glycerin. He finally entered the government to take over the Ministry of Works.[91]

Alfred Mond's passionate attempts to fit into British High Society impressed Sigmund Samuel very much. He became something of an idol for Samuel, who followed in his footsteps by entering English politics and by engaging in philanthropy.[92] According to Samuel, it was Mond who suggested that he enter British politics in the early 1920s. It took Samuel several years before he, too, ran for Parliament in the district of Litchfield as a Conservative. His first attempt to gain a seat in the House of Commons in 1929, however, was unsuccessful. A second attempt in the district of East Willesden in 1935 failed, too. When he was asked why he did not run for office in Canada, Samuel replied that he believed "he could do more for his beloved Canada in London than in Ottawa, and . . . because there was not so much religious prejudice in England."[93]

While his political ambitions in England remained unfulfilled, Samuel became one of the most important philanthropists in Toronto. He overcame anti-Semitic prejudices very common among Toronto's leisure class, but to get to this point he needed the guidance and "protection" of Sir Edmund Walker. His desire for social integration met with Walker's need for wealthy benefactors. Samuel complained in his autobiography that Toronto had been "one of the most quietly bigoted cities in Europe or America." He suggested that this religious intolerance toward Jews,

Catholics, and French Canadians derived from Toronto's localism and lack of open-minded culture, which he identified with port cities.[94]

He claimed that he had spent most of his life in the company of Christian friends but that he had suffered for his religion—although to a lesser degree than most Jews living in Canada. Samuel faced religious discrimination repeatedly when he applied "for accommodation at resorts, in politics and clubs, in newspaper reports, even in churches." When Samuel applied for membership in the National Club at the beginning of World War I, his application was turned down because one member had objected to his religion. This was especially disappointing for Samuel because club membership symbolized integration into Toronto's social elite. Jealousy and frustration characterized his attitude toward these exclusive clubs. Traces of both feelings can be found in his autobiography; in one instance he wrote about an evening when Walker invited him to dinner at the York Club. When they had finished dinner, Walker offered to give him a tour. "It was a most welcome thought," wrote Samuel, "for I had often walked past the club on my way home, wondering what was on the other side of the high brick wall which surrounds it." It was Walker who opened the doors when he suggested that Samuel join the York Club. Since Walker was its president, he could not nominate Samuel, but he arranged for two other members to do so. Samuel became the first Jewish member of the York Club—he remained its "token Jew" for years to come. However, with that acceptance, other clubs (the Toronto Hunt Club, Albany Club, and Lambton Golf and Country Club) finally opened their doors to him.[95]

Walker then persuaded him to contribute money and artifacts to the University of Toronto and the Royal Ontario Museum. For Samuel, philanthropy offered another path to social recognition, since it allowed for the public display of his economic power and his interest in all matters of education and culture. In addition, philanthropy corresponded to "his belief that those who prosper from the community have some responsibility to it and to the coming generations." In his autobiography, Samuel felt compelled to underline that he had achieved success in business on his own. He had done so through "salesmanship, hard bargaining, scrupulous honesty, and fair profits in good times and in bad." He recognized "quite early that there was no reason merely to accumulate the money thus gained, or to live extravagantly." As long as his family was comfortable, "that was enough," he wrote, "and in this view I was supported for fifty-three years by my dear wife. Rather, I have always felt an obligation to the community of which I am a member and from which my money has come."[96]

His decision not to limit his philanthropic engagement to the Jewish community made him many enemies within Toronto's Jewish community who felt that he favored general (in other words, Christian) philanthropies at the expense of Jewish causes. Furthermore, to the Jewish community, it must have seemed that Samuel was supporting the very same Christian Toronto society that maintained a prejudicial and racist stance toward the city's Jewish minority.[97]

Although he took some interest in the Holy Blossom Synagogue, Sigmund Samuel donated more to the general community. That this provoked jealousy and suspicion became clear in interviews with members of his family and the Jewish community. Jews regarded him as "aloof" and "distant." Given his father's role in the establishment of Toronto's Jewish community, Samuel was expected to do more for the Holy Blossom Synagogue. When he was asked, however, to serve as its president, he replied that he did not have the time. Samuel thus walked a very thin line, since he risked being an outcast in the Jewish community before he was really accepted into the social circles of old Toronto.[98]

Yet, since Samuel gained social recognition and integration into the philanthropic establishment after the ROM had already been established and after many Christian benefactors had already provided financial and material support, this situation resulted in some unforeseen obstacles. In March 1920, Samuel wrote to the ROM board, offering £5,000 sterling with the understanding that he was "to become the donor of the objects set forth in a letter from the Chairman to him, as follows:

1. Grecian and Etruscan vases acquired by the Museum from Dr. Sturge.
2. Tanagra figurines acquired by the Museum from Dr. Sturge.
3. Previous collection of Greek and Italian vases acquired by the Museum through Professor Currelly's efforts over a series of years.
4. Tanagra and other figurines acquired in the same manner.
5. Bronze vases and four bronze statuettes of Greek origin acquired in the same manner.
6. The Greek Venus."

This offer, while generous, was problematic because the Sturge collection had already been "paid for out of a grant by the Ontario Government to the extent of £3,000." Since the museum director did not want to lose Samuel's donation, he asked the trustees "to permit the gift of Mr. Samuel to that extent to be used to release objects pledged for the indebtedness due by Mr. Currelly. This will release the Egyptian collection of necklaces and they may now be regarded as objects for which the grant of the Government has been used to the extent of the said £3,000."[99]

This episode sheds light on several aspects of the philanthropic practices of Sigmund Samuel. Prevented from participating in the creation of the ROM until 1920, he did not want to finance merely small art objects that would barely be visible to the visitor. He wanted to link his name to an important piece of art or even a complete art collection. The exhibition of this collection would always be connected with his name and thus display his economic power and his artistic taste. The museum faced the challenge that it needed to redirect funds and rename collections, since it depended on the future support of philanthropists such as Sigmund Samuel. Furthermore, Samuel was allowed to attach his name to a collection that had been purchased using government funds about two years earlier, in October 1917, before Samuel announced his gift. In his autobiography, Samuel gives a different account of this story. He claims that he was approached during the war by Walker and Currelly, who hoped to win him over to purchase a collection of Greek and Italian vases and statuettes from Allen Sturge, a distinguished London physician and an amateur archaeologist, who wanted to sell this collection to a museum in the English world. Sturge first considered the British Museum, but was persuaded to consider the ROM. Samuel, who confessed that he "knew nothing of Greek and Italian vases,"[100] needed little persuasion before he offered the £5000 requested by Sturge. The minutes of the board of trustees do not substantiate Samuel's version of the story but provide a detailed description of the problems encountered by the museum when they learned about the donation in the spring of 1920.

From 1920 onwards, Samuel became one of the most active philanthropists in Toronto. With Mrs. H. D. Warren, he provided a financial safety net for the ROM and the University of Toronto.[101] Among his larger donations to the ROM was the famous Chinese library that made Toronto "one of the chief centres of study in Chinese art and literature on this continent."[102] When in 1933 Bishop William C. White, the Anglican bishop of Honan Province in China, informed the president of the University of Toronto, Dr. Henry John Cody, of the possibility that a very large private library and collection (considered the finest in Peking) would become available for purchase, Sigmund Samuel and Sir Robert Mond provided the necessary funding.[103] Furthermore, both agreed to contribute to the necessary funds for an extension of the museum that was to house the new collection.

It was an accident of his eight-year-old daughter Florence that led Sigmund Samuel to become involved in supporting Toronto Western Hospital. When he returned to the hospital to thank the doctors for their treatment of his daughter, Samuel asked if he could do anything in return. Faced with such a question, the hospital director invited him to join the board of governors, on which Samuel served as president and honorary president for many years. During this time, Samuel contributed significant amounts to the expansion of the hospital and made sure that his family's name was attached to the building. When a new radiology wing was opened, it was named after his wife. His involvement with this enterprise brought with it further distancing from his Jewish origin, since he joyfully participated in its annual Christmas staff parties. All of these endeavors were, however, surpassed by his involvement in the construction of a new university library. When the university's president, Sydney Smith, spoke with Samuel in 1951 about the necessity of constructing a new university library, Samuel readily donated CAD$500,000, which represented one-quarter of the total construction costs. It

FIGURE 5.1. Sigmund Samuel laying the cornerstone for the new library building of the University of Toronto on October 23, 1953. Courtesy of the University of Toronto Archives & Records Management Services.

FIGURE 5.2. Painting of Sigmund Samuel, LLD, University of Toronto and University of Western Ontario, by Archibald Barnes, from the booklet for the Sigmund Samuel Library at the University of Toronto. Courtesy of the University of Toronto Archives & Records Management Services.

was agreed that this new library building would be named in his honor—the Sigmund Samuel Library.[104]

After the library was opened to the public, Sigmund Samuel agreed with the university board that a brochure should be printed to explain his interest in this project. Furthermore, he covered the cost of printing and mailing 1,000 copies of this brochure (CAD\$5,076.18).[105] Its cover features a picture of him sitting in a chair and dressed in his graduation robe. Underneath this picture are listed his many philanthropic accomplishments, but there is no mention of his business achievements. First one learns that Samuel received an honorary LLD from the University of Toronto and from the University of Western Ontario. Then a long list of titles follows:

> Dr. Sigmund Samuel, donor of the Canadiana Gallery of the Province of Ontario and of the Royal Ontario Museum, Member of the Board of Gover-

FIGURE 5.3. Glass window at the entrance of the Sigmund Samuel
Library at the University of Toronto displaying Sigmund
Samuel's coat of arms. Courtesy of the University of
Toronto Archives & Records Management Services.

nors of the University of Toronto, a large contributor to the new Library Building of the University of Toronto, after whom it is named, Vice-President of
the Royal Ontario Museum, Hon.-President of Western Hospital of Toronto
. . . Fellow of the Royal Historical Society of England . . . Fellow of the Royal
Geographical Society of England . . . and recipient of the Cross of Lorraine
from the Government of France for his collection of "Canadiana" of the French
Regime in Canada.[106]

The second page displays the coat of arms of Sigmund Samuel's family, which has been prominently positioned on top of the main entrance door to the library on a stained glass window. The inscription in its lower part reads, "Honos Alit Artis" (Honor exalts the arts) and is derived from Cicero's *Tusculanae disputationes*. The next three pages include speeches by Rabbi Abraham L. Feinberg of Holy Blossom Temple, university president Sydney Smith, and Sigmund Samuel.

In 1948 Samuel gave CAD$150,000 for the construction of a building on Queen's Park Crescent West to house his Canadiana Gallery on the ground floor and the provincial archives on the upper two floors.[107] He again insisted that his name be visibly attached to the building. It was agreed that there would be a plaque on one side of the main entrance bearing the words "THE SIGMUND SAMUEL CANADIANA GALLERY OF THE ROYAL ONTARIO MUSEUM." In the vestibule the words "THIS GALLERY WAS ERECTED, AND THE CONTENTS COLLECTED AND GIVEN, BY SIGMUND SAMUEL, LL.D., F. R. HIST SOC (ENG) MCMXLVIII" were to be inscribed.[108] The plaque and the inscription served Samuel's desire to publicly display his philanthropic achievements. The publication of a second booklet, *The Sigmund Samuel Story,* was perfectly in line with these personal ambitions. In contrast to the first brochure, published on the occasion of the stone-laying ceremony for the Sigmund Samuel Library, the title page of the second brochure referred to both his economic and philanthropic successes by displaying the building that housed his Canadiana Collection as well as the building that housed the headquarters of his enterprise. On page 2, however, we again find the picture of Sigmund Samuel in his graduation robe—the picture of an academic, not a businessman. The text beside the picture does not mention any of his business successes but lists all his philanthropic engagements and memberships in learned societies. The first headline introduces Samuel as "Connoisseur . . . Benefactor . . . Industrialist . . ." The rest of this brochure is divided into two parts: the first part tells the story of Samuel's life and economic success, including the story of the family business in five pages; the second part is dedicated to his philanthropic engagement for the University of Toronto, the ROM, and the Canadiana Collection and covers sixteen pages.

Sigmund Samuel, as Lorne Pierce points out, "has not, as some benefactors, contented himself with signing the cheques for the acquisitions. He has selected them with discrimination."[109] As it becomes clear from the exchanges of letters between Samuel, the university administration, and the director of the ROM in the early 1950s, he also remained deeply involved in the spending of the money he donated and the acquisition of art objects. In 1952 he assigned the net income from the estate of his late wife (the estate was in excess of $1 million) to the "Governors of the University for their own use."[110] He insisted, however, that half of the annual return of $30,000 from the Leah May Samuel Estate should be available for special purchases that he would conduct on his own. It was not unusual that the ROM would receive invoices for acquisitions for the Canadiana Collection that Samuel had arranged without consulting the administration.[111] He clearly intended to have a word in what would be shown in the Canadiana Collection, even after he had turned it over to the university and the museum.

In addition to the financial contributions to the construction of a new wing for the ROM, the Sigmund Samuel Library of the University of Toronto, and the

FIGURE 5.4. Toronto Personalities: Sigmund Samuel, by Jack Moranz (Globe and Mail, December 17, 1932). Courtesy of the Toronto Public Library.

provincial archives building, Samuel donated the Sturge Collection, more than 1,000 Japanese prints and 2,000 pieces of fine Japanese silk brocades, and a large collection of fossils to the paleontological collection of the ROM, and together with Robert Mond the Mu Library. His gifts to the university and the ROM alone are estimated at about CAD$1 million. The total of all his donations to public institutions amount to more than CAD$2 million.[112]

Samuel's philanthropic engagement brought him recognition from Toronto's Christian elites and proximity to academics and intellectuals. In 1933 the university conferred upon him, Sir Robert Mond, and Mrs. H. D. Warren the honorary degree of Doctor of Law for their philanthropic support to the ROM and the university. Unlike other philanthropists who received honorary degrees, Samuel went ahead and even published *The Seven Years' War in Canada, 1756–1763: Being a Volume of Records and Illustrations Together with a Pictorial Travelogue Showing the Stage of Development Which America Had Reached Seventy Years after the Seven Years' War* (Toronto: Ryerson Press, 1934). This was not a scholarly treatment of the war but a compilation of tracts, letters, documents, and pictures. His pride in his "academic achievement" transcended public and private life. Although he lacked a university education, he insisted, after he had received the honorary doctorate, that all his grandchildren call him "Dr. Samuel."[113]

Unlike Alfred Mond, Sigmund Samuel had the feeling of being an accepted Jew, a so-called white Jew, within Toronto High Society. Although he complained about the anti-Semitic climate of Toronto up until the 1960s, it was his philanthropic engagement that probably contributed to the integration of other Jews into Toronto society. Nevertheless, Samuel was one of the few Jews whose philanthropy was accepted by the establishment prior to World War II. This may have been because of the public appearance and pronounced distance of Samuel from the Jewish community. He was socially and politically connected to influential circles in London, and he was socially active and insisted on contacts with the Christian establishment of Toronto. His education at the Model School (although short) brought him into contact with many future businessmen and thus provided the basis for a social network. Samuel's aspirations to be an English gentleman and his high regard for the arts and education won him great influence in Toronto's philanthropic establishment.[114]

His decision to remain aloof from the Jewish community—socially, financially, and even geographically (his house at Forest Hill Drive was far from the traditional Jewish neighborhood)—was not an easy one. Samuel had to give up important elements of traditional Jewish life and accept certain elements of Christian life. He did not go, however, as far as the Mond family, as Samuel occasionally went to synagogue. Nevertheless, Samuel decided that his children would attend Trinity College—the most conservative and Anglican college of the University of Toronto—because he wanted to make sure they were integrated into Toronto society. Several of his grandchildren were sent to the Bishop Strachan School and raised Anglican.[115]

The philanthropic engagement of Sigmund Samuel is an exemplary case for the transformation of economic capital into social capital. His success in business was insufficient to gain recognition from the social elites of his home city. His religion proved to be an obstacle to gaining entrance into clubs and to receiving recognition from other wealthy families. The doors of Toronto's High Society remained closed to him for a long time. His economic success provided him, however, with the necessary financial means to engage in philanthropic activities, which in turn brought him recognition from the established elites. His contributions surpassed those of wealthy Christian Toronto businessmen. These contributions allowed Samuel also to attach his name to institutions of High Culture and Higher Learning and thus to intellectual pursuits and fame. Buildings and collections have been named after him, books dedicated to him, honorary degrees bestowed upon him, and his picture preserved in many publications. The naming of buildings after him (plaques and inscriptions in stone), the inclusion of his coat of arms above the library entrance, and the publication of his booklet were an integral part of Sigmund Samuel's philanthropic engagement and clearly demonstrate the public character of the exchange of economic capital into social capital. Samuel remarked in his autobiography that even a dinosaur was named after him—the *Struthiomimus samueli*. Philanthropy was always an exchange process for Samuel. In his autobiography, he stated, "I have really received more from the Museum than I ever gave to it, because it has brought me together with men of great learning and, I might say humbly, of similar tastes to myself."[116]

Conclusion

The shift from a focus on national history to a topical history across various regions and countries allows us to reconsider the importance of the nation-state and national identity in the long nineteenth century. Even though the nation-state has shaped nineteenth-century society and the way historians write the history of that period, it should not become an analytical cage. Daniel T. Rodgers reminded us of the transnational character and context of all major historical movements and events in American history from the American Revolution to the antislavery movement and the creation of modern social policy.[1] The culture of nineteenth-century elite philanthropy in particular can only be understood within this transnational and transatlantic context. There was no distinct American, Canadian, or German philanthropy, but one universal phenomenon resulted from frequent intercultural transfers and adaptations. The social elites of Leipzig, London, Boston, New York, and Toronto were connected by travel and migration. Travelers and migrants acted as agents of intercultural transfer and thus contributed to the exchange of ideas and concepts with regard to urban organization and social domination. Even though these elites were separated by the Atlantic Ocean, they were united by a common value system and the claim to social leadership.

Philanthropy was given a central place in that value system and recognized as a tool for the formation of cohesive social groups. Throughout the nineteenth century, old elites instigated various major philanthropic projects that were to solidify their grip on power and to provide a second layer of domination parallel to the political government. Participation in these projects was restricted to individuals of the right background and socioeconomic standing. These institutions were surrounded by the air of exclusivity. One's participation in these projects was dependent on selection and invitation. Having received such an invitation was equal to social approval and inclusion in High Society. The boards of trustees and the projects themselves became the target of a heated contest between old and new elites. While in this contest the large-scale exclusion of the new elites from the institutions of the old elites in New York resulted in the creation of a divided philanthropic culture, old elites in Boston and Toronto, albeit for different reasons, avoided such a division of philanthropic activities and culture.

In contrast, the integration of women and Jews who aspired to places on the boards of museums and social housing companies occurred without much public notice. Women advanced from caregivers to members of charitable associations to board members of social housing companies and trustees of museums. This was an incremental process, in which women attained positions of responsibility as well as economic and social power. The idea that women would provide care for the destitute was certainly part of Victorian thinking about women's place in society, but it was not intended to encourage women to become involved in shaping nineteenth-century urban society. Many but not all wealthy Jews recognized the value of nonsectarian philanthropy for their integration into Christian-dominated urban society. Jewish engagement for major philanthropic projects did not arise from open confrontation but, as the example of Sigmund Samuel suggests, from negotiation between organizers of philanthropic projects and individual Jews. These negotiations resulted in the inclusion of few selected Jews into the leading circles of society. Its result, however, was by no means an integrated multireligious leisure class. Religious prejudice and anti-Semitism simply run too deep.

This book's focus on elite philanthropy runs somehow against newer approaches in American and British scholarship in which philanthropy is no longer seen as an exclusive elite phenomenon or limited to significant financial contributions. Small donations, memberships in charitable associations, and volunteer work have received their due attention. However, should one really treat all actions, from volunteering time to paying a membership fee of a few cents or dollars to providing an endowment of several hundred thousand dollars, as expressions of the same phenomenon? Or is there a difference between donating time and establishing a foundation? German scholars of philanthropy differentiate between *Spenden* (donating small amounts of money) and *Stiften* (creating a foundation or an endowment).[2] While Stiften is mostly reserved for the elites, Spenden is a phenomenon that transcends social class and can be found in all sections of society. Such a differentiation seems to be useful for future research about philanthropy. While there is no doubt that members of all social classes engaged in Spenden and volunteering, Stiften was a typical elite phenomenon. Stiften differs from Spenden not only by the amounts of money provided but also by the intentions of the philanthropist and the outcome. Philanthropists created foundations and endowments or co-financed the establishment of museums and hospitals for reasons of commemoration and the desire to imprint their ideas on the public sphere. The result of their action was never hidden but, instead, was intended to create public interest and recognition beyond one's death.

Further, Stiften allowed its protagonists to create institutions that seem to offer social control over urban society. In museums, museum makers had a word in what was exhibited. Often collections were purchased and given to museums with precise instructions about how they were to be put on display. The selection of what to show in museums allowed philanthropists to influence public taste and trends. In the case of social housing enterprises, its founders were even in a position to materialize ideas about the desired family structure and social relations between lower-class families. In the eyes of philanthropists, Stiften established a cultural countergovernment that provided a power structure parallel to the political realm. While both power structures could and indeed did overlap for most of the nineteenth century, they could also offer different options for domination of urban society.

Notes

INTRODUCTION

1. The prime examples of this newer trend in historiography are Thomas Bender, *A Nation among Nations: America's Place in World History* (New York: Hill and Wang, 2006) and Daniel T. Rodgers, *Atlantic Crossings: Social Politics in a Progressive Age* (Cambridge: Belknap Press of Harvard University Press, 1998).

2. For the concept of intercultural transfer, see Matthias Middell, ed., *Kulturtransfer und Vergleich* (Leipzig: Leipziger Universitätsverlag, 2000); Gabriele Lingelbach, "Erträge und Grenzen zweier Ansätze: Kulturtransfer und Vergleich am Beispiel der französischen und amerikanischen Geschichtswissenschaft während des 19. Jahrhunderts," in Christoph Conrad und Sebastian Conrad, eds., *Die Nation schreiben: Geschichtswissenschaft im internationalen Vergleich* (Göttingen: Vandenhoeck & Ruprecht, 2002), 333–59; Johannes Paulmann, "Internationaler Vergleich und interkultureller Transfer: Zwei Forschungsansätze zur europäischen Geschichte des 18. bis 20. Jahrhunderts," *Historische Zeitschrift* 267 (1998): 649–85. Only a few American scholars have adopted the concept of intercultural transfer. See, e.g., Kirsten Belgum, "Reading Alexander von Humboldt: Cosmopolitan Naturalist with an American Spirit," in Lynne Tatlock and Matt Erlin, eds., *German Culture in Nineteenth-Century America: Reception, Adaptation, Transformation* (Rochester, N.Y.: Camden House, 2005), 107–27.

3. Matthias Middell, "Kulturtransfer und Historische Komparatistik—Thesen zu ihrem Verhältnis," in Middell, *Kulturtransfer und Vergleich,* 18.

4. Belgum, "Reading Alexander von Humboldt," 107.

5. Bernd Kortländer, "Begrenzung—Entgrenzung: Kultur- und Wissenschaftstransfer in Europa," in Lothar Jordan and Bernd Kortländer, eds., *Nationale Grenzen und internationaler Austausch: Studien zum Kultur- und Wissenschaftstransfer in Europa* (Tübingen: Niemeyer, 1995), 1–11.

6. Michel Espagne and Michael Werner, "Deutsch-Französischer Kulturtransfer als Forschungsgegenstand. Eine Problemskizze," in Michel Espagne and Michael Werner, eds., *Transferts: Les relations interculturelles dans l'espace franco-allemand (XVIIIᵉ et XIXᵉ Siècle)* (Paris: Editions Recherche sur les civilisations, 1988), 14.

7. Michel Espagne, "Kulturtransfer und Fachgeschichte der Geisteswissenschaften," in Middell, *Kulturtransfer und Vergleich,* 58–59; Daniel T. Rodgers, "Exceptionalism," in Anthony Molho and Gordon S. Wood, eds., *Imagined Histories: American Historians Interpret the Past* (Princeton, N.J.: Princeton University Press, 1998), 21–40; Belgum, "Reading Alexander von Humboldt," 108; Stefan Berger and Peter Lambert, "Intellectual Transfers and Mental Blockades: Anglo-German Dialogues in Historiography," in Stefan Berger, Peter Lambert, and Peter Schumann, eds., *Historikerdialoge: Geschichte, Mythos,*

und Gedächtnis im deutsch-britischen kulturellen Austausch, 1750–2000 (Göttingen: Vandenhoeck & Ruprecht, 2003), 12.

8. Florian Steger and Kay Peter Jankrift, "Einleitung," in Florian Steger and Kay Peter Jankrift, eds., *Gesundheit—Krankheit: Kulturtransfer medizinischen Wissens von der Spätantike bis in die Frühe Neuzeit* (Cologne: Böhlau, 2004), 3–4.

9. Sven Beckert, "Die Kultur des Kapitals: Bürgerliche Kultur in New York und Hamburg im 19. Jahrhundert," in Warburg-Haus, ed., *Vorträge aus dem Warburg-Haus* (Berlin: Akademie, 2000), 4:143–75.

10. Mary Louise Pratt, *Imperial Eyes: Travel Writing and Transculturation* (New York: Routledge, 1992).

11. George Ticknor, *Journals*, vol. 2 (September 1816 to October 1816), September 22–23 (Dresden Public Library).

12. Thomas Adam, "Germany Seen through American Eyes: George and Anna Eliot Ticknor's German Travel Logs," in Hartmut Keil, ed., *Transatlantic Cultural Contexts: Essays in Honor of Eberhard Brüning* (Tübingen: Stauffenburg, 2005), 151–63.

13. Smithsonian Archives of American Art, George Comfort deposit reel 4276 T 6814 (microfilm): *A Metropolitan Art Museum in the City of New York: Proceedings of a Meeting Held at the Theatre of the Union League Club, Tuesday Evening, November 23, 1869* (New York: Printed for the Committee, 1869), 9.

14. Espagne and Werner, "Deutsch-Französischer Kulturtransfer," 21.

15. William Stowe, *European Travel in Nineteenth-Century American Culture* (Princeton, N.J.: Princeton University Press, 1994), 10, 12.

16. Thomas Adam, "Cultural Baggage: The Building of the Urban Community in a Trans-atlantic World," in Thomas Adam and Ruth Gross, eds., *Traveling between Worlds: German-American Encounters* (College Station: Texas A&M University Press, 2006), 87–93.

17. David C. Hammack, ed., *Making the Nonprofit Sector in the United States: A Reader* (Bloomington: Indiana University Press, 1998); Walter W. Powell and Richard Steinberg, eds., *The Nonprofit Sector: A Research Handbook* (New Haven, Conn.: Yale University Press, 2006).

18. Manuel Frey, *Macht und Moral des Schenkens: Staat und bürgerliche Mäzene vom späten 18. Jahrhundert bis zur Gegenwart* (Berlin: Fannei & Walz, 1999); Jürgen Kocka and Manuel Frey, eds., *Bürgerkultur und Mäzenatentum im 19. Jahrhundert* (Berlin: Fannei & Walz, 1998); Thomas W. Gaehtgens and Martin Schieder, eds., *Mäzenatisches Handeln: Studien zur Kultur des Bürgersinns in der Gesellschaft* (Berlin: Fannei & Walz, 1999).

19. It would be misleading to translate Bürgertum as "bourgeoisie." For the German research on Bürgertum, see Jonathan Sperber, "Bürger, Bürgertum, Bürgerlichkeit, Bürgerliche Gesellschaft: Studies of German (Upper) Middle Class and Its Sociocultural World," *Journal of Modern History* 69 (June 1997): 271–97; Thomas Mergel, "Die Bürgertumsforschung nach 15 Jahren: Für Hans-Ulrich Wehler zum 70. Geburtstag," *Archiv für Sozialgeschichte* 41 (2001): 515–38.

20. See, e.g., Frederic Cople Jaher, *The Urban Establishment: Upper Strata in Boston, New York, Charleston, Chicago, and Los Angeles* (Urbana: University of Illinois Press, 1982). A prominent exception is Sven Beckert, *The Monied Metropolis: New York City and the Consolidation of the American Bourgeoisie, 1850–1896* (Cambridge: Cambridge University Press, 2001).

21. For the following argumentation, see Thorstein Veblen, *The Theory of the Leisure Class: An Economic Study of Institutions* (New York: Modern Library, 1934), 68–101.

22. Ibid., 76.

23. Ibid., 84.

24. Kathleen McCarthy, "Women and Political Culture," in Lawrence J. Friedman and Mark D. McGarvie, eds., *Charity, Philanthropy, and Civility in American History* (Cambridge: Cambridge University Press, 2003), 179, 190.

25. For the recent scholarship on Jewish philanthropy, see the contributions by Benjamin Maria Baader, Tobias Brinkmann, and Simone Lässig in Thomas Adam, ed., *Philanthropy, Patronage, and Civil Society: Experiences from Germany, Great Britain, and North America* (Bloomington: Indiana University Press, 2004), 163–218, and Benjamin Maria Baader, *Gender, Judaism, and Bourgeois Culture in Germany, 1800–1870* (Bloomington: Indiana University Press, 2006); Simone Lässig, "Juden und Mäzenatentum in Deutschland: Religiöses Ethos, kompensierendes Minderheitsverhalten, oder genuine Bürgerlichkeit?" *Zeitschrift für Geschichtswissenschaft* 46 (1998): 211–36.

26. Kathleen D. McCarthy, *Noblesse Oblige: Charity and Cultural Philanthropy in Chicago, 1849–1929* (Chicago: University of Chicago Press, 1982), 23.

27. Kathleen D. McCarthy, *American Creed: Philanthropy and the Rise of Civil Society, 1700–1865* (Chicago: University of Chicago Press, 2003), 30–48; Richard Stites, *The Women's Liberation Movement in Russia: Feminism, Nihilism, and Bolshevism, 1860–1930* (Princeton, N.J.: Princeton University Press, 1978), 68.

1. Cultural Excursions

1. For information on Frauenkirche Dresden, see its webpage, www.frauenkirche-dresden.org; "Stiftung: Wideraufbau der Frauenkirche schuldenfrei finanziert," in *Leipziger Volkszeitung*, October 28, 2005.

2. Wolfgang Klötzer, "Über das Stiften—Zum Beispiel Frankfurt am Main," in Bernhard Kirchgässner and Hans-Peter Becht, eds., *Stadt und Mäzenatentum* (Sigmaringen: Jan Thorbecke, 1997), 15; Judith Metz and Claudia B. Reschke, "Kollektives Mäzenatentum: Freundeskreise und Fördervereine an Kunstmuseen in Deutschland und ein Blick in die USA," in Thomas W. Gaehtgens and Martin Schieder, eds., *Mäzenatisches Handeln: Studien zur Kultur des Bürgersinns in der Gesellschaft* (Zwickau: Fannei & Walz, 1998), 196–215; Karsten Borgmann, "Kultur des Reichtums: Philanthropy, Wohltätigkeit, und Elite in den Vereinigten Staaten von Amerika," in Gaehtgens and Schieder, *Mäzenatisches Handeln,* 216–34. See B. Hills Bush, "Amerika, das Land der großzügigen Spender," in *Frankfurter Allgemeine Zeitung,* February 9, 1991, 13; August Everding, "Alles besser in Amerika? Zur privat finanzierten Kultur," in *Süddeutsche Zeitung,* March 30, 1996, 32.

3. Gabriele Lingelbach, "Cultural Borrowing of Autonomous Development: American and German Universities in the Late Nineteenth Century," in Thomas Adam and Ruth Gross, eds., *Traveling between Worlds: German-American Encounters* (College Station: Texas A&M, 2006), 116.

4. Daniel T. Rodgers, *Atlantic Crossings: Social Politics in a Progressive Age* (Cambridge, Mass.: Belknap Press of Harvard University Press, 1998).

5. Neil Harris, *The Artist in American Society: The Formative Years, 1790–1860* (New York: George Braziller, 1966), 146.

6. Eberhard Brüning, "'Saxony Is a Prosperous and Happy Country': American Views of the Kingdom of Saxony in the Nineteenth Century," in Adam and Gross, *Traveling between Worlds,* 20–50.

7. A. B. Meyer, *Über Museen des Ostens der Vereinigten Staaten von Nord-Amerika* (Berlin: A. Friedländer, 1900–1901).

8. Kathleen D. McCarthy, *Noblesse Oblige: Charity and Cultural Philanthropy in Chicago, 1849–1929* (Chicago: University of Chicago Press, 1982), 156–57; Jay Pridmore, *Inventive Genius: The History of the Museum of Science and Industry, Chicago* (Chicago: Museum of Science and Industry, 1996), 11–22; Jay Pridmore, *Museum of Science and Industry, Chicago* (Chicago: Harry N. Abrams, 1997), 17–25. For the life of Julius Rosenwald, see M. R. Werner, *Julius Rosenwald: The Life of a Practical Humanitarian* (New York: Harper & Brothers, 1939), and Peter M. Ascoli, *Julius Rosenwald: The Man Who Built Sears, Roebuck and Advanced the Cause of Black Education in the American South* (Bloomington: Indiana University Press, 2006).

9. For descriptions of these museums and art galleries by American travelers, see Henry E. Dwight, *Travels in the North of Germany in the Years 1825 and 1826* (New York: G. & C. & H. Carvill, 1829), 354–56, 369–72, and J. Bayard Taylor, *Views A-foot; or, Europe Seen with Knapsack and Staff* (New York: George Putnam, 1952), 129–33. For a general overview, see Eberhard Brüning, "'It Is a Glorious Collection': Amerikanische Bildungsbürger des 19. Jahrhunderts auf 'Pilgerfahrt' zur Dresdner Gemäldegalerie," in *Jahrbuch der Staatlichen Kunstsammlungen Dresden* 1996/97, 99–105. For William Cullen Bryant, see *The Letters of William Cullen Bryant*, vol. 2: *1836–49*, ed. William Cullen Bryant II and Thomas G. Voss (New York: Fordham University Press, 1977), 287–418. For George Ticknor, see *Life, Letters, and Journals of George Ticknor*, 2 vols. (London: Sampson Low, Marston, Searle & Rivington, 1876; Boston: Houghton Mifflin, 1909), 2:299ff.

10. Will Irwin, Earl Chapin May, and Joseph Hotchkiss, *A History of the Union League Club of New York City* (New York: Dodd, Mead, 1952), 16–17, 24.

11. Francis Gerry Fairfield, *The Clubs of New York: With an Account of the Origin, Progress, Present Condition, and Membership of the Leading Clubs; an Essay on New York Club Life* (New York: Henry L. Hinton, 1873), 114–15.

12. Washington Irving, *Letters*, vol. 1, 1802–23, ed. Ralph M. Aderman et al. (Boston: Twayne, 1978), 727–36; Washington Irving, *Journals and Notebooks*, vol. 3, *1819–27*, ed. Walter A. Reichart (Madison: University of Wisconsin Press, 1970), 92–157; James Franklin Beard, ed., *The Letters and Journals of James Fenimore Cooper* (Cambridge, Mass.: Belknap Press of Harvard University Press, 1960), 418–28.

13. William W. Stowe, *Going Abroad: European Travel in Nineteenth-Century American Culture* (Princeton, N.J.: Princeton University Press, 1994), 5.

14. *Letters of William Cullen Bryant*, 2:287–421.

15. Winifred E. Howe, *A History of the Metropolitan Museum of Art with a Chapter on the Early Institutions of Art in New York* (New York: Gilliss Press, 1913; reprint, New York: Arno Press, 1974), 100–101; Leo Lerman, *The Museum: One Hundred Years and the Metropolitan Museum of Art* (New York: Viking Press, 1969), 12.

16. *The Letters of William Cullen Bryant*, vol. 5, *1865–71*, ed. William Cullen Bryant II and Thomas G. Voss (New York: Fordham University Press, 1992), 344–45; Charles H. Brown, *William Cullen Bryant* (New York: Charles Scribner's Sons, 1971), 486.

17. *A Metropolitan Art Museum in the City of New York: Proceedings of a Meeting Held at the Theatre of the Union League Club, Tuesday Evening, November 23, 1869* (New York: Printed for the Committee, 1869), 9. Stored on George Comfort deposit reel 4276 T 6814 (microfilm), Smithsonian Archives of American Art (hereafter Comfort reel).

18. For a biography, see David Tatham, *George Fiske Comfort,* pamphlet of the Syracuse University Library Associates. A comprehensive biography of Comfort needs still to be written. However, two manuscripts that provide excellent accounts of his life are available in the Syracuse University Archive's Comfort Papers: Barbara Hall Cruttenden, "George Fisk Comfort, a Biography," master's thesis, Syracuse University, 1956, and David Tatham, "George Fisk Comfort" (undated).

19. George Fiske Comfort to Reverend John Makan, April 14, 1866, Comfort reel.

20. *A Metropolitan Art Museum in the City of New York,* 15. For the Kensington Museum, see Clive Wainwright, "The Making of the South Kensington Museum, I–IV," ed. Charlotte Gere, *Journal of the History of Collections* 14 (2002): 3–78; and Anthony Burton, "The Uses of the South Kensington Art Collections," *Journal of the History of Collections* 14 (2002): 79–95. For a less favorable contemporary account, see J. C. Robinson, "On Our National Art Museums and Galleries," *Nineteenth Century* 32 (1892): 1029ff.

21. Steven Conn, *Museums and American Intellectual Life, 1876–1926* (Chicago: University of Chicago Press, 1998), 195–97.

22. *A Metropolitan Art Museum in the City of New York,* 15–16.

23. "Dean Comfort's Departure," Syracuse University Archive, Comfort Family Papers, box 1.

24. Comfort to Makan, April 14, 1866, Comfort reel.

25. "Sketch of My Life," handwritten account by George Fiske Comfort, Comfort Family Papers, box 1.

26. Manuel Frey, *Macht und Moral des Schenkens: Staat und bürgerliche Mäzene vom späten 18. Jahrhundert bis zur Gegenwart* (Zwickau: Fannei & Walz, 1999), 66; James J. Sheehan, *Museums in the German Art World from the End of the Old Regime to the Rise of Modernism* (New York: Oxford University Press 2000), 101–11.

27. Thomas Adam, "Die Kommunalisierung von Kunst und Kultur als Grundkonsens der deutschen Gesellschaft ab dem ausgehenden 19. Jahrhundert: Das Beispiel Leipzig," *Die Alte Stadt* 26 (1999): 86. For an excellent account of the history of the Leipzig Art Association, see Anett Müller, *Der Leipziger Kunstverein und das Musuem der bildenden Künste: Materialien einer Geschichte (1836–1886/87)* (Leizpig: Nouvelle Alliance, 1995). See also Margaret Eleanor Menninger, "Art and Civic Patronage in Leipzig, 1848–1914," Ph.D. diss., Harvard University, 1998, 79–94.

28. Thomas Adam, "Stiften in deutschen Bürgerstädten vor dem Ersten Weltkrieg: Das Beispiel Leipzig," *Geschichte und Gesellschaft* 33 (2007): 46–72.

29. Andreas Hansert, *Bürgerkultur und Kulturpolitik in Frankfurt am Main: Eine historisch-soziologische Rekonstruktion* (Frankfurt am Main: Waldemar Kramer, 1992), 88–106; Andreas Hansert, *Geschichte des Städelschen Museums-Vereins Frankfurt am Main* (Frankfurt am Main: Umschau, 1994).

30. Walter Grasskamp, *Museumsgründer und Museumsstürmer: Zur Sozialgeschichte des Kunstmuseums* (Munich: C. H. Beck, 1981), 36–39. For the royal museums, see Manuel Frey and Tilman von Stockhausen, "Potlatsch in Preußen? Schenkriten an der Berliner Gemäldegalerie im 19. Jahrhundert," in Jürgen Kocka and Manuel Frey, eds., *Bürgerkultur und Mäzenatentum im 19. Jahrhundert* (Zwickau: Fannei & Walz, 1998), 18–37. For the bourgeois art museums, see Menninger, "Art and Civic Patronage in Leipzig," 78–79.

31. Adam, "Die Kommunalisierung von Kunst und Kultur," 85–93; Menninger, "Art and Civic Patronage in Leipzig," 94–105.

32. Judith Huggins Balfe and Thomas A. Cassilly, " 'Friends of . . . ': Individual Patronage through Arts Institutions," in Judith Huggins Balfe, ed., *Paying the Piper: Causes and Consequences of Art Patronage* (Urbana: University of Illinois Press, 1993), 119; Victoria D. Alexander, *Museums and Money: The Impact of Funding on Exhibitions, Scholarship, and Management* (Bloomington: Indiana University Press, 1996), 19; Calvin Tomkins, *Merchants and Masterpieces: The Story of the Metropolitan Museum of Art* (New York: Henry Holt, 1989), 21, 31. Wolfgang Ismayr does not even deal with the nineteenth century. See Ismayr, "Cultural Federalism and Public Support for the Arts in the Federal Republic of Germany," in Milton C. Cummings and Richard S. Katz, eds., *The Patron State: Government and the Arts in Europe, North America, and Japan* (New York: Oxford University Press, 1987), 45–67.

33. "Biographical Sketch of Dr. George F. Comfort," 4–5, Comfort Family Papers, box 1. Comfort mentioned that he intended to propagate the idea of establishing art museums in the United States in his letters to Ferdinand Karl Wilhelm Piper, a professor at the University of Berlin. See Piper to Comfort, August 24, 1866, and June 19, 1868, Comfort reel. See also George Fisk Comfort, *Art Museums in America* (Boston: H. O. Houghton, 1870).

34. Extracts from the address of Professor Comfort before the Syracuse Chamber of Commerce regarding a museum of fine arts, 15, Comfort reel.

35. Ibid., 17–19.

36. Howe, *Metropolitan Museum,* 119.

37. Menninger, "Art and Civic Patronage in Leipzig," 90–91, 94–99; Müller, *Der Leipziger Kunstverein,* 44–51, 86–93.

38. A complete list can be found in Howe, *Metropolitan Museum,* 116–17.

39. Ibid., 125.

40. Fairfield, *The Clubs of New York,* 57–83; Reginald T. Townsend, *Mother of Clubs: Being the History of the First Hundred Years of the Union Club of the City of New York, 1836–1936* (New York: Printing House of William Edwin Rudge, 1936), 9–24.

41. The first available membership list appears in the *Sixth Annual Report of the Trustees of the Association for the Year Ending May 1, 1876,* 86–90. For Leipzig see Müller, *Der Leipziger Kunstverein,* 46–47.

42. Howe, *Metropolitan Museum,* 129–30.

43. Wainwright, "The Making of the South Kensington Museum I–IV"; Burton, "The Uses of the South Kensington Art Collections." See also A. B. Meyer, *Studies of the Museums and Kindred Institutions of New York City, Albany, Buffalo, and Chicago, with Notes on Some European Institutions* (Washington: Smithsonian Institution, 1905), 529–30. Also Conn, *Museums and American Intellectual Life,* 195–97.

44. Howe, *Metropolitan Museum,* 134.

45. Ibid., 119; Conn, *Museums and American Intellectual Life,* 197; Menninger, "Art and Civic Patronage in Leipzig," 113–18.

46. *A Metropolitan Art Museum in the City of New York,* 16.

47. C. W. Colby, "Sir Edmund Walker," *Caduceus* 5, no. 3 (June 1924): 7, Sir Edmund Walker Papers MS 1, box 41, Fisher Rare Book Library, University of Toronto (hereafter Walker Papers).

48. Colby, "Sir Edmund Walker," *Caduceus,* 8.

49. Charles R. McCullough, "Sir Edmund Walker," *Hamilton Spectator,* April 18, 1942, Walker Papers, box 41:29.

50. Howe, *Metropolitan Museum,* 143–84.

51. Ibid., 138–39, 164; Tomkins, *Merchants and Masterpieces,* 38–41, 45.

52. For an overview of the exhibition in the Douglas Mansion, see Howe, *Metropolitan Museum,* 167–70; for the museum building in Central Park, 189–225.

53. Katherine A. Lochnan, "The Walker Journals: Reminiscences of John Lavery and William Holman Hunt," *Revue d'art canadienne* 9 (1982): 58, Walker Papers, box 41:34.

54. Fergus Cronin, "The Great Toronto Crusade: The Story of the Art Gallery of Ontario," manuscript from the archive of the Art Gallery of Ontario, 1976, 1:2. See also Harold G. Needham, "Origins of the Royal Ontario Museum," M.A. thesis, University of Toronto, 1970, 142.

55. See James Mavor, *My Windows on the Street of the World,* 2 vols. (London: J. M. Dent & Sons; New York: E. P. Dutton, 1923); Martin L. Friedland, *The University of Toronto: A History* (Toronto: University of Toronto Press, 2002), 117–19.

56. Travel log, James Mavor Papers MS 119, box 56A: 22, Fisher Rare Book Library, University of Toronto; Mavor, *My Windows,* 377–81; Thomas Adam, "Philanthropic Landmarks: The Toronto Trail from a Comparative Perspective, 1870s to the 1930s," *Urban History Review* 30 (2001): 7–8.

57. Art Gallery of Toronto, 4, Mavor Papers MS 119, box 56B, B No. 5 B.

58. *Annual Reports of the Trustees of the Association of the Metropolitan Museum of Art.*

59. Adam, "Philanthropic Landmarks," 11.

60. Art Gallery of Toronto, Mavor Papers; Agreement Made the Twentieth Day of January AD 1911 between the Art Museum of Toronto . . . and the Municipal Corporation of the City of Toronto, Walker Papers, no. 27 A 7.

61. Howe, *Metropolitan Museum,* 163.

62. Meyer, *Studies of the Museums,* 321, 322.

63. Ibid., 325, 326.

64. Ibid., 328.

65. Ibid., 348; Adam, "Philanthropic Landmarks," 8.

66. Meyer, *Studies of Museums,* 328.

67. A. B. Meyer, *Über einige europäische Museen und verwandte Institute* (Berlin: A. Friedländer, 1902).

68. Adam, "Philanthropic Landmarks," 9, 13–16; Charles Trick Currelly, *I Brought the Ages Home* (Toronto: Ryerson Press, 1956), 129; Lovat Dickson, *The Museum Makers: The Story of the Royal Ontario Museum* (Toronto: Royal Ontario Museum), 11–18.

69. "Biographical Sketch of Professor Henry Montgomery," ROM archive.

70. "Report of Museums by Henry Montgomery," May 1906, 33–40, ROM archive.

71. Ibid., 35.

72. Adam, "Philanthropic Landmarks," 14–15; "The Ten Friends of the Arts" (six-page manuscript). I would like to thank Wentworth Walker, the grandson of Sir Edmund Walker, for providing this copy to me. The copy sheds light on the financing scheme of the ROM.

73. Walter Muir Whitehill, *Museum of Fine Arts, Boston: A Centennial History,* 2 vols. (Cambridge, Mass.: Belknap Press of Harvard University Press, 1970), 1:179; Museum of Fine Arts, Boston, *The Museum Commission in Europe* (January 1905), 1:6–7, 65–75, 85–88.

74. MFA, *Museum Commission in Europe,* 3:86.

75. Whitehill, *Museum of Fine Arts, Boston,* 1:221.

76. Woldemar von Seidlitz, "Museumsvereine," *Museumskunde* 9 (1913): 36–43; Karsten Borgmann, "'The Glue of Civil Society': A Comparative Approach to Art Museum Philanthropy at the Turn of the Twentieth Century," in Thomas Adam, ed., *Philanthropy, Patronage, and Civil Society: Experiences from Germany, Great Britain, and North America* (Bloomington: Indiana University Press, 2004), 34–54.

77. Michael Harris, "The Purpose of the American Public Library: A Revisionist Interpretation of History," *Library Journal* 98 (1973): 2510; David B. Tyack, *George Ticknor and the Boston Brahmins* (Cambridge, Mass.: Harvard University Press, 1967), 208–10. For Ticknor's travels to Germany and his experience in Göttingen, Dresden, Leipzig, and Berlin, see the European travel journals of George and Anna Ticknor in the years 1816–19 and 1835–38, Dartmouth College Library. Ticknor was not the only Massachusetts citizen who was inspired by the Dresden library to establish a similar institution back home. Joseph Lee tells the story of John Smith, a wealthy flax manufacturer of Andover, Mass., who established a library in his hometown after he had visited the Dresden library. See Joseph Lee, *Constructive and Preventive Philanthropy* (New York: Macmillan, 1902), 11–12.

78. For Ticknor's first stay in Germany, see Frank G. Ryder, "An American View of Germany—1817," *American-German Review* 25 (1959): 3, 16–19, and "George Ticknor on the German Scene," *American-German Review* 25 (1959): 4, 28–30.

79. Steven Allaback and Alexander Medlicott Jr., eds., *A Guide to the Microfilm Edition of the European Journals of George and Anna Ticknor* (Hanover, N.H.: Dartmouth College Library, 1978), v.

80. Tyack, *George Ticknor,* 53, 54.

81. For the history of the Royal Saxon Library in Dresden, see Wolfgang Frühauf, "Von der kurfürstlichen Privatbibliothek zur Sächsischen Landesbibliothek," in Lothar Koch, ed., *Von der Liberey zur Bibliothek: 440 Jahre Sächsische Landesbibliothek* (Dresden, 1996), 13–27.

82. Dwight, *Travels in the North of Germany,* 359–60.

83. *Life, Letters, and Journals of George Ticknor,* 2:299.

84. Ticknor, *Journal III* (October 26, 1835–May 4, 1836), April 1836, 178.

85. *Life, Letters, and Journals of George Ticknor,* 2:299–300.
86. Ibid., 2:303 (Edward Everett to George Ticknor); Tyack, *George Ticknor,* 209.
87. Harry Miller Lydenberg, *History of the New York Public Library Astor, Lenox and Tilden Foundations* (New York: New York Public Library, 1923), 3–4, 6, 21.
88. Ibid., 2; Tyack, *George Ticknor,* 54–55.
89. Lydenberg, *History of the New York Public Library,* 3.
90. See letters printed in ibid., 1–25, esp. 21 and 24.
91. Tyack, *George Ticknor,* 209.
92. *Life, Letters, and Journals of George Ticknor,* 2:301–303.
93. Walter Muir Whitehill, *Boston Public Library: A Centennial History* (Cambridge, Mass.: Harvard University Press, 1956), 27–33.
94. Neil Harris, *Cultural Excursions: Marketing Appetites and Cultural Tastes in Modern America* (Chicago: University of Chicago Press, 1990), 85–86.
95. *Life, Letters, and Journals of George Ticknor,* 2:305; Whitehill, *Boston Public Library,* 22, 34–37; Tyack, *George Ticknor,* 211; *Annual Report of the Trustees of the City Library,* 1853, 4.
96. *Annual Report of the Trustees of the City Library,* 1853, 4.
97. *Tenth Annual Report of the Trustees of the Public Library,* November 1862, 11 (Bates Fund $50,000; Phillips Fund $30,000; Lawrence Fund $10,000; Townsend Fund $4,000; Bigelow Fund $1,000).
98. *Life, Letters, and Journals of George Ticknor,* 2:313. Ticknor relied heavily on Felix Flügel, son of Dr. J. G. Flügel, a vice consul of the United States in Leipzig. See Eberhard Brüning, *Das Konsulat der Vereinigten Staaten von Amerika zu Leipzig unter besonderer Berücksichtigung des Konsuls Dr. J. G. Flügel (1839–1855)* (Berlin: Akademie, 1994).
99. *Report of the Trustees of the Public Library of the City of Boston,* July 1852, 17.
100. Abigail A. Van Slyck, *Free to All: Carnegie Libraries and American Culture, 1890–1920* (Chicago: University of Chicago Press, 1995).
101. Constantin Nörrenberg, "Congress und Conferenz der Bibliothekare in Chicago," *Centralblatt für Bibliothekswesen* 11 (1894): 70–77, 97–103.
102. Constantin Nörrenberg, *Die Volksbibliothek ihre Aufgaben und ihre Reform* (Berlin, 1895); Constantin Nörrenberg, *Die Bücher- und Lesehalle eine Bildungsanstalt der Zukunft* (Köln: Greven & Bechtold 1896).
103. For the perceived picture of the American library, see Eduard Reyer, "Amerikanische Bibliotheken," in *Centralblatt für Bibliothekswesen* 3 (1886): 121–29. For the history of the American library movement from a German point of view, see Johannes Langfeldt, ed., *Handbuch des Büchereiwesens* (Wiesbaden: Otto Harrassowitz, 1973), 273–93, 386–422. For an overview of the German public library movement, see Wolfgang Thauer, *Die Bücherhallenbewegung* (Wiesbaden: Harrassowitz, 1970); Langfeldt, *Handbuch des Büchereiwesen,* 567–621; Peter Vodosek, "Zwischen Philanthropismus und Sedativ: 'Die Bücherhallenbewegung,'" in Mark Lehmstedt and Andreas Herzog, eds., *Das bewegte Buch: Buchwesen und soziale, nationale, und kulturelle Bewegungen um 1900* (Wiesbaden: Harrassowitz, 1999), 397–407.
104. Thauer, *Die Bücherhallenbewegung,* 11; Vodosek, "Zwischen Philanthropismus und Sedativ," 401.

2. HEAVY LUGGAGE

1. David Ward, "Population Growth, Migration, and Urbanization, 1860–1920," in Thomas F. McIlwraith and Edward K. Muller, eds., *North America: The Historical Geography of a Changing Continent* (Lanham, Md.: Rowman & Littlefield, 2001), 285–305; Lawrence J.

Vale, *From the Puritans to the Projects: Public Housing and Public Neighbors* (Cambridge, Mass.: Harvard University Press, 2000), 51–62.

2. Anthony Jackson, *A Place Called Home: A History of Low-Cost Housing in Manhattan* (Cambridge, Mass.: MIT Press, 1976), 5.

3. *The Tenement Houses of New York City: A Contribution to the Study by the Tenement House Building Company* (New York: Albert B. King, 1891), 3–4.

4. For the view of the housing problem as a part of the public health issue, see Alan Marcus, *Plague of Strangers: Social Groups and the Origins of City Services in Cincinnati, 1819–1870* (Columbus: Ohio State University Press, 1991), 141–43; Roy Lubove, *The Progressives and the Slums: Tenement House Reform in New York City, 1890–1917* (Pittsburgh: University of Pittsburgh Press, 1962), 20–23. For the state response to the social housing problem in the United States, see Robert B. Fairbanks, "From Better Dwellings to Better Neighborhoods: The Rise and Fall of the First National Housing Movement," in John F. Bauman, Roger Biles, and Kristin M. Szylvian, eds., *From Tenements to the Taylor Homes* (University Park: Pennsylvania State University Press, 2000), 21–42; Robert W. De Forest and Lawrence Veiller, eds., *The Tenement House Problem Including the Report of the New York State Tenement House Commission of 1900,* 2 vols. (New York: Macmillan, 1903).

5. *The Tenement Houses of New York City,* 3.

6. For Bowditch, see "Letter from the Chairman of the State Board of Health, Concerning Houses for the People, Convalescent Homes, and the Sewage Questions," in *Second Annual Report of the State Board of Health of Massachusetts, January 1871* (Boston: Wright & Potter, State Printers, 1871), 181–243; David M. Culver, "Tenement House Reform in Boston, 1846–1898," Ph.D. thesis, Boston University, 1972, 140–44. For White, see Richard Plunz, *A History of Housing in New York City: Dwelling Type and Social Change in the American Metropolis* (New York: Columbia University Press, 1990), 92.

7. Thomas Adam, "Transatlantic Trading: The Transfer of Philanthropic Models between European and North American Cities during the Nineteenth and Early Twentieth Centuries," *Journal of Urban History* 28 (2002): 328–51. See also Emil Münsterberg, "Principles of Public Charity and of Private Philanthropy in Germany," *American Journal of Sociology* 2, no. 4 (January 1897): 589.

8. Culver, "Tenement House Reform in Boston," 145–48; Plunz, *A History of Housing in New York City,* 89–93.

9. *Seventeenth Annual Report of the Boston Co-operative Building Company* (Boston, 1888), 10–11.

10. Robert H. Bremner, "'An Iron Scepter Twined with Roses': The Octavia Hill System of Housing Management," *Social Service Review* 39 (1965): 222–31.

11. Eugenie Ladner Birch and Deborah S. Gardner, "The Seven-Percent Solution: A Review of Philanthropic Housing, 1870–1919," *Journal of Urban History* 7 (1981): 403–38.

12. Gerald Daly, "The British Roots of American Public Housing," *Journal of Urban History* 15 (1989): 399–434.

13. Kathleen Woodroofe, *From Charity to Social Work in England and the United States* (Toronto: University of Toronto Press, 1962), 90; William B. Cohen, "Epilogue: The European Comparison," in Lawrence J. Friedman and Mark D. McGarvie, eds., *Charity, Philanthropy, and Civility in American History* (New York: Cambridge University Press, 2003), 407.

14. Daniel T. Rodgers, *Atlantic Crossings: Social Politics in a Progressive Age* (Cambridge, Mass.: Belknap Press of Harvard University Press, 1998), 2; Daniel T. Rodgers, "Exceptionalism," in Anthony Molho and Gordon S. Wood, eds., *Imagined Histories: American Historians Interpret the Past* (Princeton, N.J.: Princeton University Press, 1998), 21–40.

15. Axel R. Schäfer, *American Progressives and German Social Reform, 1875–1920: Social Ethics, Moral Control, and the Regulatory State in a Transatlantic Context* (Stuttgart: Franz Steiner, 2000).

16. Thomas Adam, "Stiften in deutschen Bürgerstädten vor dem Ersten Weltkrieg: Das Beispiel Leipzig," *Geschichte und Gesellschaft* 33 (2007): 47–48; Andrew Lees, *Cities, Sin, and Social Reform in Imperial Germany* (Ann Arbor: University of Michigan Press, 2002); Stephen Pielhoff, *Paternalismus und Stadtarmut: Armutswahrnehmung und Privatwohltätigkeit im Hamburger Bürgertum, 1830–1914* (Hamburg: Verein für Hamburgische Geschichte, 1999); Thomas Küster, *Alte Armut und neues Bürgertum: Öffentliche und private Fürsorge in Münster von der Ära Fürstenberg bis zum Ersten Weltkrieg, 1756–1914* (Münster: Aschendorff, 1995); Meinolf Nitsch, *Private Wohltätigkeitsvereine im Kaiserreich: die praktische Umsetzung der bürgerlichen Sozialreform in Berlin* (Berlin: W. de Gruyter, 1999).

17. Jean H. Quataert, *Staging Philanthropy: Patriotic Women and the National Imagination in Dynastic Germany, 1813–1916* (Ann Arbor: University of Michigan Press, 2001).

18. Thomas Adam, "Bürgerliches Engagement und Zivilgesellschaft in deutschen und amerikanischen Städten des 19. Jahrhunderts im Vergleich," in Ralph Jessen, Sven Reichardt, and Ansgar Klein, eds., *Zivilgesellschaft als Geschichte: Studien zum 19. und 20. Jahrhundert* (Wiesbaden: Verlag für Sozialwissenschaften, 2004), 155–74; Renate Kastorff-Viehmann, "England, Frankreich, Preußen: Programme für den Arbeiterwohnungsbau im Industriegebiet im 19. Jahrhundert," *Westfälische Forschungen* 44 (1994): 140–51; Renate Kastorff-Viehmann, *Wohnungsbau für Arbeiter: Das Beispiel Ruhrgebiet bis 1914* (Aachen: Klenkes, 1981), 153–59; Wolfgang Ismayr, "Cultural Federalism and Public Support for the Arts in the Federal Republic of Germany," in Milton C. Cummings and Richard S. Katz, eds., *The Patron State: Government and the Arts in Europe, North America, and Japan* (New York: Oxford University Press, 1987), 45–67; Helmut K. Anheier and Wolfgang Seibel, "Germany," in Lester M. Salamon and Helmut K. Anheier, eds., *Defining the Nonprofit Sector: A Cross-National Analysis* (Manchester: Manchester University Press, 1997), 131.

19. Lees, *Cities, Sin, and Social Reform*, 394–95.

20. William Stowe, *European Travel in Nineteenth-Century American Culture* (Princeton, N.J.: Princeton University Press, 1994), 10.

21. See, e.g., Anthony Oberschall, *Empirical Social Research in Germany, 1848–1914* (Paris: Mouton, 1965).

22. Sharon Marcus, *Apartment Stories: City and Home in Nineteenth-Century Paris and London* (Berkeley: University of California Press, 1999), 104. See also the extensive discussion of the literature for the case of London in the same book, 246n63. See also Peter Keating, *Into Unknown England, 1866–1913: Selections from the Social Explorers* (Manchester: Manchester University Press, 1976); Deborah Epstein Nord, "The Social Explorer as Anthropologist: Victorian Travellers among the Urban Poor," in William Sharpe and Leonard Wallock, eds., *Visions of the Modern City* (Baltimore: Johns Hopkins University Press, 1987), 122–34.

23. Adelheid Popp, *The Autobiography of a Working Woman* (Westport, Conn.: Hyperion Press, 1983), 10.

24. Elisabeth Dietzmann, *Die Leipziger Einrichtungen der Armenpflege bis zur Übernahme der Armenverwaltung durch die Stadt 1881* (Leipzig: F. Ernst Steiger, 1932), 50–55; Stadtarchiv Leipzig, Armen- und Fürsorgeamt 15–20, vol. 5, 151 (Liagre), vol. 6, 70, 71 (Liagre); Nr. 148, vol. 1, 181 (Meyer), vol. 3, 205–14.

25. H. Mehner, "Der Haushalt und die Lebenshaltung einer Leipziger Arbeiterfamilie," *Jahrbuch für Gesetzgebung, Verwaltung, und Volkswirthschaft im Deutschen Reich* 11 (1887): 301–34.

26. Hans-Günter Zmarzlik, "Traugott Ernst Friedrich Hasse," in *Neue Deutsche Biographie* (Berlin: Duncker & Humblot, 1969), 8:39–40; *Alldeutsche Blätter: Mitteilungen des*

Alldeutschen Verbandes 18, no. 3 (January 18, 1908): 18–20, and no. 6 (February 8, 1908): 45–46; *Biographisches Jahrbuch und Deutscher Nekrolog* 13 (Berlin, 1910): 38; Ernst Hasse, *Nachrichten über die Familie Hasse und einige verwandte Familien*, 3rd ed. (Leipzig: Wilhelm Engelmann, 1903), 53–56. For the emergence of statistics as a science in Saxony, see Daniel Schmidt, "'Volk' und Bevölkerungsstatistik," in Petra Overath and Daniel Schmidt, eds., *Volks-(An)Ordnung: Einschließen, ausschließen, einteilen, aufteilen!* (Leipzig: Leipziger Universitätsverlag, 2003), 49–64.

27. Ernst Hasse, *Die Wohnungsverhältnisse der ärmeren Volksklassen in Leipzig* (Leipzig: Duncker & Humblot, 1886). See also Ernst Hasse, *Die Stadt Leipzig in hygienischer Beziehung* (Leipzig: Duncker & Humblot, 1892), 19–20, 23–29.

28. Jan Palmowski, *Urban Liberalism in Imperial Germany: Frankfurt am Main, 1866–1914* (Oxford: Oxford University Press, 1999), 221; Nicholas Bullock and James Read, *The Movement for Housing Reform in Germany and France, 1840–1914* (Cambridge: Cambridge University Press, 1985), 63–70. For the Verein für Sozialpolitik, see Oberschall, *Empirical Social Research in Germany*, 21–27; Erik Grimmer-Solem, *The Rise of Historical Economics and Social Reform in Germany, 1864–1894* (Oxford: Clarendon Press, 2003).

29. For the state response to the housing problem, see Adelheid von Saldern, *Häuserleben: Zur Geschichte städtischen Arbeiterwohnens vom Kaiserreich bis heute* (Bonn: J. H. W. Dietz Nachfolger, 1995).

30. *Entwerfen, Anlage, und Einrichtung der Gebäude: Des Handbuches der Architektur. Vierter Teil. 2. Halb-Band: Gebäude für die Zwecke des Wohnens, des Handels und Verkehres. 1. Heft: Wohnhäuser*. Von Karl Weissbach (Stuttgart: Arnold Bergsträsser Verlagsbuchhandlung A. Kröner, 1902), 223–80, esp. 232–37.

31. Culver, "Tenement House Reform in Boston," 94–95. See also Vale, *From the Puritans to the Projects*, 57–62.

32. Bowditch, "Letter from the Chairman," 191.

33. *First Annual Report of the Bureau of Statistics of Labor* (Boston: Wright & Potter, State Printers, 1870), 164–85; *Second Annual Report of the Bureau of Statistics of Labor* (Boston: Wright & Potter, State Printers, 1871), 517–31; *Third Annual Report of the Bureau of Statistics of Labor* (Boston: Wright & Potter, State Printers, 1872), 437–43.

34. *Address to the Public: Constitution and By-Laws and Visitor's Manual of the Association for the Improvement of the Condition of the Poor* (New York: John S. Taylor, 1844), 10. For a description of the poor relief system in Leipzig, established in 1803, see Dietzmann, *Die Leipziger Einrichtungen der Armenpflege*. For a description of the famous Elberfeld system established in 1853, see George Steinmetz, *Regulating the Social: The Welfare State and Local Politics in Imperial Germany* (Princeton, N.J.: Princeton University Press, 1993), 157–63; Young-Sun Hong, *Welfare, Modernity, and the Weimar State, 1919–1933* (Princeton, N.J.: Princeton University Press, 1998), 19–21; Charles Richmond Henderson, *Modern Methods of Charity: An Account of the Systems of Relief, Public and Private, in the Principal Countries Having Modern Methods* (London: Macmillan, 1904), 5–12; Christoph Sachße and Florian Tennstedt, *Geschichte der Armenfürsorge in Deutschland vom Spätmittelalter bis zum Ersten Weltkrieg* (Stuttgart: W. Kohlhammer, 1980), 214–22, 286–89; Eberhard Orthbandt, *Der Deutsche Verein in der Geschichte der deutschen Fürsorge* (Frankfurt am Main: Eigenverlag des Deutschen Vereins für öffentliche und private Fürsorge, 1980), 69–81; Jürgen Reulecke, "Formen bürgerlich-sozialen Engagements in Deutschland und England im 19. Jahrhundert," in Jürgen Kocka, ed., *Arbeiter und Bürger im 19. Jahrhundert* (Munich: Oldenbourg, 1986), 263–67.

35. *Address to the Public*, 8.

36. Quoted after Jackson, *A Place Called Home*, 12.

37. *Fiftieth and Fifty-first Annual Reports of the New York Association for Improving the Condition of the Poor* (New York, October 1894), 24, 27, 38.

38. Jacob August Riis, *How the Other Half Lives: Studies among the Tenements of New York* (New York: Charles Scribner's Sons, 1907), 10, 11. For Riis, see the introduction by Donald N. Bigelow in Riis, *How the Other Half Lives* (New York: Hill and Wang, 1957), vii–xiv; Lubove, *The Progressives and the Slums,* 49–80.

39. Marcus T. Reynolds, *The Housing of the Poor in American Cities* (Baltimore: Press of Guggenheim, Weil, 1893).

40. E. R. L. Gould, *The Housing of the Working People,* eighth special report of the commissioner of labor (Washington, D.C.: Government Printing Office, 1895).

41. Victor Aimé Huber, "Die Wohnungsnot," in *V. A. Hubers Ausgewählte Schriften über Socialreform und Genossenschaftswesen* (Berlin: Verlag der Aktien-Gesellschaft Pionier, 1894), 594; Susannah Morris, "Private Profit and Public Interest: Model Dwellings Companies and the Housing of the Working Classes in London, 1840–1914," Ph.D. diss., Oxford University, 1998, 25.

42. Rudolf Elvers, *Victor Aimé Huber: Sein Leben und Wirken* (Bremen: C. Ed. Müller, 1874), 2:210–11; V. A. Huber, "Die Wohnungsreform," in *V. A. Hubers Ausgewählte Schriften,* 1051–53; John Nelson Tarn, *Five Per Cent Philanthropy: An Account of Housing in Urban Areas between 1840 and 1914* (Cambridge: Cambridge University Press, 1973), 16–17.

43. Elvers, *Huber,* 302. Huber made the argument, perhaps for nationalist purposes, that the German cooperative movement developed without English influences. See V. A. Huber, *Die genossenschaftliche Selbtshülfe der arbeitenden Klassen* (Elberfeld: N. L. Fridrichs, 1865), 44. For Huber's interest in English cooperatives and his propagation of these ideas, see V. A. Huber, *Über die cooperativen Arbeiterassociationen in England: Ein Vortrag, veranstaltet von dem Central-Verein für das Wohl der arbeitenden Klassen, gehalten am 23. Februar 1852* (Berlin: Wilhelm Hertz, 1852), and his *Sociale Fragen: V. Die Rochdaler Pioniers: Ein Bild aus dem Genossenschaftswesen* (Nordhausen: Ferd. Förstemanns, 1867).

44. Victor Aimé Huber, *Über innere Colonisation. Aus d. Janus, Heft. VII. VIII.,* besonders abgedruckt zum Besten des Berliner Handwerkervereins (Berlin: Justus Albert Wohlgemuth, 1846), 34–36, 41ff.; Elvers, *Huber,* 193–97.

45. Michael A. Kanther and Dietmar Petzina's claim that Huber's text in fact sparked the founding of the first German limited dividend company, the Berliner gemeinnützige Baugesellschaft, seems to be exaggerated. See Kanther and Petzina, *Victor Aimé Huber (1800–1869): Sozialreformer und Wegbereiter der sozialen Wohnungswirtschaft* (Berlin: Duncker & Humblot, 2000), 75. In his book about the founding of this company, Edmund Krokisius does not even mention Huber. See Krokisius, *Die unter dem Protektorat Seiner Majestät des Kaisers und Königs Wilhelm II. stehenden Berliner gemeinnützige Bau-Gesellschaft und Alexandra-Stiftung 1847 bis 1901* (Berlin: Ferd. Dümmler Verlagsbuchhandlung, 1901), 10. Carl Wilhelm Hoffmann mentions Huber's influence in his treatment of the founding of this company. See Hoffmann, *Die Wohnungen der Arbeiter und Armen I. Heft: Die Berliner gemeinnützige Bau-Gesellschaft* (Berlin: E. H. Schroeder, 1852), 20.

46. Carl Wilhelm Hoffmann, *Die Aufgabe einer Berliner gemeinnützigen Baugesellschaft* (Berlin: Hayn, 1847).

47. Hoffmann, *Die Wohnungen der Arbeiter und Armen,* 19–24; Krokisius, *Berliner gemeinnützige Bau-Gesellschaft,* 12–13.

48. The bylaws of this company can be found in Hoffmann, *Die Wohnungen der Arbeiter und Armen,* 37–57. For the starting of this company, see also Dr. Gaebler, *Idee und Bedeutung der Berliner gemeinnützigen Baugesellschaft* (Berlin: Commissions-Verlag von Carl Heymann, 1848).

49. Elvers, *Huber,* 272–77; Huber, "Die Wohnungsreform," 1062–65; Kanther and Petzina, *Victor Aimé Huber,* 75–79; Walter Vossberg, *Die deutsche Baugenossenschafts-Bewegung* (Halle a. S., 1905), 8–9.

50. A. Grävell, *Die Baugenossenschafts-Frage: Ein Bericht über die Ausbreitung der gemeinnützigen Bauthätigkeit durch Baugenossenschaften, Aktienbaugesellschaften, Bauvereine etc. in Deutschland während der letzten 12 Jahre* (Berlin: Im Selbstverlage des Centralverbandes städtischer Haus- und Grundbesitzer-Vereine Deutschlands, 1901), 111.

51. For the development of this company until the turn of the century, see Krokisius, *Berliner gemeinnützige Bau-Gesellschaft*.

52. Institut für Stadtgeschichte Frankfurt am Main, "Aufforderung zur Gründung einer gemeinnützigen Baugesellschaft in Frankfurt am Main," 1860.

53. Dr. E. Marcus, "Dr. Georg Varrentrapp," in *Jahresbericht über die Verwaltung des Medizinalwesens der Stadt Frankfurt a. M. 1886*, 264ff.; Alexander Spiess, "Georg Varrentrapp gestorben den 15. März 1886," *Deutsche Vierteljahresschrift für öffentliche Gesundheitspflege* 18 (1886): xi ff.

54. Georg Varrentrapp, *Tagebuch einer medicinischen Reise nach England, Holland, und Belgien* (Frankfurt am Main: Franz Varrentrapp, 1839).

55. Spiess, "Georg Varrentrapp"; Marcus, "Dr. Georg Varrentrapp," 264–66; Georg Varrentrapp, *Über Pönitentiarsysteme, insbesondere über die vorgeschlagene Einführung des pensylvanischen Systems* (Frankfurt am Main: Franz Varrentrapp, 1841); Georg Varrentrapp, *De l'emprisounement individuel sous le rapport sanitaire et des attaques dirigées contre lui par M. M. Charles Lucas et Leon Faucher* (Paris: Guillaumain, 1844); Georg Varrentrapp, *Über Entwässerung der Städte, über Werth und Unwerth der Wasserclosette, über deren angebliche Folgen: Verlust werthvollen Düngers, Verunreinigung der Flüsse, Benachtheiligung der Gesundheit* (Berlin: Hirschwald, 1868).

56. Institut für Stadtgeschichte Frankfurt am Main, "Aufforderung zur Gründung," 4–6, 20–30; *Die Gemeinnützige Bautätigkeit in Frankfurt am Main* (Frankfurt am Main: Verlag des Vereins für Förderung des Arbeiterwohnungswesens und verwandte Bestrebungen, 1915), 22–25; Henriette Kramer, "Die Anfänge des sozialen Wohnungsbaus in Frankfurt am Main, 1860–1914," *Archiv für Frankfurts Geschichte und Kunst*, 1978, 135–38.

57. Institut für Stadtgeschichte Frankfurt am Main, Magistratsakten MA T 2054.

58. *Reichsgesetzblatt*, no. 11: "Gesetz, betreffend die Erwerbs- und Wirthschaftsgenossenschaften vom 1. Mai 1889." For Huber's observations of the English situation in the 1850s, see V. A. Huber, *Reisebriefe aus England im Sommer 1854* (Hamburg: Agentur des Rauhen Hauses, 1855), 462–64.

59. Rudolf Albrecht, *Die Aufgabe, Organisation und Tätigkeit der Beamten-Baugenossenschaften im Rahmen der deutschen Baugenossenschafts-Bewegung* (Stuttgart: Ferdinand Enke, 1911), 38–39.

60. Wilhelm Ruprecht, "Gesunde Wohnungen," in *Göttinger Arbeiterbibliothek* 1, no. 6 (1896): 81–96; F. Bork, "Der Spar- und Bauverein, E.G.m.beschr. Haftpflicht in Hannover," in *Die Spar- und Bau-Vereine in Hannover, Göttingen und Berlin. Eine Anleitung zur praktischen Betätigung auf dem Gebiete der Wohnungsfrage* (Schriften der Centralstelle für Arbeiter-Wohlfahrtseinrichtungen Nr. 3) (Berlin: Carl Heymann, 1893), 1–93.

61. Grävell, *Die Baugenossenschafts-Frage*, table II b No. 83.

62. Ibid., 117. See also table II b.

63. *Die Spar- und Bau-Vereine in Hannover, Göttingen, und Berlin*.

64. Albrecht, *Die Aufgabe, Organisation, und Tätigkeit der Beamten-Baugenossenschaften*, 41.

65. See Thomas Adam, *125 Jahre Wohnreform in Sachsen: Zur Geschichte der sächsischen Baugenossenschaften, 1873–1998* (Leipzig: Antonym, 1999), 134, 143–44.

66. Ibid., 136–37.

67. For the history of housing foundations in German cities, see Kaete Radke, "Wohnstifte in Lübeck und Köln: Ihre historische Entwicklung und sozialpolitische Bedeutung, zugleich ein Beitrag zum Stiftungswesen," Ph.D. diss., University of Tübingen, 1924; Michael Eissenhauer, *Die Hamburger Wohnstiftungen des 19. Jahrhunderts. "Ein Denkmal, welches theilnehmende Liebe gestiftet hat . . ."* (Hamburg: Hans Christians Verlag, 1987).

68. Marion Tietz-Strödel, *Die Fuggerei in Augsburg: Studien zur Entwicklung des sozialen Stiftungsbaus im 15. und 16. Jahrhundert* (Tübingen: J. C. B. Mohr, 1982), 24–35; Hermann Kellenbenz and Maria Gräfin Preysing, "Jakob Fuggers Stiftungsbrief von 1521," *Zeitschrift des Historischen Vereins für Schwaben* 68 (1974): 95–116; Josef Weidenbacher, *Die Fuggerei in Augsburg: Die erste deutsche Kleinhaus-Stiftung* (Augsburg, 1926), 52–55; Franz Karg, "Emersacker im 17. Jahrhundert: Zur Erwerbung durch die Fuggerschen Stiftungen," *Jahrbuch des Historischen Vereins Dillingen* 93 (1991): 391–403. All these sources are from the Archive of the Fuggersche Stiftung in Dillingen.

69. Charles Eliot Norton, "Model Lodging-Houses in Boston," *Atlantic Monthly*, June 1860, 673–80. Vale mentions this project only briefly in his account of Boston public housing. See Vale, *From the Puritans to the Projects*, 63.

70. Culver, "Tenement House Reform in Boston," 132.

71. Eissenhauer, *Die Hamburger Wohnstiftungen des 19. Jahrhunderts*, 54.

72. Franklin Parker, *George Peabody: A Biography* (Nashville, Tenn.: Vanderbilt University Press, 1995), 105–109. For a more extensive account of Peabody's life, see Franklin Parker, "George Peabody, Founder of Modern Philanthropy," Ph.D. thesis, George Peabody College for Teachers, University of Illinois, 1956. See also the biographical article about Peabody in Robert T. Grimm Jr., ed., *Notable American Philanthropists: Biographies of Giving and Volunteering* (Westport, Conn.: Greenwood Press, 2002), 242–46.

73. Susannah Morris, "Changing Perceptions of Philanthropy in the Voluntary Housing Field in Nineteenth- and Early Twentieth-Century London," in Thomas Adam, ed., *Philanthropy, Patronage, and Civil Society: Experiences from Germany, Great Britain, and North America* (Bloomington: Indiana University Press, 2004), 150.

74. Parker, *George Peabody*, 126, 127; David Owen, *English Philanthropy 1660–1960* (Cambridge, Mass.: Belknap Press of Harvard University Press, 1964), 381; Bowditch, "Letter from the Chairman," 195.

75. Parker, *George Peabody*, 127–28, 178; Morris, "Changing Perceptions," 149.

76. Tarn, *Five Per Cent Philanthropy*, 46–47; Owen, *English Philanthropy*, 380; Bowditch, "Letter from the Chairman," 195–96.

77. Owen, *English Philanthropy*, 381.

78. Parker, *George Peabody*, 127; Morris, "Changing Perceptions," 150.

79. Bowditch, "Letter from the Chairman," 199 (Bowditch quotes here an anonymous critic of Peabody).

80. Woodroofe, *From Charity to Social Work*, 92–93.

81. Susannah Morris, "Market Solutions for Social Problems: Working-Class Housing in Nineteenth-Century London," *Economic History Review* 54 (2001): 528; Morris, "Changing Perceptions," 144ff.

82. George Smalley, *The Life of Sir Sydney Waterlow, Bart., London Apprentice, Lord Mayor, Captain of Industry, and Philanthropist* (London: Edward Arnold, 1909).

83. This view is contradicted by Smalley. See ibid., 60. Smalley gives a detailed account about Waterlow's housing company on pages 56–86.

84. Bowditch, "Letter from the Chairman," 204.

85. Owen, *English Philanthropy*, 379; Tarn, *Five Per Cent Philanthropy*, 50–51.

86. Morris, "Private Profit and Public Interest," 61.

87. Morris, "Changing Perceptions," 139ff.; Woodroofe, *From Charity to Social Work*, 18.

88. Morris, "Market Solutions for Social Problems," 538.

89. Morris, "Private Profit and Public Interest," 189; Bowditch, "Letter from the Chairman," 205; Paul Felix Aschrott, "Die Arbeiterwohnungsfrage in England," in *Die Wohnungsnoth der ärmeren Klassen in deutschen Großstädten* (Leipzig: Duncker & Humblot, 1886), 133.

90. Smalley, *Life of Sir Sydney Waterlow*, 68.

91. Volker Then, *Eisenbahnen und Eisenbahnunternehmer in der Industriellen Revolution: Ein preußisch/deutsch-englischer Vergleich* (Göttingen: Vandenhoeck & Ruprecht, 1997), 315ff. See also Lubove, *The Progressives and the Slums,* 38.

92. For an account of her life, see Nancy Boyd, *Josephine Butler, Octavia Hill, Florence Nightingale: Three Victorian Women Who Changed Their World* (London and Basingstoke: Macmillan, 1982), 95–163; Gillian Darley, *Octavia Hill* (London: Constable, 1990); William Thompson Hill, *Octavia Hill: Pioneer of the National Trust and Housing Reformer* (London: Hutchinson, 1956); E. Moberly Bell, *Octavia Hill: A Biography* (London: Constable, 1942); C. Edmund Maurice, *Life of Octavia Hill as Told in Her Letters* (London: Macmillan, 1913).

93. Tarn, *Five Per Cent Philanthropy,* 72.

94. Morris, "Private Profit and Public Interest," 24–25.

95. Enid Gauldie, *Cruel Habitations: A History of Working-Class Housing, 1780–1918* (London: Allen & Unwin, 1974), 214.

96. Boyd, *Josephine Butler, Octavia Hill, Florence Nightingale,* 107–108.

97. Octavia Hill, "Organized Work among the Poor: Suggestions Founded on Four Years' Management of a London Court," *Macmillan's Magazine* 20 (May–October 1869): 219.

98. Octavia Hill, "Cottage Property in London," *Fortnightly Review* 6 (August 15– December 1, 1866): 682.

99. Hill, "Organized Work among the Poor," 219.

100. Ibid., 220.

101. Ibid.

102. Quoted in Robert Owen, *A New View of Society and Other Writings* (London: J. M. Dent & Sons/New York: E. P. Dutton, 1949), 16.

103. Hill, "Organized Work among the Poor," 220.

104. Hill, "Cottage Property in London," 682; Bremner, "Iron Scepter," 223.

105. Octavia Hill, "Common Sense and the Dwellings of the Poor," *Nineteenth Century* 82 (December 1883): 928.

106. Hill, "Cottage Property in London," 681.

107. Octavia Hill, *Homes of the London Poor,* 2nd ed. (London: Macmillan, 1883). For her other writings, see *The Befriending Leader: Social Assistance without Dependency,* ed. James L. Payne (Sandpoint, Idaho: Lytton, 1997); Elinor Southwood Ouvry, ed., *Extracts from Octavia Hill's "Letters to Fellow-Workers," 1864 to 1911* (London: Adelphi Book Shop, 1933); *House Property and Its Management: Some Papers on the Methods of Management Introduced by Miss Octavia Hill and Adapted to Modern Conditions* (London: George Allen & Unwin, 1921).

108. Octavia Hill, *Homes of the London Poor* (New York, 1875) (Publications of the State Charities Aid Association No. 8); Bremner, "Iron Scepter," 227; Anthony S. Wohl, *The Eternal Slum: Housing and Social Policy in Victorian London* (London: Edward Arnold, 1977), 181.

109. Jennifer Robinson, "Octavia Hill Women Housing Managers in South Africa: Femininity and Urban Government," *Journal of Historical Geography* 24, no. 4 (1998): 459–81.

110. Bremner, "Iron Scepter," 225–26.

111. W. T. Hill, *Octavia Hill,* 184–86; Darley, *Octavia Hill,* 160–71.

112. For the transnational/transatlantic character of social reform, see also Anja Schüler, *Frauenbewegung und soziale Reform: Jane Addams und Alice Salomon im transatlantischen Dialog, 1889–1933* (Stuttgart: Franz Steiner, 2004); Kathryn Kish Sklar, Anja Schüler, and Susan Strasser, eds., *Social Justice Feminists in the United States and Germany: A Dialogue in Documents, 1885–1933* (Ithaca, N.Y.: Cornell University Press, 1998).

113. Wohl, *The Eternal Slum,* 181; Adam, "Transatlantic Trading," 334–47.

114. "Brahmin caste of New England" was coined by Oliver Wendell Holmes in his 1861 novel *Elsie Venner: A Romance of Destiny* (Cambridge: Riverside Press, 1891), 1–6.

115. Frederic Cople Jaher, "The Boston Brahmins in the Age of Industrial Capitalism," in Jaher, ed., *The Age of Industrialism in America: Essays in Social Structure and Cultural Values* (New York: Free Press, 1968), 190.

116. *The National Cyclopaedia of American Biography* (New York: James T. White, 1929), 6:377–78; *Boston, Past and Present: Being an Outline of the History of the City as Exhibited in the Lives of Its Prominent Citizens* (Cambridge: Riverside Press, 1874), 103–106; Alfred Stanford, *Navigator: The Story of Nathaniel Bowditch* (New York: William Morrow, 1927); Robert Elton Berry, *Sextant and Sails: The Story of Nathaniel Bowditch* (New York: Dodd, Mead, 1943).

117. *The National Cyclopaedia of American Biography* (New York: James T. White, 1924), 8:214; *Biographical Encyclopaedia of Massachusetts of the Nineteenth Century* (New York: Metropolitan Publishing and Engraving Co., 1879), 303–306; John C. Rand, ed., *One of a Thousand: A Series of Biographical Sketches of One Thousand Representative Men Resident in the Commonwealth of Massachusetts AD1888–89* (Boston: First National Publishing Co., 1890), 68–69; *Harvard Graduates Magazine* 1 (1892–93): 38–43.

118. Vincent Y. Bowditch, *Life and Correspondence of Henry Ingersoll Bowditch*, 2 vols. (Boston: Houghton Mifflin, 1902), 1:189.

119. Quoted in Bowditch, "Letter from the Chairman," 194.

120. John F. Fulton, "Henry Ingersoll Bowditch," in *Dictionary of American Biography* (New York: Scribner, 1934), 2:493.

121. Culver, "Tenement House Reform in Boston," 135–37.

122. Bowditch, "Letter from the Chairman," 182; Bowditch, *Life and Correspondence*, 2:326.

123. Bowditch, "Letter from the Chairman," 212.

124. Ibid., 198–99.

125. Ibid., 202.

126. *First Annual Report of the Boston Co-operative Building Co. with the Act of Incorporation and By-Laws* (Boston: W. L. Deland, 1872); Culver, "Tenement House Reform in Boston," 145–64; Christine Cousineau, "Tenement Reform in Boston, 1870–1920: Philanthropy, Regulation, and Government-Assisted Housing" (working paper presented at the Third National Conference on American Planning History, November 30–December 2, 1989, in Cincinnati), 6–8; Joseph Lee, *Constructive and Preventive Philanthropy* (New York: Macmillan, 1902), 70–71; David P. Handlin, *The American Home: Architecture and Society, 1815–1915* (Boston: Little, Brown, 1979), 252–63. Vale mentions this company only briefly in his account of Boston public housing. See Vale, *From the Puritans to the Projects*, 63–64.

127. *Third Annual Report of the Boston Co-Operative Building Company* (Boston: W. L. Deland, 1874), 14.

128. *Twenty-third Annual Report of the Boston Co-Operative Building Company 1894* (Boston: W. L. Deland, 1894), 12.

129. Ellen Chase, *Tenant Friends in Old Deptford* (London: Williams & Norgate, 1929).

130. W. T. Hill, *Octavia Hill*, 184, 229.

131. "Certain Aspects of the Housing Problem in Philadelphia. Report Prepared by the Octavia Hill Association," *Annals of the American Academy of Political and Social Sciences* 20 (July–December 1902): 120; Helen L. Parrish, "Friendly Rent Collecting," in *Town Development*, June 1914, 52–54.

132. For White, see Lubove, *The Progressives and the Slums*, 34–39; Lee, *Constructive and Preventive Philanthropy*, 71–73.

133. Plunz, *A History of Housing in New York City*, 89.

134. Lubove, *The Progressives and the Slums*, 34. For the Improved Dwellings Association, see *Report of the Tenement House Committee as Authorized by Chapter 479 of the Laws*

of 1894, transmitted to the Legislature January 17, 1895 (Albany: James B. Lyon, State Printer, 1895), 119–21.

135. *Report of the Tenement House Committee,* 101; *First Annual Report of the City and Suburban Homes Company* (New York: Federal Housing Administration, Division of Economics and Statistics, 1897); Lee, *Constructive and Preventive Philanthropy,* 73–75.

136. *Report of the Tenement House Committee,* 9.

137. Birch and Gardner, "The Seven-Percent Solution"; Edith Elmer Wood, *Recent Trends in American Housing* (New York: Macmillan, 1931), 206ff.; Robert B. Fairbanks, "From Better Dwellings to Better Community: Changing Approaches to the Low-Cost Housing Problem, 1890–1925," *Journal of Urban History* 11 (1985): 321; Robert B. Fairbanks, *Making Better Citizens: Housing Reform and the Community Development Strategy in Cincinnati, 1890–1960* (Urbana: University of Illinois Press, 1988), 35–36.

138. Gerard Noel, *Princess Alice: Queen Victoria's Forgotten Daughter* (London: Constable, 1974), 107, 108. For the relation between Victoria and Alice, see Wilfried Rogasch, "'Vicky' und Alice—zwei coburgische Prinzessinnen in Preußen und Hessen," in *Ein Herzogtum und viele Kronen: Coburg in Bayern und Europa* (Regensburg: Pustet, 1997), 74–80.

139. Darley, *Octavia Hill,* 160.

140. Eckhardt G. Franz, "Victorias Schwester in Darmstadt: Großherzogin Alice von Hessen und bei Rhein," in Rainer von Hessen, ed., *Victoria Kaiserin Friedrich (1840–1901): Mission und Schicksal einer englischen Prinzessin in Deutschland* (Frankfurt/New York: Campus, 2002), 85. This argument is supported by *Alice Grand Duchess of Hesse, Princess of Great Britain and Ireland: Biographical Sketch and Letters* (New York: G. P. Putnam's Sons, 1884), 400. According to this biographical sketch, Alice, who was just 19, "married the husband of her choice."

141. *Alice Grand Duchess of Hesse,* 240, 242–44; Franz, "Victorias Schwester in Darmstadt," 88. For the emergence of Alice's women's associations, see Quataert, *Staging Philanthropy.* For Büchner, see Ruth-Ellen Boetcher Joeres, "Luise Büchner 1821–1877 'Wir sind mehr als wir scheinen,'" in Luise F. Pusch, ed., *Schwestern berühmter Männer: Zwölf biographische Portraits* (Frankfurt am Main: Insel, 1985), 291–321; Margarete Dierks, ed., *"Gebildet, ohne gelehrt zu sein": Essays, Berichte, und Briefe von Luise Büchner zur Geschichte ihrer Zeit* (Darmstadt: Justus von Liebig, 1991).

142. *Alice Grand Duchess of Hesse,* 294. For accounts of this women's parliament, see Dierks, *"'Gebildet, ohne gelehrt zu sein,'"* 131–38; Margaret J. Shaen, ed., *Memorials of Two Sisters: Susanna and Catherine Winkworth* (London: Longmans, Green, 1908), 288–92; Franz, "Victorias Schwester in Darmstadt," 90; Stadtarchiv Darmstadt ST G 1770, Stenographischer Bericht über die Erste ordentliche Generalversammlung des 1869 gegründeten Verbandes deutscher Frauen- und Erwerbsvereine, gehalten am 10. & 11. October 1872 zu Darmstadt (Darmstadt: Arnold Bergsträßer, 1873).

143. Darley, *Octavia Hill,* 161.

144. Letter quoted after Noel, *Princess Alice,* 221–22. See also Darley, *Octavia Hill,* 161–62.

145. Darley, *Octavia Hill,* 166–71; Noel, *Princess Alice,* 222, 230; *Alice Grand Duchess of Hesse,* 358–59.

146. For Schwab, see Stadtarchiv Darmstadt: Schwab, Wilhelm, 1816–1891. For Liagre, see Thomas Adam, *Die Anfänge industriellen Bauens in Sachsen* (Leipzig: Quadrat, 1998), 27–28.

147. Gustav de Liagre, "Ein Versuch zur Beschaffung guter Wohnungen für Arme in Leipzig," in Ernst Hasse, *Die Wohnungsverhältnisse der ärmeren Volksklassen in Leipzig* (Leipzig: Duncker & Humblot, 1886), 95.

148. Archive of the Catholic Church in Leipzig (Katholisches Propsteipfarramt Leipzig), files: Trauung Carl Benedict Franz de Liagre und Ottilie Küstner (1832/34/8); Carl Benedict Franz de Liagre (1855/470/6) Chronik der Propsteipfarrei 1891–1932, vol.

1: 1908 Superior und Pfarrer, Monsignore Hubert Schnittmann, General-Consul De Liagre †; Festschrift zur Goldenen Jubelfeier des Vincentius-Vereins Leipzig und Jahresberichte der Zweigkonferenzen (Dresden, 1905), 18–19, 67, 69, 73; Festschrift zur goldenen Jubelfeier des St. Elisabeth-Vereins zu Leipzig 1861–1911, 47; Sächsisches Staatsarchiv Leipzig, Amtsgericht Leipzig, No. 6762 (Testamentsangelegenheiten): Last Will of Charles de Liagre (1855), 8–21; Johannes Hohlfeld, *Leipziger Geschlechter,* vol. 3: *Die Reformierte Bevölkerung Leipzigs 1700–1875* (Leipzig: Zentralstelle für deutschen Personen- und Familiengeschichte, 1939), 16–18.

149. Archive of the Catholic Church in Leipzig, Kirchenaustritt 1873/Nr. 6 (Gustav de Liagre).

150. Josef Reinhold, *Zwischen Aufbruch und Beharrung: Juden und jüdische Gemeinde in Leipzig während des 19. Jahrhunderts* (Dresden: Sächsische Druck- und Verlagshaus AG, 1999), 20; Josef Reinhold, "Die Entstehung einer jüdischen Großgemeinde: Vor 150 Jahren konstituierte sich die Israelitische Religionsgemeinde zu Leipzig," *Sächsische Heimatblätter* 43 (1997): 130–31; Hans Heinrich Ebeling, *Die Juden in Braunschweig: Rechts-, Sozial-, und Wirtschaftsgeschichte von den Anfängen der Jüdischen Gemeinde bis zur Emanzipation (1282–1848)* (Braunschweig: Stadtarchiv, 1987), 332; Ernst Kroker, *Die Gesellschaft Harmonie in Leipzig 1776 bis 1926: Zum Hundertfünfzigjährigen Bestehen* (Leipzig: Gesellschaft Harmonie, 1926), 109; Hohlfeld, *Leipziger Geschlechter,* 3:16–20.

151. Adam, *Die Anfänge industriellen Bauens,* 28.

152. Paul Felix Aschrott, *25 Jahre gemeinnütziger Tätigkeit für Kleinwohnungen: Zum 25 jährigen Bestehen des Vereins zur Verbesserung der kleinen Wohnungen in Berlin* (n.p., n.d.), 5–6.

153. Gustav de Liagre, *Wohnungen für Unbemittelte: Vortrag des Herrn G. de Liagre aus Leipzig gehalten am 4. Mai 1888 auf Veranlassung Ihrer Majestät der Königin von Sachsen als Protektorin des Johannesvereins in Dresden* (Leipzig: Bibliographisches Institut, 1888); Gustav de Liagre, *Wohnungen für Unbemittelte: Vortrag von Gustav de Liagre. Öffentlicher Abend der "Sozial-Wissenschaftlichen Vereinigung" in Leipzig, am 21. November 1896* (Leipzig: O. de Liagre, 1896); Gustav de Liagre, "Ein Versuch zur Beschaffung guter Wohnungen für Arme in Leipzig," in *Die Wohnungsnoth der ärmeren Klassen* (Leipzig: Duncker & Humblot, 1886), 383–88.

154. Thomas Adam, *Arbeitermilieu und Arbeiterbewegung in Leipzig, 1871–1933* (Cologne: Böhlau, 1999), 24–32.

155. Palmowski, *Urban Liberalism in Imperial Germany,* 229–32.

156. Johann Heinrich Andreas Hermann Albrecht, Graf von Bernstorff, *Social Reforms in Germany* (n.p., 1910), 18–19.

157. Wilhelm Ruprecht, *Väter und Söhne: Zwei Jahrhunderte Buchhändler in einer deutschen Universitätsstadt* (Göttingen: Vandenhoeck & Ruprecht, 1935), 203–205; Wilhelm Ruprecht, "Der Spar- und Bauverein, E.G.m.beschr.Haftpflicht in Göttingen," in *Die Spar- und Bau-Vereine in Hannover, Göttingen und Berlin* (Berlin: Carl Heymann, 1893), 95–101; Ruprecht, "Gesunde Wohnungen," 89–96.

158. Wilhelm Ruprecht, *Die Wohnungen der arbeitenden Klassen in London. Mit besonderer Berücksichtigung der neueren englischen Gesetzgebung und ihrer Erfolge* (Göttingen: Vandenhoeck & Ruprecht, 1884), iii.

159. Ibid., 100–101.

160. Morris, "Market Solutions for Social Problems," 538; Ruprecht, *Die Wohnungen,* 105–106; Aschrott, "Die Arbeiterwohnungsfrage in England," 133.

161. Ruprecht, *Die Wohnungen,* 102–106, 126.

162. For the rejection of the housing cooperative idea, see Ruprecht, *Die Wohnungen,* 100. He refers to Ernst von Plener, *Englische Baugenossenschaften* (Vienna: Gerold, 1873).

163. Ruprecht, "Gesunde Wohnungen."

164. Ibid., 95–96; Paul Lechler, *Wohlfahrtseinrichtungen über ganz Deutschland durch gemeinnützige Aktiengesellschaften: Ein Stück sozialer Reform* (Stuttgart: W. Kohlhammer, 1892).

165. "Aufzeichnungen über den Geheimen Kommerzienrat Sigmund Aschrott (1826–1915) und dessen Bedeutung für die wirtschaftliche und städtebauliche Entwicklung von Kassel," manuscript from the Stadtarchiv Kassel; W. E. Mosse, *Jews in the German Economy: The German-Jewish Economic Élite, 1820–1935* (Oxford: Clarendon Press, 1987), 147–50, 181–82.

166. Schmidt, "'Volk' und Bevölkerungsstatistik," 57–64; Alain Desrosières, *The Politics of Large Numbers: A Social History of Statistical Reasoning* (Cambridge, Mass.: Harvard University Press, 1998), 179ff.; Hendrik S. Houthakker, "An International Comparison of Household Expenditure Patterns, Commemorating the Century of Engel's Law," *Econometrica* 25 (1957): 532–51; Carle C. Zimmerman, "Ernst Engel's Law of Expenditures for Food," *Quarterly Journal of Economics* 47, no. 1 (November 1932): 78–101.

167. Hauptstaatsarchiv Düsseldorf, Bestand Gerichte Rep. 11, no. 1474, vols. 3 and 4; Universitätsarchiv Leipzig, Phil. Fak. Prom. 4196. About Friedberg, see S. Wininger, ed., *Große Jüdische National-Biographie* (Cernauti: Druck "Orient," 1927), 2:324–25; Erich Döhring, "Friedberg, Heinrich v.," in *Neue Deutsche Biographie* (Berlin: Duncker & Humblot, 1961), 5:444–45.

168. Paul Felix Aschrott, "Die Arbeiterwohnungsfrage in England," in *Die Wohnungsnoth der ärmeren Klassen in deutschen Großstädten und Vorschläge zu deren Abhülfe. Gutachten und Berichte herausgegben vom Verein für Socialpolitik* (Leipzig: Duncker & Humblot, 1886), 96–146.

169. Ibid., 130–32.

170. Ibid., 146.

171. Aschrott, *25 Jahre gemeinnütziger Tätigkeit für Kleinwohnungen*, 5–10.

172. Lees, *Cities, Sin, and Social Reform*, 330–33; Georg Jahn, "Albrecht, Heinrich Karl Wilhelm," in *Neue Deutsche Biographie*, 1:181.

173. Heinrich Albrecht, *Die Wohnungsnot in den Großstädten und die Mittel zu ihrer Abhülfe* (München: R. Oldenbourg, 1891); Albrecht, "Wohnungen für die Armen," *Deutsche Rundschau* 65 (October–December 1890): 368–84.

174. Albrecht, *Die Wohnungsnot in den Großstädten*, 8.

175. Ibid., 66–67.

176. Andrew Lees, "Victor Böhmert," in Gerald Wiemers, ed., *Sächsische Lebensbilder* (Leipzig: Sächsischen Akademie der Wissenschaften zu Leipzig, 2003), 5:13–43; Lees, *Cities, Sin, and Social Reform*, 191–221.

177. Albrecht, *Die Wohnungsnot in den Großstädten*, 65; Lees, "Victor Böhmert," 32.

178. Albrecht, *Die Wohnungsnot in den Großstädten*, 72, 73–74.

179. Heinrich Albrecht and Alfred Messel, *Das Arbeiterwohnhaus: Gesammelte Pläne von Arbeiterwohnhäusern und Ratschläge zum Entwerfen von solchen auf Grund praktischer Erfahrungen* (Berlin: Robert Oppenheim [Gustav Schmidt], 1896).

180. Heinrich Albrecht, *Handbuch der Sozialen Wohlfahrtspflege in Deutschland* (Berlin: Carl Heymanns, 1902), 226–89.

181. Jahn, "Albrecht," 181.

182. Rodgers, *Atlantic Crossings*, 62.

183. Jacob A. Riis, *The Battle with the Slum* (New York: Macmillan, 1902), 129.

184. "Wright, Carroll Davidson," in *The National Cyclopaedia of American Biography* (New York: James T. White, 1926), 19:422.

185. Rodgers, *Atlantic Crossings*, 62–63. For Wright, see James Leiby, *Carroll Wright and Labor Reform: The Origin of Labor Statistics* (Cambridge, Mass.: Harvard University Press, 1960).

186. Gould, *The Housing of the Working People*, 13, 19.

187. Ibid., 221–22.

188. Ibid., 292, 296.

189. *First Annual Report of the City and Suburban Homes Company* (New York, May 17, 1897), 1; Riis, *The Battle with the Slum,* 128–29.

190. *Fiftieth Annual Report of the City and Suburban Homes Company* (New York, May 1946), 6.

191. Eugene J. Johnson, *Style Follows Function: Architecture of Marcus T. Reynolds* (Albany/ New York: Washington Park Press/Mount Ida Press, 1993), 1, 11, 12.

192. For an overview of the topics and published essays, see *Publications of the American Economic Association* 9, no. 1, *Hand Book of the American Economic Association 1894. Together with Report of the Sixth Annual Meeting,* University of Chicago, September 11–15, 1893 (January 1894), 8–9.

193. Reynolds, *The Housing of the Poor in American Cities,* 81, 85, 86.

194. Ibid., 107.

195. Shirley Campbell Spragge, "The Provision of Workingmen's Housing: Attempts in Toronto, 1904–1920," M.A. thesis, Queen's University Kingston, 1974, 59–60; Paul A. Bator, "Slums and Urban Reform in Toronto, 1910–1914," Level 2000 Paper, City of Toronto Archives, 3.

196. P. F. W. Rutherford, introduction to Herbert B. Ames, *The City below the Hill: A Socio- logical Study of a Portion of the City of Montreal, Canada* (1897; reprint, Toronto: Uni- versity of Toronto Press, 1972), viii.

197. Mélanie Méthot, "Herbert Brown Ames: Political Reformer and Enforcer," *Urban History Review* 31, no. 2 (Spring 2003): 21, 26–28; Ames, *The City below the Hill,* 110; Sean Purdy, "Industrial Efficiency, Social Order, and Moral Purity: Housing Reform Thought in English Canada, 1900–1950," *Urban History Review* 25, no. 2 (March 1997): 32; Méthot, "Herbert Brown Ames," 26–28.

198. W. D. Lighthall, "Rehousing in Canada," *Canadian Public Health Journal* 3, no. 8 (August 1912): 447–48; John Sutton Nettlefold, *Practical Housing* (Letchword: Garden City Press, 1908), 116–20.

199. James Pitsula, "The Relief of Poverty in Toronto, 1880–1930," Ph.D. thesis, York Uni- versity, 1979, vi.

200. James Mavor, *My Windows on the Street of the World* (New York: E. P. Dutton, 1923), 2:124–36. For the Working Man's Dwelling Company in Glasgow, see Gould, *The Housing of the Working People,* 260–68. The biography of Smith by Elisabeth Wallace briefly mentions his friendship with Mavor, but it is mute on Smith's involvement in Toronto philanthropy. Elisabeth Wallace, *Goldwin Smith: Victorian Liberal* (Toronto: University of Toronto Press, 1957).

201. Spragge, "Provision of Workingmen's Housing," 69, 78.

202. Lorna F. Hurl, "The Toronto Housing Company, 1912–1923: The Pitfalls of Painless Philanthropy," *Canadian Historical Review* 65, no. 1 (March 1984): 31.

203. Spragge, "Provision of Workingmen's Housing," 87–90.

204. Dr. Charles Hastings, "Report of the Medical Health Officer Dealing with the Recent Investigations of Slum Conditions in Toronto Embodying Recommendations for the Amelioration of the Same" (Toronto, 1911), 4. For Hastings's report, see Bator, "Slums and Urban Reform," 1–8; Paul Adolphus Bator, "'Saving Lives on the Wholesale Plan': Public Health Reform in the City of Toronto, 1900 to 1930," Ph.D. thesis, University of Toronto, 1979, 194–95; Spragge, "Provision of Workingmen's Housing," 107–109.

205. Spragge, "Provision of Workingmen's Housing," 109.

206. Nettlefold, *Practical Housing,* 132–38.

207. Bator, "'Saving Lives on the Wholesale Plan,'" 196; Hurl, "Toronto Housing Company," 28–29. Bates makes this claim on 206.

208. Percy E. Nobbs, "The Statistics of Housing and Co-Partnership Schemes," *Public Health Journal* 3, no. 8 (August 1912): 454.

209. Spragge, "Provision of Workingmen's Housing," 103–106.

210. Hurl, "Toronto Housing Company," 34–37; Spragge, "Provision of Workingmen's Housing," 121–24.

211. Hurl, "Toronto Housing Company," 35; Spragge, "Provision of Workingmen's Housing," 117, 118.

212. Bator, "'Saving Lives on the Wholesale Plan,'" 207.

213. Sean Purdy, "Class, Gender, and the Toronto Housing Company, 1912–1920," *Urban History Review* 21, no. 2 (March 1993): 78.

214. Tarn, *Five Per Cent Philanthropy,* 53.

215. Jackson, *A Place Called Home,* 111.

216. Spragge, "Provision of Workingmen's Housing," 119; Bator, "'Saving Lives on the Wholesale Plan,'" 204; Hurl, "Toronto Housing Company," 37. A list of the THC shareholders can be found in City of Toronto Archives, *Better Housing in Canada: The Ontario Plan,* first annual report of the Toronto Housing Company, Ltd., 1913, 23–24.

217. Spragge, "Provision of Workingmen's Housing," 125–26.

218. Hurl, "Toronto Housing Company," 38, 40–41; Spragge, "Provision of Workingmen's Housing," 143–44. See also Purdy, "Class, Gender, and the Toronto Housing Company," 79.

219. Hurl, "Toronto Housing Company," 41.

220. Spragge, "Provision of Workingmen's Housing," 139, 158.

3. How to Become a Gentleman

1. Daniel M. Fox, *Engines of Culture: Philanthropy and Art Museums* (Madison: State Historical Society of Wisconsin for the Department of History, University of Wisconsin, 1963), 27.

2. It could, of course, be argued that philanthropy and philanthropic practices were integral to the construction of status hierarchies since the beginning of urban life in Western civilization. See, e.g., Paul Veyne, *Bread and Circuses: Historical Sociology and Political Pluralism* (London: Penguin Press, 1990), and Sandra Cavallo, *Charity and Power in Early Modern Italy: Benefactors and Their Motives in Turin, 1541–1789* (Cambridge: Cambridge University Press, 1995).

3. Peter Dobkin Hall, "A Historical Overview of Philanthropy, Voluntary Associations, and Nonprofit Organizations in the United States, 1600–2000," in Walter W. Powell and Richard Steinberg, eds., *The Nonprofit Sector: A Research Handbook,* 2nd ed. (New Haven, Conn.: Yale University Press, 2006), 38. See also Francie Ostrower, *Why the Wealthy Give: The Culture of Elite Philanthropy* (Princeton, N.J.: Princeton University Press, 1995); Frank K. Prochaska, "Philanthropy," in F. M. L. Thompson, ed., *The Cambridge Social History of Britain, 1750–1950* (Cambridge: Cambridge University Press, 1990), 3:357–93; Lawrence J. Friedman and Mark D. McGarvie, eds., *Charity, Philanthropy, and Civility in American History* (Cambridge: Cambridge University Press, 2003); Thomas Adam, ed., *Philanthropy, Patronage, and Civil Society: Experiences from Germany, Great Britain, and North America* (Bloomington: Indiana University Press, 2004).

4. Tamara Plakins Thornton, *Cultivating Gentlemen: The Meaning of Country Life among the Boston Elite, 1785–1860* (New Haven, Conn.: Yale University Press, 1989), 15.

5. Judith Martin, *Star-Spangled Manners* (New York: W. W. Norton, 2003), 168.

6. Junius Henri Browne, *The Great Metropolis: A Mirror of New York* (Hartford: American, 1869; reprint, New York: Arno Press, 1975), 33, 35, 36. For the background to the term *Knickerbocker,* see Chase Viele, "The Knickerbockers of Upstate New York," *Halve Maen* 47 (October 1972): 2.

7. David C. Hammack, *Power and Society: Greater New York at the Turn of the Century* (New York: Russell Sage Foundation, 1982), 71; Frederic Cople Jaher, "Nineteenth-Century Elites in Boston and New York," *Journal of Social History* 6, no. 1 (Fall 1972): 54.

8. Martin, *Star-Spangled Manners,* 168.

9. Eberhard Brüning, "'Saxony Is a Prosperous and Happy Country': American Views of the Kingdom of Saxony in the Nineteenth Century," in Thomas Adam and Ruth Gross, eds., *Traveling between Worlds: German-American Encounters* (College Station: Texas A&M University Press, 2006), 20–50; Eberhard Brüning, "Sachsen mit amerikanischen Augen gesehen: Das Sachsenbild amerikanischer Globetrotter im 19. Jahrhundert," *Neues Archiv für sächsische Geschichte* 67 (1996): 109–31; Eberhard Brüning, "'It Is a Glorious Collection': Amerikanische Bildungsbürger des 19. Jahrhunderts auf 'Pilgerfahrt' zur Dresdner Gemäldegalerie," *Jahrbuch der Staatlichen Kunstsammlungen Dresden,* 1996/97, 99–105; Thomas Adam, "Germany Seen through American Eyes: George and Anna Eliot Ticknor's German Travel Logs," in Hartmut Keil, ed., *Transatlantic Cultural Contexts: Essays in Honor of Eberhard Brüning* (Tübingen: Stauffenburg, 2005), 151–63; William W. Stowe, *Going Abroad: European Travel in Nineteenth-Century American Culture* (Princeton, N.J.: Princeton University Press, 1994); Christopher Mulvey, *Transatlantic Manners: Social Patterns in Nineteenth-Century Anglo-American Travel Literature* (New York: Cambridge University Press, 1990).

10. Till von Rahden, *Juden und andere Breslauer: Die Beziehungen zwischen Juden, Protestanten, und Katholiken in einer deutschen Großstadt von 1860 bis 1925* (Göttingen: Vandenhoeck & Ruprecht, 2000), 41–42.

11. Allen Churchill, *The Upper Crust: An Informal History of New York's Highest Society* (Englewood Cliffs, N.J.: Prentice-Hall, 1970), 21–22; Ruth Brandon, *The Dollar Princesses: Sagas of Upward Nobility, 1870–1914* (New York: Alfred Knopf, 1980), 12–22; Gail MacColl and Carol McD. Wallace, *To Marry an English Lord* (New York: Workman, 1989), 13; Maureen E. Montgomery, *"Gilded Prostitution": Status, Money, and Transatlantic Marriages, 1870–1914* (London: Routledge, 1989), 40–41; Frederic Cople Jaher, "Style and Status: High Society in Late-Nineteenth-Century New York," in Frederic Cople Jaher, ed., *The Rich, the Wellborn, and the Powerful: Elites and Upper Classes in History* (Urbana: University of Illinois Press, 1973), 258–84; Eric Homberger, *Mrs. Astor's New York: Money and Social Power in a Gilded Age* (New Haven, Conn.: Yale University Press, 2002), 182–202; Dixon Wecter, *The Saga of American Society: A Record of Social Aspiration, 1607–1937* (London: Scribner's, 1937), 216–23; Samuel Ward McAllister, *Society as I Have Found It* (New York: Arno Press, 1975), 207–17.

12. Stowe, *Going Abroad;* Mulvey, *Transatlantic Manners;* Brüning, "'Saxony Is a Prosperous and Happy Country'"; Sven Beckert, *The Monied Metropolis: New York City and the Consolidation of the American Bourgeoisie, 1850–1896* (Cambridge: Cambridge University Press, 2001), 258–59; Thomas Adam, "Die Kommunalisierung von Kunst und Kultur als Grundkonsens der deutschen Gesellschaft ab dem ausgehenden 19. Jahrhundert: Das Beispiel Leipzig," *Die Alte Stadt* 26 (1999): 79–99; Nick Prior, "Museums: Leisure between State and Distinction," in Rudy Koshar, ed., *Histories of Leisure* (New York: Berg, 2002), 31–33.

13. Ostrower, *Why the Wealthy Give,* 3.

14. Margherita Arlina Hamm, *Famous Families of New York: Historical and Biographical Sketches of Families Which in Successive Generations Have Been Identified with the Development of the Nation,* 2 vols. (New York: G. P. Putnam's Sons, n.d.); *Prominent Families of New York: Being an Account in Biographical Form of Individuals and Families Distinguished as Representatives of the Social, Professional, and Civic Life of New York City* (New York: Historical Co., 1897).

15. Browne, *The Great Metropolis*, 596, 598, 602. See also Douglas T. Miller, *Jacksonian Aristocracy: Class and Democracy in New York, 1830–1860* (New York: Oxford University Press, 1967), 164–65; Churchill, *The Upper Crust*, 114.

16. For Boston, see *Boston, Past and Present: Being an Outline of the History of the City as Exhibited in the Lives of Its Prominent Citizens* (Cambridge: Riverside Press, 1874); Mary Caroline Crawford, *Famous Families of Massachusetts*, 2 vols. (Boston: Little, Brown, 1930). For Toronto, see *Leading Financial and Business Men in Toronto: A Work of Artistic Color Plates Designed to Portray One Hundred Leading Men of Toronto, Both Financially and Socially* (Toronto, 1912); Edward Marion Chadwick, *Ontarian Families: Genealogies of United Empire Loyalists and Other Pioneer Families of Upper Canada* (Lambertville, N.J.: Hunterdon House, 1894); A. Maude Cawthra Brock and A. H. Young, eds., *Past and Present: Notes by Henry Cawthra and Others* (Toronto: James and Williams, 1924).

17. Waldemar Schupp, "Der Weg der Zentralstelle für deutsche Personen- und Familiengeschichte in Leipzig: Ein Abriss von den Anfängen in den Jahren 1900/1904 bis zu ihrer Reorganisation im Jahre 1990," in Friedrich Beck and Eckart Henning, eds., *Vom Nutz und Frommen der Historischen Hilfswissenschaften* (Herold Studien 5) (Neustadt an der Aisch: Degener, 2000), 91–110; Johannes Hohlfeld, *Fünfundzwanzig Jahre Zentralstelle für Deutsche Personen- und Familiengeschichte e.V. in Leipzig 1904–16. Februar–1929* (Leipzig, 1929); Zentralstelle für Deutsche Personen- und Familiengeschichte e.V., *Verzeichnis der Mitglieder, Tauschvereine und der Bezieher der Familiengeschichtlichen Blätter* (Leipzig, 1922).

18. Johannes Hohlfeld, *Leipziger Geschlechter*, 3 vols. (Leipzig, 1933–39), and Hohlfeld, *Das Bibliographisches Institut: Festschrift zu seiner Jahrhundertfeier* (Leipzig: Bibliographisches Institut, 1926). For a biographical account on Hohlfeld, see Volkmar Weiss, "Johannes Hohlfeld, von 1924 bis 1950 Geschäftsführer der Zentralstelle für Deutsche Personen- und Familiengeschichte in Leipzig, zum 50. Todestag," *Genealogie* 49 (2000): 65–83.

19. T. W. Gwilt Mapleson, *A Hand-book of Heraldry* (New York: John Wiley, 1851), 7–8.

20. Ibid., 25. William Berry and Robert Glover, *Encyclopædia heraldica, or Complete Dictionary of Heraldry*, 3 vols. (London: Sherwood, Gilbert and Piper, 1828).

21. Mapleson, *A Hand-book of Heraldry*, 58–59.

22. McAllister, *Society as I Have Found It*, 230; Homberger, *Mrs. Astor's New York*, 197; Brandon, *The Dollar Princesses*, 17.

23. *Prominent Families of New York*, 99.

24. Brandon, *The Dollar Princesses*, 1. See also MacColl and Wallace, *To Marry an English Lord*, 36–47; Beckert, *The Monied Metropolis*, 259–60.

25. Brandon, *The Dollar Princesses*, 3–4.

26. Montgomery, "Gilded Prostitution," 43–44, 167.

27. Beckert, *The Monied Metropolis*; Hammack, *Power and Society*; Frederic Cople Jaher, *The Urban Establishment: Upper Strata in Boston, New York, Charleston, Chicago, and Los Angeles* (Urbana: University of Illinois Press, 1982); John N. Ingham, *The Iron Barons: A Social Analysis of an American Urban Elite, 1875–1965* (Westport, Conn.: Greenwood Press, 1978); Peter Dobkin Hall, *The Organization of American Culture, 1700–1900: Private Institutions, Elites, and the Origins of American Nationality* (New York: New York University Press, 1982); Ronald Story, *The Forging of an Aristocracy: Harvard and the Boston Upper Class, 1800–1870* (Middletown, Conn.: Wesleyan University Press, 1980); Thornton, *Cultivating Gentleman*; Stowe, *Going Abroad*.

28. Simone Lässig, "Bürgerlichkeit, Patronage, and Communal Liberalism in Germany, 1871–1914," in Adam, ed., *Philanthropy, Patronage, and Civil Society*, 210.

29. Robert F. Dalzell Jr., *Enterprising Elite: The Boston Associates and the World They Made* (Cambridge, Mass.: Harvard University Press, 1987), 160; Kathleen McCarthy, "Women

and Political Culture," in Lawrence J. Friedman and Mark D. McGravie, eds., *Charity, Philanthropy, and Civility in American History* (Cambridge: Cambridge University Press, 2003), 190.

30. Cleveland Amory, *The Proper Bostonians* (New York: E. P. Dutton, 1947), 178.

31. Betty G. Farrell, *Elite Families, Class, and Power in Nineteenth-Century Boston* (Albany: State University of New York Press, 1993), 31.

32. James J. Sheehan, *Museums in the German Art World from the End of the Old Regime to the Rise of Modernism* (New York: Oxford University Press, 2000), 84, 85; Gisela Weiß, *Sinnstiftung in der Provinz: Westfälische Museen im Kaiserreich* (Paderborn: Ferdinand Schöningh, 2005), 32–34.

33. Eileen Diana Mak, "Patterns of Change, Sources of Influence: An Historical Study of the Canadian Museum and the Middle Class, 1850–1950," Ph.D. diss., University of British Columbia, Vancouver, 1996, 4; H. Glenn Penny, *Objects of Culture: Ethnology and Ethnographic Museums in Imperial Germany* (Chapel Hill: University of North Carolina Press, 2001).

34. Neil Harris, *Cultural Excursions: Marketing Appetites and Cultural Tastes in Modern America* (Chicago: University of Chicago Press, 1990), 85–86.

35. Penny, *Objects of Culture*, 142–43.

36. Walter Muir Whitehill, *Museum of Fine Arts, Boston: A Centennial History*, 2 vols. (Cambridge: Belknap Press of Harvard University Press, 1970), 1:15; Calvin Tomkins, *Merchants and Masterpieces: The Story of the Metropolitan Museum of Art* (New York: Henry Holt, 1989), 61–83; Winifred E. Howe, *A History of the Metropolitan Museum of Art*, vol. 2, *1905–1941: Problems and Principles in a Period of Expansion* (New York: Columbia University Press, 1946), 49–50; Roy Rosenzweig and Elizabeth Blackmar, *The Park and the People: A History of Central Park* (Ithaca, N.Y.: Cornell University Press, 1992), 359–63.

37. Metropolitan Museum of Art, New York, N.Y., *Report of the Trustees—Metropolitan Museum of Art*, vols. 1–25 (1870–94), 501.

38. Ibid., 501, 573. For an opposing view, see Beckert, *The Monied Metropolis*, 268.

39. *Museum of Fine Arts, Boston, Thirty-fourth Annual Report for the Year 1909* (Boston: Metcalf Press, 1910), 47; *Museum of Fine Arts, Boston, Thirty-eighth Annual Report for the Year 1913* (Boston: T. O. Metcalf, 1914), 12.

40. Margaret Menninger, "The Serious Matter of True Joy: Music and Cultural Philanthropy in Leipzig, 1781–1933," in Adam, *Philanthropy, Patronage, and Civil Society*, 131.

41. Thomas Adam, *Arbeitermilieu und Arbeiterbewegung in Leipzig, 1871–1933* (Cologne: Böhlau, 1999), 143–55; Frank Heidenreich, *Arbeiterkulturbewegung und Sozialdemokratie in Sachsen vor 1933* (Cologne: Böhlau, 1995), 300–337.

42. Neil Harris, *The Artist in American Society: The Formative Years, 1790–1860* (New York: George Braziller, 1966), 159.

43. Nick Prior, "Museums: Leisure between State and Distinction," 32.

44. Harris, *Cultural Excursions*, 85.

45. John Stuart Mill, "General Intelligence," *Journal of Social Science* 5 (1873): 137–38 (originally a letter to a committee of the American Social Science Association, 1869). See also H. S. Frieze, "Art Museums and Their Connection with Public Libraries," in *Public Libraries in the United States of America: Their History, Condition, and Management*, special report provided by the Department of the Interior, Bureau of Education, part 1 (Washington, D.C.: Government Printing Office, 1876), 438.

46. Steven Conn, *Museums and American Intellectual Life, 1876–1926* (Chicago: University of Chicago Press, 1998), 11, 13.

47. Miles Orvell, *The Real Thing: Imitation and Authenticity in American Culture, 1880–1940* (Chapel Hill: University of North Carolina Press, 1989), 49.

48. Tomkins, *Merchants and Masterpieces,* 86; Metropolitan Museum of Art, New York, N.Y., *Report of the Trustees,* 502–503. For a general assessment with regard to American museums, see Laurence Vail Coleman, *The Museum in America: A Critical Study,* 3 vols. (Washington, D.C.: American Association of Museums, 1939), 2:237.

49. Edward P. Alexander, *The Museum in America: Innovators and Pioneers* (Walnut Creek, Calif.: AltaMira Press, 1997), 20–21.

50. Penny, *Objects of Culture,* 139.

51. Coleman, *Museum in America,* 1:31.

52. Quoted from Tomkins, *Merchants and Masterpieces,* 89.

53. John Michael Kennedy, "Philanthropy and Science in New York City: The American Museum of Natural History, 1868–1968," Ph.D. diss., Yale University, 1968, 65.

54. Edward Shorter, *The Making of the Modern Family* (New York: Basic Books, 1977), 227.

55. Verein für Erbauung billiger Wohnungen in Leipzig-Lindenau, Generalbericht for April 1891 to July 1895, 5, Meyersche Stiftung archive. For the architectural structure of the apartment buildings of the Meyersche Stiftung, see Thomas Adam, *Die Anfänge industriellen Bauens in Sachsen* (Leipzig: Quadrat, 1998), 18–28.

56. *Third Annual Report of the Boston Co-operative Building Company* (Boston, 1874), 14–15.

57. Sharon Marcus, *Apartment Stories: City and Home in Nineteenth-Century Paris and London* (Berkeley: University of California Press, 1999), 105–106.

58. Eduard Führ and Daniel Stemmrich, *"Nach gethaner Arbeit verbleibt im Kreise der Eurigen": Bürgerliche Wohnrezepte für Arbeiter zur individuellen und sozialen Formierung im 19. Jahrhundert* (Wuppertal: Peter Hammer, 1985), 118, 120.

59. Shorter, *Making of the Modern Family,* 227.

60. Siebenter Bericht März 1902, 2, Stiftung für Erbauung billiger Wohnungen in Leipzig, Meyersche Stiftung archive.

61. City Archive Leipzig Kap. 35 Nr. 748, Geschäftsbericht des Vereins Ostheim Leipzig für das Jahr 1905 (Leipzig, 1906), 8, 11; Rossbach, "Meine Lebensarbeit," 2, Niedersächsisches Staatsarchiv Bückeburg, Dep. 47, No. 1027. See also Thomas Adam, "Das soziale Engagement Leipziger Unternehmer—die Tradition der Wohnstiftungen," in Ulrich Heß, Michael Schäfer, Werner Bramke, and Petra Listwenik, eds., *Unternehmer in Sachsen: Aufstieg—Krise—Untergang—Neubeginn* (Leipzig: Leipziger Universitätsverlag, 1998), 115.

62. Führ and Stemmrich, *"Nach gethaner Arbeit verbleibt im Kreise der Eurigen,"* 114–30; Peter R. Gleichmann, "Wandlungen in wohnwirtschaftlichen Machtdifferentialen und im Modellieren der Mieterbeziehungen," in *AIAS. Informationen der Arbeitsgemeinschaft für interdisziplinäre angewandte Sozialforschung 1977,* 137–47; Peter R. Gleichmann, "Wandlungen im Verwalten von Wohnhäusern," in Lutz Niethammer, ed., *Wohnen im Wandel: Beiträge zur Geschichte des Alltags in der bürgerlichen Gesellschaft* (Wuppertal: Hammer, 1979), 65–88.

63. Annual report, 1908, Meyersche Stiftung archive.

64. Thomas Adam, "Meyersche Stiftung—'Es hat keinerlei Unternehmergewinn zu erfolgen,'" in *Leipziger Kalender 1997* (Leipzig: Leipziger Universitätsverlag, 1997), 149–52; John Nelson Tarn, *Five Per Cent Philanthropy: An Account of Housing in Urban Areas between 1840 and 1914* (New York: Cambridge University Press, 1973), 45–50.

65. Carol E. Harrison, *The Bourgeois Citizen in Nineteenth-Century France: Gender, Sociability, and the Uses of Emulation* (Oxford: Oxford University Press, 1999), 3.

66. Jaher, *The Urban Establishment,* 68–74, 202–208. Here Jaher corrects Edward Pessen's assumption that only a very small fraction of New York's upper class could be considered self-made men. Edward Pessen, *Riches, Class, and Power before the Civil War* (Lexington, Mass.: D. C. Heath, 1973), 62–64, 84–87; Edward Pessen, "The Egalitarian Myth and the American Social Reality: Wealth, Mobility, and Equality in the 'Era of the Common

Man,'" *American Historical Review* 76 (October 1971): 989–1034; Jaher, "Nineteenth-Century Elites in Boston and New York," 32–77; Homberger, *Mrs. Astor's New York,* 182–84.

67. Sarah Van Brugh Livingston Jay (1756–1802) was the daughter of William Livingston, the governor of New Jersey. She descended from a Scottish family of royal descent, which fled first to Holland and later to the British colonies in North America, where they arrived in 1674. The Livingstons became a highly influential family in New York, intermarrying with old Dutch families such as the Beekmans. Hamm, *Famous Families of New York,* 2:3–17.

   Caroline Webster Schermerhorn Astor (1830–1908) was the daughter of a wealthy merchant. Related to many old Dutch families, including the Beekmans, the Van Cortlandts, and the Suydams, she was able to trace her family to the very first settlers among the Dutch colonists. The Schermerhorn family was founded by Jacob Jansen, who came to North America in 1636. In 1662 Jansen established the village that was later called Schenectady. Hamm, *Famous Families of New York,* 2:117–24.

68. Churchill, *The Upper Crust,* 22.

69. The list of the famous 400 is printed in Cleveland Amory, *Who Killed Society?* (New York: Harper, 1960); Churchill, *The Upper Crust,* 114; Jerry E. Patterson, *The First Four Hundred: Mrs. Astor's New York in the Gilded Age* (New York: Rizzoli, 2000); Jaher, "Style and Status."

70. Homberger, *Mrs. Astor's New York,* 212.

71. Ibid., 224–33; Churchill, *The Upper Crust,* 134.

72. Edward Pessen, "Philip Hone's Set: The Social World of the New York City Elite in the 'Age of Egalitarianism,'" *New-York Historical Society Quarterly* 56, no. 4 (October 1972): 286–308. For London's social clubs, see Anthony Lejeune, *The Gentlemen's Clubs of London* (London: McDonald and Jane's, 1979).

73. Francis Gerry Fairfield, *The Clubs of New York: With an Account of the Origin, Progress, Present Condition, and Membership of the Leading Clubs; an Essay on New York Club-Life* (New York: Henry L. Hinton, 1873), 11.

74. Paul Porzelt, *The Metropolitan Club of New York* (New York: Rizzoli, 1982), 3. See also *Club Men of New York. Their Occupations, and Business, and Home Addresses: Sketches of Each of the Organizations: College Alumni Associations* (New York: Republic Press, 1893).

75. Porzelt, *The Metropolitan Club of New York,* 3; Pessen, "Philip Hone's Set," 291–92.

76. George Austin Morrison, *History of the Saint Andrew's Society of the State of New York, 1756–1906* (New York: St. Andrew's Society, 1906).

77. Fairfield, *The Clubs of New York,* 60.

78. Reginald T. Townsend, *Mother of Clubs: Being the History of the First Hundred Years of the Union Club of the City of New York, 1836–1936* (New York: Printing House of William Edwin Rudge, 1936), 9–24; Fairfield, *The Clubs of New York,* 57–83.

79. [William J. Dunn], *Knickerbocker Centennial: An Informal History of the Knickerbocker Club, 1871–1971* (New York: Knickerbocker Club, 1971), 15.

80. Townsend, *Mother of Clubs,* 72.

81. *Constitution and Rules, Officers and Members of the Knickerbocker Club* (New York: De Witt C. Gardner, 1877), 11–12.

82. For Belmont, see Gustav Phillip Körner, *Das Deutsche Element in den Vereinigten Staaten von Nordamerika, 1818–1848* [1880], edited and with an introduction in English by Patricia A. Herminghouse (New York: Peter Lang, 1986), 112–16. The membership list of the Knickerbocker Club can be found in *Constitution and Rules, Officers and Members of the Knickerbocker Club,* 25–36.

83. Kennedy, "Philanthropy and Science in New York City," 39; *First Annual Report of the American Museum of Natural History January, 1870* (New York, 1871), 17–18. See also

Henry Fairfield Osborn, *The American Museum of Natural History: Its Origin, Its History, the Growth of Its Departments to December 31, 1909* (New York: Irving Press, 1911).

84. Rosenzweig and Blackmar, *The Park and the People,* 351.

85. Winifred E. Howe, *A History of the Metropolitan Museum of Art with a Chapter on the Early Institutions of Art in New York* (New York, 1913), 2:103; for a list of the Committee of Fifty Gentlemen, see 116–17.

86. Hamm, *Famous Families of New York,* 2:158; *Prominent Families of New York,* 540.

87. For Morton, see *Prominent Families of New York,* 2:416; Stephen Fiske, *Off-Hand Portraits of Prominent New Yorkers* (New York: Geo. R. Lockwood & Son, 1884), 249–53.

88. See Harry Miller Lydenberg, *History of The New York Public Library* (New York: New York Public Library, 1923). The Lennox Library is discussed on pages 95–128; Phyllis Dain, *The New York Public Library: A History of Its Founding and Early Years* (New York: New York Public Library: Astor, Lennox and Tilden Foundation, 1972).

89. *Prominent Families of New York,* 1:335.

90. David Bryson Delavan, *Early Days of the Presbyterian Hospital in the City of New York* (New York: published privately, 1926), 18, 20; David Bryson Delavan, "The Origin, Birth, and Infancy of the Presbyterian Hospital," *Alumnae Association of the Presbyterian Hospital School of Nursing in the City of New York: The Quarterly Magazine 1924,* 3–14.

91. *Charter of the Society of The New-York Hospital, and the Laws relating thereto, with the By-Laws and Regulations of the Institution and Those of the Bloomingdale Asylum for the Insane* (New York: Daniel Fanshaw, 1856); *An Account of the New-York Hospital* (New York: Mahlon Day, 1829); *The Society of the New York Hospital: One Hundred and Twenty-fourth Annual Report, for the Year 1894; Charter of the Society of the New York Hospital Granted June 13, 1771, Together with the New York Laws Relating Thereto and History of the Charter* (New York: Corlies, Macy, 1953); Eric Larrabee, *The Benevolent and Necessary Institution: The New York Hospital, 1771–1971* (Garden City, N.Y.: Doubleday, 1971), 16–17; Virginia D. Harrington, *The New York Merchant on the Eve of the Revolution* (New York: Columbia University Press, 1935), 36; *So Near the Gods* (New York: Society of the New York Hospital, 1938); *The Society of the New York Hospital, 1771–1921* (New York, 1921); Society of the New York Hospital, *Biographical Catalogue Descriptive of the Portraits Belonging to the Society of the New York Hospital* (New York, 1909). For an overview of the history of hospitals in New York, see Sandra Opdycke, *No One Was Turned Away: The Role of Public Hospitals in New York City since 1900* (New York: Oxford University Press, 1999), 18–23; Harry F. Dowling, *City Hospitals: The Undercare of the Underprivileged* (Cambridge, Mass.: Harvard University Press, 1982), 31–33.

92. *Fiftieth and Fifty-first Annual Reports of the New York Association for Improving the Condition of the Poor* (October 1894), 96–98. See also John Fletcher Richmond, *New York and Its Institutions, 1609–1872* (New York: E. B. Treat, 1872), 505–508. For Rockefeller, see the biographical article in Robert T. Grimm Jr., ed., *Notable American Philanthropists: Biographies of Giving and Volunteering* (Westport, Conn.: Greenwood Press, 2002), 260–65.

93. Winifred Howe, *A History of the Metropolitan Museum of Art with a Chapter on the Early Institutions of Art in New York* (New York, 1913), 129–30; Tomkins, *Merchants and Masterpieces,* 35.

94. *The First Annual Report of the American Museum of Natural History January, 1870* (New York: Major & Knapp Engraving, 1870), 16.

95. Rosenzweig and Blackmar, *The Park and the People,* 349–66; Homberger, *Mrs. Astor's New York,* 270–72; Lloyd Morris, *Incredible New York: High Life and Low Life of the Last Hundred Years* (New York: Random House, 1951), 190–93.

96. Churchill, *The Upper Crust,* 135.

97. Anett Müller, *Der Leipziger Kunstverein und das Museum der bildenden Künste: Materialien einer Geschichte (1836–1886/87)* (Leipzig: Nouvelle Alliance, 1995), 23–26,

160–64; Karsten Hommel, *Carl Lampe: Ein Leipziger Bildungsbürger, Unternehmer, Förderer von Kunst und Wissenschaft zwischen Romantik und Kaiserreich* (Beucha: Sax, 2000), 122–24.

98. Margaret Eleanor Menninger, "Art and Civic Patronage in Leipzig, 1848–1914," Ph.D. diss., Harvard University, 1998, 89–94. For the older American tradition of thought, see Judith Huggins Balfe and Thomas A. Cassilly, "'Friends of . . .': Individual Patronage through Arts Institutions," in Judith Huggins Balfe, ed., *Paying the Piper: Causes and Consequences of Art Patronage* (Urbana: University of Illinois Press 1993), 119; Victoria D. Alexander, *Museums and Money: The Impact of Funding on Exhibitions, Scholarship, and Management* (Bloomington: Indiana University Press, 1996), 19; Tomkins, *Merchants and Masterpieces,* 21, 31.

99. Menninger, "Art and Civic Patronage in Leipzig," 89–94; Müller, *Der Leipziger Kunstverein und das Museum der bildenden Künste,* 23–26, 160–64.

100. Ernst Kroker, *Die Gesellschaft Harmonie in Leipzig 1776 bis 1926* (Leipzig: B. G. Teubner, 1926), 3–4; Friedrich August Eckstein, *Die Harmonie in dem ersten Jahrhundert ihres Bestehens* (Leipzig: B. G. Teubner, 1876), 1–8. See also Margaret Menninger, "The Serious Matter of True Joy: Music and Cultural Philanthropy in Leipzig, 1781–1933," in Adam, *Philanthropy, Patronage, and Civil Society,* 124, and Menninger, "Art and Civic Patronage in Leipzig," 55–58.

101. Herbert Helbig, *Die Vertrauten, 1680–1980* (Stuttgart: Anton Hiersemann, 1980); Gustav Wustmann, *Die Vertraute Gesellschaft* (Leipzig: Alexander Edelmann, 1880). See also Menninger, "The Serious Matter of True Joy," 124.

102. Menninger, "Art and Civic Patronage in Leipzig," 116–17, 120–21, 127–30, 135–36.

103. For the history of the Bibliographisches Institut, see Johannes Hohlfeld, *Das Bibliographische Institut: Festschrift zu seiner Jahrhundertfeier* (Leipzig: Bibliographisches Institut, 1926); Armin Human, *Carl Joseph Meyer und das Bibliographische Institut von Hildburghausen-Leipzig: Eine kulturhistorische Skizze* (Hildburghausen, 1896); Karl Heinz Kalhöfer, "125 Jahre Meyers Lexikon," *Zentralblatt für Bibliothekswesen* 78 (1964): 459–71.

104. Volker Titel, "Geschichte der Buchstadt Leipzig: Ein Überblick," in Sabine Knopf and Volker Titel, eds., *Der Leipziger Gutenbergweg: Geschichte und Topographie einer Buchstadt* (Beucha: Sax, 2001), 7–46; Andreas Herzog, ed., *Das Literarische Leipzig: Kulturhistorisches Mosaik einer Buchstadt* (Leipzig: Edition Leipzig, 1995), 147–225.

105. Herrmann Julius Meyer, Stiftung für Erbauung billiger Wohnungen in Leipzig, archival material.

106. Thomas Adam, *Arbeitermilieu und Arbeiterbewegung in Leipzig 1871–1933* (Cologne: Böhlau, 1999); Michael Rudloff, Thomas Adam, and Jürgen Schlimper, *Leipzig—Wiege der deutschen Sozialdemokratie* (Berlin: Metropol, 1996).

107. Edwin G. Burrows and Mike Wallace, *Gotham: A History of New York City to 1898* (New York: Oxford University Press, 1999), 1003.

108. For a biography of Pommer, see Adam, *Die Anfänge industriellen Bauens in Sachsen,* and Adam, "Max Pommer (1847–1915)," in *Sächsische Heimatblätter* 44, no. 2 (1998): 84–94.

109. Correspondence between Herrmann Julius Meyer and Max Pommer, September 22, 1886, and February 12, 1887, Meyersche Stiftung archive; Verein für Erbauung billiger Wohnungen in Leipzig-Lindenau, Generalbericht from April 1891 to July 1895, Meyersche Stiftung archive; *Leipzig und seine Bauten* (Leipzig: J. M. Gebhardt, 1892), 450–55; *Leipziger Zeitung,* October 1, 1895, 3940; *Centralblatt der Bauverwaltung* 1890, no. 19, 184–85, and 1900, no. 43, 262–63; *Leipziger Tageblatt,* November 1, 1898, 8162; Max Pommer, "Praktische Lösungen der Wohnungsfrage," *Leipziger Kalender 1904,* 79–84. Two unpublished studies were helpful for this discussion: Kunibert Jung, "Die

Meyer'schen Häuser in die sie prägenden Zusammenhänge gestellt" (Freie Studienarbeit am Fachbereich Architektur der Universität Hannover, Institut für Bau- und Kunstgeschichte) and "Baugeschichtliche Dokumentation und denkmalpflegerische Zielsetzung für die ehemaligen Verlags- und Druckereibetriebe Bibliographisches Institut und Notendruckerei C. G. Röder" (Pro Leipzig). See also Adam, *Die Anfänge industriellen Bauens in Sachsen,* 18–28; Adam, "Meyersche Stiftung," 135–54.

110. E. R. L. Gould, *The Housing of the Working People,* eighth special report of the commissioner of labor (Washington, D.C.: Government Printing Office, 1895), 292–96.

111. Fritz Jaeger, "Geheimer Hofrat Professor Dr. Hans Meyer, Leipzig," *Jahrbuch über die deutschen Kolonien* 7 (1904): 1–8; *Kunst aus Benin: Afrikanische Meisterwerke aus der Sammlung Hans Meyer* (Leipzig: Museum für Völkerkunde zu Leipzig, Grassimuseum Leipzig, 1994), 124–33; H. Schmitthenner, "Hans Meyer †," *Geographische Zeitschrift* 36 (1930): 129–45; Barbara Rosonsky, "Die Stellung der deutschen Geographen zur Kolonialpolitik des Deutschen Reiches," manuscript, Leibnitz Institut für Länderkunde, Nachlaß Hans Meyer, 19–34. See also Heinz Peter Brogiato, ed., *Die Anden Geographische Erforschung und künstlerische Darstellung: 100 Jahre Andenexpedition von Hans Meyer und Rudolf Reschreiter, 1903–2003* (Munich: Deutschen und Österreichischen Alpenverein, 2003); Welse von Volkmann, *Hans Meyer, "Der Mann von Kilimandscharo": Verleger, Forscher, und Mäzen* (Munich: Deutschen und Österreichischen Alpenverein, 2002); Matthias Middell, *Weltgeschichtsschreibung im Zeitalter der Verfachlichung und Professionalisierung: das Leipziger Institut für Kultur- und Universalgeschichte, 1890–1990,* vol. 1: *Das Institut unter der Leitung Karl Lamprechts* (Leipzig: Akademische Verlagsanstalt, 2005), 335–409.

112. Rolf Krusche, "Unpublished Material on the Ethnography of the Upper Xingú Region (Mato Grosso, Brazil)," *Jahrbuch des Museums für Völkerkunde zu Leipzig* 31 (1977): 177–84.

113. *Die Privatkolonien von Dr. Herrmann Meyer in Rio Grande do Sul (Südbrasilien): Ansichten aus Dr. Herrman Meyers Ackerbaukolonien Neu-Württemberg und Xingu in Rio Grande do Sul (Südbrasilien)* (Leipzig, 1904); "Die deutschen Kolonien in Südbrasilien in ihren geographischen Beziehungen," manuscript, Leibnitz Institut für Länderkunde, Nachlaß Hans Meyer; Rudolf Becker, *Deutsche Siedler in Rio Grande do Sul: Eine Geschichte der deutschen Einwanderung* (Ijuhn, Rio Grande do Sul: Verlag der Serra-Post, 1938), 70–71; Mercedes Gassen Kothe, "Die deutsche Auswanderung nach Brasilien, 1890–1914," Ph.D. diss., University of Rostock, 1992, 74. See also the entries on Hans and Herrmann Meyer by Heinz Peter Brogiato in Thomas Adam, ed., *Germany and the Americas: Culture, Politics, and History* (Santa Barbara: ABC-CLIO, 2005), 2:746–49.

114. Paul J. Dimaggio, "Cultural Entrepreneurship in Nineteenth-Century Boston: The Creation of an Organizational Base for High Culture in America," *Media Culture and Society* 4, no. 1 (1982): 47. This article was reprinted in Dimaggio's *Nonprofit Enterprise in the Arts: Studies in Mission and Constraint* (New York: Oxford University Press, 1986), 41–61.

115. The biographies of these families are included in *Boston, Past and Present; Biographical Encyclopedia of Massachusetts of the Nineteenth Century* (New York: Metropolitan Publishing and Engraving Co., 1879); William Richard Cutter, *Genealogical and Personal Memoirs Relating to the Families of Boston and Eastern Massachusetts,* 4 vols. (New York: Lewis Historical Publishing Co., 1908); Samuel Atkins Eliot, ed., *Biographical History of Massachusetts: Biographies and Autobiographies of the Leading Men in the State,* 10 vols. (Boston: Massachusetts Biographical Society, 1911–19); and Crawford, *Famous Families of Massachusetts.*

116. Nathaniel I. Bowditch, *A History of the Massachusetts General Hospital [to August 5, 1851]* (reprint: New York: Arno Press and New York Times, 1972), 3, 31, 410–16, 423–32. For

the context of the founding of the Massachusetts General Hospital, see Dowling, *City Hospitals*, 29–32.

117. *"Our First Men": A Calendar of Wealth, Fashion, and Gentility; Containing a List of Those Persons Taxed in the City of Boston, Credibly Reported to Be Worth One Hundred Thousand Dollars, with Biographical Notices of the Principal Persons* (Boston: Published by all the Booksellers, 1846), 29; Thomas L. V. Wilson, *The Aristocracy of Boston; Who They Are, and What They Were: Being a History of the Business and Business Men of Boston. For the Last Forty Years. By One Who Knows Them* (Boston: Published by the Author, 1848), 23–25; A. Forbes and J. W. Greene, *The Rich Men of Massachusetts: Containing a Statement of the Reputed Wealth of About Fifteen Hundred Persons, with Brief Sketches of More than One Thousand Characters* (Boston: Fetridge, 1851), 38–39; *List of Persons, Copartnerships, and Corporations, Who Were Taxed on Six Thousand Dollars and Upwards, in the City of Boston, in the Year 1850, Specifying the Amount of Tax on Real and Personal Estate, Severally Conformably to an Order of the City Council* (City Document.—No. 14) (Boston: J. H. Eastburn, City Printer, 1851), 72.

118. Jaher, *The Urban Establishment*, 50, 51.

119. Forbes and Greene, *The Rich Men of Massachusetts*, 61; *List of Persons, Copartnerships, and Corporations*, 117.

120. Bowditch, *History of the Massachusetts General Hospital*, 16, 418.

121. *Proceedings at the Opening of the Museum of Fine Arts with the Reports for 1876, A List of Donations, the Act of Incorporation, By-laws, etc.* (Boston: Alfred Mudge & Son, 1876), 12; Walter Muir Whitehill, *Museum of Fine Arts, Boston: A Centennial History* (Cambridge, Mass.: Belknap Press of Harvard University Press, 1970), 1:5–8.

122. *Proceedings at the Opening of the Museum of Fine Arts*, 12.

123. Ibid., 13. See also Whitehill, *Museum of Fine Arts, Boston*, 14–15.

124. *Proceedings at the Opening of the Museum of Fine Arts*, 13, 21–32; Whitehill, *Museum of Fine Arts, Boston*, 15–16.

125. *Biographical Encyclopaedia of Massachusetts of the Nineteenth Century* (New York: Metropolitan Publishing and Engraving Co., 1879), 306–308.

126. Ibid., 114, 116.

127. Jaher, *The Urban Establishment*, 50–51.

128. For his biography, see G. P. de T. Glazebrook, *Sir Edmund Walker* (London: Oxford University Press, 1933); Katharine A. Jordan, *Sir Edmund Walker, Print Collector: A Tribute to Sir Edmund Walker on the Seventy-fifth Anniversary of the Founding of the Art Gallery of Ontario* (Toronto: Art Gallery of Ontario, 1974); C. W. Colby, "Sir Edmund Walker," *Caduceus* 5, no. 3 (June 1924): 3–18, and C. W. Colby, "Sir Edmund Walker," *Canadian Banker* 56, no. 2 (Spring 1949): 93–101, both in Sir Edmund Walker Papers MS 1, box 41:30, Fisher Rare Book Library, University of Toronto (hereafter Walker Papers); Dorothy Walker Webb, "Biography of Sir Edmund Walker," manuscript, family archive of Conrad Heidenreich. See also Victor Ross, *A History of the Canadian Bank of Commerce with an Account of the Other Banks Which Now Form Part of Its Organization* (Toronto: Oxford University Press, 1922), 2:71–74, 100–102, 374–76, 553–55. Walker's philanthropic achievements are not sufficiently discussed in either of these publications. See Webb's chapter on the Royal Ontario Museum and Harold G. Needham, "Origins of the Royal Ontario Museum," M.A. thesis, 1970, 141–63, ROM archive.

129. Colby, "Sir Edmund Walker," *Caduceus*, 4.

130. Ibid., 5; Ross, *Canadian Bank of Commerce*, 2:72–73.

131. *Toronto Star*, 25 July 1918, Walker Papers, box 41:17; *Jubilee of Sir Edmund Walker* (private print), 25–28.

132. Colby, "Sir Edmund Walker," *Caduceus*, 7.

133. Ross, *Canadian Bank of Commerce*, 2:100–101.

134. Eleanor Creighton, Memorandum Sir Edmund Walker, 15, 21, Walker Papers, box 41:6.

135. *Argus* 9, no. 2 (June 1924): 19–2, Walker Papers.

136. Colby, "Sir Edmund Walker," *Caduceus,* 10.

137. Colby, "Sir Edmund Walker," *Canadian Banker,* 94–95; Colby, "Sir Edmund Walker," *Caduceus,* 8–10; Charles R. McCullough, "A Biographical Sketch of a Hamilton Old-Boy," *Hamilton Spectator,* April 18, 1942, Walker Papers, box 41:29.

138. Colby, "Sir Edmund Walker," *Canadian Banker,* 99.

139. Ibid.

140. Dean Beeby, "Industrial Strategy and Manufacturing Growth in Toronto, 1880–1910," *Ontario History* 76, no. 3 (September 1984): 199–232; J. M. S. Careless, "Some Aspects of Urbanization in Nineteenth-Century Ontario," in F. H. Armstrong, H. A. Stevenson, and J. D. Wilson, eds., *Aspects of Nineteenth-Century Ontario: Essays Presented to James J. Talman* (Toronto: Published in association with the University of Western Ontario by University of Toronto Press, 1974), 75; Peter G. Goheen, *Victorian Toronto, 1850 to 1900: Pattern and Process of Growth* (University of Chicago, Department of Geography, Research Paper No. 127, 1970), 58, 64–65; Stephen Spencer, "The Good Queen of Hogs: Toronto, 1850–1914," *Urban History Review,* no. 1 (1975): 38–42; C. Pelham Mulvany, *Toronto, Past and Present: A Handbook of the City* (Toronto: W. E. Caiger, 1884), 9–34. See also Randall White, *Ontario, 1610–1985: A Political and Economic History* (Toronto: Dundurn Press, 1985), 106–11, 152–54.

141. Fergus Cronin, "The Great Toronto Crusade: The Story of the Art Gallery of Ontario," Art Gallery of Ontario archive, 1976, 1:4; Art Gallery of Toronto, *Catalogue of Inaugural Exhibition January 29th to February 28th Nineteen Hundred and Twenty-six,* 68.

142. Goheen, *Victorian Toronto,* 75–77.

143. Careless, "Some Aspects of Urbanization," 75.

144. Brock and Young, eds., *Past and Present.*

145. Goheen, *Victorian Toronto,* 77.

146. Sigmund Samuel, *In Return: The Autobiography of Sigmund Samuel* (Toronto: University of Toronto Press, 1963), 139.

147. Newspaper article collection (microfilm), Art Gallery of Ontario archive.

148. Elisabeth Wallace, *Goldwin Smith: Victorian Liberal* (Toronto: Toronto University Press, 1957), 60–61.

149. Cronin, "The Great Toronto Crusade," 1:18; James Mavor, *My Windows on the Street of the World* (Toronto: J. M. Dent & Sons, 1923), 2:135–36.

150. Wallace, *Goldwin Smith,* 129; Creighton, Memorandum Sir Edmund Walker, 18–19.

151. Art Gallery of Toronto, 4, Mavor Papers MS 119, box 56B, B No. 5 B, Fisher Rare Book Library, University of Toronto; Agreement Made the Twentieth Day of January, A.D. 1911 between the Art Museum of Toronto . . . and the Municipal Corporation of the City of Toronto, Walker Papers MS 1, no. 27 A 7.

152. Tomkins, *Merchants and Masterpieces;* Adam, "Die Kommunalisierung von Kunst und Kultur."

153. Michael Bliss, *A Canadian Millionaire: The Life and Business Times of Sir Joseph Flavelle, Bart., 1858–1939* (Toronto: Macmillan, 1978), 160, 161, 205.

154. Scrapbook Biographies of People, 20:921, Metropolitan Toronto Library.

155. Charles Trick Currelly, *I Brought the Ages Home* (Toronto: Ryerson Press, 1956), 129; Lovat Dickson, *The Museum Makers: The Story of the Royal Ontario Museum* (Toronto: Royal Ontario Museum, 1986), 11–18; Mak, "Patterns of Change," 57–62.

156. Dickson, *The Museum Makers,* 27.

157. Currelly, *I Brought the Ages Home,* 183.

158. Dickson, *The Museum Makers,* 28.

159. No. 27 D: 13 (Letter from Walker, June 23, 1914), No. 27 D: 19 (Letter from the Canadian Bank of Commerce in London to Sir Edmund Walker, February 11, 1915), Walker Papers MS 1.

160. Minutes of the Board of Trustees, Royal Ontario Museum, vol. 1 (1911–20); vol. 2 (1921–26), 89–92, ROM archive.
161. Minutes of the Board of Trustees, Royal Ontario Museum, vol. 2 (1921–26), 4–5, ROM archive.
162. Ibid., 7; *Bulletin of the Royal Ontario Museum of Archaeology,* no. 1 (May 1923): 16.

4. Bountiful Ladies

1. Frank K. Prochaska, *Women and Philanthropy in Nineteenth-Century England* (Oxford: Clarendon Press, 1980), 1.
2. For the concept of public and private sphere, see Jürgen Habermas, *The Structural Transformation of the Public Sphere: An Inquiry into a Category of Bourgeois Society* (Cambridge, Mass.: MIT Press, 1989). For challenges to Habermas's concept, see Geoff Eley, "Nations, Publics, and Political Cultures: Placing Habermas in the Nineteenth Century," in Craig Calhoun, ed., *Habermas and the Public Sphere* (Cambridge, Mass.: MIT Press, 1992), 289–339; Anthony LaVopa, "Conceiving a Public: Ideas and Society in Eighteenth-Century Europe," *Journal of Modern History* 64 (1992): 79–116; Dena Goodman, "Public Sphere and Private Life: Toward a Synthesis of Current Historiographical Approaches to the Old Regime," *History and Theory* 31 (1992): 1–20; James van Horn Melton, *The Rise of the Public in Enlightenment Europe* (New York: Cambridge University Press, 2001), 1–15.
3. Ute Frevert, *Women in German History: From Bourgeois Emancipation to Sexual Liberation* (New York: Berg, 1988), 109, 113. See also Sharon Marcus, *Apartment Stories: City and Home in Nineteenth-Century Paris and London* (Berkeley: University of California Press, 1999), 90, 235–36n21.
4. For an overview of this historiographical tradition, see Stefan-Ludwig Hoffmann, *Geselligkeit und Demokratie: Vereine und zivile Gesellschaft im transnationalen Vergleich, 1750–1914* (Göttingen: Vandenhoeck & Ruprecht, 2003), 16–18, 45–46, 88–89. For a wider discussion of the relation between public/private sphere and gender, see Joan B. Landes, *Women and the Public Sphere in the Age of the French Revolution* (Ithaca, N.Y.: Cornell University Press, 1988). Landes's contention that the bourgeois public sphere was essentially masculine has been refuted by a number of historians including Keith Michael Baker, Dena Goodman, Colin Jones, and Belinda Davis. See Baker, "Defining the Public Sphere in Eighteenth-Century France: Variations on a Theme by Habermas," in Craig, *Habermas and the Public Sphere,* 181–211; Goodman, "Public Sphere and Private Life"; Jones, "The Great Chain of Buying: Medical Advertisement, the Bourgeois Public Sphere, and the Origins of the French Revolution," *American Historical Review* 101 (1996): 13–40; Davis, "Reconsidering Habermas, Gender, and the Public Sphere: The Case of Wilhelmine Germany," in Geoff Eley, ed., *Society, Culture, and the State in Germany, 1870–1930* (Ann Arbor: University of Michigan Press, 1997), 397–426.
5. See, for example, Marion Kaplan, "Prostitution, Morality Crusades, and Feminism: German-Jewish Feminists and the Campaign against White Slavery," *Women's Studies International Forum* 5, no. 6 (1982): 619–27.
6. Benjamin Maria Baader, "Rabbinic Study, Self-Improvement, and Philanthropy: Gender and the Refashioning of Jewish Voluntary Associations in Germany, 1750–1870," in Thomas Adam, ed., *Philanthropy, Patronage, and Civil Society: Experiences from Germany, Great Britain, and North America* (Bloomington: Indiana University Press, 2004), 163, 169.
7. Frevert, *Women in German History,* 69.
8. Jean H. Quataert, *Staging Philanthropy: Patriotic Women and the National Imagination in Dynastic Germany, 1813–1916* (Ann Arbor: University of Michigan Press, 2001), 6.

9. Kathleen D. McCarthy, *American Creed: Philanthropy and the Rise of Civil Society, 1700–1865* (Chicago: University of Chicago Press, 2003), 31.

10. Frank K. Prochaska, *Women and Philanthropy in Nineteenth-Century England* (New York: Oxford University Press, 1980), 6.

11. Anne M. Boylan, *The Origin of Women's Activism: New York and Boston, 1797–1840* (Chapel Hill: University of North Carolina Press, 2002), 54.

12. Prochaska, *Women and Philanthropy*, 17.

13. Henry Ingersoll Bowditch, "Letter from the Chairman of the State Board of Health, Concerning Houses for the People, Convalescent Homes, and the Sewage Questions," in *Second Annual Report of the State Board of Health of Massachusetts, January 1871* (Boston: Wright & Potter, State Printers, 1871), 214.

14. McCarthy, *American Creed*, 39.

15. J. J. Maclaren, "Moral Reform in Ontario: An Encouraging Outlook," in Isabel C. Barrows, ed., *Proceedings of the National Conference of Charities and Correction at the Twenty-fourth Annual Session Held in Toronto, Ontario, July 7–14, 1897* (Boston: Geo. H. Ellis/London: P. S. King & Son, 1898), 349.

16. Prochaska, *Women and Philanthropy*, 5.

17. Richard Stites, *The Women's Liberation Movement in Russia: Feminism, Nihilism, and Bolshevism, 1860–1930* (Princeton, N.J.: Princeton University Press, 1978), 68.

18. Frances Willard quoted in Kathleen D. McCarthy, *Noblesse Oblige: Charity and Cultural Philanthropy in Chicago, 1849–1929* (Chicago: University of Chicago Press, 1982), 32

19. Eugenie Ladner Birch and Deborah S. Gardner, "The Seven-Percent Solution: A Review of Philanthropic Housing, 1870–1910," *Journal of Urban History* 7, no. 4 (August 1981): 430. See also Marion Brion, *Women in the Housing Service* (London: Routledge, 1995).

20. Quataert, *Staging Philanthropy*, 112.

21. McCarthy, *American Creed*, 30–41.

22. Thomas Adam, "Philanthropic Landmarks: The Toronto Trail from a Comparative Perspective, 1870s to the 1930s," *Urban History Review* 30 (2001): 5; Adam, "Ein Schritt in die bürgerliche Öffentlichkeit?" *Ariadne*, no. 42 (November 2002): 28.

23. Prochaska, *Women and Philanthropy*, 34.

24. McCarthy, *Noblesse Oblige*, 20, 23, 24, 30, 43–44; McCarthy, *American Creed*, 186. For the legal regulations with regard to married women's rights to property in Germany, see Arne Duncker, *Gleichheit und Ungleichheit in der Ehe: Persönliche Stellung von Frau und Mann im Recht der ehelichen Lebensgemeinschaft, 1700–1914* (Cologne: Böhlau, 2003), 1020–23. For Ontario, see Lori Chambers, *Married Women and Property Law in Victorian Ontario* (Toronto: University of Toronto Press, 1997).

25. *Ariadne: Forum für Frauen und Geschlechtergeschichte*, no. 42 (November 2002): special issue, *Stifterinnen—Zeit, Geld, und Engagement: Vom Mittelalter bis ins 21. Jahrhundert*.

26. For a comparative legal study of laws with regard to inheriting in the United States and Germany, see Jens Beckert, *Unverdientes Vermögen: Soziologie des Erbrechts* (Frankfurt am Main: Campus, 2004).

27. Michael Bliss, *A Canadian Millionaire: The Life and Business Times of Sir Joseph Flavelle, Bart., 1858–1939* (Toronto: Macmillan, 1978), 145.

28. C. K. Clarke, *A History of the Toronto General Hospital Including an Account of the Medal of the Loyal and Patriotic Society of 1812* (Toronto: William Briggs, 1913), 122.

29. Frederic Cople Jaher, *The Urban Establishment: Upper Strata in Boston, New York, Charleston, Chicago, and Los Angeles* (Urbana: University of Illinois Press, 1982), 202–208; Edward Pessen, *Riches, Class, and Power before the Civil War* (Lexington, Mass.: D. C. Heath, 1973), 31–91.

30. Women received the right to vote in national elections in Canada in 1918, in Germany in 1919, and in the United States in 1920.

31. Diana Pedersen, "'Building Today for the Womanhood of Tomorrow': Businessmen, Boosters, and the YMCA, 1890–1930," *Urban History Review* 15, no. 3 (February 1987): 226, 227.

32. Kathleen McCarthy, "Women and Political Culture," in Lawrence J. Friedman and Mark D. McGravie, eds., *Charity, Philanthropy, and Civility in American History* (Cambridge: Cambridge University Press, 2003), 190, 194. See also Peter Dobkin Hall, *Inventing the Nonprofit Sector and Other Essays on Philanthropy, Voluntarism, and Nonprofit Organizations* (Baltimore: Johns Hopkins University Press, 1992), 41–49.

33. Quataert, *Staging Philanthropy,* 5–6.

34. The following discussion is based on an evaluation of the gender structure of the membership organizations and donor groups already discussed in chapter 3.

35. Alexis de Tocqueville, *Democracy in America,* trans. Henry Reeve (New York: Bantam Classic, 2000), 640–45; Hoffmann, *Geselligkeit und Demokratie,* 8; Robert D. Putnam, "Bowling Alone: America's Declining Social Capital," *Journal of Democracy* 6 (1995): 65–78.

36. Metropolitan Museum of Art, New York, *Report of the Trustees—Metropolitan Museum of Art,* vols. 1–25 (1870–94), 383–84, 407. For her various gifts to the AMNH, see American Museum of Natural History, *Annual Report of the Trustees, Act of Incorporation, Constitution, By-Laws, and List of Members for the Year 1885–86* (New York: Wm. C. Martin, 1886), 1; American Museum of Natural History, *Annual Report of the Trustees, Act of Incorporation, Contract with City, By-Laws, and List of Members for the Year 1888–89* (New York: Printed for the Museum, 1889), 8.

37. This question is inspired by the discussion of feminine and masculine qualities of acts of charity in Adele Lindenmeyr, *Poverty Is Not a Vice: Charity, Society, and the State in Imperial Russia* (Princeton, N.J.: Princeton University Press, 1996), 13.

38. Edwin P. Hoyt, *The Vanderbilts and Their Fortunes* (Garden City, N.Y.: Doubleday, 1962), 217–20.

39. Prochaska, *Women and Philanthropy,* 5.

40. Stites, *The Women's Liberation Movement in Russia,* 68.

41. This information is based on documentation from several members of the Warren family in Toronto (especially Hillary Nichols) and the family archive (in the possession of John T. Band).

42. Biographical information based on the biographical file on H. D. Warren, Seeley G. Mudd Manuscript Library, Princeton University.

43. For this story see the genealogical webpage www.tracycrocker.com/p105.htm#i1027.

44. *Descriptive Catalogue of Fire Department Supplies* (Gutta Percha & Rubber Mfg. Co. Toronto); William C. Geer, *The Reign of Rubber* (London: Allan & Unwin, 1922).

45. *Descriptive Catalogue of Fire Department Supplies;* Geer, *The Reign of Rubber;* obituary, Harry Dorman Warren, *Globe,* March 6, 1909, Biographical Scrapbooks, vol. 16, Metropolitan Toronto Library.

46. Article from the *Toronto Star,* 1987, Biographical Scrapbooks, vol. 16, Metropolitan Toronto Library.

47. Theodore Allen Heinrich, *Art Treasures in the Royal Ontario Museum* (Toronto: McClelland and Stewart, 1963), 7.

48. Protocol of an interview with Mrs. Charles Band, daughter of Mrs. H. D. Warren. The document is available in the family archive (in the possession of John T. Band).

49. Collection of documents on Mrs. H. D. Warren from the Archive of the Girl Guides of Canada (provided by Margaret Machell): Jean Graham, "Among Those Present XLII.—Mrs. H. D. Warren."

50. Collection of documents on Mrs. H. D. Warren from the Archive of the Girl Guides of Canada (provided by Margaret Machell): *Canadian Guider* 6, no. 1 (January 1937).

51. Graham, "Among Those Present XLII.—Mrs. H. D. Warren."

52. See Catherine L. Cleverdon, *The Woman Suffrage Movement in Canada,* with an introduction by Ramsay Cook (Toronto: University of Toronto Press, 1974).

53. Biographical Scrapbooks, 16:213, Metropolitan Library, Toronto.

54. Article from the *Toronto Star,* 1987, Biographical Scrapbooks, vol. 16, Metropolitan Toronto Library; Cleverdon, *Woman Suffrage,* 44–45.

55. McCarthy, "Women and Political Culture," 190.

56. Stites, *The Women's Liberation Movement in Russia,* 68.

57. Arminius, *Die Großstädte in ihrer Wohnungsnoth und die Grundlagen einer durchgreifenden Abhilfe* (Leipzig: Duncker & Humblot, 1874); Gerlinde Kämmerer and Anett Pilz, eds., *Leipziger Frauengeschichten: Ein historischer Stadtrundgang* (Leipzig, 1995), 176, 183. For the importance of this book for the history of German city planning, see Werner Hegemann, *Das steinerne Berlin: Geschichte der größten Mietskasernenstadt der Welt* (Braunschweig/Wiesbaden: Friedr. Vieweg & Sohn, 1988), 260–66; Maja Binder, "Arminius—eine Stadttheoretikerin in der zweiten Hälfte des 19. Jahrhunderts," in Sigrun Anselm and Barbara Beck, eds., *Triumph und Scheitern in der Metropole: Zur Rolle der Weiblichkeit in der Geschichte Berlins* (Berlin: Dietrich Reimer, 1987), 56–74; Ursula Gräfin Dohna, "Gegen 'Bemooste Vorurtheile,'" *Das Gartenamt* 4 (1971): 170–73.

58. For an overview on the urbanization in Germany, see Jürgen Reulecke, *Geschichte der Urbanisierung in Deutschland* (Frankfurt am Main: Suhrkamp, 1985). For a case study, see Thomas Adam, *Arbeitermilieu und Arbeiterbewegung in Leipzig, 1871–1933* (Cologne: Böhlau, 1999), 24–56.

59. Hegemann, *Das steinerne Berlin,* 261–62; Binder, "Arminius," 61–62; Elisabeth Meyer-Renschhausen and Hartwig Berger, "Bodenreform," in Diethart Kerbs and Jürgen Reulecke, eds., *Handbuch der deutschen Reformbewegungen, 1880–1933* (Wuppertal: Peter Hammer, 1998), 266.

60. Arminius, *Die Großstädte in ihrer Wohnungsnoth,* 134; Anke Schekahn, *Spurensuche, 1700–1933: Frauen in der Disziplingeschichte der Freiraum- und Landschaftsplanung* (Universität Gesamthochschule Kassel, 2000), 57–61; Lydia Buchmüller, "Ausradierte Geschichte: Dohna-Poninska und die Anfänge der Stadtplanungstheorie," *Dokumente und Informationen zur Schweizerischen Orts-, Regional- und Landesplanung* 120 (January 1995): 11–17.

61. Hegemann, *Das steinerne Berlin,* 260; Binder, "Arminius," 60–61.

62. Max Schwarz, *MdR: Biographisches Handbuch der Reichstage* (Hanover: Verlag für Literatur und Zeitgeschehen, 1965), 298.

63. Dohna, "Gegen 'Bemooste Vorurtheile,'" 170; Hermann Wilhelm Albrecht Graf zu Dohna-Kotzenau, *Die freien Arbeiter im Preußischen Staate* (Leipzig: O. Wigand, 1847); Hermann zu Dohna Kotzenau, *Das Einkommen des Arbeiters vom nationalökonomischen Standpunkte* (Berlin: Schneider, 1855); Ursula Gräfin Dohna to Thomas Adam, July 2005.

64. Bernhard Dohna, *Analyse der socialen Noth* (Berlin, 1856).

65. Morris, *Private Profit and Public Interest,* 25–26.

66. Theodor Freiherr von der Goltz, *Die ländliche Arbeiterfrage und ihre Lösung* (Danzig: A. W. Kafemann, 1872).

67. Kurt Munier, *Theodor Freiherr von der Goltz: Ein Bild seines Lebens und Schaffens* (Berlin: Verlag für Landwirtschaft, Gartenbau und Forstwesen, 1921); *Neue Deutsche Biographie* (Berlin: Duncker & Humblot, 1959), 4:635–36.

68. Arminius, *Die Großstädte in ihrer Wohnungsnoth,* 61–64, 89–106.

69. Ibid., 101–102, 110–11, 118.

70. Ibid., 120–30.

71. Newman quoted in Birch and Gardner, "Philanthropic Housing," 430.

72. *The First Annual Report of the Boston Co-operative Building Company,* 3–4, 10, 16–17.

73. Ulrike König, "Das Wirken des Architekten Arwed Rossbach in Leipzig im letzten Drittel des 19. Jahrhunderts," unpublished Diplomarbeit, University of Leipzig 1988), 56n58.

74. Stadtarchiv Leipzig, Kap. 35, Nr. 748, Geschäftsbericht des Vereins Ostheim Leipzig für das Jahr 1904 (Leipzig 1905), 5–6, 23; Bettina Kaun, "Der Architekt Max Arwed Rossbach und sein Wirken für Leipzig—Eine Laudatio," *Leipziger Kalender,* 1995, 156.

75. Adam, "Meyersche Stiftung—'Es hat keinerlei Unternehmergewinn zu erfolgen,'" in *Leipziger Kalender 1997,* 137–39.

76. In October 1876 she gave birth to her first daughter, who died within six months; in November 1877 her son was born, and in October 1880 her second daughter was born, but she too died within one month. Ernst Hasse, *Nachrichten über die Familie Hasse und einige verwandte Familien,* 3rd ed. (Leipzig: Wilhelm Engelmann, 1903), 53–56.

77. Manfred Hötzel, "Die Hasseschen Häuser in der Breitenfelder Straße—Ein kleines Beispiel sozialen Wohnungsbau in Gohlis vor über 100 Jahren," in *Historisches des Stadtteil Gohlis* (www.stadtinfo2000.de/gohlis/chg-wohnungsbau.html).

78. Stadtarchiv Leipzig, GR Gohlis no. 115, 55–56.

79. Stadtarchiv Leipzig, Kap. 24, no. 662, vol. 1, 10–13.

80. E. R. L. Gould, *The Housing of the Working People,* Eighth Special Report of the Commissioner of Labor (Washington, D.C.: Government Printing Office, 1895), 295–96. See also *Handbuch der Architektur Vierter Teil: Entwerfen, Anlage, und Einrichtung der Gebäude* 2. Halb-Band: *Gebäude für die Zwecke des Wohnens, des Handels und Verkehres.* 1. Heft: *Wohnhäuser* (Stuttgart: Arnold Bergsträsser/A. Kröner, 1902), 262–63.

81. Emma Hasse sold the buildings in 1897.

82. *Eine Glückliche: Hedwig von Holstein in ihren Briefen und Tagebuchblättern,* 3rd ed. (Leipzig: H. Haessel, 1907), 6, 17; Gerhart Glaser, *Franz von Holstein: Ein Dichterkomponist des 19. Jahrhunderts* (Leipzig: Schwarzenberg und Schumann, 1930), 8–40; Geck, "Nicht nur Komponisten Gattin," 291–92. For Franz von Holstein's biography and his literary work, see *Franz von Holstein: Seine nachgelassenen Gedichte herausgegeben und mit einer biographischen Einleitung versehen* (Leipzig: Breitkopf und Härtel, 1880).

83. Bibliothek der Hochschule für Musik und Theater "Felix Mendelssohn-Bartholdy," Leipzig, I 2.5.1, I 2.5.3/2, 2.5.4/2 (Holsteinstift); Stadtarchiv Leipzig, Kap. 36 H No. 42, vol. 1; *Eine Glückliche,* 319–20. See also Glaser, *Franz von Holstein,* 41. Glaser, however, is wrong when he assumes that this foundation ceased to exist during World War I. According to the documents in the archive of the Leipzig Conservatory and the City Archive, the Holstein foundation was fully functioning at least until December 1945. The foundation capital at this point was 212,740.22 Reichsmark.

84. *Eine Glückliche,* 286–87.

85. Ibid., 381; H. Geffcken and H. Tykorinski, *Stiftungsbuch der Stadt Leipzig* (Leipzig: Bär und Hermann, 1905), 563.

86. *Eine Glückliche,* 467; König, "Das Wirken des Architekten Arwed Rossbach," 55n57.

87. Bibliothek der Hochschule für Musik und Theater "Felix Mendelssohn-Bartholdy," Leipzig, I 2.5.1, 2.5.3/2, 2.5.4/2 (Holsteinstift); *Eine Glückliche,* 382–83.

88. Stadt Leipzig, Amt für Bauordnung und Denkmalpflege, Bauakten-Archiv, Acten des Rathes der Stadt Leipzig in Baupolizeisachen über das Grundstück No. 51–53 an der Oststrasse und No. 21 an der Eilenburger Strasse (Salomonstift) (letter of Arwed Rossbach to the city council of Leipzig, March 6, 1890); Bibliothek der Hochschule für Musik und Theater "Felix Mendelssohn-Bartholdy," Leipzig, I 2.5.1, 2.5.3/2, 2.5.4/2 (Holsteinstift).

89. *Leipzig und seine Bauten* (Leipzig 1892), 459–60; Bernard Riedel, "Gruppenbauten in und um Leipzig," *Leipziger Kalender* 9 (1912): 173–83; Robert Bruck, *Arwed Rossbach und seine Bauten* (Berlin 1904), 71.

90. See the contributions by Jörg Roesler and Richard Klinkhardt in Ulrich Heß, Michael Schäfer, Werner Bramke, and Petra Listwenik, eds., *Unternehmer in Sachsen: Aufstieg—Krise—Untergang—Neubeginn* (Leipzig: Leipziger Universitätsverlag, 1998), 221–42, 283–304.

91. City of Leipzig, Amt für Bauordnung und Denkmalpflege, Akten des Rates der Stadt Leipzig in Baupolizeisachsen, Ostheimstraße 1, 1b, 1–4.

92. City of Leipzig, Amt für Bauordnung und Denkmalpflege, Akten des Rates der Stadt Leipzig in Baupolizeisachsen, Ostheimstraße 3a, b, 1–2, 18c.

93. Professor Dr. Ernst Hasse and Emma Hasse, letter to the city council of Gohlis, October 25, 1888, Stadtarchiv Leipzig, Kap. 24, Nr. 662, vol. 1, 13.

94. Bruck, *Arwed Rossbach und seine Bauten*. For Max Pommer, see Thomas Adam, *Die Anfänge industriellen Bauens in Sachsen* (Leipzig: Quadrat, 1998).

95. Sächsisches Staatsarchiv Leipzig, Bezirksschulrat Borna 396, 3v.; Niedersächsisches Staatsarchiv Bückeburg, Dep. 47, No. 1027 (unnumbered biographical page about Therese Rossbach).

96. Therese Rossbach, "Meine Lebensarbeit," 1–2, Niedersächsisches Staatsarchiv Bückeburg, Dep. 47, No. 1027.

97. Betina Kaun, "Der Architekt Max Arwed Rossbach und sein Wirken für Leipzig—Eine Laudatio," *Leipziger Kalender* 1995, 153–56; Robert Bruck, *Arwed Rossbach und seine Bauten* (Berlin: Wachsmuth, 1904).

98. For this conflict see James Retallack, ed., *Saxony in German History: Culture, Society, and Politics, 1830–1933* (Ann Arbor: University of Michigan Press, 2000); Retallack, "'Why Can't a Saxon Be More Like a Prussian?' Regional Identities and the Birth of Modern Political Culture in Germany, 1866–67," *Canadian Journal of History* 32 (1997): 26–55. For the problem of German regionalism, see Celia Applegate, *A Nation of Provincials: The German Idea of Heimat* (Berkeley: University of California Press, 1990); Alon Confino, *The Nation as a Local Metaphor: Württemberg, Imperial Germany, and National Memory, 1871–1918* (Chapel Hill: University of North Carolina Press, 1997).

99. Eberhard Brüning, "'Saxony Is a Prosperous and Happy Country': American Views of the Kingdom of Saxony in the Nineteenth Century," in Thomas Adam and Ruth Gross, eds., *Traveling between Worlds: German-American Encounters* (Texas A&M, 2006), 20–50; Eberhard Brüning: *Das Konsulat der Vereinigten Staaten von Amerika zu Leipzig: Unter besonderer Berücksichtigung des Konsuls Dr. J. G. Flügel (1839–1855).* Sitzungsberichte der Sächsischen Akademie der Wissenschaften zu Leipzig. Phil.-hist. Klasse, vol. 134, Heft 1 (Berlin: Akademie, 1994), 59. For Leipzig's fairs, see Hartmut Zwahr, Thomas Topfstedt, and Günter Bentele, eds., *Leipzigs Messen, 1497–1997: Gestaltwandel, Umbrüche, Neubeginn,* 2 vols. (Cologne: Böhlau, 1999).

100. Thomas Adam, "Das soziale Engagement Leipziger Unternehmer—die Tradition der Wohnstiftungen," in Ulrich Heß et al., *Unternehmer in Sachsen,* 115–16.

101. Adolf Diamant, *Chronik der Juden in Leipzig* (Chemnitz/Leipzig: Heimatland Sachsen, 1993), 192; Josef Reinhold, *Zwischen Aufbruch und Beharrung: Juden und jüdische Gemeinde in Leipzig während des 19. Jahrhunderts* (Leipzig: Ephraim Carlebach Stiftung, 1999), 20.

102. Reinhold, *Zwischen Aufbruch und Beharrung,* 20. For the emancipation of Jews in Saxony, see Josef Reinhold, "Die Entstehung einer jüdischen Großgemeinde: Vor 150 Jahren konstituierte sich die Israelitische Religionsgemeinde zu Leipzig," *Sächsische Heimatblätter* 43 (1997): 122–24. For the history of the Jewish community in Leipzig, see Reinhold, *Zwischen Aufbruch und Beharrung;* Reinhold, "Die Entstehung einer jüdischen Großgemeinde"; Diamant, *Chronik der Juden in Leipzig;* Ephraim Carlebach Stiftung, ed., *Judaica Lipsiensia: Zur Geschichte der Juden in Leipzig* (Leipzig: Edition Leipzig, 1994); Vorstand der Israelitischen Religionsgemeinde Leipzig, *Aus Geschichte*

und Leben der Juden in Leipzig. Festschrift zum 75 jährigen Bestehen der Leipziger Gemeinde—Synagoge (Leipzig: A. Pries, 1930); Ernst Hasse, "Die Israeliten," in *Die Stadt Leipzig in hygienischer Beziehung* (Leipzig: Duncker, 1891), 149ff.

103. Archive of the Catholic Church in Leipzig (Katholisches Propsteipfarramt Leipzig): Festschrift zur Goldenen Jubelfeier des Vincentius-Vereins Leipzig und Jahresberichte der Zweigkonferenzen (Dresden, 1905), 18–19, 67, 69, 73.

104. Reinhold, *Zwischen Aufbruch und Beharrung,* 20; Reinhold, "Die Entstehung einer jüdischen Großgemeinde," 131.

105. Archive of the Catholic Church in Leipzig (Katholisches Propsteipfarramt Leipzig): files: Kirchenaustritt Gustav de Liagre (1873/No. 6); Konversionen (1958/39/2); Trauung Albert Heinrich de Liagre und Anna Marie Samson (1858/310/14).

106. For Rossbach's biography, see Kaun, "Der Architekt Max Arwed Rossbach," 153–59.

107. Kroker, *Die Gesellschaft Harmonie in Leipzig;* Menninger, "Art and Civic Patronage in Leipzig," 55–56.

108. Stadtarchiv Leipzig, Kap. 35, Nr. 748, Geschäftsbericht des Vereins Ostheim Leipzig für das Jahr 1904, 6.

109. Stadtarchiv Leipzig, Kap. 35, Nr. 748, Geschäftsbericht des Vereins Ostheim Leipzig für das Jahr 1905 (Leipzig 1906), 8, 11; Rossbach, "Meine Lebensarbeit," 2.

110. Stadtarchiv Leipzig, Kap. 35, Nr. 748, Geschäftsbericht des Vereins Ostheim Leipzig für das Jahr 1904, 9; Rossbach, "Meine Lebensarbeit," 2.

111. Stadtarchiv Leipzig, Kap. 35, Nr. 748, Geschäftsbericht des Vereins Ostheim Leipzig für das Jahr 1904, 5; Rossbach, "Meine Lebensarbeit," 2.

112. Robert Treat Paine, "The Housing Conditions in Boston," *Annals of the American Academy of Political and Social Science* 20 (July 1902–December 1902): 125.

113. *Sixteenth Annual Report of the Boston Co-operative Building Company* (Boston 1887), 22. Niedersächsisches Staatsarchiv.

114. *Forty-first Annual Report of the Boston Co-operative Building Company* (Boston 1912), 8.

115. Stadtarchiv Leipzig, Kap. 35, Nr. 748, Akten den Verein Ostheim betreffend, 247.

116. Rossbach, "Meine Lebensarbeit," 3–5.

117. For Ida von Kortzfleisch and the Reifensteiner Verband, see Ortrud Wörner-Heil, *Frauenschulen auf dem Lande: Reifensteiner Verband (1897–1997)* (Kassel: Archiv der Deutschen Frauenbewegung, 1997), 60ff.; Anna von Heydekampf, *Ida von Kortzfleisch, ihr Leben und ihr Werk* (Gotha: Schmidt & Thelow, 1927); Elisabeth Heimpel-Michel, *Ida von Kortzfleisch: Frauenbewegung und Frauendienstpflicht* (Gotha, 1932); Ida von Kortzfleisch, *Das Maiden-Buch: Mit Tafeln und hübschen Textilillustrationen von Elisabeth Molter* (Gotha: Schmidt, 1910); Ida von Kortzfleisch, "VI. Unsere zwölfjährige Erfahrungen in den wirtschaftlichen Frauenschulen auf dem Lande," in *Frauenschulen: Referate über von Frauen gegründete, in der Praxis bewährte Fortbildungsanstalten für Frauen gesammelt und herausgegeben von der Berliner Ortsgruppe des Deutsch-Evangelischen Frauenbundes* (Leipzig/Berlin: Teubner, 1901), 42–53.

118. Rossbach, "Meine Lebensarbeit," 5–22; Niedersächsisches Staatsarchiv Bückeburg, Dep. 47, No. 980 (Haus- und landwirtschaftliche Frauenschule Arvedshof in Elbisbach), 2–9; Niedersächsisches Staatsarchiv Bückeburg, Dep. Reifensteiner Verband, *Reifensteiner Maidenzeitung* 1, no. 3 (March 1916): 44–45; no. 8 (August 1916): 123–24; 2, no. 7 (July 1917): 100–101; 3, no. 1 (January 1918): 7–8; Sächsisches Staatsarchiv Leipzig, Bezirksschulrat Borna 396; Wörner-Heil, *Frauenschulen auf dem Lande,* 171–73.

119. Rossbach, "Meine Lebensarbeit," 22–23. For the further history of Arvedshof, see *2. Bericht der Wirtschaftschaftlichen Frauenschule Arvedshof in Elbisbach von Oktober 1925 bis September 1926,* Sächsische Landesbibliothek, Dresden; Wörner-Heil, *Frauenschulen auf dem Lande,* 173.

120. R. Julien, "Ein Werk der Menschenliebe: Neues aus Arwedshof," *Die Gutsfrau* 4, no. 3 (1915–16): 46–47. For a nationalistic concept of labor, see Frank Trommler, "Die Nationalisierung der Arbeit," in Reinhold Grimm and Jost Hermand, eds., *Arbeit als Thema in der deutschen Literatur vom Mittelalter bis zur Gegenwart* (Königstein/Ts.: Athenäum, 1979), 102–25.

121. Jeremy Noakes and Geoffrey Pridham, eds., *Nazism, 1919–1945: A Documentary Reader*, vol. 2, *State, Economy and Society, 1933–1939* (Exeter: University of Exeter Press, 1997), 453; Gisela Bock, "Antinatalism, Maternity, and Paternity in National Socialist Racism," in David F. Crew, ed., *Nazism and German Society, 1933–1945* (New York: Routledge, 1997), 121–29.

5. Giving for Good

1. Kathleen Woodroofe, *From Charity to Social Work in England and the United States* (Toronto: University of Toronto Press, 1962), 18.

2. Derek J. Penslar, "Philanthropy, the 'Social Question,' and Jewish Identity in Imperial Germany," *Leo Baeck Institute Year Book* 38 (1993): 52; Sachsse and Florian Tennstedt, *Geschichte der Armenfürsorge in Deutschland vom Spätmittelalter bis zum Ersten Weltkrieg* (Stuttgart: W. Kohlhammer, 1980), 227–33. For the history of the concepts of charity and philanthropy as well as the religious roots of charity, see Robert H. Bremner, *Giving: Charity and Philanthropy in History* (New Brunswick, N.J.: Transaction, 1994).

3. Stephen A. Speisman, "Munificent Parsons and Municipal Parsimony: Voluntary vs. Public Poor Relief in Nineteenth-Century Toronto," *Ontario History* 65, no. 1 (March 1973): 33.

4. Ibid., 46.

5. Rainer Liedtke, *Jewish Welfare in Hamburg and Manchester c. 1850–1914* (Oxford: Clarendon Press, 1998), 232, 234, 235; David Sorkin, *The Transformation of German Jewry, 1780–1840* (New York: Oxford University Press, 1987). See also Andreas Reinke, *Judentum und Wohlfahrtspflege in Deutschland: Das Jüdische Krankenhaus in Breslau, 1726–1944* (Hanover: Hahnsche Buchhandlung, 1999), 118–31.

6. Derek J. Penslar, "The Origins of Modern Jewish Philanthropy," in Warren F. Ilchman, Stanley N. Katz, and Edward L. Queen II, eds., *Philanthropy in the World's Traditions* (Bloomington: Indiana University Press, 1998), 208, 209.

7. Tobias Brinkmann, "Ethnic Difference and Civic Unity: A Comparison of Jewish Communal Philanthropy in Nineteenth-Century German and U.S. Cities," in Thomas Adam, ed., *Philanthropy, Patronage, and Civil Society: Experiences from Germany, Great Britain, and North America* (Bloomington: Indiana University Press, 2004), 193; Tobias Brinkmann, *Von der Gemeinde zur "Community" Jüdische Einwanderer in Chicago, 1840–1900* (Osnabrück: Rasch University Press, 2002), 253–59.

8. Jacob Rader Marcus, *United States Jewry, 1776–1985*, vol. 3: *The Germanic Period*, part 2 (Detroit: Wayne State University Press, 1993), 367.

9. E. Digby Baltzell, *The Protestant Establishment: Aristocracy and Caste in America* (New York: Random House, 1964), 356. For the changes that occurred after World War II, see David Hammack, "Patronage and the Great Institutions," in Adam, *Philanthropy, Patronage, and Civil Society*, 88–92.

10. Thomas Adam, "Philanthropic Landmarks: The Toronto Trail from a Comparative Perspective, 1870s to the 1930s," *Urban History Review* 30 (2001): 3–21.

11. German historians have paid much attention to philanthropy and Jewish integration. See the contributions by Benjamin Maria Baader, Tobias Brinkmann, and Simone Lässig in Adam, *Philanthropy, Patronage, and Civil Society*, 163–218. For the integration

of Jews into the German Bürgertum, see Simone Lässig, *Jüdische Wege ins Bürgertum: Kulturelles Kapital und sozialer Aufstieg im 19. Jahrhundert* (Göttingen: Vandenhoeck und Ruprecht, 2004); Till van Rahden, *Juden und andere Breslauer: Die Beziehungen zwischen Juden, Protestanten, und Katholiken in einer deutschen Großstadt von 1860 bis 1925* (Göttingen: Vandenhoeck und Ruprecht, 2001); Michael Dorrmann, *Eduard Arnhold (1849–1925): Eine biographische Studie zu Unternehmer- und Mäzenatentum im Deutschen Kaiserreich* (Berlin: Akademie, 2002); Erika Bucholtz, *Henri Hinrichsen und der Musikverlag C. F. Peters: Deutsch-Jüdisches Bürgertum in Leipzig von 1891 bis 1938* (Tübingen: Mohr Siebeck, 2001); Olaf Matthes, *James Simon: Mäzen im Wilhelminischen Zeitalter* (Berlin: Bostelmann und Siebenhaar, 2000); Elisabeth Kraus, *Die Familie Mosse: deutsch-jüdisches Bürgertum im 19. und 20. Jahrhundert* (Munich: C. H. Beck, 1999).

12. Marcus, *United States Jewry*, 3:367.

13. Naomi W. Cohen, *Encounter with Emancipation: The German Jews in the United States, 1830–1914* (Philadelphia: Jewish Publication Society of America, 1984), 116–17.

14. Marcus, *United States Jewry*, 3:369. For anti-Jewish prejudice in the United States, see Cohen, *Encounter with Emancipation*, 249ff.; E. Digby Baltzell, "The Development of a Jewish Upper Class in Philadelphia, 1782–1940," in Marshall Sklare, ed., *The Jews: Social Patterns of an American Group* (Glencoe, Ill.: Free Press, 1960), 275–76, 282. See also Alan T. Davies, *Antisemitism in Canada: History and Interpretation* (Waterloo, Ont.: Wilfrid Laurier University Press, 1992), and Irving Abella and Harold Troper, *None Is Too Many: Canada and the Jews of Europe, 1933–1948* (New York: Random House, 1983).

15. Marcus, *United States Jewry*, 3:369. For accounts of Rosenwald and his many philanthropies, see Peter M. Ascoli, *Julius Rosenwald: The Man Who Built Sears, Roebuck and Advanced the Cause of Black Education in the American South* (Bloomington: Indiana University Press, 2006); M. R. Werner, *Julius Rosenwald: The Life of a Practical Humanitarian* (New York: Harper & Brothers, 1939); Philip P. Bregstone, *Chicago and Its Jews: A Cultural History* (privately published, 1933), 121–27; Jay Pridmore, *Inventive Genius: The History of the Museum of Science and Industry, Chicago* (Chicago: Museum of Science and Industry, 1996), 11–22.

16. William V. Shannon, *The American Irish* (New York: Macmillan, 1963), 182–83; Peter Dobkin Hall, *The Organization of American Culture, 1700–1900: Private Institutions, Elites, and the Origins of American Nationality* (New York: New York University Press, 1982), 198–206.

17. Frederic Cople Jaher, "The Politics of the Boston Brahmins, 1800–1860," in Ronald P. Formisano and Constance K. Burns, eds., *Boston, 1700–1980: The Evolution of Urban Politics* (Westport, Conn.: Greenwood Press, 1984), 60–63, 70; Thomas H. O'Connor, *The Boston Irish: A Political History* (Boston: Northeastern University Press), 62–63.

18. Paul Dimaggio, "Cultural Entrepreneurship in Nineteenth-Century Boston: The Creation of an Organizational Base for High Culture in America," *Media Culture and Society* 4, no. 1 (1982): 47. This article was reprinted in Paul J. Dimaggio, *Nonprofit Enterprise in the Arts: Studies in Mission and Constraint* (New York: Oxford University Press, 1986), 41–61.

19. Betty G. Farrell, *Elite Families: Class and Power in Nineteenth-Century Boston* (Albany: State University of New York Press, 1993), 31. The Boston Symphony Orchestra will not be discussed here. See Dimaggio, "Cultural Entrepreneurship," 40–49; M. A. De Wolfe Howe, *The Boston Symphony Orchestra, 1881–1931* (Boston: Houghton Mifflin, 1931); Bliss Perry, *Life and Letters of Henry Lee Higginson* (Boston: Atlantic Monthly Press, 1921), 291–324.

20. Kathleen McCarthy, "Women and Political Culture," in Lawrence J. Friedman and Mark D. McGravie, eds., *Charity, Philanthropy, and Civility in American History* (Cambridge: Cambridge University Press, 2003), 190; Dimaggio, "Cultural Entrepreneurship," 40.

21. Cleveland Amory, *The Proper Bostonians* (New York: E. P. Dutton, 1947), 37ff., 178. For Paine, see *The Harvard Graduates Magazine* 19 (1910–11): 390–92. For Endicott, see William Richard Cutter, ed., *Genealogical and Personal Memoirs Relating to the Families of Boston and Eastern Massachusetts,* 4 vols. (New York: Lewis Historical, 1908), 1:133–41.

22. This argumentation is based on Dimaggio, "Cultural Entrepreneurship," 38–39. His use of the term *non-profit corporation,* however, is inadequate, since all philanthropic institutions under discussion relied on making profits. In the case of the BCBC, a certain part of the profit was evenly distributed among the philanthropists/shareholders. For the phenomenon of limited dividend companies, see the second chapter of this book.

23. Dimaggio, "Cultural Entrepreneurship," 38.

24. Robert F. Dalzell Jr., *Enterprising Elite: The Boston Associates and the World They Made* (Cambridge, Mass.: Harvard University Press, 1987), 128.

25. *Biographical Encyclopaedia of Massachusetts of the Nineteenth Century* (New York: Metropolitan Publishing and Engraving Co., 1879), 306–308; Walter Muir Whitehill, *Museum of Fine Arts Boston: A Centennial History* (Cambridge, Mass.: Belknap Press of Harvard University Press, 1970), 1:11–12.

26. The following analysis is based upon my biographical databases, which have been created from the *Proceedings at the Opening of the Museum of Fine Arts: with the Reports for 1876, a List of Donations, the Act of Incorporation, By-Laws etc* (Boston, 1876), 21–32; *Trustees of the Museum of Fine Arts: Twentieth Annual Report for the Year Ending December 31, 1895* (Boston: Alfred Mudge & Son, Printers, 1896), 34–46.

27. Leona Bean McQuiston, ed., *The McQuiston, McCuiston, and McQuesten Families, 1620–1937* (Louisville, Ky.: Standard Press, 1937), 68–69, 164.

28. For a discussion of the ability of the Brahmins to absorb new men and capital, see Jaher, "The Politics of the Boston Brahmins: 1800–1860," 70.

29. William A. Braverman, "The Ascent of Boston's Jews, 1630–1918," Ph.D. diss., Harvard University, 1990, 90; Ellen Smith, "'Israelites in Boston,' 1840–1880," in Jonathan D. Sarna and Ellen Smith, eds., *The Jews of Boston: Essays on the Occasion of the Centenary (1895–1995) of the Combined Jewish Philanthropies of Greater Boston* (Boston: Combined Jewish Philanthropies of Greater Boston, 1995), 62.

30. Braverman, "The Ascent of Boston's Jews," 113.

31. Sarna and Smith, *The Jews of Boston,* 329; John Koren, *Boston, 1822 to 1922: The Story of Its Government and Principal Activities during One Hundred Years* (Boston: City of Boston Printing Department, 1923), 205; Braverman, "The Ascent of Boston's Jews," 116–17; Smith, "'Israelites in Boston,' 1840–1880," 57.

32. Martin Green, *The Problem of Boston: Some Readings in Cultural History* (London: Longmans, Green, 1966), 44–45; Koren, *Boston,* 205; Stephan Thernstrom, *The Other Bostonians: Poverty and Progress in the American Metropolis, 1880–1970* (Cambridge, Mass.: Harvard University Press, 1973), 112.

33. Oscar Handlin, *Boston's Immigrants: A Study in Acculturation* (Cambridge, Mass.: Belknap Press of Harvard University Press, 1959), 184.

34. Shannon, *The American Irish,* 182.

35. For a discussion that focuses on the conflict in the field of education and schooling, see Barbara Miller Solomon, *Ancestors and Immigrants: A Changing New England Tradition* (Cambridge: Harvard University Press, 1956), 44–52.

36. Thernstrom, *The Other Bostonians,* 112.

37. N. I. Bowditch, *A History of the Massachusetts General Hospital* (New York: Arno Press and New York Times, 1972), 423–31.

38. Green, *The Problem of Boston,* 49; Dalzell, *Enterprising Elite,* 131.

39. Farrell, *Elite Families,* 35.

40. Shannon, *The American Irish,* 185.
41. Green, *The Problem of Boston,* 49.
42. Dalzell, *Enterprising Elite,* 153–54; Walter Muir Whitehill, *Boston Public Library: A Centennial History* (Cambridge, Mass.: Harvard University Press, 1956), 34–36.
43. Koren, *Boston,* 114; Whitehill, *Boston Public Library,* 19, 22.
44. Neil Harris, "The Gilded Age Revisited: Boston and the Museum Movement," *American Quarterly* 14, no. 4 (Winter 1962): 549, 559; Whitehill, *Museum of Fine Arts,* vol. 1.
45. Jaher, "The Politics of the Boston Brahmins," 73.
46. Handlin, *Boston's Immigrants,* 190.
47. Charles Theo. Russell Jr., *Disfranchisement of Paupers: Examination of the Law of Massachusetts* (Boston: Little, Brown, 1878), 7–8.
48. Handlin, *Boston's Immigrants,* 205.
49. See New York Sven Beckert, "Democracy and Its Discontents: Contesting Suffrage Rights in Gilded Age New York," *Past and Present* 174 (2002): 116–57.
50. Russell, *Disfranchisement of Paupers,* 4.
51. Dimaggio, "Cultural Entrepreneurship," 40; Jaher, "The Politics of the Boston Brahmins," 64; Ronald Story, *The Forging of an Aristocracy: Harvard and the Boston Upper Class, 1800–1870* (Middletown, Conn.: Wesleyan University Press, 1980).
52. Geoffrey Blodgett, "Yankee Leadership in a Divided City: Boston, 1860–1910," in Formisano and Burns, *Boston,* 90.
53. For a discussion of philanthropy and power, see David Hammack, "Patronage and the Great Institutions of the Cities of the United States: Questions and Evidence, 1800–2000," in Adam, *Philanthropy, Patronage, and Civil Society,* 79–100.
54. Dalzell, *Enterprising Elite,* 160.
55. Jaher, "The Politics of the Boston Brahmins," 60.
56. Adam, "Philanthropy and the Shaping of Social Distinctions," in Adam, *Philanthropy, Patronage, and Civil Society,* 15–33.
57. Dimaggio, "Cultural Entrepreneurship," 40.
58. Shannon, *The American Irish,* 186.
59. Thernstrom, *The Other Bostonians,* 133.
60. Handlin, *Boston's Immigrants,* 216.
61. Ernest S. Griffith, *The Modern Development of City Government in the United Kingdom and the United States* (London: Oxford University Press, 1927), 111n1.
62. Handlin, *Boston's Immigrants,* 222–23; Shannon, *The American Irish,* 186–87.
63. *Report of the Toronto General Hospital: Annual Report for the Year Ending 30th September 1906* (Toronto, 1906), 82–91. The information for the Royal Ontario Museum is based on minutes of its board of trustees, vol. 1 (1911–20) and vol. 2 (1921–26), ROM archive. The membership list for the Art Gallery of Toronto can be found in its *Catalogue of Inaugural Exhibition January 29th to February 28th Nineteen Hundred and Twenty-six,* 68–71. For the members of the Toronto Housing Company, see City of Toronto archives, *Better Housing in Canada: The Ontario Plan,* first annual report of the Toronto Housing Company, Ltd., 1913, 23–24. See also Glen Eker, *Jewish Residents of Toronto in the 1861–1901 Censuses of Canada* (1908), 234, 185; Peter G. Goheen, *Victorian Toronto, 1850 to 1900: Pattern and Process of Growth* (University of Chicago Department of Geography Research Paper No. 127, 1970), 76; Adam, "Philanthropic Landmarks," 5–7.
64. For a discussion of political-economic ways to social integration, see Alan Gordon, "Taking Root in the Patronage Garden: Jewish Businessmen in Toronto's Conservative Party, 1911–1921," *Ontario History* 88, no. 1 (March 1996): 31–46.
65. Sigmund Samuel, *In Return: The Autobiography of Sigmund Samuel* (Toronto: University of Toronto Press, 1963), viii.
66. The following discussion of Pierre Bourdieu's capital concept is based on Simone Laessig's interpretation of Bourdieu. Simone Laessig, *Jüdische Wege ins Bürgertum:*

Kulturelles Kapital und sozialer aufstieg im 19. Jahrhundert (Göttingen: Vandenhoeck und Ruprecht, 2004), 26-30.

67. One could make an argument that such clubs are still very important in American and Canadian life. See Lawrence Otis Graham, *Member of the Club: Reflections on Life in a Racially Polarized World* (New York: HarperCollins, 1995).

68. Samuel, *In Return,* 8.

69. Stephen A. Speisman, *The Jews of Toronto: A History to 1937* (Toronto: McClelland and Stewart, 1979), 22ff.; Alan Gordon, "Taking Root in the Patronage Garden," 34.

70. Samuel, *In Return,* 11, 39, 41; Speisman, *The Jews of Toronto,* 32-33; file on Lewis and Sigmund Samuel, Holy Blossom Temple archive.

71. Samuel, *In Return,* 52.

72. Ibid., 53.

73. Ibid., 62, 65, 100.

74. *Maclean's Magazine,* July 1, 1954, in Scrapbook Biographies of People, 81:40, Metropolitan Toronto Library.

75. Samuel, *In Return,* 84, 89-90; Sigmund Samuel LLD 1933, University of Toronto Archives, A 73-0026/396 (53).

76. *The Sigmund Samuel Story,* University of Toronto Archives, LE 3T59S27.

77. Samuel, *In Return,* 97.

78. Jean Goodman, *The Mond Legacy: A Family Saga* (London: Weidenfeld and Nicolson, 1982), 7-25; American Institute of the History of Pharmacy Collection, Kremers Reference Files, Madison, Wis.: "Britain's Biggest Alkali-works," *Chemist and Druggist,* January 30, 1897, 165-66; "Ludwig Mond," *Pharmaceutical Era,* September 26, 1895; "Manufacture of Ammonia," *Pharmaceutical Era,* October 1889, 383-84.

79. Goodman, *The Mond Legacy,* 31.

80. Todd M. Endelman, *The Jews of Georgian England, 1714-1830: Tradition and Change in a Liberal Society* (Ann Arbor: University of Michigan Press, 1999), 119.

81. Goodman, *The Mond Legacy,* 31.

82. For the biography of Henriette Hertz and her relationship to Frieda and Ludwig Mond, see Julia Laura Rischbieter, *Henriette Hertz: Mäzenin und Gründerin der Bibliotheca Hertziana in Rom* (Stuttgart: Franz Steiner, 2004).

83. Goodman, *The Mond Legacy,* 34, 39, 43, 59.

84. Ibid., 62-65.

85. J. M. Cohen, *The Life of Ludwig Mond* (London: Methuen, 1956), 222.

86. Goodman, *The Mond Legacy,* 79-80.

87. George Edward Cokayne, *The Complete Peerage; or A History of the House of Lords and All Its Members from the Earliest Times,* revised and much enlarged, ed. H. A. Doubleday and Lord Howard de Walden, vol. 13: *Peers Created 1901 to 1938* (London: St. Catherine Press, 1940), 445-46.

88. Sir Bernard Burke and Ashworth P. Burke, *A Genealogical and Heraldic History of the Peerage and Baronetage, the Privy Council, Knightage, and Compagnionage,* 80th ed, (London: Burke, 1921), 1562.

89. Goodman, *The Mond Legacy,* 92.

90. Ibid., 30, 75, 97.

91. Ibid., 93-94, 97-100.

92. Samuel, *In Return,* 108.

93. Scrapbook Biographies of People, 20:919, 929, Metropolitan Toronto Library.

94. Samuel, *In Return,* 125. For a slightly different view, see Gordon, "Taking Root in the Patronage Garden," 34-35.

95. Samuel, *In Return,* 125-27; Scrapbook Biographies of People, 20:923, Metropolitan Toronto Library.

96. Samuel, *In Return,* viii, 133.

97. Interview with Elizabeth Samuel, July 28, 2002.

98. Interview with David Hart, historian of Holy Blossom Temple, July 30, 2002.

99. Minutes of the Royal Ontario Museum board of trustees, vol. 1 (1911–20), 135, 171–72, ROM archive.

100. Samuel, *In Return,* 103.

101. This (financial/philanthropic) aspect of the history of the University of Toronto still remains unexplored. Martin L. Friedland, *The University of Toronto: A History* (Toronto: University of Toronto Press, 2002) does little to fill this gap.

102. Biographical file on Robert Ludwig Mond based on newspaper clippings, University of Toronto Archives, A 73-0026/331(08).

103. Samuel, *In Return,* 133–35; Scrapbook Biographies of People, 20:929, Metropolitan Toronto Library.

104. Sigmund Samuel LLD 1933, University of Toronto Archives, A 73-0026/396 (53); Samuel, *In Return,* 140, 142.

105. "Sigmund Samuel Donation," University of Toronto Archives, A 82-0036/032 (Endowments Sigmund Samuel).

106. Brochure about Sigmund Samuel on the occasion of laying the first stone for the new library building on October 23, 1953, University of Toronto Archives.

107. Samuel, *In Return,* 149–51.

108. Letter "Re: Sigmund Samuel Canadiana Building," 2, University of Toronto Archives A 82-0036/032 (Endowments Sigmund Samuel).

109. Charles W. Jefferys, ed., *A Catalogue of the Sigmund Samuel Collection Canadiana and Americana* (Toronto: Ryerson Press, 1948), xiii.

110. "Memorandum Sigmund Samuel Trust(s)," 2, University of Toronto Archives A 82-0036/032 (Endowments Sigmund Samuel).

111. A. G. Rankin to Dr. S. E. Smith, January 13, 1955, and F. R. Stone (Vice President) to H. M. Turner, August 17, 1955, University of Toronto Archives A 82-0036/032 (Endowments Sigmund Samuel).

112. Sigmund Samuel LLD 1933, University of Toronto Archives, A 73-0026/396 (53); Scrapbook Biographies of People, 20:921, 932, Metropolitan Toronto Library.

113. Interview with Edith Samuel, Toronto, August 7, 2002.

114. Interview with Elizabeth Samuel, Toronto, July 28, 2002.

115. Ibid.; interview with Edith Samuel.

116. Samuel, *In Return,* 139.

Conclusion

1. Daniel T. Rodgers, *Atlantic Crossings: Social Politics in a Progressive Age* (Cambridge, Mass.: Belknap Press of Harvard University Press, 1998), 2.

2. See for this differentiation the contributions to the special issue *Schenken, Stiften, Spenden* of the journal *Geschichte und Gesellschaft* 33, no. 1 (2007). See also Gabriele Lingelbach, *Spenden und Sammeln: Die Entwicklung des bundesrepublikanischen Spendenmarktes von den späten 1940er bis in die frühen 1980er Jahren* (Göttingen: Wallstein, 2009).

Index

Abbott, Edwin Hale, 114, 157
Academy of Music (New York), 103, 107
Adams, Charles Francis, 53
Agassiz, Louis, 29
Albany, 27, 78
Albrecht, Heinrich, 66, 71–74
Albrecht, Rudolf, 51
Alden, John, 134
Alice, Grand Duchess of Hesse-Darmstadt, 10, 63–64, 66, 83; Hülfsverein, 63; Lyceum, 63; Society for Aid to the Sick and Wounded, 63; Society for the Education and Employment of Women, 63
Allen, Matthew, 55
American Economic Association, 46, 78, 79
American Museum of Natural History (AMNH), 23, 26, 28, 29, 92, 96, 98, 100, 105, 106, 107, 108, 109, 132–133; financing of building, 23; founding of, 104–105; membership organization, 105–107, 132–133
American School of Classical Studies at Athens, 133
Ames, Evan Fisher, 80
Ames, Herbert Brown, 80–81

Amory, Cleveland, 157
Amory (family), 113
Amsterdam, 31, 49
Anson (family), 93
Appleby Boys School, 118
Appleton, Thomas Gold, 115
Appleton (family), 113
Applied Arts Museum (Leipzig), 92, 96, 109, 132; museum association membership, 109, 132
Arbeiterbildungsinstitut Leipzig, 98–99
Art Associations (Kunstvereine), 15, 17–18, 19–21, 108
Art galleries, 13, 14, 15, 16, 24, 85, 95, 99, 100, 102, 115, 124, 128, 131, 133
Art Museum (Gallery) (Leipzig), 14, 19–20, 21, 24, 26, 92, 96, 110, 132; art association, 18, 19, 21, 26, 31; membership, 132
Art Museum (Springfield, Massachusetts), 28
Artisans Dwellings Company in Glasgow, 82
Artisans Dwellings Company (Toronto), 81
Artizans', Labourers' and General Dwellings Company, 46
Arvedshof, 150–151
Aschrott, Paul Felix, 58, 66, 68, 69–71, 72, 76
Aschrott, Sigmund, 69

Ashley, Lord (later Lord Shaftesbury), 47, 53, 138
Aspinwell, William H., 20
Aspinwell (family), 106
Association for Improving the Condition of the Poor (AICP), 45, 76, 92, 106–107
Association Opposed to Women's Suffrage (in Canada), 136
Astor, John Jacob, 35–36, 37, 104; public library, 36, 37
Astor, Mrs. Caroline Schermerhorn, 103, 107
Astor, Mrs. William, 90, 94
Astor (family), 106
Athenæum (Boston), 114–115, 156
Augsburg, 51, 143

Baader, Benjamin Maria, 126
Baby-Castle (England), 149
Baden, 63
Baedecker, Fritz, 146, 147
Baltimore, 61, 80
Bank of Upper Canada, 117
Barnardo, Thomas John, 149–150
Barrington (Mass.), 78
Bartlett, Sidney, 157
Basel, 49
Bates, Joshua, 6, 37, 161; library donation, 37
Bator, Paul Adolphus, 82
Bauer, Catherine, 128, 140
Bavaria, 63
Bayard, Balthazar, 105
Beckert, Sven, 4

Beekman (family), 105, 106
Beer, George Frank, 80, 82, 83, 84–85
Belgium, 16, 30, 49, 75
Belgum, Kirsten, 3
Belmont, August, 104
Berlin, 10, 15, 16, 17, 19, 22, 31, 33, 36, 37, 43, 48, 49, 50, 51, 63, 64, 68, 69, 70, 138, 139, 145, 151; Academy of Fine Arts, 17, 22; New Museum, 18; Old Museum, 18, 22; Royal Library, 17; Seminar for Royal Prussian Statistics, 42; University of, 17, 22, 59, 70, 71, 72, 112
Berliner Gemeinnützige Baugesellschaft, 48, 50
Berliner Spar- und Bauverein, 73
Beverly (Mass.), 158
Bibliographisches Institut, 110
Bickmore, Albert, 100
Bigelow, Erastus Brigham, 116
Bigelow (family), 160
Binder, Maja, 137
Birch, Eugene Ladner, 40, 128, 140
Birmingham (England), 80, 138
Bishop (family), 106
Bliss (family), 106
Blodgett, William T., 20, 105
Bochum, 43
Böhmert, Victor, 73
Bourdieu, Pierre, 165
Boston, 5, 9, 10, 11, 15, 23, 27, 29, 30, 31, 32, 35, 36, 37, 40, 41, 44–45, 51, 59–60, 61, 79, 83, 84, 91, 92, 96, 98, 99, 102, 107, 112–116, 119, 121, 125, 127, 131, 132, 133, 154, 155, 156–164; 181; Board of Health of the City of, 44; City Council, 115, 161, 164; city government, 161, 163; High Society of, 94, 164; Irish/Catholics, 95, 113, 114, 154–155, 156–158, 160–164;

Jews, 159–160; Music Hall, 115; philanthropic establishment, 156, 159, 163, 164; Water Power Company, 115
Boston and Worcester Railroad, 158
Boston City Hospital, 59
Boston Cooperative Building Company (BCBC), 61, 62, 79, 92, 96, 101, 114, 115, 140, 141, 148–149, 156, 157, 159, 160, 161, 163; membership, 157. See also Limited dividend (housing) companies
Boston Public Library (BPL), 6, 14, 15, 31, 35, 36, 37, 38, 156, 157, 161
Boston Symphony Orchestra, 156
Boulton, D'Arcy, 121
Boulton, William Henry, 121
Bowditch, Henry Ingersoll, 40, 44–45, 53, 54, 58, 59–62, 66, 68, 69, 74, 76, 79, 81, 84, 110, 113, 114, 127, 140, 149, 157
Bowditch, Nathaniel, 59
Bowditch, Nathaniel I., 113
Bowditch, William, 59
Bowditch (family), 158
Boylan, Anne M., 127
Bradlee (family), 158
Brahmins (Boston), 9, 35, 37, 59, 114, 115, 116, 156–164; Brahmin elite, 102, 113; Brahmin society, 113, 116
Brandeis, Louis D., 159
Brandeis, Mrs. Louis D., 159
Braunbehrens, Reichsgerichtsrat, 146
Braverman, William, 160
Bremen, 17, 18, 49
Bremner, Robert H., 40
Breslau (Silesia), 31, 43, 64, 147
Brimmer, Martin, 61, 114, 115, 116, 157
Brimmer, Martin, II, 116
Brimmer, Martin, III, 116
Brimmer (family), 115–116, 158
Brinkmann, Tobias, 154, 155

British Museum, 105
British Town Planning Institute, 83
Brockhaus, Heinrich, 108
Brockhaus (publishing house), 110
Brown, Caroline, 80
Brown, James, 104, 106
Browne, Junius Henri, 90, 91
Brussels (Austrian Netherlands), 65
Bryant, William Cullen, 15, 16
Büchner, Luise, 63, 64
Buffalo (New York), 27
Burdett-Coutts, Baroness Angela, 129
Bürgertum, 7; Bildungs-bürgertum, 7; Wirt-schaftsbürgertum, 7. See also Leisure class
Burlington & Missouri River Railroad, 158

Cabot (family), 160
Cadwalader (family), 106
Caledonia (Ontario), 116
Calvin, Johannes, 146
Cambridge (Mass.), 27, 28
Canadian Bank of Commerce, 23, 24, 116, 117, 118, 119, 123, 168
Canadian Club (Toronto), 83
Canadian Council of the Girl Guides Association, 136
Canadian Girl Guides movement, 136
Canadiana Gallery of the Province of Ontario (of the Royal Ontario Museum), 174, 176
Carnegie, Andrew, 78
Carpenter, Mary, 64
Cauchon, Noulan, 83
Cawthra, Joseph, 120
Cawthra (family), 92, 120
Celle (Hanover), 31
Center (family), 104
Central London Dwellings Improvement Company, 46
Century Club (New York), 16, 105
Cesnola, Louis P. di, 98, 100

Charity, 126–128, 153–154, 155, 182
Charity Organizations Society (New York), 106
Charlestown (Mass.), 113, 114
Chase, Ellen, 62
Chelsea (Mass.), 113
Chemnitz (Saxony), 43
Chicago, 27, 38, 80, 129, 154, 155; Jewish hospital, 154; Museum of Science and Industry, 14
Chicago, Burlington & Quincy Railroad, 158
Church (family), 107
Cincinnati, 62
Cité ouvrière, 138
City and Suburban Homes Company (CSHC), 62, 76, 80, 82, 92, 140, 148. See also Limited dividend (housing) companies
Civil society, 13, 41, 131
Clason (family), 104
Clauss, Gustav M., 108
Clinton (Mass.), 116
Clydach (Wales), 169
Cobb, Samuel, 99
Cody, Henry John, 173
Cogswell, Joseph Green, 36
Cohen, J. M., 169
Cohen, Sir Louis, 167
Cohen, William B., 40
Cohnheim, Julius, 146
Cohnheim, Mrs. Julius, 146
Cohnheim, Marta, 146
Colby, C. W., 23, 119
Coleraine (Northern Ireland), 158
Cologne, 16, 168
Columbia University, 78, 106
Comfort, George Fisk, 6, 15, 16–20, 31
Concert Hall (Leipzig), 98–99
Conn, Steven, 99
Connecticut, 105, 134
Conspicuous Consumption, 7–8. See also Veblen, Thorstein
Cooke, Jay, 23
Coolidge (family), 113
Cooper, James Fenimore, 16
Copenhagen, 49, 72

Cöpenick (Prussia), 70
Cox, George A., 119, 122
Creighton, Eleanor, 118
Crenshaw, Hannah Fox, 62
Cronin, Fergus, 24
Council of Women (of Canada), 83
Cruger, S. van Rensselaer, 104
Cummings, John, 116
Currelly, Charles Trick, 29, 118, 122–123, 124, 134, 136, 172
Curtis, Miranda Lampson, 53
Cutting, Robert Fulton, 76

Dalwigk, Reinhard Carl Friedrich von, 63
Daly, Gerald, 40
Dalzell, Robert, 95, 157, 163
Darley, Gillian, 63
Darmstadt, 30, 63, 64, 66; New Grand Ducal Museum, 30
Denmark, 75
De Peyster, Catherine M. van Cortlandt, 105
De Peyster (family), 93, 106
Deutsches Museum (Nuremberg), 14, 22
Die Vertrauten, 108–109
Dimaggio, Paul, 162
Dodge, William E., 106
Dodge (family), 106
Dohna, Bernhard, 138
Dohna, Hermann, 138
Dollfuß, Jean, 138
Dominion Bank of Canada, 84
Dortmund (Westfalen), 43
Dresden, 5, 9, 13, 14, 15, 16, 17, 18–19, 31, 33, 35, 36, 38, 49, 51, 72, 147, 159; Albertinum, 24; art association, 21; art gallery/museum (Green Vault), 14, 15, 18, 19, 24, 27, 31, 33; Frauenkirche, 13; Japanese Palace, 34, 35; nobility, 5; Palace of the Grosse Garden, 24; royal court, 5, 33; Royal Zoological, Anthropological, and Ethnographical

Museum, 27; Technical Institute, 73
Dresdner Mietzinssparkasse, 72–73
Dudley, Joseph, 105
Duncker & Humblot (publishing house), 138
Dunham (family), 104
Dunlap, David Alexander, 123
Düsseldorf (Westfalen), 16
Duyckinck (family), 106
Dwight, Henry E., 35
Dwight, H. P., 81

Ealing Tenants Ltd. (London), 82, 83
Eaton, Timothy, 122
Eaton (family), 120
Education of women, 136, 145, 150, 151
Edwards, W. C., 123
Elberfeld (Westfalen), 43; Landgericht, 71
Elbisbach (Saxony), 150
Elites, 7, 9, 11, 81, 99, 182; new, 10, 11, 94, 95, 96, 99, 102, 181; old, 8, 10, 11, 94, 95, 96, 99, 102, 181; Boston, new, 102, 112–116, 159–160; Boston, old, 112–116, 156–164, 181; Leipzig, new (industrial), 108–112, 163; Leipzig, old (mercantile), 108–112; New York, new, 102, 103–108, 110, 116, 163, 181; New York, old, 103–108, 110, 116, 181; philanthropic, 137, 147, 155; Toronto, new, 112, 113, 116–125, 165–179; Toronto, old, 112, 113, 116–125, 164–179, 181
Elliot, Charles William, 158
Elvers, Rudolf, 47
Emancipation, 128, 131, 134, 136, 137
Endicott, William, Jr., 114, 157, 158
Endicott (family), 158
Engel, Ernst, 70
England, 16, 17, 30, 46, 49, 51, 64, 69, 70, 81, 105, 116, 120, 167, 168–169, 170

Erbpacht, 67
Espagne, Michel, 3, 4
Essen (Westfalen), 43
Ethnographic Museum
    (Leipzig), 100, 110, 112;
    museum association
    membership, 110
Eutritzsch (Saxony), 111
Everett, Edward, 31, 32, 33,
    36–37

Factory villages, 68
Fairfield, Francis Gerry, 103
Family: concept of, 100–102,
    131, 163; heraldry, 93,
    94; histories/identities,
    making of, 91–94
Farnworth (England), 168
Farrell, Betty G., 156
Feinberg, Abraham L., 176
Field, Benjamin H., 104, 105
Field (family), 106
First International Congress
    on Public Hygiene in
    Brussels, 49
Flavelle, Joseph W., 84, 119,
    120, 121–122, 129
Flensburger Arbeiter-
    bauverein, 50
Four Per Cent Industrial
    Dwellings Company
    (London), 46
France, 3, 16, 31, 49, 75, 80,
    99, 120, 138
Frankfurt am Main, 10,
    19, 31, 40, 48–49, 139;
    Städelsche Art Institute,
    18, 19
Franz, Eckhardt G., 63
Free lending library, 6, 9,
    31, 36–37, 38; as educa-
    tional institution, 37–38
Freiesleben, Georg Otto,
    146, 147
Frevert, Ute, 126
Frey, Manuel, 17
Friedberg, Heinrich von, 70
Friendly visiting, 52, 56, 62,
    65–66, 71, 102, 110, 140,
    143, 144, 148. See also
    Hill, Octavia
Fugger, Jacob, 51
Fuggerei, 51, 143

Gardner, Deborah S., 40,
    128, 140

Gardner, John Lowell, 114,
    157
Gemeinnützige
    Baugesellschaft in
    Frankfurt am Main,
    49–50
Gerhard, Wilhelm, 108
Gesellschaft der Freunde
    (Leipzig), 146
Gesellschaft Harmonie, 65,
    108, 111, 146, 147
Gibson, Sir John, 84
Gibson, Lady, 84
Glasgow, 80, 81, 106;
    Working Man's
    Dwelling Company, 81
Goelet (family), 106
Goetze, Sigismund, 169
Goetze, Violet (later Mond),
    169–170
Gohlis (Saxony), 142; city
    council of, 142, 145
Goldschmidt, Johanna, 64
Goltz, Theodor Freiherr von
    der, 138
Gooderham (family), 120
Göring, H., 100
Gotha (Thuringia), 19, 65,
    110
Göttingen, 33, 35, 37, 51, 66;
    University of, 31, 32, 36,
    59; university library, 35
Göttinger Spar- und
    Bauverein, 68
Gottschald, Julius, 142
Gould, Elgin Ralston Lovell,
    46, 62, 66, 74–78, 80, 84,
    110, 143
Grasskamp, Walter, 18
Grävell, A., 50
Gray, William, 141
Green, Martin, 160
Griffith, Ernest S., 164
Griswold (family), 104
Groningen (Netherlands),
    49
Grosse, Ernst, 30
Gutta-Percha & Rubber
    Manufacturing
    Company in Brooklyn,
    135

Habermas, Jürgen, 126
Hall, Peter Dobkin, 89
Halle (Prussia), 31, 33, 49,
    67

Hamburg, 4, 18, 30, 40,
    49, 52, 64, 65, 154;
    Kunsthalle, 30
Hamilton (Ontario), 117,
    118
Hammack, David, 90
Hammerslough, Julius,
    155–156
Handlin, Oscar, 160, 162,
    163
Hanna, William J., 85;
    Hanna Act, 85
Hanover, 50; Spar- und Bau-
    verein, 50, 69; Technical
    University of, 71
Harkort, Gustav, 108
Harris, Neil, 13–14, 97, 99
Härtel, Hermann, 108
Harvard University
    Museum, 28
Hasse, Emma, 66, 76, 131,
    142–143, 145, 147
Hasse, Ernst, 42–43, 74, 137,
    142–143, 145
Hastings, Charles, 82
Hegemann, Werner, 137,
    138
Heidenstam, Adèle Marie
    von, 134
Heidenstam, Gerhard
    Balthazar von, 134
Helferich, J. A. R., 70
Hertz, Henriette, 168
Hesse-Darmstadt, Duchy
    of, 63
High Society, 94–95, 155,
    156, 181
Hill, Florence, 64
Hill, Octavia, 10, 51, 52,
    56–59, 60–62, 63, 64–
    66, 68, 69, 71, 72, 73, 79,
    127, 137, 142, 145, 147;
    housing management
    system, 40, 64, 68, 70,
    72, 75–76, 78, 80–81,
    102, 140, 144, 148
Hingham (Mass.), 113
Hirsch, Jenny, 64
Hirt, Arnold, 146, 147
Hirzel, Georg Theodor
    Salomon, 146–147
Hirzel, Salomon, 147
Hirzel (publishing house),
    147
Hochefried, Countess
    Catherine Anne de, 134

Hoffmann, Carl Wilhelm, 48, 50, 139
Hoffmann, Stefan-Ludwig, 126
Hohlfeld, Johannes, 93
Holstein, Franz von, 143
Holstein, Hedwig von, 131, 143–144
Holsteinstift, 143
Home Buildings in Brooklyn, 62
Home for Incurables (Chicago), 129
Home for Incurables (Fordham), 133
Hospitals, 89, 95, 124, 131, 155, 157, 182. *See also* Massachusetts General Hospital; New York Hospital; Toronto General Hospital
Housing cooperatives, 43, 46, 49, 50–51, 69, 72, 73, 82, 83, 138; housing companies/enterprises, philanthropic, 55, 56, 69, 83, 84, 139
Housing foundation/trust, 40, 43, 51, 52, 81, 140, 143, 144. *See also* Meyer's Housing Foundation (trust) in Leipzig; Peabody (housing) Trust
Housing reform, 10, 39, 40, 41, 42–43, 46–47, 49, 58, 60, 62, 63, 64, 66, 68, 69, 70, 71, 72, 73, 75, 79, 81, 82, 83, 101, 137, 138–139, 142, 145, 147, 148, 149
Huber, Victor Aimé, 46–48, 49, 50, 63, 66, 138
Hurl, Lorna F., 81, 82, 83, 84

Ilford (England), 149
Improved Dwellings Association (New York), 62
Improved Industrial Dwellings Company (IIDC or Waterlow Company), 46, 55, 56, 58, 61, 68, 70, 71, 75, 148. *See also* Limited dividend (housing)

companies; Waterlow, Sydney
Intercultural transfer (transatlantic transfer), 3–4, 5–6, 9–10, 13–85, 181; agents of, 5–6, 10, 14, 24, 29, 41, 52, 82–83; of library concepts, 31–38; of models for social housing enterprises, 39–85; of museum concepts, 18–31; professionalization of, 26–31, 66–79
Ireland, 49, 81
Ireland (family), 104
Irving, Washington, 16
Isham (family), 106
Iselin, Adrian, 104
Italy, 16, 30, 99

Jackson, Anthony, 39
Jackson, James, 113
Jackson (family), 113, 160
Jaher, Frederic Cople, 59, 90, 114, 129, 163
Jay, John, 16, 104
Jay, Mrs. John, 90, 103
Jena (Thuringia), 33
Jenks, Mrs. William F., 62
Jesup, Morris K., 106
Johann Heinrich Andreas Hermann Albrecht, Graf von Bernstorff, 67
John E. Thayer & Brother (banking house), 158
Johns Hopkins University, 74
Johnson, Eugene J., 78
Johnston, John Taylor, 106
Johnston (family), 106

Karlsruhe (Baden), 18; Art Hall, 18
Kassel (Hesse-Kassel), 69, 168
Kennedy, John Michael, 100
Kennedy, John Stuart, 106
Kensington (England), 17; South Kensington Museum, 17, 21
Keys, Ella M., 82
Kidder, Henry Purkitt, 114, 157, 158
Kidder (family), 158
Kidder, Peabody and Co. (investment firm), 158

Kiel (Holstein), 38; university library, 38
Kirkbride, Mrs. Thomas S., 62
Kleinzschocher (Saxony), 111
Knapp, Friedrich, 70
Knauth, Nachod & Kühne (banking house), 146
Knickerbocker Club (New York City), 15, 104
Knickerbocker families (New York City), 20, 59, 79, 90, 93, 94, 104, 106, 107; Knickerbocker elite, 93, 96, 103, 104, 105, 106, 116; Knickerbocker society, 90, 103
Koblenz (Rhineland), 147
Kopenhagen Arbeiter-bauverein, 50
Koren, John, 161
Kortländer, Bernd, 4
Kortzfleisch, Ida von, 150
Kotzenau (Silesia), 138
Krefeld (Rhineland), 31, 43
Krupp, 73; settlements, 72. *See also* Factory villages
Kuhnow, Anna, 134
Küstner, Heinrich, 65
Küstner, Ottilie, 65
Kylie, Edward, 84
Kyrle Society (Glasgow), 81. *See also* Hill, Octavia

Laird, Alexander, 84
Lambton Golf and Country Club, 171
Lampe, Carl, 108
Lash, Zebulon Aiton, 84, 85, 123
Lathrop, John, 157
Lawrence, Abbott, 51–52, 113, 114
Lawrence, Amos, 113
Lawrence, Timothy Bigelow, 114–115
Lawrence, Mrs. T. B., 115, 158
Lawrence (Mass.), 113
Lechler, Paul, 69
Lees, Andrew, 41
Leipzig, 9, 10, 14, 15, 16, 17, 18, 21, 24, 31, 33, 37, 40, 41, 43, 49, 51, 64–66, 67,

69, 72, 74, 75–77, 84, 91, 92, 96, 98, 101, 102, 108–112, 113, 115, 119, 121, 125, 131, 132, 134, 137, 138, 142, 143, 145–149, 151, 155, 163, 181; city council, 144, 145, 146; city government, 121, 144–145, 146; city parliament, 146; Conservatory of, 143; fairs, 146; High Society of, 94, 143, 146, 147; Jewish community of, 146, 147; Reichsgericht, 146, 148; Statistical Office of the city of, 42, 142; University of, 42, 59, 67, 71, 110, 111–112, 146, 147, 148

Leipziger Kunstverein (Leipzig Art Association), 108, 109

Leisure class, 7–8, 11, 89, 102, 127–128, 130, 154; Frankfurt's, 49; Leipzig's, 145, 147; New York's, 15, 24, 94, 104, 105, 155; Toronto's, 116, 122, 124, 125, 154, 165, 170. *See also* Elites

Lennox, James, 106

Leonhard, Colonel R. W., 123

Liagre, Albert de, 65, 147

Liagre, Charles, 147

Liagre, Charles Benoit François, 65

Liagre, Gustav de, 42, 64–66, 72, 142, 145, 147, 149

Libraries, 3, 8, 9, 13, 14, 15, 16, 35, 37, 38, 85, 89, 95, 99, 100, 102, 115. *See also* Boston Public Library; Royal Saxon Library

Lichtwark, Alfred, 30

Liedtke, Rainer, 154

Lighthall, William Dow, 80–81

Limited dividend (housing) companies, 43, 46, 48, 49, 50, 51, 62, 76, 79, 80, 82, 149; in Berlin, 48–49, 50; in Boston, 52, 140; in Frankfurt

am Main, 49; in Leipzig, 142–143, 144, 146, 148; in London, 46–47, 48, 55–56, 68, 71, 81; in Toronto, 81, 82. *See also* Boston Cooperative Building Company; City and Suburban Homes Company; Toronto Housing Company

Lindenau (Saxony), 110–111, 143

Lingelbach, Gabriele, 13

Litchfield (New Hampshire), 159

Little, James L., 114, 157

Liverpool (England), 16, 31, 167

Livingston, Robert, 105

Livingston, Robert J., 104

Livingston (family), 93, 104, 106

Lochnan, Katherine, 24

Lodge, Anna Cabot, 141

London, 3, 10, 15, 31, 32, 36, 37, 40, 46–47, 49, 51, 52–59, 60–61, 62, 63, 64, 65, 66, 67–68, 69, 70, 71, 72, 74, 78, 81, 84, 117, 122, 123, 138, 142, 148, 149–150, 167, 170, 172, 178, 181; social clubs of, 15, 103, 104

London (Ontario), 118

Louisville (Kentucky), 159

Lowell (Mass.), 113, 114, 116

Lowell (family), 113

Lübeck, 31

Ludington, C. H., Jr., 62

Ludwig, Duke of Hesse, 63

Lybrand, Mrs. William M., 62

Lyman, Arthur Theodore, 114, 157

Lyman, Theodore, Sr., 116

Lyman (family), 113

M. & L. Samuel (commission and wholesale merchants), 166

Macdonald, J. A., 81

Macdonald (family), 120

Mackenzie, William, 119, 122

Maclaren, John James, 127

Mak, Eileen, 97

Makan, John, 16, 17

Manchester (England), 154

Mandelson, Leah May (later Leah May Samuel), 167

Manhattan Club (New York City), 16, 105

Mapleson, Gwilt, 93

Marcus, Jacob Rader, 154

Marlborough, Duke of, 94

Marriages, transatlantic, 94

Married Women's Property Act, 128–129

Martin, Judith, 90

Mason, Harry, 167

Mason, Will, 167

Massachusetts, 16, 60, 74, 80, 105, 114, 115, 135, 159, 162; Bureau of Labor, 74; Bureau of Statistics of Labor of, 45; legislature, 162; General Court, 161; State Board of Health, 44, 60

Massachusetts General Hospital (MGH), 59, 92, 96, 113–114, 156, 157, 159, 161; subscribers, 113, 114, 157, 160–161

Massey, Chester D., 122, 123

Massey, H. O., 119

Mavor, James, 24, 25, 26, 81–82, 121

May, Abby W., 141

Mayflower Association (New York City), 103

McAllister, Ward, 90, 94, 103

McCarthy, Kathleen, 8, 9, 11, 14, 95, 127, 129, 130, 137, 156

McIntosh, Hector, 62

McQuesten, George E., 158–159

McQuesten, William, 158–159

Mehner, Dr. H., 42

Menninger, Margaret, 108, 109, 110

Messel, Alfred, 71, 73

Metropolitan Association for Improving the Dwellings of the Industrious Classes (MAIDIC) (London), 46, 48, 56, 70, 71. *See also* Limited dividend (housing) companies

Metropolitan Museum of
Art, 5–6, 9, 14, 24, 26,
27, 28, 29, 31, 92, 95,
96, 98, 100, 103, 104,
106, 107, 108, 119, 132,
133; Art Association,
20, 21, 24, 26, 31;
financing of building,
23; founding of, 15–23,
105; membership
organization, 19–21,
23–24, 26, 29–30,
105–107, 132; opening
hours, 27
Metropolitan Opera House
(New York City),
107–108
Meyer, Adolf Bernhard, 6,
27–28
Meyer, Hans, 110, 111–112
Meyer, Herrmann, 110, 112
Meyer, Herrmann Julius,
42, 66, 72, 73, 75, 84,
93, 101, 102, 110–111,
140, 143
Meyer, Oscar, 146
Meyer (family), 110–112
Meyer & Co. (banking
house), 146
Meyer's Housing Foundation
(trust) in Leipzig, 72,
73, 75, 93, 101, 102,
110–111, 140, 143,
144, 145, 147, 148, 152.
See also Philanthropy,
"pure"
Migration, 13, 39, 79, 181;
German migration
to Brazil, 112; Irish
migration to Boston,
158, 160; Irish
migration to Toronto,
120
Mill, John Stuart, 99
Mitchell, Samuel Latham
Barlow, 105
Model Lodging-House
Association (Boston),
51–52. See also Limited
dividend (housing)
companies
Mond, Frida (formerly Frida
Löwenthal), 168
Mond, Henry, 170
Mond, Ludwig, 168, 169
Mond, Sir Alfred (later Lord

Melchett), 123, 134, 156,
165, 168–170, 178
Mond, Sir Robert Ludwig,
165, 168, 169, 173, 178
Mond brothers, 123,
168–169
Mond (family), 168–170,
178
Mond Nickel Company,
168, 169
Montclair (New Jersey), 135
Montgomery, Henry, 28–29
Montgomery, Maureen
E., 94
Montreal (Quebec), 10,
79, 80
Moore, Edward C., 100
Moore, Mr., 75
Moran, Benjamin, 54
Morgan, Junius Spencer, 53
Morgenstern, Lina, 64
Morris, Lewis, 105
Morris, Lloyd, 107
Morris, Susannah, 54,
55–56, 68, 85
Morris (family), 106
Morton, George, 105
Morton, Levi P., 105
Mudge, Enoch Redington,
116
Mühlhausen (Alsatia), 138
Mulock, Cawthra, 124,
129–130
Mulock, Sir William, 129
Mulock (family), 129
Munich, 14, 17, 18, 31, 49,
70; art gallery, 24
Murton, Fanny, 117
Murton, J. W., 117
Murton, Mrs. William, 117
Museum of Comparative
Zoology (Cambridge,
Mass.), 29
Museum of Fine Arts
(MFA), 23, 29, 30, 92,
96, 98, 99, 113, 114,
115, 132, 133, 156,
157–158, 159, 160,
161–163; access to the
public, 161; architecture
of, 30; membership
organization, 29–30,
115–116, 132, 157–158
Museum of Regional
Geography (Leipzig),
110

Museums, 8, 9, 13, 14, 15,
16, 17, 19, 27, 28, 29,
30, 31, 37, 85, 89, 95,
96–98, 99–100, 102,
107, 108, 109, 113, 124,
128, 130, 131, 133, 134,
136, 155, 157, 181–182;
admission and opening
times, 27–28, 97, 98; of
applied arts, 22, 131;
architecture of, 29–30;
of art, 16, 18, 21, 22,
108, 114, 115, 119–121;
associations, 3, 6, 9, 31,
89, 91, 102, 124, 131,
133, 134; education and
social control through,
17, 22–23, 27–29, 97, 99;
of natural history, 131

Nachod, Friedrich, 146, 149
Nachod, Jacob, 146
National Academy of Design
(New York City), 16
National Club (Canada), 171
National Museum of Natural
History (Washington,
D.C.), 28, 29
Natural Science Museum
(Springfield,
Massachusetts), 28
Netherlands (Holland), 16,
30, 49, 58, 64, 65, 75
Nettlefold, John Sutton, 80
New Haven (Conn.), 28
New Jersey, 105, 134
New York City (formerly
New Amsterdam), 4, 9,
10, 14, 15, 16, 17, 19, 20,
21, 23, 24, 26, 27, 28, 29,
31, 35, 36, 39, 40, 41, 44,
58, 61, 62, 79, 80, 82, 83,
90, 91, 92, 93, 94, 96, 98,
100, 102–108, 109, 112,
113, 115, 116, 118, 119,
120, 121, 122, 125, 127,
131, 132, 133, 148, 155,
162, 163, 165, 166, 181;
city council, 26; High
Society, 78, 94, 103–108;
social clubs, 20, 89, 103,
104, 108
New York Historical Society,
16, 105
New York Hospital (NYH),
92, 96, 106

New York Public Library, 35–36, 106
New York (State), 105, 134, 166
Newburg (New York), 159
Newman, Bernard, 140
Nicholls, Fredric, 119
Niemeyer, Max, 67
Nightingale, Florence, 63
Nobbs, Percy E., 82
Nobility, 18, 94, 107, 108, 134, 170
Noel, Gerard, 63
Nörrenberg, Constantin, 6, 31, 38
Nottingham (England), 135
Nova Scotia, 85
Nuremberg, 16, 17, 19, 22; art gallery, 24

Octavia Hill Association of Philadelphia, 62
Olmstedt, Fredrick Law, 20
Ontario, 28, 137; legislature (parliament), 85, 123; Province of, 120; provincial government of, 28, 29, 84–85, 121, 122, 172
Ontario Society of Artists (OSA), 24, 119
Orange (New Jersey), 134
Orvell, Miles, 100
Osler, Sir Edmund (formerly Edmund B.), 84, 118, 122–123
Osnabrück (Hanover), 43
Ostheim (Stuttgart), 73
Ostrower, Francie, 91
Ottawa, 170; Ottawa Planning Commission, 83
Ottendorfer, Oswald, 107
Owen, David, 54, 55
Owen, Robert, 57

Paine (family), 104
Paine, R. T., Jr., 157
Palmowski, Jan, 43
Paris, 16, 31, 36, 126; university of, 59
Parks, William Arthur, 122
Parrish, Helen L., 62
Peabody, George, 51, 52–54, 56, 58, 59, 60–61, 66, 68, 73, 75, 79, 81

Peabody (family), 158
Peabody (housing) Trust, 53, 54, 58, 60–61, 66, 68, 70–71, 72, 73, 75, 81, 102
Peck, Clarissa, 129
Pederson, Diana, 130
Pellatt, Lady of Casa Loma, 136
Penny, H. Glenn, 97, 100
Penslar, Derek, 153, 154
Pessen, Edward, 103, 129
Philadelphia, 23, 27, 61, 62, 79, 80, 83, 127; Philadelphia Housing Association, 140
Philanthropic culture, 9, 10, 107, 125, 144, 168; contested, 10; counterculture, 113; divided, 10, 102–112, 181; unified, 10, 11, 102, 112–125, 181
Philanthropic establishment, 99, 103, 105, 111, 120, 154–155, 159; housing enterprises, 61, 63, 65, 72, 73, 74, 75, 78, 79, 80, 127, 139, 140, 142
Philanthropy, 3, 7, 8, 9, 11, 20, 24, 26, 27, 40, 41, 43, 47, 49, 50, 51, 54, 55, 58, 59, 60–61, 62, 63, 68, 69, 75, 78, 79, 85, 89–90, 91, 95, 100, 101, 102, 105, 106, 110, 111, 112, 114, 115, 116, 120, 121, 122, 123, 124, 126, 127, 128, 129, 130, 131, 133, 134, 136, 137, 142, 145, 148, 149, 151, 152, 153, 154, 156, 157, 158, 160, 163, 165, 169, 171, 178, 179, 181–182; and 5 Percent (investment philanthropy), 46, 48, 50, 51, 54–55, 61, 68, 69, 76–78, 80, 81, 82, 83, 137, 139, 148, 149; Boston's, 114, 115, 157, 161, 162–163; Chicago's, 129; collective, 19, 31, 148; cultural, 116, 118, 119, 121, 122, 128, 129, 131, 132, 135, 136, 155, 169; educational, 121,

132, 143, 155; New York's, 102–108, 155; "pure," 54, 60–61, 73; social, 59, 85, 116, 119, 127, 128, 129, 131, 132, 143, 155; Toronto's, 83, 85, 119, 120, 124, 125, 135, 164–179
Philanthropy and Catholics, 89, 95, 147, 153, 158–159; and colonialism, 112, 169; and German nationalism, 41, 152; and Jews, 8, 11, 89, 95, 146–147, 153–154, 155, 164–179, 181–182; and Protestants, 89, 146–147; and religion, 11, 153–179, 182; and women, 8, 11, 41, 63–64, 89, 95, 126–152, 181–182
Philanthropy as cultural countergovernment, 8–9, 95, 130, 131, 137, 155, 162–163, 182; empowering function of, 8, 109–110, 131, 156; as social and cultural domination, 41, 89
Phillips, John, 159
Phillips, William, 113
Pierce, Lorne, 176
Plauen (Saxony), 147
Plymouth (Mass.), 113, 116
Pommer, Max, 73, 101, 110, 111, 143, 144, 145, 147
Pońinska, Adelheid Gräfin (also Arminius; formerly Adelheid Gräfin zu Dohna-Schlodien), 131, 137–139
Pońinska, Adolph Graf, 138
Pońinska, Ignaz Graf, 138
Posen (Preußen), 17
Potter, Howard, 105
Prague, 24, 49, 159
Presbyterian Hospital (New York City), 106
Prior, Nick, 99
Private Sphere, 126
Prochaska, Frank, 127, 128, 134
Prüfer, Hermann Bernhard Arthur, 146, 147

Prussia, 63, 70, 146, 151;
  Statistical Bureau of the
  Kingdom of, 70
Public Sphere, 8, 126, 127,
  130–131, 137, 155;
  women's integration
  into, 128, 134
Putnam, George P., 16, 19, 20

Quartaert, Jean H., 41, 127,
  128, 152
Quincy, Josiah, Jr., 161

Rastede (Oldenbourg), 71
Reclam, Hans Heinrich,
  146, 147
Reclam (publishing house),
  110
Reid, George A., 24, 119
Reifenstein (Thuringia), 150
Reudnitz (Saxony), 110,
  111, 143
Reynolds, Marcus T., 45, 58,
  66, 74, 78–79
Rhinelander, Frederick W.,
  104
Rhinelander (family), 105
Riehl, Wilhelm Heinrich, 70
Rietschel, Georg, 144
Riis, Jacob August, 45, 74, 78
Roberts, Marshall O., 105
Robinson, Edward, 29
Rockefeller, John D., 107
Roden, Thomas, 84
Rodgers, Daniel T., 13, 14,
  40–41, 74, 181
Rogers, Henry B., 141
Rogers, William Barton, 158
Roscher, Wilhelm, 67
Rosenwald, Julius, 14, 156
Rosenwald Fund, 156
Rossbach, Arwed, 144, 145,
  146, 147, 149
Rossbach, Therese, 66, 101,
  131, 141–142, 144–152
Royal Geographical Society
  of England, 175
Royal Historical Society of
  England, 175
Royal Ontario Museum
  (ROM), 24, 28, 29,
  92, 96, 116, 118, 119,
  121–125, 132, 133, 134,
  135–136, 154, 155, 165,
  169, 171, 172, 173, 174,
  175, 176–177, 178, 179;

financing scheme, 29,
  122–123; membership
  association and
  members, 29, 124, 128,
  132, 164
Royal Saxon Library, 5, 14,
  15, 31, 33–35, 36, 38
Ruprecht, Wilhelm, 58,
  66–69, 71, 72
Ruskin, John, 56
Rutherford, P. F. W., 80
Rutherfurd, Walter, 105

Salem (Mass.), 59, 113
Salomon, Julius, 143
Salomon Stift, 76–77,
  143–144, 145
Samuel, Florence, 173
Samuel, Lewis, 165–166
Samuel, Mark, 166
Samuel, Sigmund, 121, 123,
  134, 136, 155, 156,
  165–168, 170–179, 182
Samson, Anna Marie, 147
Samson, Hermann, 65, 147
Sawyer, Emma S., 158
Saxony, 5, 19, 104, 133,
  150, 151; Kingdom of
  Saxony, 16
Schäfer, Axel, 41
Schermerhorn (family), 93,
  107
Scheuer, Edmund, 165
Schletter, Heinrich Adolf, 19
Schlobach, Paul Georg Otto,
  111
Schmoller, Gustav, 70, 72
Schneidemühl (Western
  Prussia), 159
Schomburgk, Heinrich, 147
Schönberg, Gustav von, 67
Schuyler, Louisa Lee, 58, 62
Schuyler (family), 93
Schwab, Wilhelm, 64, 66
Scotland, 49, 158
Seckelman, Kate (later Kate
  Samuel), 165–166
Seidlitz, Woldemar von, 31
Self-help, concept of, 47,
  49, 50, 68, 72. See also
  Housing cooperatives
Seligman, Jefferson, 107
Seligman (family), 165
Sellerhausen (Saxony), 144
Sellin (Rügen), 151
Sembritzky, Johanna, 145

Shannon, William, 161, 163
Shattuck, George Otis, 114
Shattuck (family), 160–161
Shedd, John G., 14
Sheehan, James, 97
Shuman, Abraham, 159
Sieveking, Amalie, 52
Simson, Anna, 64
Singer, Jacob, 165
Smalley, George, 56
Smethwick (England), 169
Smith, Ellen, 159–160
Smith, Goldwin, 26, 80, 81,
  119, 121
Smith, Harriet Elizabeth
  (formerly Harriet
  Elizabeth Mann Dixon),
  26, 121
Smith, Southwood, 56
Smith, Sydney, 176
Smithsonian Institution, 28
Social housing, 41, 50, 52,
  54, 74, 83, 85, 145,
  163; architecture of,
  73, 100–102, 131;
  associations/companies/
  enterprises/projects, 3,
  8, 9, 39, 40, 41, 42, 49,
  50, 52, 59, 60, 62, 66, 70,
  73, 74, 75, 82, 85, 89, 91,
  95, 100, 101, 102, 110,
  114, 128, 130, 131, 142,
  157, 181–182
Social reform, 10, 14, 39, 40,
  41, 42, 43, 44, 49, 59, 62,
  64, 66, 67, 71, 74, 75,
  76, 78, 79–80, 81, 83,
  101, 102, 110, 112, 138,
  147, 152
Société industrielle, 138
Society for Improving
  the Condition of the
  Labouring Classes
  (SICLC) (London), 46,
  47, 48, 49, 53, 138. See
  also Limited dividend
  (housing) companies
Sohn, Rudolf, 146, 147
Soltau, Mrs., 150
Somerville (Mass.), 114
Sorkin, David, 154
Spain, 5, 16, 99
Speck-Sternburg, Max von,
  108
Speisman, Stephen A., 153
Spenden, 182

Spragge, Shirley Campbell, 83–84
Springfield (Illinois), Jewish Community, 155
St. Andrews Society (New York City), 103
St. Luke's Hospital (New York City), 133
St. Nicholas Society (New York City), 103
Städel, Johann Friedrich, 18
Stanley, Edward George G. F. S. (the 14th Earl of Derby), 53, 54–55
State Charities Aid Association of New York (SCAA), 58
Steward, D. Jackson, 105
Stewart, Alexander T., 105
Stiften, 182
Stites, Richard, 11, 128, 134
Stockholm, 24
Story, Ronald, 162
Stowe, William, 6
Stuart, Alexander, 106
Stuart, Robert L., 104, 105, 106
Sturge, Allen, 172
Sturges, Jonathan, 106
Sturgis, R. Clipston, 29
Stuttgart (Württemberg), 31, 49
Stuyvesant, Peter, 105
Stuyvesant, Rutherfurd, 20, 105
Stuyvesant (family), 93, 104, 105, 106, 107
Sudbury (Ontario), 169
Suffrage for women (in Canada), 136–137; restrictions for Irish in Massachusetts, 162
Sullivan, James, 114
Sullivan, Richard, 114
Sulzbach (Bavaria), 165
Suydam (family), 104
Sweden, 58, 75, 120
Switzerland, 30, 64, 146, 147
Syracuse (New York), 18, 19, 166; museum of fine arts, 19

Tarn, John Nelson, 54, 56
Taylor, James, 138
"Ten Friends of Art" (Toronto), 123, 134, 135

Tennent, Sir James Emerson, 53
Thayer, Nathaniel, 115
Then, Volker, 56
Thernstrom, Stephan, 163
Ticknor, George, 5, 6, 9, 14, 15, 16, 31–37, 59
Tiffany (family), 105
Tocqueville, Alexis de, 131
Tomkins, Calvin, 23
Toronto (formerly York), 9, 10, 11, 14, 23, 24, 29, 40, 79, 81–85, 91, 92, 96, 102, 107, 112–113, 115, 116–125, 131, 132, 134–137, 153, 154, 155, 163, 164–179, 181; Anglicans, 164, 165; Baptists, 164; Bishop Strachan School, 178; Catholics, 164; City Council, 83, 85, 121; City Council Civic Improvement Committee, 83; City government, 122, 153; District Labour Council (DLC), 84; Hebrew Congregation (Holy Blossom), 166, 171–172, 176; Hebrew Ladies' Sick and Benevolent Society, 153; High Society, 84, 94, 113, 166, 168, 178; Irish, 120; Jarvis Street Collegiate Institute, 166; Jewish community, 95, 155, 165, 166, 171–172, 178; Jews, 154, 155, 164–165; Methodists, 164, 167; Model School, 166, 178; Mutual Improvement Society (MIS), 166–167; Normal School, 117; philanthropic establishment, 120, 155, 156, 165, 172, 178; Presbyterian, 164, 168; social clubs, 165, 171; Toronto Associated Charities, 81; Toronto Mechanics Institute, 166; Upper Canada College, 28, 166
Toronto Art Gallery (TAG) (Art Gallery of

Ontario), 14, 23, 24, 26, 28, 29, 81, 92, 96, 116, 118, 119–121, 122, 124, 125, 132, 133, 134, 135–136, 154; admission, 121; Grange, 26, 81, 121; membership classes and members, 24–26, 119–120, 132, 164; Toronto Art Museum Association, 24, 26
Toronto General Hospital (TGH), 92, 95, 96, 116, 120, 121–122, 129, 154; membership and members, 120, 124, 164
Toronto Housing Company (THC), 82, 83–85, 92, 96, 116, 120, 135, 140, 141; membership and members, 120, 124, 128, 164
Toronto Western Hospital, 165, 173, 175
Townsend (family), 105
Transatlantic history, 3, 181
Transnational history, 3, 181
Travel, 5, 6, 13, 14, 24–25, 27, 28, 29–30, 66, 90, 181; American travels in Germany, 16, 18, 90; American travel to Europe, 15, 16, 59, 91, 99; Canadian travels in Germany, 24; reports, 59
Trübner, Nikolaus, 67
Trumbull, Jonathan, 134
"Twenty Friends of Art" (Toronto), 123

Union Club (New York City), 15, 20, 103–104
Union College (Schenectady), 133
Union League Club (New York City), 15, 16, 20, 104, 105
Universities, 13, 15, 17, 155
University of Toronto, 24, 28, 81, 83, 84, 118, 122, 123, 155, 166, 167, 171, 173, 175, 176, 177–178; Leah May Samuel Estate, 176; museum of, 28; museum of archaeology, 122; Museum of

Paleontology, 118–119; Sigmund Samuel Library, 165, 173–176
Urban culture, 89–90, 96; Boston, 113; contested, 89; New York's, 104–105, 107–108

Van Cortlandt (family), 104
Van Lennep, Augustus Oscar, 135
Van Lennep (family), 134
Van Rensselaer, Bayard, 78
Van Rensselaer (family), 93, 104
Vandenhoeck & Ruprecht Press, 66
Vanderbilt, Alva Smith, 107
Vanderbilt, Consuela, 94
Vanderbilt, Cornelius, 62
Vanderbilt, William H., 94, 130
Vanderbilt (family), 105, 106
Vandervoort (family), 104
Varrentrapp, Johann Conrad, 49
Varrentrapp, Johann Georg, 49, 63, 66, 139
Veblen, Thorstein, 7–8, 99
Verein für Deutsche Personen- und Familiengeschichte, 92–93
Verein für Socialpolitik, 43, 70
Verein Ostheim (Leipzig), 92, 96, 101, 128, 140, 141–142, 144–149, 151; membership, 146–147, 148, 149
Verein zur Verbesserung der kleinen Wohnungen in Berlin, 66, 71
Vienna, 49, 137, 138
Villa Heimkehr (Sellin), 151

Village Home for Girls, 149–150
Vincentius Verein (Leipzig), 147
Vivian, Henry, 82, 83

Wagner, Adolph, 72
Walker, Alfred, 117
Walker, Edmund, Jr., 122
Walker, Mary Alexander, 23, 119
Walker, Sir Edmund (formerly Byron), 6, 11, 23–26, 28, 29, 83, 113, 116–125, 135, 165, 167–168, 169, 170, 171, 172
Walker, Thomas, 117
Walker (family), 119
Wallace, Elisabeth, 121
Walsh, Frank J., 81
Walter, Hermann, 20, 21
Warburg, Felix, 4
Ward, Samuel, 36
Warren, Arthur, 135
Warren, Harry Dorman, 129, 134, 135
Warren, Mrs. H. D. (formerly Sarah Trumbull van Lennep), 120, 123, 131, 134–137, 165, 173, 178
Warren, John C., 113
Warren, Samuel D., 29, 30
Warren (family), 135, 158, 160–161
Washington, D.C., 27, 40, 62
Waterlow, Sydney, 51, 52, 55–56, 58, 59, 60–61, 62, 66, 68, 71, 75, 76, 78, 79, 84, 149
Watson, George, 116
Watson, Sarah, 116
Weisbach, Valentin, 71

Werner, Michael, 3, 4
Weymouth (Mass.), 135
Wheelwright, Edmund M., 29
White, Alfred Treadway, 40, 62, 66, 74, 79
White, William C., 173
Whitney, Sir James, 85, 122–123
Whittredge (family), 105
Willard, Frances, 128
Windsor (Ontario), 118
Winkworth, Catherine, 64
Winkworth, Susanna, 64
Winterton, Lord, 170
Winthrop, John, 105
Winthrop, Robert, 54
Winthrop (family), 105
Wolfe, John David, 104, 133
Wolfe, Miss Catharine Lorillard, 133
Women's associations, 126–127
Women's Parliament (Darmstadt), 64
Wood, Edith Elmer, 128, 140
Woodbury (family), 158
Woodroofe, Kathleen, 54, 153
Woodward, George, 62
Work ethic: neo-Puritan, 6; Protestant, 41
Worthington (family), 105
Worts (family), 120
Wright, Carroll Davidson, 74

Yale University, 28
Yardley, John, 60
Yardley, Olivia, 60
Yonkers (New York), 23; Browning Society in, 23
York Club (Toronto), 165, 171
Yorkshire (England), 120

William H. Schneider, editor. *Rockefeller Philanthropy and Modern Biomedicine: International Initiatives from World War I to the Cold War*

Bradford Smith, Sylvia Shue, Jennifer Lisa Vest, and Joseph Villarreal. *Philanthropy in Communities of Color*

David Horton Smith, Robert A. Stebbins, and Michael A. Dover, editors. *A Dictionary of Nonprofit Terms and Concepts*

David H. Smith. *Entrusted: The Moral Responsibilities of Trusteeship*

David H. Smith, editor. *Good Intentions: Moral Obstacles and Opportunities*

Jon Van Til. *Growing Civil Society: From Nonprofit Sector to Third Space*

Andrea Walton. *Women and Philanthropy in Education*

THOMAS ADAM is Associate Professor at the University of Texas at Arlington. He teaches courses on German and modern transatlantic history. His research focuses on nineteenth-century philanthropy in the United States, Great Britain, Canada, and Germany and the inter-cultural transfer of philanthropic concepts between these countries. He has just published a book on funding higher education in Germany, 1800 to 1960, and is currently working on a comparative study of funding for university education in the United States and Germany, 1800 to 1945.